"Dawn Nothwehr combines depth of scholarship with depth of passion and prayer in a way that is simply breathtaking. *Ecological Footprints* positively *sings* with hope. While grim determination and even despair characterize all too many works on today's (admittedly overwhelming) environmental crises, this book begins and ends with the conviction that we already have the spiritual resources we need in order to live sustainably on our fragile planet. At once prayerful, scholarly, and wonderfully practical, this book is exactly the ecotheology we need today."

—Colleen Mary Carpenter
Saint Catherine University
Author of *Redeeming the Story:
Women, Suffering, and Christ*

"*Ecological Footprints* is a hopeful and profound book, one we need today as we search for a way of living as responsible members of the community of life on Earth. Dawn Nothwehr invites the reader into a Christian ecological vision and practice that is inspired by the Scriptures and wonderfully enriched by the precious Franciscan tradition of Francis, Clare, Bonaventure, and Scotus."

—Denis Edwards
Flinders University, South Australia
Author of *How God Acts* and *Ecology
at the Heart of Faith*

"*Ecological Footprints* is as vast and rich as Mother Earth. The book is comprehensive in content, exploring its 'urgent issues' in a clear, engaging manner. It is a book that can be read individually or with a group, in chapters or in its entirety. However grasped, the charges it outlines about the modern burdens of the earth are haunting and demand our action."

—Ingrid J. Peterson, OSF
Co-author of *The Franciscan Tradition*

Can the Franciscan ideal support modern
progress? — how the world works —

   (J: prophetic — rather than self-denial)
      size, scale, we do things —
Buddhist mindfulness ↔ ecological awareness

   • Studies on sustainability

Creation: as the second book of revelation —

✱ Connecting through conflict rather than
through care —

   Millenium Goals
      Good
   1) Education   Not as Good
   2) Food   1) Water
               major corporation selling it

             2) Major investors
                Robert Kennedy JR → sustainable
                               energy
                Making money being green —

             3) Laws shifted back on
              food 2008 commodity
              futures → (back)

             4) Mentality — Nigeria — trees as
              primitive: build my home &
              cut down tree —

   Caritas International
   Passionists on Simple Living

Ecological Footprints

An Essential Franciscan Guide
for Faith and Sustainable Living

Dawn M. Nothwehr, OSF

LITURGICAL PRESS

Collegeville, Minnesota

www.litpress.org

(Handwritten annotations):

p.82 How does person specifically give one access to God?

p.109 J: How did your study of mutuality influence your insight into the Franciscan Tradition?

God ↔ cosmos
manifestation ↔ participation

p.114 Christo-genesis

p.121 finding the intrinsic value of the material world, not just its instrumental value —

p.165 Global warming caused less available water in sub-Saharan African.

theo. of Holy Men + Women who lived the Christian life at this time (experience)

Francis + vernacular theology

B. McGinn
scholastic
mystic
vernacular
theology

→ 30 treatises ⟹ marked his conversion
Bonaventure & the Incarnation (wrote on St. John)
Trinity → transform neo-platonism - relational ethics

chaum:
righteousness
+ flourishing
through gift

1   2   3   4   5   6   7   8   9

Library of Congress Cataloging-in-Publication Data

Nothwehr, Dawn M., 1951–
    Ecological footprints : an Essential Franciscan guide for faith and sustainable living / Dawn M. Nothwehr.
        p.   cm.
    ISBN 978-0-8146-3374-8 — ISBN 978-0-8146-3957-3 (e-book)
    1. Human ecology—Religious aspects—Catholic Church.   2. Ecotheology.
3. Sustainable living.   4. Franciscans—Theology.   I. Title.

BX1795.H82N68   2012
261.8'8—dc23   2012029293

Contents

PART 2

St. Francis and St. Clare:
Models of Faith and Sustainable Living

CHAPTER 3

CHAPTER 4

PART 3

St. Bonaventure of Bagnoregio:
Creator, Christ, Creatures, Cosmos

CHAPTER 5 ⌄

Who Is God? Christ in the Middle of a Love Triangle   103

PART 4

Blessed John Duns Scotus: One in a Million

CHAPTER 6

Sacred Subtle Thoughts Concerning Creation   129

PART 5

What Is Ours to Do: Urgent Issues

CHAPTER 7

Human-Caused Global Warming: A Leper Awaiting Our Embrace   155

CHAPTER 8

Flowing Water for Life: A Human Right   187

Preface

"His highest aim, and foremost desire, and greatest intention was to pay heed to the Holy Gospel in all things and through all things, to follow the teachings of Our Lord Jesus Christ and to retrace his footsteps completely with all vigilance and all zeal and all desire of his soul and all the fervor of his heart." [1]

"They entered the Order of the Lesser Ones, obliging themselves to follow, according to the particular grace given to them by God, the poverty and the footsteps of Christ and his most blessed servant, Francis." [2]

"His whole aim, in public and in private, was to reproduce in himself and in others those footprints of Christ which had been covered over and forgotten." [3]

"In the twelfth hundredth twenty sixth year of the Incarnation, on the fourth day before the Nones of October, the day he had foretold, having completed

---

[1] *The Life of St. Francis* by Thomas of Celano (1228–1229), bk. I, chap. I, 88, in *Francis of Assisi: Early Documents*, vol. I, *The Saint*, trans. and ed. Regis J. Armstrong, J. A. Wayne Hellmann, and William J. Short (New York: New City Press, 1999), 131, emphasis added. Hereafter citations will follow this pattern: "Document Title" (date), chapter, section, line, in FAED, vol. I, *The Saint*, page number.

[2] *The Legend of the Three Companions* (1241–1247), chap. XVIII, 73, in *Francis of Assisi: Early Documents*, vol. II, *The Founder*, trans. and ed. Regis J. Armstrong, J. A. Wayne Hellmann, and William J. Short (New York: New City Press, 2000), 110, emphasis added. Hereafter citations will follow this pattern: "Document Title" (date), chapter, section, line, in FAED, vol. II, *The Founder*, page number.

[3] *The Tree of the Crucified Life of Jesus*, Book Five (Excerpts), by Umbertino DaCasale (1305), chap. III, 54, in *Francis of Assisi: Early Documents*, vol. III, *The Prophet*, trans. and ed. Regis J. Armstrong, J. A. Wayne Hellmann, and William J. Short (New York: New City Press, 2001), 148, emphasis added. Hereafter citations will follow this pattern: "Document Title" (date), chapter, section, line, in FAED, vol. III, *The Prophet*, page number.

twenty years from the time he perfectly adhered to Christ, following in the footsteps and the life of the Apostles, the apostolic man Francis, freed from the fetters of mortal life, departed happily to Christ."[4]

I grew up in the "heartland" of southwestern Minnesota, one of the richest agricultural areas of the United States. Though my family did not live on a farm (all of my friends did), we lived in a storybook small town, in a comfortably large three-bedroom house, on a huge corner lot with all sorts of hedges, trees, and flowers strategically arranged around a vast grassy lawn. Each summer my parents planted a sprawling vegetable garden that my sister (five years my elder) and I were "forced" to help weed, tend, and ultimately harvest its produce. Though I would never admit it at that time, I actually *loved* working in the garden. I was quite awestruck by the fact that you could put this hard, flat, little yellow thing in the ground, and weeks later you could find a sweet corn plant in its place! Deep down I knew my mother was right when she proclaimed, "Only God can make the garden grow!" (I didn't admit that to her until years later either!)

Some thirty years later I had the privilege of going on a pilgrimage to Assisi and the "Franciscan Holy Land" of Umbria, the region of Assisi, Italy, where St. Francis and St. Clare lived. As we journeyed from place to place, no one could miss the striking lush verdancy of the fertile fields of sunflowers and the vineyards that covered the rolling hills. As one spirited friar remarked, "Francis sure knew how to find the best real estate!" It was no wonder that St. Francis and St. Clare too saw—as I had seen—the vestiges of an incarnate God cradling them in love and mercy in that lush nest of creation.

Today I live in a large midwestern city. Though I must admit that there are many conveniences to city life, I have a real love-hate relationship with those environs. Everything is huge, impersonal, paved over, fast paced, human built, constantly in motion, competitive—often violent. For me the "saving grace" is the clearly demarcated park system that abuts Lake Michigan. There, there is some semblance of intimacy with the web of life; people actually smile and greet one another, there are trees, grass, flowers, and open sky, the lake stretches out to the horizon, and the rhythm of the waves lapping against the sands of extensive

---

[4] *The Remembrance of the Desire of a Soul* by Thomas of Celano (1245–1247), bk. II, chap. CLXVI, 220, in FAED, vol. II, *The Founder*, 390, emphasis in the original.

beaches sets the tone and pace of more peaceful living. There is a sense of the sacred there, quite distinct from that found in all the cavernous cathedrals that dot numerous street corners in the sprawling metropolis. Yes, St. Francis was definitely on to something!

As Franciscan scholar Ingrid J. Peterson, OSF, notes, Franciscan spirituality "is sacramental in that all created things are also seen as signs pointing to God as creator."[5] Francis knew this in various ways—as we do today—by observing the beauty and splendor of the natural world and in the loving ways we touch each other's lives. But Giovanni Francesco di Bernardone was not always so aware! In fact, as we will elaborate in chapter 4, in his youth he was a carousing spoiled brat of an up-and-coming cloth merchant, who went off to war as a knight in the Crusades hoping to gain fame and fortune! But he soon discovered that none of that met his deepest heart's desire. It was only after Giovanni embraced a leper and did a 360-degree about-face on his life's journey that he found what he was looking for.

What he had been trashing in his early life was the reality that it is in truly caring for people and God's creation that there is potential to arrive where he most desired to go—to the very heart of God. The carousing and the war making, the seeking fame and fortune, his use and abuse of people and creation, only pushed him along a path directly opposite of the way to intimacy with God, people, and all creation. So it was through joining his intuition, his appreciation of the beauty of the Umbrian landscape, with God's grace that Giovanni Francesco di Bernardone became St. Francis of Assisi.

Francis's deepest desire was to "follow in the footprints of Jesus." But why follow "in the footprints"? There is an intimacy to be found in such activity. In practical terms, a footprint leaves a distinctive mark of the one who made it—a human person—on some material object such as soil, sand, or wet concrete. Forensic scientists can learn a lot from studying footprints: a person's approximate height (a foot is about 15 percent of the length of a person's height) or weight, depending on the size and depth of the impression. Footprints also have characteristics that are unique to each person: creases, flatness, horizontal or vertical ridges, or other deformities.

---

[5] Ingrid Peterson, "Franciscan Spirituality: The Footprints of Jesus in the Classroom and the Marketplace," in *As Leaven to the World: Catholic Perspectives on Faith, Vocation, and the Intellectual Life,* ed. Thomas M. Landy (Franklin, WI: Sheed & Ward, 2001), 291.

While Francis was no forensic scientist, he knew that footprints marked the physical presence of a person in a particular time and place. To attempt to place one's foot in the footprints of another requires careful attention to the original form, and thus one needs to learn something about the author of those impressions. Also, by following footprints, one likely would eventually meet face to face with the one who made them. For Francis, the "footprints of Jesus" symbolized the reality of the incarnation—Jesus, the Word made flesh, the One who came to dwell among us as one of us! It was that intuition that attracted Francis. Jesus is indeed the pattern and model for our life in God, and with all others *in this world*. And because Jesus became part of this material world, everything and everyone is now deified, made whole, holy, and sacramental. Just as a painting or a sculpture reveals something of the artist who created it, so too everything in the cosmos speaks to us of God.

Thus, to know Jesus and to walk in his footprints is to make contact with the human face of God. Francis found the footprints of Jesus in the tiny feet of the Babe of Bethlehem—the incarnation. He saw the profound love of Christ in the feet pierced by nails on the cross—the redemption. In the eucharistic bread and wine, Francis perceived the life of Christ, sifted, refined, and poured out for us—the one who walked the roads of Nazareth, Galilee, and Jerusalem and who desires to remain intimately present to us and within us. And, most clearly in the Sacred Scriptures, Jesus the Word inspires, instructs, consoles, and empowers us to see his footprints at every turn each day.

Following in the footprints of Jesus demands that we be attentive and attuned to the world with all of our senses, for they are our point of contact with reality. The best way we can keep in touch with the creative Word is to also remain in touch with *this* world—sights, sounds, smells, tastes, stories, symbols, concepts, encounters with the sacraments, and human rituals. In these ways humans come to recognize they are part of the created universe and to continually renew and restore their relationships with each other, God, and the entire cosmos. Christ, as the firstborn of all creation, stands at the center of all of this (Col 1:15-20).

Jesus is at the heart of history, but he is also the transcendent Christ who is divine and lives at the heart of the Trinity. And he lives as the Cosmic Christ permeating the heart of the entire cosmos. In all of these ways, footprints are left for us to see. We need only become attentive, opening all of our senses to see, learn, and follow. If we are attentive to the footprints and to the person of Jesus, we will come to know our truest possibilities and potentials.

In our globalized, terrorized, economically impoverished, and ecologically threatened world, we are often surrounded with the fallout from people treating others as so much chemistry or resources to be exploited for selfish profit and gain, and with impunity. In contrast to that, as Peterson reminds us, is to look at the world with the eyes of St. Francis and to see "the value of an object is never more important than the fact that it is a 'vestige' [footprint] of the divine, an object that enriches us spiritually by providing us with a contact with the presence of God."[6]

For several decades, many scientists and theologians have agreed that at the root of the ecological crisis is a more profound spiritual crisis. In St. Francis's terms, the "footprints of Christ have been covered over and forgotten."[7] The sacred relationship among God, humans, otherkind, and the cosmos has given way to pillaging, plundering, raping, and otherwise exploiting our Sister, Mother Earth, and ultimately her children—especially the poor and vulnerable.

The good news is that things have not always been this way, and they need not continue to be so! As St. Bonaventure pointed out, God loved every bit of creation into life, with a unique love, and for its own sake. The purpose of creation is not to satiate human desires but rather for each element to find its own unique way to joy, peace, and fulfillment in loving, transforming union with God. Because of our distinct capacities as humans, we are to be the guardians, nurturers, and protectors of our sisters and brothers—human and otherkind.

But St. Francis also knew the value of penance. Today "following in the footprints of Jesus" also means confronting our own particular role in "covering over and forgetting" them. It is most sobering to realize that our ecological footprints, what we take for granted and consume daily, is effectively killing our sisters and brothers and the planet! Thus, I recommend that before you read further, you (1) calculate your carbon footprint at http://coolclimate.berkeley.edu/carboncalculator; (2) calculate your water-use footprint at http://goblue.zerofootprint.net/?language=en; and (3) read about your foodprint at http://brighterplanet.com/research.[8] Each of these web sites has helpful ideas for making

---

[6] Ibid., 303.

[7] *The Tree of the Crucified Life of Jesus*, Book Five (Excerpts), by Umbertino DaCasale (1305), in FAED, vol. III, *The Prophet*, 148.

[8] Matthew Kling and Ian Hough, "The American Carbon Foodprint: Understanding Your Food's Impact on Climate Change," Brighter Planet, Inc., 2010.

lifestyle changes toward living more sustainably.[9] Conversion of heart
and habits was St. Francis's first step in following in the footprints of
Jesus, and so too it must be ours. As we continue following, we will grow
in our capacity to grasp how all things are revelations of God and divine
actions in the natural world each day. We will come to cherish hospitality
and presence in contrast to utilitarian objectification of people and other
creatures.

Our deepest self-expression moves out of our spiritual center. Our vo-
cational choices and daily actions ultimately reveal with great authority
who we are in relationship with God. Indeed, our spiritual formation
and status and will determine our environmental ethics and our ecojustice actions as well. Living sustainably on this earth must flow from a
deep-seated conviction and confidence that God will provide for our
need, but not for our greed. Such certainty can be found by following in
the footprints of Jesus. Cathy Tisel Nelson composed and recorded the
following song. It has become a kind of a theme song for my prayer and
ecojustice activities. Cathy has given her permission for me to share it
with you, and I hope you find it inspirational and helpful as you read
this book.

Before I introduce the various sections of the book, something must
be said about the meaning of "sustainability." The source and motivation
for Christian concern for ecology and the environment is the belief that
the earth is "the dwelling place of God." Early Christian communities
understood the *oikumēnē* as "the whole inhabited globe." The *oikonomia
tou theo* was known as "the economy of God," and it was an ancient way
of speaking about the redemptive transformation of the world, brought to
us through Christ incarnate. However, the 1987 United Nations–sponsored
Brundtland Commission presumed that "sustainable development"[10]
meant raising productivity, accumulation of goods, and technological
innovations.[11] But that kind of thinking caused them to fail to address
key sources of poverty—the exploitation of workers and the pillaging

---

[9] When I first worked through these calculations, I found that if everyone in the
world lived as I live, it would take no less than 4.5 earths to sustain us! I have my
work toward conversion before me!

[10] Cited in Leonardo Boff, *Cry of the Earth, Cry of the Poor* (Maryknoll, NY: Orbis
Books, 1997), 66.

[11] James B. Martin-Schramm and Robert L. Stivers, *Christian Environmental Ethics:
A Case Study Method* (Maryknoll, NY: Orbis Books, 2003), 90, cite the World Commis-
sion on Environment and Development, *Our Common Future* (New York: Oxford
University Press, 1987), 8: the Brundtland Commission coined the term "sustainable

In the Footprints of Jesus

Cathy Tisel Nelson

Refrain

May we fol-low in the foot-prints of Je - sus Christ as we make our

way— to You. In-ward-ly cleansed and en - light - ened, on fire with the

to verses

Spir - it, may we fol-low in the foot-prints of Je - sus.

Final

sus.___ May we fol-low in the foot-prints of Je - sus.___

Verses

1. Feed - ing   the   hun - gry,   shelt - 'ring   the   home - less,
2. Friend   to   the   strang - er,   hope   for   the   hope - less,
3. Sim - ple   our   liv - ing,   few   our   pos - ses - sions,
4. With   liv - ing   wa - ters,   You   have   re - freshed   us;
5. As   we   move   for - ward   in - to   the   fu - ture,

1. set - ting   the   pris - on - er   free. ___   Bring-ing Your   jus - tice
2. car - ing   for   all   those   in   need. ___   Bring-ing Your   jus - tice
3. trust-ing   in   You   for   our   needs. ___   May   we   re - mem - ber
4. now we   are   filled with Your   fire. ___   May   we   have   cour-age,
5. led   by   Your   Spir - it,   O   God, ___   grant us   a   vis - ion,

2

1. to   all   the   earth,   to   all   the   earth,   O   God. ___
2. to   all   the   earth,   to   all   the   earth,   O   God. ___
3. how we   are   called   to   serve You   all   our   days. ___
4. wis - dom and   grace,   to   do   Your   will,   O   God. ___
5. show us   the   way   that   brings   us   all   to   You. ___

of nature. Brundtland's notion of "sustainable development" is an oxymoron because its real focus was economic growth for its own sake, and the primary goal was profit making. This thinking has permeated the globalization of world markets through the present day.

By contrast, "sustainability" as it is defined in biology and ecology is "the trend of ecosystems toward equilibrium, sustained in the web of interdependencies and complementarities flourishing in ecosystems."[12] Genuine "sustainability" requires social and economic structures that support *social justice*—the right relationship between persons, roles, and institutions—and *ecological justice*, which is the right relationship with nature, sufficient access to resources, and the assurance of quality of life."[13]

A renewed vision of community is essential for interdependent sustainability.[14] Such a vision is found in early Christian sources, utilizing the rich meanings gleaned from the Greek root *oikos*. The habitability of the earth is the central reality that links "economy, ecology, and ecumenicity." "Economy in its Greek-root meaning is simply the ordering of the household for the sustenance of its members."[15] Theologian Larry Rasmussen explained the importance of this:

> Economics is *eco* (habitat as the household) + *nomos* (the rules or law). Economics means knowing how things work and arranging these "home systems" (ecosystems) so that the material requirements of the household of life are met and sustained. The household is established as hospitable habitat. The basic task of any economy, then, is *the continuation of life*, though no economist has put it that way for ages. In fact, the kind of economics generating earth's present distress resulted from three decisive moves *away* from *oikos* economics . . . to consider nature as interchangeable parts . . . to generate affluence by expanding to new worlds . . . and to shift

---

development" to mean development that "meets the needs of the present without compromising the ability of future generations to meet their own needs."

[12] Boff, *Cry of the Earth*, 66.

[13] Ibid., 105.

[14] See World Council of Churches, *Accelerated Climate Change: Sign of Peril, Test of Faith* (Geneva: WCC Publications, 1994).

[15] Ibid., cited in Larry L. Rasmussen, *Earth Community, Earth Ethics* (Maryknoll, NY: Orbis Books, 1996), 144.

economic attention from the household and its community [sustainability] to the firm or corporation [profit making].[16]

In their 1991 statement Renewing the Earth, the US Catholic bishops made a similar point, defining *authentic development* this way: "It supports moderation and even austerity in the use of material resources . . . encourages a balanced view of human progress consistent with respect for nature . . . invites the development of alternative visions of the good society and the use of economic models with richer standards of well-being than material productivity alone . . . requires affluent nations to seek ways to reduce and restructure their over consumption of natural resources . . . [encourages] the proper use of both agricultural and industrial technologies, so that . . . technology benefits people and enhances the land."[17]

My purpose in writing this book is to provide knowledge and motivation toward the spiritual renewal necessary to move us beyond the present environmental crises.[18] Here I unfold portions of the theological, spiritual, and ethical treasure trove the Christian tradition, and particularly Catholic and Franciscan traditions, has to offer for our efforts to achieve sustainable living. In part 1, I open the wonderful collection of texts that illuminate our understanding of God's creation, first in the Hebrew Testament and then in the Christian Testament. In chapter 1, I show the importance of the relationship of the Christian doctrines of redemption and creation and their importance for how we form and shape environmental ethics and our own choices for sustainable living. Chapter 2 provides greater details about how Jesus' life and ministry and the experiences of early Christians form even greater foundations for the linkages between the doctrines of creation and redemption. Here I give special attention to St. Bonaventure's development of a hope-filled vision of the New Creation, and to rich new insights from scientific concepts of emergence and evolution.

In part 2, I examine the life of St. Francis and St. Clare, the founders of the Franciscan movement, as models for sustainable living. Chapter

---

[16] Rasmussen, *Earth Community*, 91–92.

[17] United States Catholic Conference, Renewing the Earth, part III, http://www.usccb.org/issues-and-action/human-life-and-dignity/environment/renewing-the-earth.cfm, accessed December 23, 2010.

[18] This book is also an updating of my *Franciscan Theology of the Environment: An Introductory Reader* (Quincy, IL: Franciscan Press, 2002), now available from St. Anthony Messenger Press.

3 considers Clare's choice to "follow in the footprints of the poor Christ," her spirituality, and her *Form of Life* as a way marked by cosmic mutuality. Countering the common simplistic "birdbath images" of St Francis, chapter 4 unfolds the profound conversion that undergirds St. Francis's way of life, his concept of the kinship of creation, and its meaning for ecotheology and sustainable living today.

Part 3 gives voice to St. Bonaventure of Bagnoregio, the university theologian who is the most authentic interpreter of the values and vision of St. Francis in terms of systematic theology. Bonaventure's vision holds that Christ stands at the center of creation. The Seraphic Doctor's work is deeply rooted in Scripture, is focused on the Trinity, and opens the way for conversations between science and theology. Part 4 introduces John Duns Scotus and his positive view of the incarnation of Christ as the one who is "God's Masterpiece." Sin was not the motive for the incarnation. Scotus shows us the intrinsic value of each particular being in creation—a challenge to the loss of biodiversity—and his ethics point us to economics and politics that lead to justice, peace, and sustainable living.

Part 5 is most demanding in that it confronts four critical issues of our day: global warming and climate change, the right to water, the right to food, and the need to convert to the use of renewable and sustainable energy sources. Chapter 7 tackles the daunting issues of global warming. Here St. Francis exemplifies a way to face the limits of life that can free us to make the urgent, immediate, and necessary changes to heal our planet. Chapter 8 unpacks the complexities of the global water crisis. There we turn to Catholic social teaching and the spirituality of St. Francis to show us a way forward for achieving a sustainable water supply. Chapter 9 invites us to awaken to our status as earth creatures. We are sojourners and guests in God's land, and we need to care for it in sustainable ways so that present and future generations can have sufficient and nutritious food. Eating is a moral activity! Finally, in chapter 10 we examine the intersections among our own lifestyles, our use of energy, and energy policies. Again, St. Francis shows us a way of life for a hope-filled future and for sustainable living, while St. Bonaventure's virtue ethics serve as our guide.

Each chapter includes a selection from the writings of Francis, Clare, Bonaventure, or Scotus. There is an extended reflection and application on the topic at hand, followed by questions for reflection and discussion. Suggestions for action are provided, along with a prayer and recommendations for further study. It is my sincere hope that in some small way this work will assist us in returning to sustainable ways of living as a global family in justice, peace, and integrity so that there will be no one in need. To this end, to paraphrase St. Francis, I have done in part what is mine to do; may Christ continue to teach us what is ours![19]

Dawn M. Nothwehr, OSF, PhD
Catholic Theological Union, Chicago, IL
The Feast of Our Lady of Lourdes, February 11, 2012

---

[19] See *The Remembrance of the Desire of a Soul* by Thomas of Celano (1245–1247), bk. II, chap. CLXII, 214, in FAED, vol. II, *The Founder*, 386. The original quote reads, "I have done *what is mine; may Christ teach* you what is yours!"

Acknowledgments

Scripture texts in this work are taken from the *New Revised Standard Version Bible* © 1989, Division of Christian Education of the National Council of the Churches of Christ in the United States of America. Used by permission. All rights reserved.

Excerpts from the early documents of St. Clare of Assisi are from Regis J. Armstrong, ed. and trans., *The Lady—Clare of Assisi: Early Documents*, rev. ed. (New York: New City Press, 2006). Used with permission.

Excerpts from the early documents of St. Francis of Assisi are from the three-volume series *Francis of Assisi: Early Documents*, ed. Regis J. Armstrong, J. A. Wayne Hellman, and William J. Short: vol. 1, *The Saint* (New York: New City Press, 1999); vol. II, *The Founder* (New York: New City Press, 2000); and vol. III, *The Prophet* (New York: New City Press, 2001). Used with permission.

Reproduction in the preface of Cathy Tisel Nelson, "In the Footprints of Jesus," © 1993, 1998 Cathy Tisel Nelson. All Rights Reserved. Text translation used by permission of Regis Armstrong, OFM Cap., The Franciscan Institute, St. Bonaventure University, St. Bonaventure, New York 14778. Used with permission.

Portions of chapter 6 of this work have been reproduced from Dawn M. Nothwehr, OSF, *The Franciscan View of the Human Person: Some Central Elements*, Franciscan Institute Publications, St. Bonaventure, NY, © 2005. Used with permission.

In chapter 7, "Search . . ." is an unpublished poem by Eileen Haugh, OSF. Included here in loving memory of Sr. Eileen Haugh, OSF (November 3, 1928, to May 23, 2011), member of the Sisters of St. Francis, Rochester, MN, cherished teacher, and gifted poet. Used with permission of the Sisters of St. Francis, Rochester, MN.

In chapter 8, "Sister Water" is an unpublished prayer poem by Mary Goergen, OSF. Sr. Mary Goergen, OSF, is a member of the Sisters of St. Francis, Rochester, MN, a beloved elementary school teacher, gardener, and ecological justice advocate. Used with permission of the author.

"The Hydrologic Cycle" image used in chapter 8 is from the National Weather Service, http://www.srh.noaa.gov/srh/jetstream/atmos/hydro.htm, and is in the public domain. Special thanks to Dennis Cain and Steven Cooper of the National Weather Service for their assistance in providing a high-resolution version of the chart.

Excerpts in chapter 10 from Bishop Luc Bouchard's pastoral letter The Integrity of Creation and the Athabasca Oil Sands © 2010 Diocese of St. Paul, Alberta, Canada. Used with permission.

Portions of the material in the chart in chapter 10, "Norms, Themes, and Guidelines for Energy and Climate Policy," are taken or adapted from James B. Martin Schramm, *Climate Justice: Ethics, Energy, and Public Policy* (Minneapolis: Fortress Press, 2010), 38–39, 42–44, 46, and 119. Used with permission.

The "Crown of Thorns around the Earth" image in the afterword is used with permission of the artist, Clairvaux McFarland, OSF.

"The Way of the Cross and the Suffering Earth" in the afterword is by members of the Water Forum, Sisters of St. Francis, Rochester, MN: Sisters Ruth Peterson, Victorine Honerman, Verona Klein, Clairvaux McFarland, Eileen Haugh, Bernetta Quinn, Joseen Vought, DeLellis Hinrichs, Valerie Usher, Carlan Kraman, Valerie Olson, Franchon Pirkl, Adelia Marie Ryan, Mary Ann Dols, and Cojourner Janet Cramer. Used with permission from the authors and the Sisters of St. Francis, Rochester, MN.

The reflection by Mary Southard, CSJ, used in the afterword is taken from her self-published calendar. Used with permission.

Part 1

The Bible: Creation and the Word

Chapter 1

"In the Beginning . . .": The Hebrew Testament on Creation and Redemption

Introduction: St. Francis and St. Clare and the Scriptures

It is said that St. Francis of Assisi had such great reverence for the Sacred Scriptures that he would pick up from the ground pieces of paper that contained any lettering on them. He reasoned that the letters on such scraps could, literally, be put together to form the texts of the Holy Scriptures, the Word of God.[1] A similar kind of reverence for the Bible can be seen in Clare's *Second Letter to Blessed Agnes of Prague*. Praying with the Scriptures and meditating on their message was very important for the Poor Ladies of San Damiano (the Poor Clares) as a means of following the example of Jesus, or as Clare put it, to "[hold] fast to the footprints (1 Pet 2:21) of Him to Whom you have merited to be joined as a Spouse."[2]

---

[1] Thomas of Celano, *The Life of Saint Francis* (1228–1229), chap. XXIX, 82, in *Francis of Assisi: Early Documents*, vol. I, *The Saint*, trans. and ed. Regis J. Armstrong, J. A. Wayne Hellmann, and William J. Short (New York: New City Press, 1999), 251–52.

[2] Clare of Assisi, "Second Letter to Blessed Agnes of Prague," in *Clare of Assisi: Early Documents*, trans. and ed. Regis J. Armstrong (St. Bonaventure, NY: Franciscan Institute Publications, 1993), 40.

One need not look far to realize the importance of Scripture in the lives of St. Francis and St. Clare.[3] Clearly, for Francis and Clare the sacred texts revealed Jesus Christ, the incarnate Word in whose footprints all must follow.[4] To follow in the footprints of Jesus meant to conform one's ways of being, thinking, and acting to the life, teachings, and example of Jesus. And so it is with this same respect that we, like St. Francis and St. Clare of Assisi, begin our study of Franciscan understandings of the environment, with a focus on the Bible. We will see that the Hebrew Testament (Old Testament) and the Christian Scriptures (New Testament) are helpful for understanding in light of Christian faith the current discussions about ecology and the present threats to the world's natural environment.

Another way we know of Francis's deep regard for the Scriptures is through his *Testament*, the document he gave the first Franciscan friars in which he explained his most important teachings. Further, St. Francis regarded the Gospel itself as the very center of the Rule for the Friars and the Poor Ladies.[5] Clare and the Poor Ladies of Assisi joined Francis in taking up a life in pursuit of Gospel perfection.[6] The daily practice of the Poor Ladies included times in which they meditated together on the Scriptures. And then they engaged in the ordinary tasks of living in community and assisting the poor—practicing and integrating the insights they gained through their contemplation, the Word that had grasped their heart.[7]

Finally, it is rare to find something written by St. Francis or St. Clare that does not include at least a paraphrase of some portion of a biblical text. Given that Francis and Clare lived in thirteenth-century Assisi, Italy, we find that they often understood the biblical texts as a narrative or

---

[3] For works by Francis, see the three volumes of *Francis of Assisi: Early Documents*. For works by Clare, see *Clare of Assisi: Early Documents*.

[4] Francis of Assisi, "A Letter to Brother Leo" (1224–1226), in FAED, vol. I, *The Saint*, 122–23.

[5] See Francis of Assisi, "The Undated Writings—The Admonitions," VII, in FAED, vol. I, *The Saint*, 132. See also Francis of Assisi, "The Testament" (1226), 14–15, in FAED, vol. I, *The Saint*, 124–27. In addition, see Regis J. Armstrong and Ignatius C. Brady, trans. and eds., *Francis and Clare: The Complete Works* (New York: Paulist Press, 1982), 4, 12, 17–18, 108n2.

[6] See Armstrong and Brady, trans. and eds., *Francis and Clare*, 170, 172, 178.

[7] See Ingrid J. Peterson, *Clare of Assisi: A Bibliographical Study* (Quincy, IL: Franciscan Press, 1993), 279, 283–84.

story of faith, in a literal[8] or analogical[9] sense, and as a means of providing authority to what they say concerning the topic at hand.[10] At that
time, they lacked the tools developed by more recent Scripture scholars
for gaining a deeper understanding of the Bible. Both Francis and Clare
are "at home" with Scripture as one is comfortable with a good friend.
Unfortunately, we have more of St. Francis's writings than we have of
St. Clare's, so most of what we say here will be from his perspective.[11]
However, there is plenty of evidence that Clare had a lot of influence on
how Francis thought.[12]

Within the various works of Francis and Clare— prayers, letters,
poems, the rules for the first, second, and third Franciscan orders, etc.—
we find extensive use of scriptural texts that show God as the Creator
of the universe and how God is revealed through the natural world.[13]
Intuitively, Francis wove this revelation from Scripture together with his
personal knowledge of Jesus the Christ Incarnate, the One who became
part of the material world and through whom the world was brought
into existence.

For Francis, who was very familiar with the natural beauty of the
Umbrian region around Assisi, Italy, who knew much of the Bible from
memory, and who had an intimate relationship with Jesus, it seemed
quite clear that the Bible tells one story of God's relationship to the world.

---

[8] The literal sense of Scripture refers to a way of interpreting the biblical texts
stressing the obvious common meaning of each word in light of the kind of work
(poem, song, historical record, etc.) it is. *Litera* is the Latin word for "letter."

[9] The analogical sense of Scripture is a way of interpreting the biblical texts by
finding a symbolic meaning for the words concerning human destiny or purpose
(beyond the literal meaning). *Anagein* is the Greek word for "to refer."

[10] Thomas of Celano, *The Major Legend of St. Francis of Assisi* (1260–1263), chap. X,
2, in FAED, vol. II, *The Founder*, ed. Regis J. Armstrong, J. A. Wayne Hellmann, and
William J. Short (New York: New City Press, 2000), 613.

[11] For an explanation of this situation, see Margaret Carney, "Franciscan Women
and the Theological Enterprise," in *The History of Franciscan Theology*, ed. Kenan B.
Osborne (St. Bonaventure, NY: The Franciscan Institute, 1994), 331–45, especially 333.

[12] See Ingrid J. Peterson, *Clare of Assisi: A Biographical Study.*

[13] For a small sampling of such texts, see Francis of Assisi, "The Later Admonition
and Exhortation to the Brothers and Sisters of Penance," 61; Francis of Assisi, "Exhortation to the Praise of God," 138; Francis of Assisi, "The Praises to Be Said at All
the Hours," 161; and Thomas of Celano, *The Life of Saint Francis* (1228–1229), chap.
XXIX, 80–81, in FAED, vol. I, *The Saint*, 49, 138, 161–62, 250–51. See also Thomas of
Celano, *The Major Legend of St. Francis* (1260–1263), chap. VIII, in FAED, vol. II, *The
Founder*, 586–95.

This relationship began from the first moment of creation; it continued through the many moments when people rejected and then returned to God and through God's many promises and covenants with people. That story came to a climax in the birth, life, death, and resurrection of Jesus. Today theologians talk about this reality as the connection between the Christian doctrines of creation and redemption. Unfortunately, what was so obvious for St. Francis was not always so for theologians and the church, and it was nearly lost.

Where early Christians, Francis and Clare, and medieval theologians such as Bonaventure of Bagnoregio, Thomas Aquinas, and John Duns Scotus saw the created world as a "second book of revelation" that was enhanced and explained in the Scriptures, the numerous connections to the natural world found in the Bible were grossly neglected in the telling of the story of salvation in modern times. There was a strong emphasis on the "saving of souls," and the natural world beyond humanity was seen as unimportant. Only when it seemed that scientific theories conflicted with a literal reading of the Bible (e.g., Galileo and the heliocentric universe, or Charles Darwin and his theory of biological evolution) did the church and Christian theologians deal with scientific matters. It was left to science to deal with the natural world. Some Catholic Scripture scholars developed a theory of "special revelation" and joined debates of the nineteenth and twentieth centuries and attempted to defend the literal reading of the Bible against biological evolution. They claimed that God acted directly to create every new species. Another debate centered on the meaning of Genesis 1:28 concerning humans having "dominion over all living creatures."

Two important developments took place to help the church and Catholic Scripture scholars return to more authentic ways of understanding the Bible in relation to the environment, ecology, and the whole creation. In 1943 Pius XII published an encyclical, *Divino Afflante Spiritu*,[14] that directed biblical scholars to use ancient language studies (Hebrew, Greek, Aramaic, and other languages of the original ancient biblical manuscripts) and other modes of modern biblical criticism to interpret the Scriptures. The second development was the publication of *Dei Verbum*, The Dogmatic Constitution on Divine Revelation of the Second Vatican

[14] An encyclical is a pastoral teaching document circulated to the whole church by the pope. See Pope Pius XII, *Divino Afflante Spiritu*, http://www.vatican.va/holy_father/pius_xii/encyclicals/documents/hf_p-xii_enc_30091943_divino-afflante-spiritu_en.html, accessed July 11, 2010.

Council (1965), which stressed that Sacred Scripture, taken together with the church's tradition, is the supreme rule of Catholic faith.[15] These developments brought new opportunities for conversations between science and religion. It quickly became evident that where science seeks to explain the workings of the universe, religion and the Bible address the meaning of the universe; it is in God that the ultimate meaning of all creatures is found. There is no conflict between religion and science. Today we have the benefit of some 850 more years (beyond the lifetimes of St. Francis and St. Clare) of Scripture scholarship to assist us in discovering the relationship between biblical wisdom and questions of our day. As we seek to uncover a Franciscan theology of the environment, we need to follow Francis and Clare and utilize Scripture as a major source.

The Unity of the Stories of Creation and Redemption

When Christians think about the environment, ecology, or the natural world, the story of creation in Genesis usually comes to mind. But, as we will see, there are several creation accounts in the Bible, and other texts in books such as Job, Sirach, Proverbs, and Wisdom show how creation is connected to the bigger story of redemption, the major focus of the Bible. Taken together, these stories give us a rich and deep vision of the thoroughgoing relationship of God, humans, living beings, and nonliving beings in the entire universe.

Indeed, it is important to recall that the God who created is the same God who redeems. "And this God creates not only Israel, but all other peoples and the whole world in which human history is enacted."[16] If

---

[15] See *Dei Verbum*, http://www.vatican.va/archive/hist_councils/ii_vatican_council/documents/vat-ii_const_19651118_dei-verbum_en.html, accessed July 11, 2010. *Dei Verbum* presents three broad principles for interpreting biblical texts: (1) the primary message of any biblical text is the meaning intended by its author(s); therefore, the language, history, and culture of the Bible must be studied (no. 12); (2) it is important to examine themes in light of how the Bible as a whole treats them; and (3) taking into account the entire tradition of the church, the interpreter should study how a particular passage was used and understood in the earlier life of the church (no. 12). These three principles of biblical interpretation affirm Roman Catholicism as an ever-evolving tradition concerned with illuminating and responding to the changing signs of the times.

[16] Zachary Hayes, *A Window to the Divine: A Study of Christian Creation Theology* (Quincy, IL: Franciscan Press, 1997), 18.

we are to understand what the Bible has to say about environmental and ecological issues, we need to see how the biblical texts deal with the interactions between God, humans, living, and nonliving beings. Clearly, for the Hebrew Testament writers, the only divine being was God. Yet everything God created was "good and beautiful" (Gen 1; Hebrew = *tob*), capable of revealing something about the creator; was to be shared among the creatures; and was respected because it was "of God." Second, there was no absolute separation between the spiritual and the material because "The earth is the LORD's and all that is in it, the world, and those who live in it" (Ps 24:1). Humans and all creation are to serve God and follow the divine commandments. Human service to God is not enslavement but a loving covenanted relationship for the flourishing of the entire creation. Various expressions of the covenant are woven through the whole Bible, but especially in the Hebrew Testament. The Hebrew Testament also shows God as the origin of goodness and life, while evil and sin originate in history where human beings have not responded to God.[17]

Creation and Redemption in Genesis 1–11

Even though today the Hebrew Testament begins with the creation stories of Genesis, the older of the two creation narratives in Genesis is the one found in Genesis 2:4b-25. Scripture scholars refer to this version as the Yahwist source, and they think it was written about 1010–930 BCE. God is the main character in this story. A human being is formed by God out of the mud of the earth, and God breathes the very breath of life (Hebrew = *rûah*) into its nostrils, making it a living person (v. 7).[18] This creature was needy, so God placed it in the Garden of Eden, a lush place of plenty, and directed the person to cultivate and care for it (v. 15). God also created the animals, and the animals and the humans share in the status of being "living souls" or "living creatures" (Hebrew = *nefesh chayah*).[19] Further, the human is asked to give the animals names and find a companion among them (v. 19). This act of naming was considered

[17] Ibid., 19.

[18] See also Ps 104:30; Eccl 3:19, 21; and Gen 1:24-26.

[19] Jeanne Kay, "Concepts of Nature in the Hebrew Bible," in *Franciscan Theology of the Environment: An Introductory Reader*, ed. Dawn M. Nothwehr (Quincy, IL: Franciscan Press, 2002), 27.

an act of intimacy, of creating an orderly bond and caring relationship between the human and the other creatures.

According to Scripture scholars, the Genesis 1 account, often called the "Days of Creation," is dated about the sixth century BCE and is authored by the Priestly writer. This is an example of what Franciscan theologian Zachary Hayes calls "a physical cosmology which manifest clear parallels with the accounts of origins in other religions of the ancient world, though these elements have been shaped and reformed by the confrontation with Israel's own religious experience." [20] This account contains God's directives to humans to "subdue" the earth and to have "dominion over" it. In keeping with proper methods of biblical interpretation, we need to understand this text in its original setting and then see what meaning it can have for us today. The Priestly writer stressed Israel's belief that God created order out of chaos, and this story includes a day of rest for praising that God. We need to recall that this text was written when Israel was being held captive in Babylon.

The Genesis 1 story is very similar to the Babylonian creation myth, the *Enuma Elish*,[21] but the differences are most significant.[22] In the *Enuma Elish*, there is a horrible battle in which the goddess Taimat is killed as an act of vengeance by the god Marduk. Her carcass is then used by Marduk to create the world. By contrast, the God of Israel creates order out of chaos by simply speaking a word. In fact, the Spirit of God, the *rûah* of God, moves over the waters, giving the life energy to all of creation (v. 2). In Genesis, the heavenly bodies and the fertility of the natural world are simply creatures of God, whereas the Babylonians considered them sacred. In the *Enuma Elish*, humans were created from the blood of an evil god, killed by other gods, and thus became slaves of the gods. In Genesis 1:26-27, the sixth day saw the creation of humans and animals, and God called them "very good, beautiful" (Hebrew = *tob*). Humans need to remember their common creaturely status *with* the animals, as St. Francis did, and respect them accordingly.

The Hebrew Testament tells us that humans were created in God's "image and likeness" (Gen 1:26-27). According to Scripture scholar Claus

---

[20] Zachary Hayes, *A Window to the Divine*, 20–21.

[21] See Bernard W. Anderson, *Creation versus Chaos: The Reinterpretation of Mystical Symbolism in the Bible* (New York: Association Press, 1967). Also see Alexander Heidel, *The Babylonian Genesis* (Chicago: University of Chicago Press, 1951).

[22] Susan Power Bratton, "Christian Ecotheology and the Hebrew Scriptures," in *Franciscan Theology of the Environment: An Introductory Reader*, ed. Nothwehr, 51–52.

Westermann, this reflects language used by ancient Egyptian and Meso-potamian kings, who were considered representatives of their gods or as trustees of the gods' possessions.[23] This understanding was a source of dignity for the exiled Jewish people, who could thus see themselves as entrusted with the privilege of representing God and as delegated to care for creation as God cares for it. But more significantly, this indicated the spiritual capacity of the humans that enables them to relate to God in a distinct way. However, humans remain creatures among others of God's creation.[24]

After declaring humans to be made in the image of God, the text states: "God blessed them, and God said to them, 'Be fruitful and multiply, and fill the earth and subdue it; and have dominion over the fish of the sea and over the birds of the air and over every living thing that moves upon the earth'" (Gen 1:28).

In Genesis, the creation of humans is for the service of living creatures with which humans share an earthly kinship. To keep the meaning of "subdue" and "dominion" in perspective, it is helpful to recall that these stories were written during the Neolithic Age, when likely little was known about egalitarian relationships. So humans (Hebrew = *adam*) are to rule over the biota (Gen 2:19), the Leviathan over the sea (Job 40:25-32; 41:1-22), and the Behemoth over the land (Job 40:15-24). But all of those "ruling" are ultimately accountable to God, who is their Creator, the loving God of the covenant.

Scripture scholars have shown how all of the creatures are involved with different kinds of relationships with each other.[25] The human role of "dominion" is held in perspective by the "mocking of the human in-ability to understand nature beyond that which has been domesticated."[26] The plants and animals empathize with human joys and sorrows.[27] Isaiah 34–35 exemplifies how nature chastises humans, sympathizes with them, and also rejoices in their redemption. "And the streams of Edom shall

---

[23] See Claus Westermann, *Genesis 1–11: A Commentary*, trans. John J. Scullion (Minneapolis: Augsburg Publishing House, 1974), 153.

[24] Susan Power Bratton, "Christian Ecotheology and the Hebrew Scriptures," 56.

[25] See Clarence J. Glacken, *Traces on the Rhodian Shore: Nature and Culture in Western Thought from Ancient Times to the End of the Eighteenth Century* (Berkeley: University of California Press, 1967). See Gen 1:30; Ps 104:14-20; 145:16; 147:8-9; Job 38:39-41; Job 39:1-8, 28.

[26] See Jeanne Kay, "Concepts of Nature in the Hebrew Bible," 29. See Job 38:25-27; 39:9-12; and Eccl 11:5.

[27] See Joel 1:12; Amos 1:2; Jonah 3:7-7; and Isa 14:7-8.

be turned into pitch, and her soil into sulfur; her land shall become burning pitch. . . . The hawk and the hedgehog shall possess it; the owl and
the raven shall live in it. . . . Thorns shall grow over its strongholds,
nettles and thistles in its fortresses. . . . Wildcats shall meet with hyenas,
goat-demons shall call to each other. . . . There too the buzzards shall
gather, each one with its mate" (34:9-15).

During Israel's future salvation, however, "the wilderness and the dry
land shall be glad, the desert shall rejoice and blossom; like the crocus
it shall blossom abundantly, and rejoice with joy and singing" (35:1-2).
The environment deteriorates when people sin; nature is often God's
tool of reward and punishment. Nature's beneficence depends on human
morality. Humans' dominion over nature, then, is strictly conditioned
on their moral fitness. Humans who sin bestialize the divine image and
diminish their authority over nature (Gen 9:7). The full meaning of "dominion" emerges later in Genesis in the story of the Great Flood.

In Genesis 6, God grieves over the immense wickedness of humans,
initiating the onslaught of an ecological disaster of worldwide proportions. Only Noah and his family were faithful and thus exempted from
the Great Flood that destroyed all other humans, "together with animals
and creeping things and birds of the air" (v. 7). Noah followed God's
instruction to build an ark and bring "two of every kind . . . to keep
them alive" (v. 20). This action exemplified the true meaning of "having
dominion"—to affirm morality and to care and save the other living
creatures.

After the Flood, God indicated that from this time forward, a reckon-
ing will be required from humans and from every beast alike (Gen 9:1-4).
Then God established a covenant with Noah's family, their descendants,
and all living creatures (vv. 9-11) that is symbolized by God's "bow in
the clouds" (v. 13). The story of Noah and the Flood illustrates that
human offenses potentially threaten the rest of creation. "Dominion,"
enacted by a representative of God in Noahic covenant partnership,
clearly ruled out anthropocentricism or the exploitation of nonhuman
nature. Today, with every "bow in the clouds," we too are invited to
recall this Noahic covenant that God made with the earth and all of its
inhabitants.

Genesis 1:28 also includes God's command that humans "fill the earth
and subdue it." The Hebrew term for "subdue" (Hebrew = *kabas*) means
"to bring into bondage." However, according to biblical scholar James
Barr, and in light of the use of the term throughout the Bible, "subdue"

simply means to inhabit the land that God has given as a gift, transforming it into a home where God can be worshiped.[28] Subduing the earth cannot be equated with a license to exploit nonhuman creation. In fact, the premeditated decimation of nature is uniquely God's prerogative, not that of humans (Ps 29:5-6, 9; Zech 11:1-3; and Hab 3:5-8). Human arrogance against nature is actually considered blasphemous against God (2 Kgs 19:23-24; Isa 9:9-11; 10:13-19; 14:24; Hab 2:17; Judg 6:3-6; Ezek 29:3-59). Humans indirectly bring about environmental destruction as an outcome of sin, so to do so directly is foolish arrogance. In the Hebrew Testament, crimes against God are also crimes against the natural landscape in which they were committed (Gen 4:10; Lev 18:25; Ezek 12:19; Hos 1:1-3). Reciprocal justice governs human-nature relationships. All moral and immoral deeds have a positive or a negative impact on the land in which they are perpetrated, and the land responds accordingly. Humans do not commit evil in isolation or without effects on the entire community. The masses suffer for the crimes of a few. This reality places a heavy weight on individuals to act responsibly and morally. "The entire Torah could be considered as a guidebook for environmental maintenance. The belief that all human offenses potentially imperil nature is the Bible's strongest statement about human domination over the environment."[29]

 In summary, Genesis 1 confesses belief in a God who creates, bringing order out of chaos in a nonviolent manner. In this context, the commission given by God to humankind, made in God's image, is to protect the balance of life that God's ordering word has built into the earth, and to promote the continuation of all species having a place in that delicate balance.

Creation and Redemption beyond Genesis

Second Isaiah

The place that most clearly connects the themes of creation and redemption is the second part of the book of Isaiah, known as Second

---

[28] James Barr, "Man and Nature: The Ecological Controversy and the Old Testament," in *Ecology and Religion in History*, ed. David and Ellen Spring (New York: Harper & Row, 1974), 63–64.

[29] Jeanne Kay, "Concepts of Nature in the Hebrew Bible," 36.

Isaiah (chaps. 40–50). This text was composed at about the same time as Genesis 1. The context of its writing is that the author is directed by God to "speak tenderly to Jerusalem [because] her service [as an exile in Babylon] is at an end" (Isa 40:1). Here we have some reflections on the theological significance of the end of Israel's exile and the new exodus to the Promised Land. The prophet links God's redemption of Israel and God's re-creation of the earth. An important Hebrew word that shows this connection is *bara*. This word is used frequently in the creation stories of Genesis and also in Second Isaiah. It means "making full" or literally "fattening" in a way that only God can perform. "The same word is used for the original creation as for God establishing his loving kindness toward Israel."[30] Both actions are very personal and responsible acts of God.

God leads the Israelites through the wilderness to a new occupation of the Promised Land, a kind of redemption that is God's gift. During this new exodus, valleys are filled in and mountains leveled so that the glory of God can be revealed anew (Isa 40:4-5). The new creation is also God's gift. Echoing Genesis 1, Second Isaiah encourages a depressed and impoverished Israel to trust in God: "For thus says the LORD, who created the heavens (he is God!), who formed the earth and made it (he established it; he did not create it a chaos, he formed it to be inhabited!): I am the LORD, and there is no other" (45:18). The word "chaos" (Hebrew = *tohu)* is a clear reference to the origins of creation, when the earth was "a formless void" and without God's ordering (Gen 1:2). For Second Isaiah, God continues to call order out of chaos through his caring involvement with all creatures, sustaining them and their survival. God invites: "Turn to me and be saved, all the ends of the earth! For I am God, and there is no other" (Isa 45:22). Clearly, in Second Isaiah *creation and redemption* are *complementary* in the deepest sense of the word.

The Prophets: Hosea and Jeremiah

The connection between creation and redemption is sometimes made in a negative way in the Hebrew Testament. Two examples of this are found in the preexilic writings of Hosea and Jeremiah. The first instance in Hosea recalls the Noahic covenant: "On that day I will answer, says the LORD, I will answer the heavens and they shall answer the earth; and

---

[30] Susan Power Bratton, "Christian Ecotheology and the Hebrew Scriptures,"53.

the earth shall answer the grain, the wine, and the oil, and they shall answer" (2:21-22). Here even the animals were given commandments by God (Hebrew = *mitzvot*) in Gen 1:22 and 8:17. But later, Hosea points out, because the people sinned, violating the covenant, God has a legal suit against Israel: "Therefore the land mourns, and all who live in it languish; together with the wild animals and the birds of the air, even the fish of the sea are perishing" (4:3). A century later Jeremiah proclaims the extension of the covenant to the earth: "Give them this charge for their masters: Thus says the LORD of hosts, the God of Israel: This is what you shall say to your masters: It is I who by my great power and my outstretched arm have made the earth, with the people and animals that are on the earth, and I give it to whomever I please" (27:4-5). The people suffer because they have failed to honor the sacred Noahic covenant relationship, and thus the land also suffers. Jeremiah calls for a "mournful dirge" on behalf of the despoiled land and all that dwell on it: "Shall I not punish them for these things? says the LORD; and shall I not bring retribution on a nation such as this? Take up weeping and wailing for the mountains, and a lamentation for the pastures of the wilderness, because they are laid waste so that no one passes through, and the lowing of cattle is not heard; both the birds of the air and the animals have fled and are gone" (Jer 9:9-10). Jeremiah maintains the people have brought this ecological crisis upon themselves by their own life choices, and thus a lament is required (8:4–10:25).

Israel's infidelity and failure resulted in defeat by Nebuchadnezzar, king of Babylon (Jer 27:5-6). Yet hope remained. What God created and what has been reduced to chaos by sin, Jeremiah suggests, can be recreated. He announced a time of a new creation is coming, when Nebuchadnezzar's kingdom will collapse (27:7), ending Israel's long period of exile (25:11-12; 29:10; 28:1).

The Psalms

God as the Creator and the natural world as the occasion of praise of God are common themes in the Psalms. Psalm 104, commonly known as the "Franciscan Psalm" because it closely resembles St. Francis's "Canticle of the Creatures," recalls the creation stories of Genesis 1 and 2, honoring God the Creator. The psalmist responds with wonder and awe to the beauty of creation (vv. 24-34) in some detail: God's splendor in the heavens (vv. 1-4), how the chaotic waters were tamed to fertilize and feed the world (vv. 5-18), and how primordial night was transformed into a gentle time of refreshment (vv. 19-23). Then the *rûah*, the Spirit, of God again appears: "When you hide your face, they are dismayed; when you take away their breath, they die and return to their dust. When you send forth your spirit, they are created; and you renew the face of the ground" (vv. 29-30).

These verses presuppose that God always creates in the Spirit. The Spirit is poured out on everything that exists, preserving and renewing it. In the Hebrew language, *rûah* (spirit/breath) is feminine, so the divine life in creation can be thought of not only in masculine images but also in feminine ones. Psalm 104 ends with hope: "Let sinners be consumed from the earth, and let the wicked be no more. Bless the LORD, O my soul. Praise the LORD!" (v. 35).

Psalm 146 speaks most clearly of the one and the same God who is the Creator and the Redeemer of all. There is no other source of salvation (v. 3) than God the Creator, the Maker of heaven and earth, the sea, and all that is in them (v. 6). It is this same God who "executes justice for the oppressed; who gives food to the hungry. The LORD sets the prisoners free; the LORD opens the eyes of the blind. The LORD lifts up those who are bowed down; the LORD loves the righteous. The LORD watches over the strangers; he upholds the orphan and the widow, but the way of the wicked he brings to ruin" (vv.7-9). In each activity, God responds to the creatures most in need, offering them the freedom of a redeemed life.

In the Wisdom literature, we find the themes of creation and redemption united in wisdom (*Hôkmah* in Hebrew and *Sophia* in Greek, both feminine nouns). Today Scripture scholars understand that "wisdom theology is creation theology." Wisdom represents the human effort to relate to creation as God has intended. The theme of redemption is closely intertwined with creation because people always struggle with the forces of chaos in their lives.

The Wisdom Literature

Another important set of texts about the environment and creation is the Wisdom literature.[31] Wisdom literature includes the biblical books of Job, Sirach, Proverbs, and Wisdom. Today we usually think of wisdom as an accumulation of insights people create or gather through experiences

---

[31] For a good basic discussion of Wisdom literature, see John H. Hayes, *Introduction to the Bible*, (Philadelphia: Westminster Press, 1971), chap. 14.

over a lifetime. But the Israelites thought of wisdom as a separate creation of God, something that guided the cosmos as well as humans. The way people gained access to wisdom was through "fear of the Lord"—deep reverence and respect for God. Wisdom is the key to understanding the universe, but it is also the way of proper action and the moral life before God. According to Scripture scholar Gerhardt von Rad, a characteristic of the Wisdom literature is "the determined effort to relate the phenomenon of the world, of 'nature' with its secrets of creation, to the saving revelation addressed to man."[32] Throughout the book of Proverbs the teacher consistently links the themes of creation and redemption in profound and penetrating ways. For example, in Proverbs 3, the teacher asserts, "The LORD by wisdom founded the earth" (v. 19).

Wisdom is personified as a woman in the first nine chapters of Proverbs, with strong suggestions of divinity.[33] In the Greek language, Wisdom is Sophia. Sophia is she who is the giver of life (Prov 4:23). In Proverbs 8, Sophia describes her character and works: "Ages ago I was set up, at the first, before the beginning of the earth" (v. 23). Sophia presents herself as existing before the rest of creation and as the very first of God's creative works, and not of the ordinary created order (vv. 22-26). She explains: "The LORD created me at the beginning of his work, the first of his acts of long ago. Ages ago I was set up, at the first, before the beginning of the earth. When there were no depths I was brought forth, when there were no springs abounding with water. Before the mountains had been shaped, before the hills, I was brought forth—when he had not yet made earth and fields, or the world's first bits of soil" (vv. 27-30).

Sophia is a creature of God and also a cocreator with God. She is involved in the activity of creation as a designer and master craftswoman: "When he assigned to the sea its limit, so that the waters might not transgress his command, when he marked out the foundations of the earth, then I was beside him, like a master worker; and I was daily his delight, rejoicing before him always" (vv. 29-30). Sophia is the model or exemplar of God's works. She is also the one who executes the creative activity of God—through her, creation happens, and she takes delight

---

[32] Gerhardt von Rad, *Old Testament Theology*, vol. 1 (New York: Harper & Row, 1962), 449.

[33] See Roger N. Whybray, *Wisdom in Proverbs: The Concept of Wisdom in Proverbs 1–9* (London: SCM Press, Ltd., 1965). Also see Roland E. Murphy, *The Tree of Life* (New York: Doubleday; The Anchor Bible Reference Library, 1990).

in creation. Sophia sustains the order of creation by opposing evil for the sake of justice (v. 13). Lady Wisdom, Sophia, invites her followers to listen to her and obey her directives. Those who follow them find life, but those who neglect her ways die (vv. 35-36).

Gleanings from Hebrew Testament Texts

The overriding viewpoint of the Hebrew Testament is that of choosing life over death.[34] As we have indicated, to "choose life" meant to keep God's commands (Hebrew = *mitzvot*). If one fulfilled the commandments, then one would have the means to produce or find food and enough to eat; protection from the extremes of weather; freedom from life-threatening dangers; sufficient capacity for human, animal, and plant reproduction; and sufficient shelter. All of this security would be accounted for as the work of God the Creator and the spiritual force (*rûah*) within all living beings. Choosing life would be continued through the capacity to have a sufficient livelihood to pass on to future generations. Today we might well call this a life based on sustainability.

Humans share the *nefesh chayah* and the *rûah* with all animate life. Jeanne Kay explains the implications of this:

> Judaism's belief in nature dependent on a single Creator God is therefore a belief in the fundamental unity of nature, rather than in its fragmentation under different powers as depicted in some forms of pantheism [worship of the objects of nature—plants, animals, rocks, rivers, etc.]. There is no textual or archaeological evidence that ancient Jews believed that God commanded humanity to deplete the environment to such an extent that its life-supporting capabilities deteriorate. In contrast, a life-sustaining environment, with sufficient rainfall and fertile soil, is considered among the most desirable of God's gifts. It is a principal reward for the demands of a Jewish life (Deut 11:14-17).[35]

The Hebrew Testament, including the creation stories of Genesis 1 and 2 and related texts, clearly shows that creation and redemption are intimately related and that there is a genuine kinship between humans and

---

[34] See Jeanne Kay, "Concepts of Nature in the Hebrew Bible," 39. Also see Deut 30:15-20.

[35] Jeanne Kay, "Concepts of Nature in the Hebrew Bible," 41.

all other creatures of God. Throughout salvation history, the God whose creative love overflows in creation also redeems, continuing to bring order out of the chaos caused by sin—all the work of a loving God.

Long before Ernest Haeckel first defined the science of ecology in 1866, the Bible presented humans and earth's other life forms as interconnected and interdependent, on religious grounds. Humans are distinct among creatures, but they are *also* profoundly *related* to all creatures. This is what St. Francis and St. Clare knew so well, exemplified with their lives, and passed on to us. St. Francis called all the animals "brother" or "sister," and we read in his story how even the wild animals came running to him as their friend and companion. And St. Clare taught that we must respect all the creatures—whether a person, a tree, or a paper wasp— because they all are made and loved by God.

In our next chapter, we will examine the Christian Scriptures, the New Testament, focusing on the theme of creation and the "new creation." We will see how the promises God made to the people of Israel are ful- filled in Jesus, the "Wisdom of God." Jesus' life and ministry are full of rich references to creation. We will examine how the Wisdom Woman of the Hebrew Testament and the parables, proverbs, and prayers of Jesus all play a part in the Christian understanding of the environment and ecological ethics.

From the Writings of St. Francis

Francis of Assisi, "The Admonitions VII:
Let Good Action Follow Knowledge"[36]

The apostle says, *the letter kills, but the spirit gives life.*

Those people are put to death by the letter who only wish to know the words alone, that they might be esteemed the wiser than others and be able to acquire great riches to give to their relatives and friends.

And those religious are put to death by the letter who are not willing to follow the spirit of the divine letter but, instead, wish only to know the words and to interpret them for others.

[36] Francis of Assisi, "The Undated Writings—The Admonitions," VII, in FAED, vol. I, *The Saint*, 132.

And those people who are brought to life by the spirit of the divine letter who do not attribute every letter they know, or wish to know, to the body, but by word and example, return them to the most high Lord God to Whom every good belongs.

Reflection and Application

The "Admonitions" are a collection of the teachings of St. Francis that were given to guide Christians who were trying to live their lives according to the Good News of Jesus. In this section, St. Francis emphasized the best motivation for Christians studying the Sacred Scriptures and what our response to their messages needs to be.

He quotes St. Paul the apostle (2 Cor 3:6) and stresses that Christians should not merely be concerned with "the letter" of the Sacred Scriptures—that is, learning facts and information *about* the biblical texts or priding themselves on how many Bible passages they can memorize and recite back to prove their point in a debate or argument with relatives or friends. To use the Sacred Scriptures in those ways would be to abuse them, taking away their "spirit." The Scriptures are not intended to be instruments for boosting our egos or drawing attention to ourselves. Doing such things makes it impossible for us or anyone else to whom we might speak to hear God's voice in the texts—"The letter kills."

Instead, St. Francis cautions, we need to live out in our daily lives what we learn when we study the Scriptures. As we have seen, the Scriptures show us a God who lovingly and generously created a good and beautiful universe for us and all of our sisters and brothers. We need to read the Bible, to reflect and pray about what touches our heart as we read the sacred texts. Then, with the help of God's grace, we will be able to make the changes necessary to form our lives, "following in the footprints of Jesus." We must love and care for creation as God the Creator loves and cares for us.

Questions for Reflection and Discussion

1. When did you first learn to regard the Bible or Sacred Scriptures differently from how you regarded other books? Compare your experience with that of St. Francis.

2. Have you ever heard a homily on the doctrine of creation? What do you remember from it? Did the preacher connect the doctrine of creation and the doctrine of redemption?

3. What kind of a relationship among humans, animals, plants, and other natural elements such as rivers, lakes, rocks, hills, or plains is given to us in the Hebrew Testament creation texts? Explain how you understand these relationships.

4. What influence might the Hebrew Testament creation texts have on how you think about "natural resources," on what you buy, or on how you invest your money?

5. When growing up, what did you learn about the doctrine of creation, especially the phrases "have dominion" and "subdue the earth"? How did that learning affect your daily life?

Suggestions for Action

1. Read and compare the Genesis 1 and Genesis 2 creation stories.

2. Go to your favorite outdoor place or observe your favorite plant, animal, or daytime or nighttime sky or earth element. Then write your own psalm telling its "creation story" and giving praise and thanks to God.

3. Read Psalm 104. Then sit quietly for a while and bask in God's generosity. In gratitude, praise God for the gift of your life within such a marvelous creation.

4. Use cloth shopping bags to save trees and reduce pollution of land and waterways with plastics that endanger all kinds of wild animals who become entangled in them or mistake them for food.

5. Replace paper napkins, towels, cups, plasticware, and plates with cloth and/or with reusable or biodegradable items.

6. Buying daily coffee in paper cups generates about 22.27 pounds of waste per person per year. Use a refillable coffee mug in the office or on the go.

7. Check out the Franciscan Action Network web site and see how you can participate in caring for the earth at http://www.franciscan action.org.

Prayer

Most high, all-powerful, and good Lord,
Thank you for the wondrous and beautiful creation you have so generously given us! And thank you for the Sacred Scriptures that tell the stories of your great love for us and for all of your creatures. We are grateful for your invitation to live together as sisters and brothers, caring for one another, just as you care for us. Give us eyes to see, ears to hear, and a voice to speak of your marvelous works! Help us to change our ways so that we might walk more closely in the footprints of Jesus. Amen.

Sources for Further Study

Bergant, Dianne. *The Earth Is the Lord's: The Bible, Ecology, and Worship*. American Essays in Liturgy. Collegeville, MN: Liturgical Press, 1998.

Delio, Ilia. *A Franciscan View of Creation: Learning to Live in a Sacramental World*. The Franciscan Heritage Series, vol. 2. St. Bonaventure, NY: The Franciscan Institute, 2003.

Hayes, Zachary. *Window to the Divine: A Study of Christian Creation Theology*. Quincy, IL: The Franciscan Press, 1997.

Nothwehr, Dawn M., ed., *Franciscan Theology of the Environment: An Introductory Reader*. Quincy, IL. The Franciscan Press, 2002.

Chapter 2

Toward a New Creation:
The Christian Testament on Creation
and Redemption

Introduction: God So Loved the World

Most people have never heard of British composer Sir John Stainer (1840–1901) or his oritorio *The Crucifixion* (1887). He was a professor of music at Oxford; however, he was never considered among the "first-rank" composers of his time. Yet, even today, one movement from this oritorio can be found in the repertoire of nearly every English-speaking church choir: "God So Loved the World."[1] Its velvet-soft, reverent, yet supple vocal harmony conspires to penetrate the heart, drawing the listener to marvel at the profound message it proclaims: "God so loved the world that he gave his only begotten Son, that whosoever believeth in Him should not perish, but have everlasting life. For God sent not his Son into the world to condemn the world, but that the world through Him might be saved" (John 3:16-17). How can these words make sense for us today? What new insights can we gain if we reflect on these words in light of evolution, quantum physics, or ecology? What does all of this have to do with St. Francis and finding sustainable ways of living today?

---

[1] To see and hear "God So Loved the World," performed on February 9, 2009, by St. Paul's Cathedral Choir, London, see http://www.youtube.com/watch?v=X5Akz6J8Rw0, accessed July 3, 2011.

Our Rich Heritage

God Created and Continues to Sustain the World

Jesus Christ, whom Christians confess to be the Son of God and Savior of the world, holds center stage in the New Testament, not the belief that God has created and is sustaining the world. However, early Christians experienced the Creator God of Genesis and understood the original goodness of creation through Jesus, his teaching, and his actions.[2] Thus, the New Testament actually presents the themes of creation and redemption as two related aspects of God's one engagement with the world in the incarnation. Simply put, through Jesus' life, death, and resurrection, God's creative activity continues as a work of redemption (healing, renewal, re-creation). The theme of creation is constantly in the background of all that Jesus says and does, and it undergirds how the early Christians viewed Jesus as the bringer of the new creation. According to Scripture scholar Barbara Bowe, "Notions of new creation [*kainē ktisis*] and ultimate destruction of 'this world' undergird the whole apocalyptic schema of Hellenistic Jewish and early Christian thought."[3]

Notions concerning the original creation are found in the New Testament Pauline and post-Pauline traditions and in the Johannine writings.[4]

---

[2] See Michael D. Guinan, *The Franciscan Vision and the Gospel of John: The San Damiano Cross; Francis and John; Creation and John*, The Franciscan Heritage Series, vol. 4 (St. Bonaventure, NY: The Franciscan Institute, 2006), 32: "Creation is not the same as 'nature'; neither is it a scientific or philosophical term. Creation is a thoroughly religious concept. Creation means that to understand everything that exists at its deepest level, it must be seen in relationship to God. Creation is concerned not only with beginnings but with every single moment of existence. Creation always implies a Creator; the two go together and mutually imply each other."

See, for example, Mark 10:6 and its parallel in Matthew 19:4. Here Jesus explains that the original and ideal relationship between men and women is an egalitarian, loving companionship, since both women and men are created in the divine image. Divorce is tolerated because people have hardness of heart. Also see 1 Corinthians 11:8-9. Here Paul discussed the ideal of following the example of Christ. Again, the reference is to Genesis 2 where initially there was no problem with sexism among men and women, who were created in the divine image—male and female. However, because of the Fall, this became problematic. In Paul's culture, women were inferior to men. However, in the new creation, in Christ, there is "neither male nor female"—all are one in Christ (Gal 3:28).

[3] Barbara Bowe, "Soundings in the New Testament Understandings of Creation," in *Earth, Wind, and Fire: Biblical and Theological Perspectives on Creation*, ed. Carol J. Dempsey and Mary Margaret Pazdan (Collegeville, MN: Liturgical Press, 2004), 59.

[4] Ibid., 59–60.

Bowe illustrates this utilizing two word studies: the Greek *ktizō* word group and the *kosmos* word group. *Ktizō* means "to intentionally establish" or "to found."[5] God, in a manner similar to a Roman emperor who founded a city, intentionally brought order out of chaos. The use of the term *ktizō* is significant because in non-Christian sources, that founding action is indicated using the term *dēmiourgeō*, meaning "to engage in the construction of something."[6] There is an important qualitative difference in that God's act of creation (*ktizō*) is not simply pragmatic or utilitarian, but rather personal, loving, and intentional.

Bowe observes that the term *kosmos* is used 186 times in the New Testament, 37 times in the Pauline writings, and 78 times in the Johannine corpus.[7] Generally, *kosmos* indicates the "arrangement" or the "order" of our world or universe. She suggests that the term originated in Hellenistic Judaism to tell of God's creating the world "out of formless matter." *Kosmos* thus indicates the "earth" that humankind inhabits, but also "humankind itself" (cf. Wis 6:24; 4 Macc 17:14). In the Gospel of John and in 1 Corinthians, "this world" refers to creation as a temporary place of sin that is marked by the absence of salvation and knowledge of God. Other uses of the term *kosmos* indicate creation as the place where God's activity takes place through Jesus; in John, the one sent; and, as Paul claims, through the Spirit.

The meaning of the term *kosmos* is further specified by Scripture scholar Sandra Schneiders.[8] First, "world" refers to this earth as God spoke all things into being (Gen 1:1–2:4a)—the very place of God's revelation (Wis 6:24; 4 Macc 17:14). This world, this universe, emerged at God's expression through the Word, and it is a place God called "very good." Second, "world" refers to "the theater of human history," this place of material existence where we humans live among other creatures. It is into this history that the "Word made flesh" (John 1:14) was born. Third, and particularly significant for Christians, the world is the place where the reign of God opens up and the place where disciples of Jesus over the ages are sent (John 17:15). And fourth, "world" refers to "a

---

[5] Ibid., 59.

[6] Ibid., 60.

[7] Ibid.

[8] Sandra Schneiders, "God So Loved the World. . . . Ministerial Religious Life in 2009," talk on vowed religious life given to the IHM Congregation, June 14, 2009, 22–24, http://www.ihmsisters.org/www/media/about_us_autogen/SSchneiders Lecture2009.pdf, accessed July 3, 2011.

synonym for evil," or the one Jesus calls Satan, who is the one with whom Jesus and his disciples struggle in the pursuit of God. It is into this multivalent world that God's creative love bursts, first as the emergence of creation and then in the redemptive action of the new creation. All in all, the world, the *kosmos*, is the place where God is revealed through what God created, and it is the object of God's abundant love—a love that dynamically continues to grow and deepen in each and every moment, bringing forth ever-new and renewed life.

Linking Original Creation and New Creation

Jesus' "Inaugural Address"

As we saw in chapter 1, beyond the Genesis creation stories there are many other texts in the Scriptures that address creation. The Synoptic Gospels (Matthew, Mark, and Luke) are most familiar and are brimming with various ways we see creation referenced. One such text is Luke 4:16-21, which gives an account of Jesus' proclamation of his mission, at the beginning of his ministry, in his "inaugural address":

> When he came to Nazareth, where he had been brought up, he went to the synagogue on the Sabbath day, as was his custom. He stood up to read, and the scroll of the prophet Isaiah was given to him. He unrolled the scroll and found the place where it was written: "The Spirit of the Lord is upon me, because he has anointed me to bring good news to the poor. He has sent me to proclaim release to the captives and recovery of sight to the blind, to let the oppressed go free, to proclaim the year of the Lord's favor." And he rolled up the scroll, gave it back to the attendant, and sat down. The eyes of all in the synagogue were fixed on him. Then he began to say to them, "Today this scripture has been fulfilled in your hearing."

The passage Jesus read was from Isaiah 61, and that text ends with a proclamation of a Sabbath Year (every seventh year), "the year of the Lord's favor." In the Sabbath Year, not only were slaves freed and debts canceled, but planting, pruning, and harvesting crops for storage were forbidden. The earth itself was given Sabbath rest in honor of the Creator (Lev 25:2-7; Deut 15:7-11). Throughout the Jubilee Year mandates, especially in light of Leviticus 25:23, we see that the ecological well-being of the land is intimately tied to the spiritual and material well-being of the people of Israel.[9] The God who owns the land is attentive to the needs of the poor and the need of the land for rest. The Levitical laws of holiness, when heeded, bring wholeness to all of creation, including human persons.

The original creation and the new creation are thus linked in the New Testament. After Jesus read Isaiah 61:1-2 in the temple (Luke 4:18-19), which refers to Isaiah 58:6 (both texts point to the Jubilee Year), he claimed what it outlined there as his own prophetic mission. Subsequently, through his ministry he also taught his followers to engage in liberating, enlightening, and saving actions, bringing about the kingdom of God. All such activities are, in some way, life giving. Such language reckons back to the great prophetic promises and talk of the new covenant (Jer 31:31-34), the resurrection (Ezek 37:1-4), and the new creation (Isa 65:17-25). All of this points to the fulfillment of the reign of God—the new creation.

Similarly, even a cursory reading of the gospels shows they are filled with sacred memories of Jesus carrying out actions that Psalm 146 attributed to the Creator. As Jesus announced it, his mission was to do what "the LORD their God, the maker of heaven and earth" had done (Ps 146:5-6). The widow and the orphan of Psalm 146 are among the poor to whom Jesus brought glad tidings, the prisoners to whom he proclaimed liberty, the blind to whom he gave sight, and the oppressed for whom he secured justice (Luke 4:18).

From the Synoptic Gospels

If we read the stories in the Synoptic Gospels of the life, teachings, and ministry of Jesus with an eye toward ecological sensitivity, we readily see how "earth friendly" Jesus was. Clearly, we cannot impose or insert today's specific issues upon the biblical texts. However, we can assert that Jesus was highly attentive to the natural world; indeed, matter mattered to him! Elizabeth A. Johnson observes, "The point is that his life

---

[9] See Moshe Greenberg, David L. Lieber, Aaron Rothkoff, and Shmuel Safrai, "Sabbatical Year and Jubilee," *Encyclopaedia Judaica*, ed. Michael Berenbaum and Fred Skolnik, vol. 17, 2nd ed. (Detroit: Macmillan Reference USA, 2007), 623–30, at 623: "Sabbatical Year and Jubilee (Hebrew שְׁמִטָּה, *shemittah*; יוֹבֵל, *yovel*). According to the Bible, during the seventh year all land had to be fallow and debts were to be remitted (Ex. 23:10-11; Lev. 25:1-7, 18-22; Deut. 15:1-11). The close of seven sabbatical cycles instituted the Jubilee (Lev. 27:16-25; Num. 36:4)."

and ministry were filled with orientations that open to the physical, earthy dimensions without strain, once the question is raised."[10]

Jesus was an excellent teacher who taught about who God is for us by using examples from the material world God created. Just as we can know something about an artist by examining her or his work—paintings, sculpture, drawings, poems, or choreography—so too something of who God is can be found in every creature in creation (panentheism). Indeed, the natural world is the place of God. The examples of Jesus' physical healings of the sick, lame, or mentally ill and his teachings using natural "visual aids" fill the pages of the gospels. The litany of examples he used in parables, sayings, and sermons is intentionally familiar: wildflowers, trees, grains, miniscule seeds, birds, fish, children, women, enemies, sheep, foxes, ants, wind, rain, sunrises, and more.

Because the world is overflowing with the grandeur of God, Jesus (often including his disciples) frequently immersed himself in natural out-of-doors settings for prayer and reflection. Common places for Jesus' life-changing encounters with God (*Abba*) were deserts, hilltops, beaches, or gardens (see Luke 6:12 and Mark 1:15-35, for example).

Through all of his teaching, Jesus shows us a radically relational God (*Abba*) who loves all of creation unconditionally, with grace, compassion, and tender mercy. Indeed, all creation is loved by God and is revelatory of God. Jesus admonished that we must love our neighbor as ourselves. But he also showed us that *we* need to love *as* God loves—and that includes our "ecological neighbors," those who live downwind and downstream from us![11]

Beyond the Synoptics: Lady Wisdom and Jesus, the Wisdom of God

The New Testament writers built on the Jewish prophetic tradition, but also on the Wisdom tradition. As we saw in chapter 1, Lady Wisdom was present at the foundation of the world. Early Christians recognized Jesus as a wisdom teacher and soon attributed to him the role of *Hôkmah/Sophia* (Sir 24:23; Prov 8). We could cite many New Testament references illustrating this, but St. Paul is most explicit when he speaks of Christ as the best revelation of God's wisdom (1 Cor 1:24, 30). Similarly, Matthew

[10] Elizabeth A. Johnson, "An Earthy Christology: 'For God So Loved the Cosmos,'" *America* 200, no. 12, whole no. 4852 (April 13, 2009): 28.

[11] See Jeanne Kay Guelke, "Looking for Jesus in Christian Environmental Ethics," *Environmental Ethics* 26/2 (2004): 123.

sees Jesus as Wisdom because of his healing and all-encompassing presence (Matt 11:20, 28). However, the role of Jesus as Wisdom is particularly poignant in the Gospel of John, "the Franciscan Gospel."[12]

Jesus the Wisdom of God in the Gospel of John

In order to understand the Gospel of John, particularly the Prologue (John 1:1-14), some background information from the Hebrew Testament is important. The Hebrew Testament speaks about God as the "wise" creator (Ps 104:24; Prov 3:19; Job 38:4-11). God is a divine artisan or skilled craftsperson who fashioned a good and beautiful universe (Sir 39:16; Gen 1:4, 10, 12, 18, 21, 25, 31).[13] Over several centuries, the fact that God created "with wisdom" became personified as "Wisdom Woman," who originated with God and who had a mission directed to humans on earth (Prov 8:22; Sir 24:3, 9). Among Wisdom Woman's activities are that she beckons us, drawing us in and through the world (Prov 1, 8, 9), and promises life and blessing for those who embrace her (Prov 1:32; 3:13-18). Through her, God is present in the world.

In the discussion of the ways of Wisdom in Job 28, the author clearly states that "God knows the way to it and he knows its place" (Job 28:23). Then in Proverbs 1–9, Wisdom Woman makes her appearance as "one more precious than jewels," "beyond compare," and a "tree of life," for "the LORD by wisdom founded the earth" (Prov 3:15-19). Further, in Proverbs 8 Wisdom Woman speaks of being God's first creature, of her presence in and through all divine creative actions, and that she delights and rejoices in her presence in the created world, including the human race (Prov 8:22-31).

---

[12] According to the critical edition of the writings of St. Francis prepared by Kajetan Esser in 1978, the Gospel of John is the most influential source for St. Francis's vision of his way of life. See *Opuscula Sancti Patris Francisci Assisiensis*, ed. K. Esser, OFM (Rome: Grottaferrata, 1978). Also see Optatus van Asseldonk, OFM Cap., "Favored Biblical Teachings in the Writings of St. Francis," *Greyfriars Review* 3 (1989): 287–314, especially 295–305; Thaddée Matura, OFM, "How Francis Reads and Interprets Scripture," in *The Gospel Life of St. Francis of Assisi Today* (Chicago: Franciscan Herald Press, 1980), 31–44; and James P. Scullion, OFM, "The Writings of St. Francis and the Gospel of John," in *Franciscans and the Scriptures: Living in the Word of God*, Washington Theological Union Symposium Papers, 2005, ed. Elise Saggau, OSF (St. Bonaventure, NY: Franciscan Institute Publications, 2006).

[13] Michael D. Guinan, "Images of God in the Wisdom Literature," *Bible Today* 38 (2000): 223–27.

Beyond all of this, there is a further development recorded in the book of Sirach. In Sirach 24, Wisdom Woman now seeks a "resting place" (v. 7), and God chose a spot for her tent "in Jacob" (v. 8). More specifically, though Wisdom continues to be present throughout creation, she rests in the "book of the covenant," the Torah, the law of Moses (vv. 22-23). So now we also see that the Torah preexisted creation (cf. Job 28:12, 20). Subsequently, we read in John 1, "In the beginning the Word [*logos*] was with God" (John 1:1a)—but not created, because "the Word was God" (John 1:1b). As Christians believe, Jesus is the fullness of the law; he is the Word made flesh, God incarnate (John 1:14).

As Guinan points out, what God created was the entire universe (Prov 3:19-20), and Wisdom provided the supporting pillars (Prov 14:31). She actually rejoices and delights in the human race (Prov 8:31) and invites everyone (all creation) to feast with her (Prov 9:2-6). Wisdom opens for us a joyful way of living; to follow in her way, the way of Wisdom, is to follow the One who in John's gospel is Jesus Christ, the Wisdom of God.

Scripture scholar Barbara Bowe utilizes the work of Josephine Massyngbaerde Ford to break open some more important insights, linking the original creation and the new creation (creation, incarnation, and redemption) themes in the Gospel of John.[14] Naturally, Bowe begins her discussion with the Prologue of the gospel:

> In the beginning was the Word, and the Word was with God, and the Word was God. He was in the beginning with God. All things came into being through him, and without him not one thing came into being. What has come into being in him was life, and the life was the light of all people. The light shines in the darkness, and the darkness did not overcome it.
>
> There was a man sent from God, whose name was John. He came as a witness to testify to the light, so that all might believe through him. He himself was not the light, but he came to testify to the light. The true light, which enlightens everyone, was coming into the world.
>
> He was in the world, and the world came into being through him; yet the world did not know him. He came to what was his own, and his own people did not accept him. But to all who received him, who believed in his name, he gave power to become children of God,

---

[14] See Bowe, "Soundings in the New Testament Understandings of Creation," 61. She cites Josephine Massyngbaerde Ford, *Redeemer, Friend, and Mother: Salvation in Antiquity and in the Gospel of John* (Minneapolis: Fortress Press, 1997).

who were born, not of blood or of the will of the flesh or of the will of man, but of God.

And the Word became flesh and lived among us, and we have seen his glory, the glory as of a father's only son, full of grace and truth. (John 1:1-14)

We read the familiar words "In the beginning . . ." (cf. Gen 1:1), but the ending of the phrase is different: ". . . was the Word" (John 1:1). Here the story of Jesus is presented as a new story of creation.[15] Bowe notes that the structure of the Prologue is patterned as "celestial-divine / terrestrial-human, alternating between realms."[16] In verse 14, Jesus the Word (*logos*) of God is identified as the one (like Wisdom) who "pitched a tent with us" joining the divine and human realms for eternity. It is through the Word (*logos*) that "all things came into being, and [emphatically] without him not one thing came into being" (v. 3). Jesus is the creative agent whose divinity is the light infused in the world (1:5), making way for the rebirth of the Spirit (3:6), the bringer of regenerating energy to the world.[17]

Bowe continues, showing how John 1 and 2 expand on the creation motif (1:29, 35, 43; and 2:1), intimating that Jesus' story begins a new week of creation (cf Gen 1:1–2:4). Jesus' act of revealing God's glory begins "on the third day" at Cana (John 2:1), and this evokes the memory of God coming to the people of Israel at Sinai "on the third day" (Exod 19:9). The fact that the occasion of Jesus' action is the wedding banquet at Cana suggests further the messianic banquet that crowns creation (2 Bar 29:5-8). That recollection, moreover, points to the "Bread of Life" discourse of John 6, especially verses 51 and 58, where the Word made flesh gives himself "for the life of the world" so that the person "who eats will live for ever."[18] In all of these instances, renewal, regeneration, and re-creation of life is brought about.

Bowe again turns to Ford's work and her interpretation of John 19, the scene of the death of Jesus on the cross. Ford raises up the provocative insight from the Syriac tradition concerning the significance of the flow of blood and water from Jesus' pierced side. Ford connects the piercing of Jesus' side with the opening of Adam's side (Gen 2:21-23) as a kind of act of giving birth to new life. In Ford's words: "I suggest that

---

[15] Bowe, "Soundings in the New Testament Understandings of Creation," 61.
[16] Ibid.
[17] Ibid.
[18] Ibid., 62.

Jesus goes to his passion and death . . . as a woman to give birth to her child by blood and water."[19] Ford suggests a similar strain of rebirthing can be seen in the giving of the Spirit (John 19:30; 20:22). Jesus "breathes upon the disciples to bring them new life and the Paraclete. . . . It may also be possible that the insufflation reflects the action of the midwife helping the newborn child to breathe."[20]

At the conclusion of John's gospel (John 20:11-18), Bowe points out, Mary Magdelene meets Jesus in a garden (*kēpos*, John 19:41; compare with *paradeisos*, Gen 2–3). She suggests that Magdalene's encounter with Jesus brings the theme of "new birth" proclaimed in the Prologue (1:12) full circle. "Mary, the *apostola apostolorum* (female apostle to the other apostles) becomes the herald, the midwife of the new creation in the family of God."[21] Indeed, the Gospel of John shows us how God's love poured out in the original creation is expressed in the incarnation and is the link that brings forth life-giving redemption.

Creation and New Creation:
Insights from an Evolutionary Worldview

Most of Christian teaching about creation and redemption for the past several centuries has utilized Aristotelian and neoplatonic models of metaphysics and the theology of Thomas Aquinas or Bonaventure of Bagnoregio and later Newtonian models of science. These models have helped us understand much about God and the known world. But today our knowledge of evolution and quantum physics opens vistas for reflecton that can enrich, renew, and revise our understanding of God, creation, and redemption. Such reflections offer new insights for understanding Christian life and our participation in the reign of God— particularly as they pertain to care for the planet and the poor.

Over a decade ago, the preeminent Bonaventure scholar Zachary Hayes set out four characteristics that must be considered in any theological reflection on creation.[22] Creation is *immense* in size and duration—well

---

[19] Josephine Massyngbaerde Ford, *Redeemer, Friend, and Mother,* 198.

[20] Ibid., 200.

[21] Bowe, "Soundings in the New Testament Understandings of Creation," 63.

[22] Zachary Hayes, "New Cosmology for a New Millennium," *New Theology Review* 12/3 (1999): 29–39.

beyond human capacities to fathom. It is between fifteen and twenty billion years old and is of such porportions that we know of billions of galaxies and billions of stars in each of them.[23]

Still, this immense universe is yet *unfinished*; in fact, it is actually expanding. According to the big bang theory, all of creation burst forth from a concentration of energy the size of a pin head some 13.7 billion years ago. Through a process of emergence of subatomic particles, protons, neutrons, and electrons, which then cooled, the cosmos as we know it today came forth.[24]

In light of today's physics, we know that creation is *interrelated* at every point. From the smallest fractal to the expanses of the universe, everything is related to everything else, and "what we think of as matter is actually the manifestation of energy, what physicists call quanta or little packets or lumps of energy manifesting themselves out of an infinite field."[25] Similarly, biologists see the world as "living systems as interrelated wholes. . . . A 'part' becomes identified as a 'pattern in an inseperable web of relationships.' "[26] Where Newton understood the world as the result of forces and trajectories, today's evolutionary thinking requires us to think in terms of change, growth, and development or in considerations of complexity.

Hayes's fourth characteristic is the *uniqueness of planet Earth*, which produced the vast diversity of life, ranging from the simple to the complex. Remarkably, the whole evolutionary process became fine-tuned to support carbon-based life as we know it. What is even more amazing is that humans are this universe come to consciousness![27] Scientists call this reality evidence of the "strong anthropic principle."[28] Had the process developed "a trillionth of a trillionth of a trillionth of one percent faster, the cosmic material would have been flung too far apart for anything significant to happen."[29]

---

[23] Today the consensus is that the age of the universe is 13.7 billion years old.

[24] Ilia Delio, *The Emergent Christ: Exploring the Meaning of Catholic in an Evolutionary Universe* (Maryknoll, NY: Orbis Books, 2011), 13–17.

[25] Ibid., 24.

[26] Ibid., 25.

[27] Ibid., 17.

[28] Ibid.

[29] See Judy Cannato, *Radical Amazement: Contemplative Lessons from Black Holes, Supernovas, and Other Wonders of the Universe* (Notre Dame: Sorin Books, 2006), 42, cited by Delio, *The Emergent Christ*, 17.

Considerations of evolution and ecology place humanity in a new light as well. Early humans appeared about 150,000 years ago. This view does not negate the biblical story of human origins but rather gives us "an understanding of how the mechanics within nature promote species diversity and development and on a cosmic level, how the universe progresses from the big bang to human life."[30] Basically, the modern theory of evolution holds that life can be explained by a combination of law, chance, and deep time. In the case of humans, this process took billions of prior forms, cataclysmic events, and extinctions before "humans" evolved. Beyond their evolution into *Homo sapiens*, humans are also products of emergence. "Philip Clayton defines emergence as 'genuinely new properties which are not reducable to what came before, although they are continuous with it.'"[31] Humans developed in complexity in a world of grace to become self-conscious beings, aware of their divine origins.

Reign of God—New Creation—Emergence

The "new creation" or the "reign of God" is at the heart of the New Testament and the activity of Jesus. As Leonardo Boff and Mark Hathaway explain, the actual Aramaic term Jesus used to name the reign of God or the kingdom of heaven is *malkuta*. The term is related to *malkatuh*, a Middle Eastern name for Mother Earth.[32] The ancients perceived a divine quality about the earth, which they found dynamic and empowering. Thus, the *malkuta* is that which provides an empowering vision rooted in the divine presence in the cosmos. Today we can understand this empowerment in terms of "liberation, as a process leading the cosmos toward ever-greater communion, differentiation, and interiority."[33] As Douglas-Klotz puts it, the image evoked is "of a fruitful arm poised to create, or a coiled spring that is ready to unwind with all

[30] Delio, *The Emergent Christ*, 21. Also see her discussion about the compatibility of evolution with Catholic Church teaching at 21–24. There is no inherent conflict between evolution and Christian doctrine.

[31] Ibid., 20.

[32] Leonardo Boff and Mark Hathaway, *The Tao of Liberation: Exploring the Ecology of Transformation* (Maryknoll, NY: Orbis Books, 2009), 331. Boff and Hathaway cite Neil Douglas-Klotz, *Prayers of the Cosmos: Meditations on the Aramaic Words of Jesus* (San Francisco: HarperSanFrancisco, 1990), 20.

[33] Boff and Hathaway, *The Tao of Liberation*, 131.

the verdant potential of the Earth."[34] Jesus reminds us that the reign of God is here, but not yet—within us, yet beyond us and around us (Luke 17:21). The implications for discipleship, "following in the footprints of Jesus," especially in caring for the earth, are vast.

Throughout Christian history, believers have talked about God and God's love by comparing their experience and understanding to some object or something more commonly and thoroughly knowable. Often comparisons or models came from science or philosophy. So it is not surprising that theologians today are doing likewise.

One important recent line of reflection concerns how we understand God as the Creator, especially in light of "emergence theory." Danish theologian Niels Henrik Gregersen points out that we can see a simpler version of emergence theory in Aristotle's principle of *entelechy*[35] or Plotinus's doctrine of *emanation*. Plotinus's neoplatonism greatly influenced Christian thought. He thought of creation as all things flowing from the One. The occurrence of new things took place as *devolution*, or a kind of dissipation of the power of the being that is in the divine principle before creation takes place. In Plotinus's thought, "emanation from the One is a sharing of being from Being . . . and hence participates in Being without becoming something new."[36] Currently, as Delio explains, "emergenists subscribe to a robust scientific naturalism, according to which mental processes supervene on biological processes, and biological processes on physical processes. Emergence is irreducable novelty of increasing complexity, a combination of holism with novelty in a way that contrasts with both physical reductionism and dualism."[37]

In light of this, we can no longer speak of God primarily as the neoplatonic *cause* of creation. Rather, we need to think about God as the *goal* toward which all things are moving. Harkening back to the big bang and the 13.75 billion-year history of the universe, God's creative activity can be understood as enabling things to evolve into something ever new. The notion of emergence gives us a different idea of what creation really

---

[34] Ibid.

[35] See Ilia Delio, "Godhead or God Ahead? Rethinking the Trinity in Light of Emergence," in *God, Grace, and Creation*, ed. Philip J. Rossi, College Theology Society Annual Volume 55 (2009), 20n91: "Entelechy refers to the internal principle of growth and perfection that directs the organism to actualize the qualities that it contains in a merely potential state."

[36] Ibid., 7.

[37] Ibid., 7–8.

is, and it also suggests a far more dynamic image of God than has been dominant in many circles in the past. We now have knowledge about the physical creation that gives us renewed insights about God, the Creator of an emerging creation. Here is a renewed way to understand God's dynamic, overflowing, generous, reconciling, and healing love in all of creation. We can build on ideas that are nacent in 2 Corinthians 5:17 and in Revelation 21:1-8. These passages speak of God who "makes all things new" and of the reality that we have "new life" in Jesus Christ. Obvserving the ongoing emergence of creation is yet another way of following in the footprints of Jesus in our day.

St. Bonaventure's Dynamic Trinity and Doctrine of Creation: A Hope-Filled Vision

St. Bonaventure's understanding of the trinitarian God and his doctrine of creation can assist us in grasping and deepening our comprehension of the Word (John 1:1), creation, and new creation. St. Bonaventure of Bagnoregio (1217–74) stands as the founder of the Franciscan theological tradition[38] and the clearest interpretive voice of St. Francis of Assisi.[39] Other important sources in Bonaventure's thought include

---

[38] See Kenan B. Osborne, ed., *The History of Franciscan Theology* (St. Bonaventure, NY: The Franciscan Institute, 1994), vii–ix. See also Zachary Hayes, "The Life and the Christological Thought of St. Bonaventure," in *Franciscan Christology: Selected Texts, Translations and Introductory Essays*, ed. Damian McElrath, Franciscan Sources, no. 1 (St. Bonaventure, NY: The Franciscan Institute, 1980), 62–64.

[39] See Timothy Johnson, "Lost in Sacred Space: Textual Hermeneutics, Liturgical Worship, and Celano's *Legenda ad usum chori*," *Franciscan Studies* 59 (2001): 109–13, especially 112. See also E. R. Daniel, *The Franciscan Concept of Mission in the High Middle Ages* (New York: The Franciscan Institute, 1975), 48.

The "common thread" sustaining the Franciscan theological tradition across time is the person and witness of Francis of Assisi, "the patron of ecology." See Pope John Paul II, apostolic letter *Inter Sanctos: Franciscus Assisiensis Caelestis Patronus Oecologiae Cultorum Eligitur*, http://www.vatican.va/holy_father/john_paul_ii/apost_letters/1979 /documents/hf_jp-ii_apl_19791129_inter-sanctos_lt.html (accessed March 18, 2009).

For a discussion of the role of a "vernacular theologian," see Bernard McGinn, *Meister Eckhart and the Beguine Mystics* (New York, Continuum, 1983), 6–7, and his *The Flowering of Mysticism: Men and Women in the New Mysticism, 1200–1350* (New York: Crossroad, 1998), 21.

Francis's theological authority originated in the gift of grace of his experience of God (*ex beneficio*), not *ex officio*. See Congregation for the Doctrine of the Faith, Instruction

neoplatonism and the work of Augustine, Pseudo-Dionysius, and Richard of St. Victor.[40]

Bonaventure's Method and Metaphysics

The metaphysical structure supporting Bonaventure's thought consists of the notions of emanation, exemplarism, and consummation.[41] Simply put, in Bonaventure's worldview we come from God, we live in God, and we return to God. Concerning *emanation*, the mystery of divine, infinite self-diffusive goodness is the basis of the life *ad intra* of the Trinity. The inner relational life of the Trinity overflows externally to creation (including humans). Thus God, creation, and humans are radically related.

Concerning *exemplarism*, God is the prototype of everything that exists, and so everything in creation expresses the divine, thus revealing the Creator. Exemplarism can be defined as "the doctrine of the relations of expression between God and creatures."[42] Using his modified notion of Plato's divine ideas, Bonaventure holds that the Word (John 1:1) expresses the Father's ideas, and thus the Word is the Exemplar of all that exists. Further, the Exemplar is the active side of that expression, namely, that which expresses itself (cf. John 1:3-4). Correlatively, that in which the Exemplar is expressed is called an *image*. As Delio puts it, "God is the exemplary cause of all things, because God in knowing himself ex-

---

on the Ecclesial Vocation of the Theologian, *Origins* 20/8 (July 5, 1990): 119. Also see United States Conference of Catholic Bishops, Doctrinal Responsibilities: Approaches to Promoting Cooperation and Resolving Misunderstandings between Bishops and Theologians, *Origins* 19/7 (June 29, 1989): 101.

Three major themes in Francis's vernacular theology irrevocably link Franciscan spirituality and Franciscan theology: the humanity of Christ, the mystery of God as generous love, and the sense of creation as family. See John 14:6-9 and St. Francis, *Admonition I*, 1–4, in *Francis and Clare*, eds. Regis Armstrong and Ignatius Brady (Mahwah, NJ: Paulist Press, 1982), 25–26.

[40] See J. Guy Bougerol, *Introduction to the Works of Bonaventure*, vol. 1, trans. José de Vinck (Patterson, NJ: St. Anthony Guild Press, 1964), especially 23–49.

[41] See Phil Hoebing, "St. Bonaventure and Ecology," in *Franciscan Theology of the Environment: An Introductory Reader*, ed. Dawn M. Nothwehr, 273–75 (Quincy, IL: Franciscan Press, 2002). These three dimensions are also interrelated. Thus, it is not easy to discuss any part of Bonaventure's theology without also referencing other dimensions; it is a carefully interwoven whole.

[42] See Leonard J. Bowman, "The Cosmic Exemplarism of Bonaventure," *The Journal of Religion* 55/2 (April 1975): 184.

presses his most perfect idea, the *rationes* or the external patterns of all possible things. Everything that exists, therefore, is in some way related to God as a copy or imitation. Bonaventure distinguishes three different degrees of resemblance: the vestige, image, and similitude. The exemplar is the pattern or original model in whose likeness all things are made. It is the basis of imitation. Because the Word expresses the Father's ideas, the Word is the exemplar of all that exists."[43]

The third major component of Bonaventure's metaphysics is *consummation* or *reduction*. Here Franciscan spirituality and Bonaventure's theology converge. While all creation images and reveals God in Christ the Exemplar, its purpose is to lead humanity back to God. "The First Principle created this perceptible world as a means of self-revelation, so that like a mirror of God or a divine footprint, it might lead [humans] to love and praise [their] Creator."[44] In fact, Bonaventure saw that the world in its ascending levels of reflecting God was like a ladder for humans to ascend in the return to God.[45] Certainly, Bonaventure grasped that nature can be admired, misunderstood, or abused. However, he insisted that true seekers of wisdom (philosophers) will try to comprehend something by first understanding its causes. The goal of understanding is to know the essential structure of a thing, a structure constituted by a thing's relationship to its causes. This process of analysis (*plena resolutio*) is a goal of wisdom and the mirror image of exemplary causality.[46] Though limited by sin, humans have the capacity of *contuition*, the ability to see God through things and to see things in God—the ultimate significance of things in the economy of exemplarism.[47]

Bonaventure's Trinitarian Theology[48]

Bonaventure's approach to explaining who God is, is (following the Cappadocians) to try to understand the relationship of the Christ of the

---

[43] Ilia Delio, *Simply Bonaventure: An Introduction to His Life, Thought, and Writings* (Hyde Park, NY: New City Press, 2001), 200–201.

[44] Bowman, "The Cosmic Exemplarism of Bonaventure," 188n47, citing *Breviloquium*, pt. 2, chap. 11, no. 2, in J. Guy Bougerol, *Introduction to the Works of Bonaventure*, vol. 1, p. 101.

[45] Ibid., 188, n. 47. Bowman cites *Breviloquium*, pt. 2, chap. 12, tome 5, p. 230.

[46] Ibid., 189, n. 53. Bowman cites *Hexaëmeron*, collation 1, no. 10, tome 5, p. 133.

[47] Ibid., 197, n. 89. Bowman cites *De Scientia Christi*, q. 4, ad. 22, tome 5, p. 26.

[48] This section draws heavily from Ilia Delio, *Simply Bonaventure*.

gospels and the God of creation.[49] Thus, Bonaventure focuses on the Divine *Persons* of the Trinity. Implicit in the notion of *persons* is the experience of relationship; to be a person is to be social, a person-in-relationship. Bonaventure describes this relationship of trinitarian persons as *circumincessio* (to move around one another in a communion of love).[50]

THE TRINITY *AD INTRA*

Bonaventure first reflects on the occasion where Jesus tells the young man that God alone is good.[51] Scripture proclaims, "No one is good but God alone" (Mark 10:18; Luke 18:19), and from this, Bonaventure concludes that God's truest name is "Good." For additional systematic support for this notion of "Good," he turns to Pseudo-Dionysius,[52] who called God "the self-diffusive goodness." So besides the notion of God as Being, revealed in Exodus 3:14, God is "that Goodness which is beyond Being, and which gives rise to being."[53] Bonaventure also utilizes the Aristotelian axiom that "to the degree that something is prior, it is fecund." Therefore, because God the Father is the Unoriginate One, he is the absolute fecund source of the entire cosmos.[54] Thus, Bonaventure calls God "Fountain Fullness" or "Font of All Goodness." God is absolute goodness; therefore, God is *necessarily* (by definition) uniquely *relational*.

[49] Ilia Delio, *Christ in Evolution* (Maryknoll, NY: Orbis Books, 2008), 55: "The question Who is Jesus Christ? then becomes the theological question integrally related to the question What kind of a God could create and become incarnate?" See also Catherine Mowry LaCugna, *God for Us: The Trinity and Christian Life* (New York: HarperCollins Publications, 1991), 53–81.

[50] Delio, *Simply Bonaventure*, 41nn4–5. Also LaCugna, *God for Us*, 272.

[51] Bonaventure, *The Soul's Journey into God*, 5:1–2, in Ewert Cousins, trans. (New York: Paulist Press, 1978), 94–95.

[52] "Dionysius, or Pseudo-Dionysius, as he has come to be known in the contemporary world, was a Christian Neoplatonist who wrote in the late fifth or early sixth century CE and who transposed in a thoroughly original way the whole of Pagan Neoplatonism from Plotinus to Proclus, but especially that of Proclus and the Platonic Academy in Athens, into a distinctively new Christian context." *Stanford Encyclopedia of Philosophy*, http://plato.stanford.edu/entries/pseudo-dionysius-areopagite, accessed July 8, 2011.

[53] Delio, *Simply Bonaventure*, 52. See her notes 9–11.

[54] LaCugna, *God For Us*, 164.

But importantly, God also *chooses* to love.[55] So, to further explain the trinitarian relations, Bonaventure turns to Richard of St. Victor.[56]

Richard of St. Victor calls God's goodness "charity" (love). By its very nature, love is dynamic and requires a second person; a lover requires a beloved. If a love is not turned in on itself, then a perfect love requires a third person for the relationship with whom the lover and the beloved can each share their love. Thus, Richard of St. Victor provides the model for the trinitarian God: the totally gratuitous love (Father), absolute love (Spirit), and both gratuitous and receptive love (Son). For Bonaventure, therefore, God is the personal, self-communicating, generous, overflowing goodness and source of all reality who desires to express the divine self *ad intra* (within the Godhead) and *ad extra* (outward). Like an infinite, intensely flowing fountain, this self-diffusive primal and eternal goodness generates the Son *ad intra* and the entire cosmos *ad extra* in a kenotic (self-emptying) expression of that goodness.

THE FATHER

Bonaventure sees the generation of the Son by the Father as the personal diffusion of the love of the Father (*per modum naturae*).[57] This is important for our purposes because "the Son, therefore, is everything the Father is in One other than the Father. The relationship between the Father and the Son, in Bonaventure's thought, is the very ground of all other relationships. An understanding of this relationship allows us to comprehend the deeper meaning of creation, and within creation, the centrality of Jesus the Christ."[58]

---

[55] See E. Gilson, *The Philosophy of Bonaventure* (Patterson, NJ: St. Anthony Guild Press, 1965), 163. The Good can diffuse itself in two ways: *per modum voluntatis* and per *modum naturae*.

[56] Zachary Hayes, introduction to *Disputed Questions on the Mystery of the Trinity*, vol. 3 of *Works of Saint Bonaventure* (St. Bonaventure, NY: The Franciscan Institute, 1979), 3–40. Richard of St. Victor "is known today as one of the most influential religious thinkers of his time. He was a prominent mystical theologian, and was prior of the famous Augustinian Abbey of St. Victor in Paris from 1162 until his death in 1173," http://en.wikipedia.org/wiki/Richard_of_Saint_Victor, accessed July 8, 2011.

[57] Delio, *Simply Bonaventure*, 52n14.

[58] Ibid., 45.

THE SON

The Son is also the "image of the Father" in the sense that, like the Father, the Son is the source of others. Indeed, the Son is the true and perfect expression of the Father. Bonaventure prefers the title "Word" for the Son because it best encompasses the reality of the Son as the Father's expression. More precisely, the Son is the *causal word*.[59] In language usage, we distinguish between the *mental word*, or internal thoughts of people and the actual spoken, written, or acted out expression of their ideas or thoughts. Similarly, then, "the eternal 'self-thinking' of the Father, that is, all the eternal ideas of the Father, [is] expressed in the Word."[60] Bonaventure thus calls the Son the "Art of the Father."[61]

Understanding the Word as the Father's expression and self-diffusive goodness gives rise to a set of relationships *ad extra*: the speaker is the Father; the audience is all of creation; the sound or expression is the incarnation; and the knowledge attained by others through the mediation of the Word is found in the Scriptures.[62]

As the Father's self-expression, the Word, though singular, is however the one through whom all of the multiple divine ideas are articulated. Thus, the vast diversity that is creation reveals something about the Father and the Son, but it is not God.[63] "When the Word becomes incarnate, the eternal Word enters into union with creation through humanity, and the mystery of the Father is uttered in history and time."[64]

THE HOLY SPIRIT

In Bonaventure's understanding of the relational triune God, the Holy Spirit is the communication of the Father's goodness by the will (*per modum voluntatis*). The Spirit proceeds from the free will of the Father

---

[59] See Bonaventure, "Sermon II on the Nativity of the Lord," in *What Manner of Man? Sermons on Christ by St. Bonaventure*, trans. Zachary Hayes (Chicago: Franciscan Herald Press, 1989).

[60] Delio, *Simply Bonaventure*, 46n18.

[61] Ibid., 46.

[62] Ibid., 53. See Zachary Hayes, *The Hidden Center: Spirituality and Speculative Christology in St. Bonaventure*, Franciscan Pathways (St. Bonaventure, NY: The Franciscan Institute, 1992), 55–63. Also see Hayes, introduction to *Disputed Questions on the Mystery of the Trinity*, 51–52.

[63] Hayes, "Christ, Word of God and Exemplar of Humanity," 11–12.

[64] Delio, *Simply Bonaventure*, 48.

and the Son. The Father is the primal source of love, and the Son is the emanation of love proceeding from pure liberality; their sharing of love as an act of the will spirates forth the Spirit. The Spirit is the fruit of mutual love. It is the gift of the Spirit in creation that unites humanity with the Father and the Son. And most significantly, the mutual trinitarian relations signal the normative mode of all moral relationships.

Bonaventure understands the Word as the *medium* between the Father and the Spirit. The Son with the Father is the source of others (all creation, the Holy Spirit); the Father and the Son together spirate the Spirit. The Holy Spirit and the Son share the characteristics of receptivity insofar as they are both generated from the Father's self-diffusive goodness. The Word is at the center of trinitarian relations *ad intra* and, as we shall see, *ad extra.*

Bonaventure's Doctrine of Creation

Simply put, for Bonaventure the triune God is the God who creates the entire cosmos. Using modified Platonic models, Bonaventure explains that the world is one where God freely created everything as ordered, oriented, and directed toward its goal in a manner such that all of creation is fully interrelated and interdependent.[65] He sees the community of creation as the product of the overflowing self-diffusive and self-expressive love of the community of the Trinity. Based on Aristotle's hylomorphism (everything is open to change) and the Platonic doctrine of seminal principles (everything has potential), creation is dynamic and open to transformation.[66] Simply put, Bonaventure holds that it was part of God's plan that all creation would desire to be perfected (to grow and develop into its best self). The Word is the Art of the Father, and the creation is the expression of the Artist. Of all in creation, human beings are those most capable of participating in and manifesting God's glory.[67]

---

[65] Bonaventure's main point still holds. He would appreciate later scientific explanations of the interconnected and evolving cosmos. See Zachary Hayes, "The Cosmos, a Symbol of the Divine," in *Franciscan Theology of the Environment*, ed. Nothwehr, 249–67.

[66] Delio, *Simply Bonaventure*, 56–57. See Zachary Hayes, "Bonaventure: Mystery of the Triune God," in *The History of Franciscan Theology*, ed. Kenan B. Osborne, 72–79.

[67] Ibid., 65. See *II Sent.* d. 1., p. 2., a. 2., q. 1., concl. (II, 44b).

God's dynamic love affirms this open process of (sometimes uncertain and painful) evolution. Literally everything in the universe participates in the process of creation. Bonaventure shows what St. Francis knew so well through faith and intuition, that everything in creation is related and moves to ever-greater perfection (read: emergence, evolution, movement toward complexity) drawn forth by God's love. Delio suggests that in light of the theory of emergence and evolution, we could rephrase Bonaventure's notion of *circumincessio* as "the movement from within to be for another so as to become more than the other."[68] She continues: "The emergent Trinity may be described as love yielding to love, an eternal movement toward personal, complexified union in love. Thus, every divine person is nested in every other person so that every divine person recapitulates God who is eternally coming to be. Thus we can say, God is that which no greater is coming to be for it is in the coming to be that God is."[69] We know from our own experience of genuine human love that the love of persons "in love" grows, deepens, and changes in its expression in different situations and on different occasions across time. So it is with the triune God; change is integral to God because God is love. Since God actively loves what God creates, we can know God in relationship to evolutionary creation as novelty and future. This dynamic activity of the triune God is the way the Creator constantly pours out life to the world. As Delio concludes, "Creation is always more than the present moment can hold. Creation therefore thrives on the threshold of the future endowed with freedom, promise, and openness to new emergent life. . . . Creation moves forward, driven by the power of love into an ever-new horizon of God, a future of newness in love, and our hope that love alone will endure."[70]

Indeed, God so loved the world that from the moment of creation divine dynamism was infused into everything to "become" until it reaches its fullest potential. God, from within atoms and protons, through variations of their valences, set life into motion to become and emerge, and the divine continues to draw the beloved creation forward to perfection. But this "becoming" of the world, in the world involves constant change and conversion.

---

[68] Delio, "Godhead or God Ahead?" 14.
[69] Ibid.
[70] Ibid., 19.

From the Writings of St. Francis

Thomas of Celano, The Life of St. Francis, *XXIX, 81*[71]

How great do you think was the delight the beauty of flowers brought to his soul whenever he saw their lovely form and noticed their sweet fragrance? He would immediately turn his gaze to the beauty of that flower, brilliant in springtime, sprouting *from the root of* Jesse [Isa 11:1]. By its *fragrance* [1 Cor 2:14] it raised up countless thousands of dead. Whenever he found an abundance of flowers, he used to preach to them and invite them to praise the Lord, just as if they were endowed with reason.

Thomas of Celano, The Remembrance of the Desire of a Soul *(1245–1247), CXXIV, 165*[72]

In art
he praises the Artist;
whatever he discovers in creatures
he guides to the Creator.
He rejoices in all the works of the Lord's hands [Ps 92:5],
and through their delightful display
he gazes on their life-giving reason and cause.
In beautiful things he discerns Beauty Itself;
All good things cry out to him [Gen 1:31]:
"The One who made us is the Best" [Ps 100:3].
Following the *footprints* imprinted on creatures,
he *follows his Beloved* everywhere [Job 23:11; Song 5:17; Matt 12:18];
out of them all he makes himself a *ladder* [Gen 28:12-13]
by which he might reach the Throne [Jb 23:3].

He embraces all things
with an intensity of unheard of devotion,
speaking to them about the Lord
and exhorting them to praise Him.

---

[71] Thomas of Celano, *The Life of St. Francis*, XXIX, 81, in *Francis of Assisi: Early Documents*, vol. 1, *The Saint*, ed. Regis J. Armstrong, J. A. Wayne Hellmann, and William J. Short (New York: New City Press, 1999), 251.

[72] Thomas of Celano, *The Remembrance of the Desire of a Soul* (1245–1247), CXXIV, 165, in *Francis of Assisi: Early Documents*, vol. II, *The Founder*, ed. Regis J. Armstrong, J. A. Wayne Hellmann, and William J. Short (New York: New City Press, 2000), 353–54.

He walked reverently over rocks, out of respect for Him who is called *the Rock* [1 Cor 10:4; Ps 61:3]. When he came to the verse "You have set me high upon the rock," in order to express it more respectfully, he would say: "You have set me high *under the feet* [Ps 18:39] of the Rock."

When the brothers are cutting wood he forbids them to cut down the whole tree, so that it might have hope of sprouting again.

Reflection and Application

In our ecologically threatened age, conversion takes on a new look. Indeed, on March 10, 2008, for the first time the Apostolic Penitentiary listed "ecological offences" among the "new forms of social sin." Moreover, the late Blessed John Paul II called for penance and ecological conversion to a life of *Christian simplicity*—a return to a relational vision and way of living.[73] In 2001, in their pastoral Global Climate Change: A Plea for Dialogue, Prudence, and the Common Good, the United States Catholic bishops called for immediate and *significant* lifestyle changes toward arresting human-caused global warming. Such change and conversion requires that we open ourselves to the love of God as St. Francis did.

St. Francis of Assisi was not always a model of one caring for creation. Thomas of Celano tells us that *only after* Francis's conversion did he truly delight in creation.[74] Falling in love with Christ drastically shifted Francis's capacity to see and to know. He made the connection between God as the Creator and the Word made flesh, Jesus Christ, through whom the world was created, but who also lived on this earth as part of the material universe. Only then did St. Francis realize that humans are also part of the natural world and that to love God is to also love God's creation.[75] And only then did he see the footprints of Jesus everywhere!

[73] Pope John Paul II, general audience address, January 17, 2001, http://conservation.catholic.org/john_paul_ii.htm, accessed May 26, 2009.

[74] See Roger D. Sorrell, *St. Francis of Assisi and Nature: Tradition and Innovation in Western Christian Attitudes toward the Environment* (New York: Oxford University Press, 1988), especially 57 and 67–68.

[75] As St. Bonaventure tells us in *The Major Legend of St. Francis* (1260–1263), in FAED, vol. II, *The Founder*, 596–97, "In beautiful things [Francis] contuited Beauty itself. . . . He savored in each and every creature . . . that fontal goodness."

With St. Francis, we are called to protect and preserve the earth and all creatures, which, in their beauty and complexity, draw us in, give us joy, inspire us to praise, and lead us to the heart of God. St. Francis's vision of the kinship of creation extends the meaning of Jesus' command to love both God and neighbor (Matt 22:37-39). Our neighbor is everyone, including every creature, plant, and cosmic element. Today our lifestyle and daily choices reveal our values and affect the health of the planet. The "new creation" is not yet here, but it is present within us and among us. It is our work to open ourselves to God's love and to create the conditions for it to emerge.

Questions for Reflection and Discussion

1. Describe your best experience of loving or of being loved. How does love stay the same? In what ways does love change? How is the love you experience like or unlike God's love expressed in creation?

2. Does thinking about creation as a process of emergence give life any less dignity than it has in your previous understanding of the origins of life?

3. In what ways do your actions of loving or being loved assist or detract from the emergence of God's new creation?

4. How well do you know the place where you live? What is its evolutionary and ecological history? How has it emerged (changed) over the years? How has human intervention shaped it—for good or for ill?

5. How does the Word of God take on the flesh of the piece of God's creation where you live?

Suggestions for Action

1. Visit a science or natural history museum in your area and learn about the geological and ecological evolution of your locale.

2. Read the Gospel of John and consider the ways in which the natural world reveals the Word made flesh.

3. Practice paying close attention to the natural world around your home. Do you know the names of the various plants, animals, rocks and minerals, and bodies of water and the creatures that live in them? Pay attention to how you feel inside whenever you see one of those "sisters or brothers."

4. What animals and plants in your area of the planet are endangered by human intervention in their habitats? Seek out a group or organization to advocate on their behalf. If no such group exists, start a group yourself!

5. Where do the poor people live in your community? What access do they have to beauty? What access do they have to clean air, water, and land that is free from pollution? Ask some of the people who live in that area how you might become allied with them in taking action against the environmental injustices they experience.

6. The next time you prepare to receive the sacrament of reconciliation, reflect on the ways you have participated in "ecological offenses" against God's creation. Pray for ecological conversion and a more sensitive heart.

7. Write your own "Canticle of Brother Sun."

Prayer[76]

You who are the Center at which all things meet and which stretches out over all things so as to draw them back into itself, I love you for the extensions of your body and soul to the farthest corners of creation through grace, through life, and through matter.

Lord Jesus, you who are as gentle as the human heart, as fiery as the forces of nature, as intimate as life itself, you in whom I can melt away and with whom I must have mastery and freedom, I love you as the world, as this world which has captivated my heart. Amen.

[76] Pierre Teilhard de Chardin, *Hymn of the Universe* (New York: Harper & Row, 1965), 7.

Sources for Further Study

Boff, Leonardo, and Mark Hathaway. *The Tao of Liberation: Exploring the Ecology of Transformation.* Maryknoll, NY: Orbis Books, 2009.

Delio, Ilia. *The Emergent Christ: Exploring the Meaning of Catholic in an Evolutionary Universe.* Maryknoll, NY: Orbis Books, 2011.

Nothwehr, Dawn M. "Called to Ecological Conversion." *New Theology Review* 22, no.1 (February 2009): 84–87.

Sorrell, Roger D. *St. Francis of Assisi and Nature: Tradition and Innovation in Western Christian Attitudes toward the Environment.* New York: Oxford University Press, 1988.

Part 2

St. Francis and St. Clare:
Models of Faith and Sustainable Living

Chapter 3

A Word from Lady Clare of Assisi on Sustainable Living

Introduction: Why Consider St. Clare?

It may seem rather odd that we would reach back into the late twelfth to early thirteenth century to find a model for twenty-first-century environmentally sustainable living. Yet if we examine the life and writings of Lady Chiara Offreduccio, better known as St. Clare of Assisi (July 16, 1194, to August 11, 1253), we can uncover important clues for ecologically healthy, moral, and Christ-centered living.[1]

It was St. Francis of Assisi who received Lady Chiara into religious life as a penitent.[2] Later Clare, her blood sisters Beatrice and Catherine (who became known as Agnes of Prague), her mother, Lady Ortulana,

---

[1] See Regis J. Armstrong, ed. and trans., "Introduction," in *The Lady—Clare of Assisi: Early Documents*, rev. ed. (New York: New City Press, 2006), especially 13–28 (hereafter TLCAED). All primary sources cited are from that translation and edition unless indicated otherwise. See list of abbreviations.

It is recommended that those not familiar with the basic outlines of St. Clare's biography and spirituality read one of the texts found in the "Sources for Further Study" section at the end of this chapter.

[2] Ingrid J. Peterson, *Clare of Assisi: A Biographical Study* (Quincy, IL: Franciscan Press, 1993), 109: "Francis heard about Clare's holiness and came to preach to her the gospel way of poverty. Clare decided to leave her home and renounce her social status on Palm Sunday 1212." See also LCl, III and IV. Also see PC, "The Twelfth Witness," 2.

and several other women moved into the cloister at San Damiano, which St. Francis of Assisi and the Lesser Brothers prepared for them, just outside of the walls of Assisi.[3] Known for their radically austere lifestyle, these women were called the "Poor Ladies."[4] Clare's ideal was to emulate "the Poor Christ, who had nowhere to lay his head."[5] In contrast to God, who is eternal and the ultimate source of our security, she believed the created world is fleeting and filled with temptation.[6] Yet, beyond this belief, Clare's life exemplified ways of being and acting that are vital for true ecological living.

Clare's Community-Minded Living

In Clare's day, the economy of Umbria was in flux, shifting from the medieval system to the mercantile system. In 1197, after the death of Emperor Henry VI, citizens of Assisi established a *commune* and elected counsels to rule the city.[7] And subsequently in 1198, when Clare was five years old, a band of Assisi's commoners (*minores*) rebelled against the ruling Duke Conrad of Urslingen and captured the Rocca Maggiore outside of Assisi. This set off a war for political control between the nobility (*majores*) and the common people that was rooted in the shift in economic systems and class mobility made possible by access to new wealth. During that time, the Offereduccio household (which belonged to the *majores*) fled for their lives and lived in exile in Perugia until the Peace of Assisi was signed in 1210. Having learned much from this violent context, her childhood religious training, and her meetings with pious women in the Offereduccio household[8] and being rooted in gospel values,[9] Clare and her sisters established a life at San Domiano charac-

---

[3] See LCl, V.

[4] See Peterson, *Clare of Assisi*, 168: "The first Clares were called Damianites—the Sisters Minor—in France, the Clarisses—but most references identify them as Poor Ladies. The title was an oxymoron. Lady implied aristocracy. Upper class included wealth. Being a lady was a matter of bloodlines. Clare could not change that. Being poor was not a matter of externals, of accident; for Clare, poorness involved a fundamental approach to God. To be poor was Clare's choice and driving passion."

[5] See 1LAg, 17–18; 4LAg, 15–23; FLCl, VI–VII, 5–15. Also see Matthew 8:20.

[6] See 1LAg, 22–23; 2LAg, 15–23; and 4LAg, 7.

[7] See Peterson, *Clare of Assisi*, 55–65.

[8] See ibid., 17–106.

[9] See John 13:4-5 and John 15:15.

terized by mutual regard, respectful admiration, humility, and the delight
of real friendship.

Reverence and Respect

As the founding abbess, Clare set the example and tone for the life of
the Poor Ladies. As a young woman of nobility, she was better educated
than most women of her day, and from her letters, Rule, and "Testament,"
we can see that she was a gifted writer. Yet she did not flaunt her status
in any way. Rather, Clare's self-deprecating manner and courtesy was
noted by all who knew her, and it is particularly evident in the letters
she exchanged with Agnes of Prague. Typical of the late twelfth-century
language of address used by nobility and fitting with Clare's style are
greetings such as "To the esteemed and most holy virgin, Lady Agnes,"
or "To the Lady most respected in Christ, and the sister to be loved before
all mortals, Agnes."[10]

While this flowery language seems a bit much to our postmodern ears,
such statements reflect the deepest affection and respect and communicate a profound sense of love. Such words of affirmation draw out and
invite self-esteem and courage and possibly even stir up a desire to treat
someone else in a similar respectful manner. For Christians, these words
recall the reality that humans are created in the image and likeness of
God and thus bear an inviolable dignity. There is no hint of domination,
manipulation, utilitarianism, one-upmanship, or objectification in these
salutations.

Clare's Example of Humility

Clare's expressions in reference to herself are humble, to the extent
that they even seem unhealthy to our ears. Typical self-deprecating statements are "Clare, the most lowly and unworthy handmaid of Christ and
servant of the Poor Ladies,"[11] or "Clare, an unworthy servant of Jesus
Christ and a *useless* servant of the enclosed Ladies of the Monastery of
San Damiano."[12]

Significantly, Clare's humility was deeply grounded in her experience
of God's unfathomable and steadfast love demonstrated in the incarnation

---

[10] See 1LAg, 1, and 3LAg, 1.

[11] 3LAg, 2.

[12] 4LAg, 2.

(God become flesh in the person of Jesus Christ, part of the material world). She accepted that she was made in the divine image and that she was loved by others as well. Clare was thus free to move beyond her status as a daughter of the nobility and to show respect and extend affirmation to others.

Poverty, charity, and humility are the virtues that recur most often in "The Form of Life of Clare of Assisi" (1253), "The Testament" (1247–1253), and Clare's letters to Agnes of Prague. But Clare herself was known primarily for her humility.[13] Though she was the abbess[14] at San Damiano, Clare lived as a humble servant to others. As "The Acts of the Process of Canonization" (1253) indicates, numerous witnesses testified that Clare even washed the mattresses of her sick sisters, cared for them, and washed their feet.[15]

Engaging the Heart

Among her writings, the most personally revealing of Clare's work are her letters to Agnes of Prague. Therein, Clare expressed her profound appreciation for Agnes's qualities and virtues. The two women shared much in common in terms of their noble upbringing, their spiritual journeys, and their rejection of a marriage proposal, and they seemed to draw out the very best from and for each other. Clare was thrilled that Agnes had become a faithful lover of God, and she desired that Agnes would know the fullness of God's friendship. There is no doubt that Agnes elicited Clare's personal fondness. In her fourth and final letter to Agnes, Clare expressed her delight in their intimate friendship. Clare wrote: "I have inscribed the happy memory of you on the tablets of my heart, holding you dearer than all others. What more can I say? Let the tongue of the flesh be silent when I seek to express my love for you; and

[13] See PC, Prologue, "The First Witness," "The Fourth Witness," "The Fifth Witness," "The Sixth Witness," "The Seventh Witness," "The Eighth Witness," and "The Tenth Witness." See also LCl, VII, 5; LCl, VIII; and LCl, XI.

[14] Peterson, *Clare of Assisi*, 144, explains that Clare cared for the sick in this "hands-on" manner not only as a humble, religious, and pious gesture, risking her status, but quite realistically, also risking her own life. During this period in history, plagues swept Europe. The disease was carried by insects, and to be bitten was to become ill. See also LCl, VIII, 12.

[15] See PC, "The First Witness," 12; "The Second Witness," 3; "The Third Witness," 9; "The Seventh Witness," 5; "The Tenth Witness," 6. Also see Peterson, *Clare of Assisi*, 144.

let the tongue of the Spirit speak, because the love that I have for you, O blessed daughter, can never be fully expressed by the tongue of the flesh, and even what I have written is an inadequate expression."[16] These words from Clare, the abbess, to Agnes, who is, technically speaking, her subject, reveal Clare's desire that Agnes receive her words with deep and unrestricted regard and fondness. This is but one example of Clare's respectful, reverential, and unbiased treatment of all of her sisters. But on the other hand, Clare does not hesitate to establish genuine bonds of adult friendship.

But what does all of this have to do with the environment? Without a doubt, Clare's focus was on God. But significantly, in a time when the predominant Christian spirituality and worldview set "spiritual things" over against "material things," Clare described Christ using the heavenly luminaries (material things) positively: "[Christ] gave Himself totally for your love, / At Whose beauty the sun and the moon marvel, / Whose rewards and their preciousness are without end."[17] Worship of God definitely did not keep her from also reverencing God's creation in all its splendor. In fact, at Clare's canonization proceedings, Sister Angeluccia testified that Clare instructed the Poor Ladies to "praise God when they saw beautiful trees, flowers, and bushes; and, likewise, always to praise Him for and in all things when they saw all peoples and creatures."[18]

Clare made a similar kind of association with the element of water. When Clare blessed her sisters with water, she would say, "My sisters and daughters, you must always remember and recall this blessed water that came from the right side of our Lord Jesus Christ as He hung upon the cross."[19] Though the dominant philosophical orientation of her day was to see the spiritual as superior to the material things of this world, through the eyes of faith, perhaps influenced by St. Francis, Clare was able to understand the sacredness of creation, reflecting the beloved Creator and Redeemer.

But also significant for our consideration of environment and sustainability is that in her "Testament" Clare entrusted the Poor Ladies with the values she hoped they would maintain after her death. She wrote a succinct and powerful statement about how the sisters were to care for

---

[16] 4LAg, 33.
[17] 3LAg, 16.
[18] PC, "The Fourteenth Witness," 9.
[19] Ibid., 8.

each other: "And loving one another with the love of Christ, may you demonstrate without in your deeds the love you have within so that, compelled by such an example, the sisters may always grow in love of God, and in mutual charity."[20]

A Community of Footwashers

No doubt influenced by her experiences at home, where especially her mother Ortulana gathered strong women together to pray and do pious deeds,[21] as well as by the example of the lives of St. Francis and the Lesser Brothers,[22] Clare went beyond the legalistic norms for religious life in the way she structured life in the San Damiano community. In her "Form of Life" (1253), Clare outlined her "way" as a horizontal, rather than a vertical, set of relationships.[23] She was concerned about gentle, mutual care; power sharing; compassion for sinners; and special treatment for the ill among the Poor Ladies.[24] About Clare's "Form of Life" Margaret Carney states: "A sisterhood which guaranteed equality combined with sensitive and affectionate regard provided a new possibility of social relationships for the women who comprised it. Freed from the social constraints and traditions of the secular and monastic forms of their day, these Poor Sisters identified, in a dramatic and unsettling way, with groups of women seeking their own place in a nascent social ecclesiastical urban reality."[25] All of the sisters were involved in decision making, and when that was not possible, Clare turned to a special group of consultors.[26] *All* of the Poor Ladies, including the abbess, openly confessed their faults[27] and sought forgiveness from one another.[28] Most

---

[20] TestCl, 56–60, at 59–60.

[21] See LCl, I, 1. Also see Armstrong, ed. and trans., "Introduction," in TLCAED, 14–16. See also Peterson, *Clare of Assisi*, 29–38, 67–78.

[22] See Margaret Carney, *The First Franciscan Woman: Clare of Assisi and Her Form of Life* (Quincy, IL: Franciscan Press, 1993), 150–59.

[23] See FLCl, IV, 9–12. Also see TestCl, 61–73, and Carney, *The First Franciscan Woman*, 146–49.

[24] See FLCl, X, 4–5. Also see LCl, VIII, 6–11, and Peterson, *Clare of Assisi*, 144.

[25] Carney, *The First Franciscan Woman*, 171.

[26] FLCl, IV, 15–17.

[27] FLCl, IX, 6–10.

[28] FLCl, IV, 16.

telling was that while under political pressure Clare reluctantly accepted the title "abbess," she never referred to herself in this way.[29]

The *Legend of Saint Clare* (1254–1255) speaks of Clare's care for the Poor Ladies this way:

> This venerable Abbess loved not only the souls of her sisters, she also took care of their little bodies with wonderful zeal of charity. Frequently, in the cold of night, she covered them with her own hands while they were sleeping. She wished that those whom she perceived unable to observe the common rigor to be content to govern themselves with gentleness. If a temptation disturbed someone, if sadness took hold of someone, as is natural, she called her in secret and consoled her with her tears. Sometimes she would place herself at the feet of the depressed [sister] so that she might relieve the force of [her] sadness with her motherly caress.[30]

All of this reverential love and respect for her sisters had deep roots in her profound comprehension of human dignity and in her own sense of being held in the heart of God, her loving Creator.

Lady Clare's Lessons for Sustainable Living

Today we have a new consciousness of the earth; its inhabitants; the serious threats of human-caused global warming; the loss of potable water, clean air, and arable soils; and vast extinctions limiting the earth's biodiversity. Yet, there is much to learn from Clare's simple, respectful, and courteous ways of relating to God and all of God's creation.

Courtesy and Civility

As children and young adults, St. Clare and St. Francis were influenced by the institution of knighthood—its warring ways as well as the luxuriant religious and social formalities that accompanied it. There were no fewer than seven knights in Clare's family, and Francis himself had dabbled (unsuccessfully) in knighthood. One of the premiere virtues of

---

[29] PC, "The First Witness," 6; "The Sixth Witness," 2; and "The Tenth Witness," 14. Also see LCl, VIII, 4–5; Carney, *The First Franciscan Woman*, 67–68; and Peterson, *Clare of Assisi*, 146–47.

[30] LCl, XXV, 1–4, brackets in original.

a knight was to behave courteously, in a polished manner, gallantly, respectfully, and with consideration, cooperation, and generosity.[31]

Marco Bartoli explains that in Clare's day, the knightly virtues to be upheld were strength, fidelity, and courage.[32] Courtesy included the virtue of solidarity in war, which became transfigured as fidelity to one's word. It also included leaving the door open to communication with one's enemies, so there was a possibility to settle disagreements without shedding blood. Knights were obliged to believe the word of another, until it was proven not trustworthy. And the virtue of courage required that knights be not self-serving but rather generous and liberal, exerting their considerable power on behalf of the vulnerable in society. Similarly, noble women were best characterized by the virtues of beauty, courtesy, and wisdom. These virtues were readily attributed to Clare by all who knew her, as is born out in the testimony of the various witnesses and recorded in "The Acts of the Process of Canonization" (1253).[33]

When corresponding with Agnes of Prague, Clare refers to the knightly character of the man Agnes had been betrothed to marry but whom she subsequently refused to wed. Instead, Agnes vowed to follow in the footprints of Jesus as a Poor Lady. Clare writes that in choosing Christ, Agnes has gained one "Whose strength is more robust, / generosity more lofty, / Whose appearance is more handsome, / love more courteous, / and every kindness more refined."[34]

The language of courtesy appears again in Clare's "The Testament" (1247–1253), and she mentions the courtly gesture of courtesy, bowing. There, too, Clare speaks of the form of life she received from Francis "to persevere in holy poverty."[35] She fought all her life for the papal approval of this form of life, which was granted by Pope Innocent IV at the time of her death. She continues: "For this reason, *on bended knees and bowing*

---

[31] *Gale Virtual Reference Library Dictionary*, s.v. "courteous": "1: marked by polished manners, gallantry, or ceremonial usage of a court; 2: marked by respect for and consideration of others; consideration, cooperation, and generosity in providing something (as a gift or privilege)."

[32] Marco Bartoli, *Saint Clare: Beyond the Legend*, trans. Frances Teresa Downing (Cincinnati, OH: St. Anthony Messenger Press, 2010), 29–43.

[33] See PC, VIII, 4: the witness spoke of Clare's integrity and mature judgment; PC, II, 2, and XVI, 2: the witness spoke of Clare's gentleness, kindness, and courtesy that revealed the nobility of her soul; and PC VIII, 2. It was publically known that she refused the proposal of marriage by men who admired her great beauty.

[34] 1LAg, 9.

[35] TestCl, 33–36.

low with both [body and soul], I commend all my sisters, both those present and those to come, to holy Mother the Roman Church, to the supreme Pontiff, and, especially, to the Lord Cardinal who has been appointed for the religion of the Lesser Brothers and for us."[36] Here Clare's stance is one of gratitude—expressed in the most respectful courtly gesture of the day—first to God, then to her beloved sisters, the church, and the cardinal protector of her order. Here again she gives herself away in order to raise up another, recognizing the dignity and worth of another person, all in the name of holy poverty.

Our postmodern consciousness rarely leads us to consider the virtue of courtesy or courtly respect. Yet today in our ecologically threatened world, we need to learn new ways to give a courtly bow to one another and to our ravaged global environment, to deal with it kindly, to be prudent about how we treat the air, water, and soil, and to protect and restore earth's beauty. Taking on an attitude of courtesy would be but a first concrete step toward healing our ravaged planet and renewing our commitment to uphold the God-given intrinsic value of God's creation. Clearly, we can speculate about whether or not Clare would have had similar thoughts in her day. Yet we know of her intimate spiritual friendship with St. Francis and the important role he played in the founding and sustaining of the community of the Poor Ladies. In his "Salutations of the Virtues" St. Francis proposes that a fitting relationship among humans and between humans and animals is that of obedience: ". . . [The person who possesses holy Obedience] is subject and submissive / to everyone in the world, / not only to people / but to every beast and wild animal as well / that they may do whatever they want with it / insofar as it *has been given* to them / *from above* by the Lord."[37]

Roger D. Sorrell called the relationship Francis refers to here "mutual deference." Just as in the relationship of chivalry between the medieval knights, who exercised the virtue of *noblesse oblige*, "a mutual regard and deference between brothers serving God together," so too Francis's view of the relationship among humans and animals was one of "sisters" and "brothers" serving the Creator.[38]

---

[36] TestCl, 44, emphasis added, brackets in original.

[37] Francis of Assisi, "The Undated Writings—A Salutation of the Virtues," 14, in *Francis of Assisi: Early Documents*, vol. I, *The Saint*, trans. and ed. Regis J. Armstrong, J. A. Wayne Hellmann, and William J. Short (New York: New City Press, 1999), 165.

[38] Roger D. Sorrell, *St. Francis of Assisi and Nature* (New York: Oxford University Press, 1989), 74.

Beloved: One among Many

As we saw in previous chapters, much took place in the graced story of the universe before the arrival of *Homo sapiens.* We present-day humans are the fruit of billions of years of intense activity on the part of the matter that preceded us. Humans are unique in that we are the universe become conscious. Yet we remain interdependent with everything else in the universe. Without clear air, potable water, and arable soil and intact global systems that keep the earth's bioregions in ecological balance, no human could survive to live and love. Indeed, as we saw in chapter 2, God is the common ground behind the creation story of evolution (which tells us *how* creation emerged) and the Genesis creation accounts (which tell us *why* creation emerged). In chapter 1, we saw that through the covenants with humans and all of creation God models for us the way toward global environmental well-being and sustainability. The Scriptures present a holistic, interdependent relationship between God and all creation and among all the elements of creation.

Heart Sight

Clare was simply in love with God. And, like all people who are in love, she saw the world differently—in all of its potentials and possibilities. The source and motive for Clare's optimism was her participation in the very life of God—a life she saw as open to all of creation. What made Clare's perception different was that she had what Franciscan theologian Eric Doyle calls "heart sight."[39] Clare, like Francis, had the capacity to see things through the "eyes of the Spirit."[40] When Clare saw her sisters, other people, or things created by God, she also perceived the reality that each had a God-given dignity all its own (intrinsic value). Like Clare, we need to reverence one another and all of creation because we reverence Christ, and each for its own sake. In light of this, it is idolatry to be self-centered, oppressive in our actions toward others, or destructive of God's creation.

---

[39] See Eric Doyle, "'The Canticle of Brother Sun' and the Value of Creation," in *Franciscan Theology of the Environment: An Introductory Reader,* ed. Dawn M. Nothwehr (Quincy, IL: Franciscan Press, 2002), 163.

[40] Francis of Assisi, "The Undated Writings—The Admonitions," I, in FAED, vol. 1, *The Saint,* 128–29.

Beyond that, we are emboldened to open ourselves to the poor and oppressed—whether they be human or otherkind. And then, like Clare, through the process of letting go of status and power, we can recognize our *inter*dependence. But also like Clare, we need to *choose* to use our personal, economic, and political power to truly love and nurture both humans and otherkind, just as God generously cares for us.

Clare understood creation to be permeated with the presence of God. Why else would she have asked the "extern sisters" to notice the beauty and wonder of creation when doing their work outside the enclosure of San Damiano? To be indifferent toward, to ignore, or even to abuse such evidence of God would be the equivalent of denying God's revelation or self-expression—and thus would be sinful.

To Have a Voice

In Clare's community, each sister, including the youngest sister, had a voice in determining the life of the sisters.[41] According to Clare's Rule, 4:15, the abbess met with the sisters "at least once a week." And, as Margaret Carney points out, throughout her "Form of Life" Clare uses the possessive form—"*our* profession," "*our* poverty," "*our* life."[42] Through this expression of inclusive valuing and providing an opportunity for all voices to be heard on a regular basis, Carney suggests that "Clare ensured a sense of mutuality" within the community.[43]

If we consider today's state of creation in this light, who today hears the voices of the glaciers, the rainforests, or the polluted air, streams, or soils? As we saw in the previous chapters, "the Earth is the Lord's" (Ps 24). We humans are to be the guardians giving voice to the needs of creation. Indeed, according to the Noahic covenant,[44] all plants and animals have value and moral standing before God. Therefore, human destruction of creation is not only foolish but also blasphemous against God and therefore sinful. We are not destined to be masters and mistresses of the universe, to rule over creation in utilitarian ways. Today there are many ways—environmental impact studies, scientific models, or even our own observations of the natural world—that allow us to "hear" the voice of the created world (see Rom 8:18-27).

---

[41] FLCl, 4:15-24.

[42] Carney, *The First Franciscan Woman*, 168, emphasis mine.

[43] Ibid.

[44] "Everlasting covenant" = Hebrew *bᵊrith ʿolam*.

By contrast with the positive effects Clare's reverence and respect had on all others, our violent destruction of creatures and ecosystems infects our very character and identity, distorting and warping it.[45] As theologian Elizabeth A. Dreyer suggests, our attitude toward the nonhuman world directly affects our development and excellence as persons.[46] We, like Clare, can genuinely care for creation and experience empathy with it rather than the need to control it. With a vision of cosmic harmony to lure us, we can put ourselves at the service of the cosmos in a spirit of sacrificial love. "To live in hope as we face possible ecological disaster is a difficult and revolutionary activity. But the mandate of the gospel demands that we use the graces of the tradition—St. Clare of Assisi is one example—and the graces of our own commitment and creative imagination in the service of the universe."[47]

From the Writings of St. Clare

"The Form of Life of St. Clare of Assisi" (1253), IV, 8–18[48]

Let whoever is elected reflect upon the kind of burden she has undertaken on herself and to Whom *she must render an account* of the flock committed to her. Let her also strive to preside over the others more by her virtues and holy behavior than by her office, so that, moved by her example, the sisters may obey her more out of love than out of fear. Let her avoid exclusive loves, lest by loving some more than others she give scandal to all. Let her console the afflicted. Let her also be *the last refuge for those who are troubled*, lest the sickness of despair overcome the weak should they fail to find in her health-giving remedies.

Let her preserve the common life in everything. . . .

[45] This statement is based on an understanding of virtue ethics. In this understanding of Christian ethics, people become good (virtuous) by doing what is good, or they become evil (vicious) by doing what is not good, or what is evil. See Richard M. Gula, "The Shifting Landscape of Moral Theology," *Church* 25/1 (Spring 2009): 44–53.

[46] Elisabeth A. Dreyer, "'[God] Whose Beauty the Sun and Moon Admire': Clare and Ecology," in *Franciscan Theology of the Environment*, ed. Nothwehr, 139.

[47] Ibid.

[48] Armstrong, ed. and trans., "The Form of Life of St. Clare of Assisi" (1253), IV, 8–18, in TLCAED, 65–66.

The abbess is bound to call her sisters together at least once a week in the chapter, where both she and her sisters should humbly confess their common and public offenses and negligences. There let her consult with all her sisters concerning whatever concerns the welfare and good of the monastery, for the Lord frequently reveals what is better to the youngest.

"The Third Letter to Agnes of Prague" (1238), 15–17[49]

And, after all who ensnare their blind lovers
in a deceitful and turbulent world
have been completely passed over,
may you totally love Him
Who gave Himself totally for your love,
At Whose beauty the sun and the moon marvel,
Whose rewards and their uniqueness and grandeur have no limits.
I am speaking of Him,
the Son of the Most High,
Whom the Virgin brought to birth
and remained a virgin after His birth.

"The Acts of the Process of Canonization:
The Fourteenth Witness" (1253), 9[50]

She also said when the most holy mother used to send the serving sisters outside the monastery, she reminded them to praise God when they saw beautiful trees, flowers, and bushes; and, likewise, always to praise Him for and in all things when they saw all people and creatures.

Reflection and Application

For centuries, the industrialized Western nations have exercised power over the "resources" of the earth with little regard for their limits. This use of power is what David Toolan cites as the "imperial ecology" of

[49] Armstrong, ed. and trans., "The Third Letter to Agnes of Prague" (1238), 15–17, in TLCAED, 46.

[50] Armstrong, ed. and trans., "The Acts of the Process of Canonization: The Fourteenth Witness" (1253), 9, in TLCAED, 178.

Bacon and Descartes, the shift to economic materialism, and the belief in the clock-maker god of Deism, which are all models of the exercise of what ethicists call "power-over."[51] Underpinning this exercise of power-over is the assertion of human superiority on all counts.

Imperial Ecology

Two key figures, Francis Bacon (1561–1626) and Rene Descartes (1596–1650), initiated what environmental historian Donald Worster calls "imperial ecology."[52] Bacon saw humans as lords and masters over nature. The agricultural revolution promoted the earth as a garden to be cultivated, and the nature of scientific and industrial revolutions held that various earth elements were parts of a machine that could be remade, according to the reason and the imagination of "man the maker" (*Homo faber*). Bacon believed that science could restore the world to paradisial conditions, bringing about the biblical "new Jerusalem."[53] Technology was the means to that end. Bacon's writings are full of metaphors for "Mother Earth" that conjure up the practice of interrogating and torturing witches. In his terms, nature was to be "bound into service," "made a slave," and "put under constraint."[54] She was to be "squeezed and dissected" and "forced out of her natural state and molded" so that "human knowledge and human power meet as one."[55] Ultimately, the new science would produce a "blessed race of heroes and supermen."[56]

Rene Descartes held that nature is nothing but a machine that could be understood by analyzing its various parts.[57] He thought that to understand nature is to discover the functional relationship between abstractly conceived processes and objects that could be translated into mathematical equations. The key is to bring natural processes into the realm of the conceptual, mathematical understandings—that is, to formulate laws so as to serve human interests. The aim of modern science, Descartes

---

[51] See David Toolan, *At Home in the Cosmos* (Maryknoll, NY: Orbis Books, 2001), especially pt. II, "The Development of Scientific Materialism," 41–74. Toolan cites Donald Worster, *Nature's Economy: A History of Ecological Ideas*, 2nd ed. (Cambridge: Cambridge University Press, 1977), 29.

[52] Ibid., 48.

[53] Ibid., 49.

[54] Ibid.

[55] Ibid.

[56] Ibid.

[57] Ibid., 49–50.

argued in *Discourse on Method* (VI.62), is to "know the power and action of fire, water, air, the stars, the heavens and all the other bodies in our environment, as distinctly as we know the various crafts of our artisans; and we could use this knowledge—as the artisans use theirs—for all the purposes for which it is appropriate, and thus make ourselves, as it were, the lords and masters of nature."[58]

David Toolan remarks that Isaac Newton (1642–1727) was Francis Bacon's dream of the "superman" come true. Newton was a genius at taking what had previously been known only as facts and novelties and formulating them into general laws and principles that could be broadly applied. Even today, every high school student learns Newton's three laws of motion. Those laws could be applied to the movement of a child's toy or the movement of comets, the moon, or the sea. Toolan puts it well: "If Descartes embodied the new detached ego of the modern West, Newton gave us its objective correlate: an objective world of deterministic law."[59] Toolan also notes that, all the while, Newton saw his "mechanical philosophy" as proceeding from the fiat of God's omnipotent will. His theories were simply fulfilling his duty to bear witness of God to others. The ultimate effect of Newton's work was to place the capstone on what Bacon had begun. As David Toolan explains, "In effect, Newton's *Principia Mathematica* convinced Western Europeans that the state of nature was that of martial law. . . . Nature's Eros and ambiguity, its randomness and unpredictability, so familiar to the ancients, are simply ignored or repressed. Turbulence or frustration became invisible."[60] Eventually, Newton's student Pierre Simon LePlace (1749–1827) argued that the universe is completely determined, "so we no longer require the hypothesis of God."[61]

In our world created by scientific materialism, there is little, if any, consideration of the intrinsic worth or the innate powers of anything other than the human. Tragically, we are now reaping the results of this arrogance and idolatry. The current water, energy, food, and climate crises reek of the scale and size of the abuse human power-over has wrought, forcing the capacities of the earth's ecosystems to their breaking point.

---

[58] Ibid., 50.
[59] Ibid., 52.
[60] Ibid.
[61] Ibid., 53.

Power and Kinds of Power

But let's be realistic! We all have power. And if one is North American, educated, and Catholic, one has more power than most individuals in the world! So how do we move from abusive power to mutuality, as Clare understood it? From being cold, mechanistic problem solvers to persons who share in mutual relations? Put simply, we need to shift our self-understanding and the focus of our choices from our presumed superiority to what we hold in common with others—especially nonhumans.

To shift our focus to commonality is not to negate all differences. Rather, it is to recognize the reality that, in the moral sense, each element of creation has God-given worth and power. The particular kind of power humans have is distinctive in that it can manipulate the natural order on a scale unknown to other creatures. How we humans use that power is our choice—for good or for ill.

When we decide to act in any moment of our day—whether on a personal scale or in setting public policy—the choices are ours concerning *whether* to engage, *who* to engage, *when* to engage, or *how* to engage. Daily we are involved with the ethics of power. Feminist ethicist Beverly Wildung Harrison's analysis of power is helpful here: "Power has long connoted the capacity to control others. . . . I believe that in situations of genuine conflict of interest, power does take on a zero-sum dynamic, but it is the goal of a genuinely transformative social ethic to identify social policies that will enhance shared, reciprocal, accountable social power, so as to press beyond zero-sum power toward more inclusive shared power and participation."[62]

Harrison provides her own definition of power as "the ability to act on and effectively shape the world around us, particularly through collective and institutional policy. To have power means to have access to physical resources and wealth, to knowledge, and to loci of social decision-making and to be able to impact institutional and social policy."[63]

---

[62] Beverly Wildung Harrison, "The Politics of Energy Policy," in *Making the Connections: Essays in Feminist Social Ethics*, ed. Carol S. Robb (Boston: Beacon Press, 1985), 174. See also Dawn M. Nothwehr, *Mutuality: A Formal Norm for Christian Social Ethics* (San Francisco: Catholic Scholars Press, 1998; repr., Eugene, OR: Wipf & Stock Publishers, 2005), 7.

[63] Beverly Wildung Harrison, "Keeping the Faith in a Sexist Church," in *Making the Connections: Essays in Feminist Social Ethics*, ed. Carol S. Robb (Boston: Beacon Press, 1985), 290. Also see Nothwehr, *Mutuality: A Formal Norm*, 67n177.

The kind of power relations the ecological future requires, and that is modeled for us by Clare of Assisi, is the exercise of "power-with"—that is, one's ability to make a difference that is "shared, reciprocal, and constrained by the limits that respectful interrelationship imposes."[64] The sort of power envisioned here is one in which the engagement of all parties—plants, animals, air, water, soil, and people—in a relationship is prized and pursued. All of this stands in contrast to "power-over," that is, the possession of control, authority, or influence over others from a hierarchical stance.[65]

But why is the use of power important? With Jewish philosopher and Holocaust survivor Elie Wiesel, I claim that "the opposite of love is not hate; it's indifference."[66] The key to genuine love is not discounting someone or something as a mere worthless object toward whom indifference can justifiably be directed (an "other" discounted even unto death). Rather, as exemplified by St. Clare, when making ordinary daily decisions, especially those affecting the natural environment, we must engage that "other" as a partner—whether human or nonhuman. Such engagement must take place on the level of the personal and the concrete, as well as the objective and the abstract. In any case, it is not only important for Christians to consider whether relationships are loving and just, but they also need to analyze the dynamics of power operative in the relationship when relating to people or the created world.

With an eye toward Clare's example of mutual relations in dealings with her sisters, I suggest that the virtue and norm of mutuality is the standard of measure that can help us make much better moral decisions, whether in regard to human or nonhuman relations. Asking questions concerning mutuality seeks out the threads of common human needs and desires, placing everything and everyone in the context of a history and a developmental continuum with a beginning, middle, and end. When utilizing the norm of mutuality, one constantly involves the potential "other" in some manner—whether through a personal conversation or an environmental impact study—toward forming a consensus that maximizes the flourishing of everyone and everything involved in

---

[64] Harrison, "The Politics of Energy Policy," 175.

[65] See Carter Heyward, *Touching Our Strength: The Erotic and the Love of God* (San Francisco: Harper & Row, 1989), 191.

[66] Elie Wiesel, "Humankind: Wisdom, Philosophy and Other Musings," *U.S. News & World Report* (October 27, 1986): 86.

the situation.[67] In recent decades, Christian feminist ethicists have carefully defined "mutuality" as a formal norm for Christian social and environmental ethics, and they have uncovered its probative value. [68] Using "mutuality" as a standard of measure helps us to examine the dynamics of power in all kinds of relationships: gender, generative, social, and cosmic. Here we will focus on "cosmic mutuality."

Mutuality Defined

Whenever we deal with a relationship, we must deal with boundaries—that is, the set of limits and capacities that define the person, plant, animal, earth element, or earth system we are engaging, as well as the patterns or dynamics of the exchange of power. For example, Clare knew and respected the needs of the individual sisters, and she cared for them accordingly. In the case of mutuality, boundaries are distinct, but the critical difference is that their engagement is determined *with* the other(s), and thus they are often more flexible and fluid. Clare's "Form of Life" required the participation of all the sisters in making decisions about all dimensions of life in the monastery. The means and the end of exchange must be geared to the common flourishing of all parties involved. How we cross boundaries in our relationships, and what we *do* once we have breached a boundary, is certainly significant. In Clare's case, she treated all of her sisters courteously, and open confession and reconciliation was a frequent practice in the life of the Poor Ladies.

Mutuality is a concept found in classical Christian theology, and it defines the maximum flourishing of humanity in relation to four areas: the cosmos, gender relationships, divine-human cogenerativity, and human sociality. The basic definition of mutuality is "the sharing of 'power-with' by and among all parties in a relationship in a way that recognizes the wholeness and particular experience of each participant toward the end of optimum flourishing of all."[69]

The form of mutuality that is most relevant to our discussion of environmental issues is "cosmic mutuality." As we saw in Clare's "Form of Life," the relationships she spoke about in her "Testament" and in her

---

[67] See Martin Buber, *Between Man and Man*, trans. Ronald Gregor Smith (London: Kegan Paul, 1947), 41–42.

[68] For an extensive treatment of mutuality in all of its forms, see Dawn M. Nothwehr, *Mutuality: A Formal Norm.*

[69] Ibid., 233.

letters to Agnes of Prague all model the social dimension of mutuality. Yet we can also find glimpses of the other forms of mutuality in Clare's work (though, admittedly, she did not use this term).[70]

Cosmic Mutuality

Evidence for cosmic mutuality is advanced from astrophysics, ecology, and quantum physics, and it demonstrates a foundational kinship of everything in the entire cosmos. In a rather negative, though persuasive, way, there is strong ecological evidence that the natural environment asserts itself as a set of living systems that "answer back" when humans defile nature.[71] In fact, humans violate the ecosystem to their own detriment. From another perspective, the social sciences have shown that the most effective social analysis takes into account how any form of power impacts the most disadvantaged, not forgetting all elements of the ecosystem, in the interest of attaining the well-being of all. Beyond that, as we saw in previous chapters, in recent years theologians have recovered a renewed understanding of the deep relationship between creation and God.

The phrase "God in the world and the world in God" expresses the age-old Christian belief that the entire creation is revelatory of God.[72] The reality that Christians proclaim in their creeds—that God is Creator, Vivifier, Redeemer, and more—is possible only in relation to creation and shows, in a certain analogous sense, need on God's part for relationship with the cosmos.[73] If we acknowledge the kinship of all creation, then the command "Love thy neighbor" must be extended to everything and everyone in a manner that reverences the God-given capacities of each.[74] In short, all of this data points to a form of mutuality that can be defined as "Cosmic Mutuality—*the sharing of 'power-with' by and among the Creator, human beings, all earth elements, and the entire cosmos in a way that recognizes their interdependence and reverences all.*"[75]

---

[70] See PC, "The Fourteenth Witness," 9.

[71] Rosemary Radford Ruether, *Gaia and God: An Ecofeminist Theology of Earth and Healing* (San Francisco: Harper, 1992), 2–3.

[72] See Bonaventure of Bagnoregio, *Hexaemeron*, XII, 14. Also see Thomas Aquinas, *Summa Theologiae* I, q. 47.

[73] See Elizabeth A. Johnson, *She Who Is: The Mystery of God in Feminist Discourse* (New York: Crossroad, 1992), 232.

[74] See Elizabeth A. Johnson, *Woman, Earth, Creator Spirit*, 1993 Madelava Lecture (New York: Paulist Press, 1993), 59–60, 66–67.

[75] Nothwehr, *Mutuality: A Formal Norm*, 233.

St. Clare of Assisi and Cosmic Mutuality

Though Clare of Assisi never studied theology or ethics, and though she was taught the dualistic neoplatonic worldview of the twelfth and thirteenth centuries, as we have seen, she keenly understood the meaning of the incarnation. In many ways, we can understand the incarnation as God's most impressive expression of mutuality (sharing of power or empowerment). God bent low to cross the boundary of this material world and became one of us, so that we might mature and grow, becoming more God-like through the saving power of Jesus.

Thus, through her profound knowledge of the Poor Christ, who humbled himself to become part of this material world, Clare clearly understood the deepest meaning of deference and courtesy, but also something of what we know as mutuality. As a humble servant of God, she readily connected the praise of God, the beauty of creation, and reverence for the human person as related to the same source of power. When we forget that this is God's planet and that we are the humble guardians charged with its care, and when we arrogantly appropriate power over one another, our fellow creatures, or the planet itself, we find ourselves in environmental crises. So, let us heed the example of the Poor Lady, St. Clare of Assisi, and take her words to heart when she exhorts, "Praise God when [you see] beautiful trees, flowers, and bushes; and, likewise, always . . . praise Him for and in all things when [you see] all peoples and creatures."[76] In doing this, we will be taking new steps in our day—just as St. Clare did in her time—to follow in the footprints of Jesus.

Questions for Reflection and Discussion

1. What are your experiences of being held in esteem?

2. Whom do you know as someone especially careful and respectful of others—including nonhuman others?

3. When are you most reverent toward others? Toward plants, animals, soil, water, air?

4. What might it feel like to be on the receiving end of someone's regard and care?

---

[76] PC, "The Fourteenth Witness," 9.

5. Is it possible to begin to practice Clare's kind of courtesy not only toward people but also toward plants, animals, water, air, or even the entire universe?

Suggestions for Action

1. Take a walk around your immediate neighborhood. Listen to the voices of your fellow earth creatures. Then respond to their cries and groaning with a courteous, loving, healing action.

2. Consider your own lifestyle in light of St. Clare's simple way of life. In what ways do your "needs" lead to pollution, abuse, or destruction of air, water, soil, or even human life?

3. Explore the internet or your local library and find a web site or book that explains the system of ocean currents across the globe, the system of air currents that creates global weather patterns, or the geological history of the place where you live. Pay attention to how all of the various parts are interdependent and interrelated.

4. Clare was known as a healer. Go the web site of the United States Conference of Catholic Bishops' Children's Health and the Environment Initiative at http://old.usccb.org/sdwp/ejp/case. Learn how pollution of air, water, and soil destroys human health—especially the health of pregnant women and unborn children.

5. Clare was known for her humility—doing the "dirty jobs" necessary to care for her sick sisters. The word "humility" is derived from the Latin word for "earth," *humus*. Humans are "earth creatures"; we have our origins in dirt (Gen 2:7). Those who do the "dirty jobs" in our society are often looked down upon. Treat your trash collector, food processing and service workers, grocery cashier, or custodian with personal courtesy and advocate for just working conditions for them so that they can have a life of dignity.

6. Go to the web site of the Catholic Coalition on Climate Change at http://catholicclimatecovenant.org. Make the St. Francis Pledge to Care for the Creation and the Poor.

7. Clare and the Poor Ladies owned no income-generating land. They maintained only the smallest parcel needed for a garden to cultivate

vegetables.[77] This is a wonderful example of sustainable living. Explore the web site of the Catholic Rural Life Conference at http://www.ncrlc.com. Learn about both sustainable and unsustainable agricultural practices and the global food crisis.

Prayer

Good and gracious Creator of all that exists, the One who loves and sustains us each day, forgive us for the times we have ignored the beautiful trees, flowers, and bushes and, likewise, failed to praise you for and in all things when we have seen people and creatures. Help us to become attuned to the voices of our sisters and brothers who are our fellow earth creatures, to treat them courteously, and to lovingly nurture and heal them. We pray in the name of the One "at Whose beauty the sun and the moon marvel." Amen.

Sources for Further Study

Secondary Sources

Bartoli, Marco. *Saint Clare: Beyond the Legend*. Translated by Frances Teresa Downing. Cincinnati, OH: St. Anthony Messenger Press, 2010.

Bodo, Murray. *Clare: A Light in the Garden*. Cincinnati, OH: St. Anthony Press, 1979.

Carney, Margaret. *The First Franciscan Woman: Clare of Assisi and Her Form of Life*. Quincy, IL: Franciscan Press, 1993.

Dreyer, Elizabeth A. "[God] 'Whose Beauty the Sun and the Moon Admire': Clare and Ecology." In *Franciscan Theology of the Environment: An Introductory Reader*, ed. Dawn M. Nothwehr, 129–41. Quincy, IL: Franciscan Press, 2002.

Peterson, Ingrid J. *Clare of Assisi: A Biographical Study*. Quincy, IL: Franciscan Press, 1993.

[77] See TestCl, 53–55.

Primary Source in English Translation

Armstrong, Regis J., editor and translator. *The Lady—Clare of Assisi: Early Documents*. Rev. ed. New York: New City Press, 2006.

Abbreviations

Abbreviation	Source
TLCAED	*The Lady—Clare of Assisi: Early Documents*
1LAg	"The First Letter to Agnes of Prague" (1234)
2LAg	"The Second Letter to Agnes of Prague" (1235)
3LAg	"The Third Letter to Agnes of Prague" (1238)
4LAg	"The Fourth Letter to Agnes of Prague" 1253)
FLCl	"The Form of Life of Clare of Assisi" (1253)
TestCl	"The Testament" (1247–1253)
BlCl	"The Blessing" (1253)
PC	"The Acts of the Process of Canonization" (1253)
LCl	*Legend of St. Clare* (1255)

Chapter 4

St. Francis's Kinship with Creation

Introduction: More Than Your Garden Variety

It is not without reason that on November 29, 1979, Pope John Paul II proclaimed St. Francis of Assisi the patron saint of ecology. Sadly, too often the power of this patronage is lost amid the saccharine and romanticized likenesses of the saint that appear in flower gardens, or the statues of the servile Francis bearing a dish of water forming a birdbath. While these images are not entirely without meaning, they certainly miss the depth of the spirit of the Poverello and all that he can teach us about the cosmos and the God of all creation. If we are to benefit from the life and teaching of St. Francis, we must "get him out of the birdbath!"[1] This requires that we learn about his life story and the profound depth of his conversion to Christ. Because the limits of this volume do not allow me to include a full spiritual biography of St. Francis, any reader not familiar with it is advised to seek out one of the several excellent accounts and study it as a complement to what is said here.[2]

St. Francis of Assisi is best characterized as an ontological poet and a nature mystic who discovered the transformation of the universe and

---

[1] See Keith Douglas Warner, "Get Him out of the Birdbath! What Does It Mean to Have a Patron Saint of Ecology?" in *Franciscan Theology of the Environment: An Introductory Reader,* ed. Dawn M. Nothwehr (Quincy, IL: Franciscan Press, 2002), 361–75.

[2] See the "Sources for Further Study" list at the end of this chapter.

the interrelatedness of all beings through a spiritual journey of conversion, penance, and praise. The journey to his conversion was arduous, and it was the subject of his entire life. In our ecologically threatened age, it is important for us to see the necessity of both the internal spiritual encounter and the external ecological effect of this spiritual journey in the life of Francis, for it points the way to our own conversion toward becoming sisters and brothers in the cosmos. As we will see, Brazilian theologian Leonardo Boff gives three main explanations that can be advanced for how Francis "arrived at sympathy and synergy with all things."[3]

Now few have come as close to living as a brother (or sister) to all of creation as St. Francis did, though thousands have tried and many have speculated about it. As theologian William Short, OFM, explains, there are several important themes that run through everything that St. Francis did, wrote, and taught.[4] The first is the reality of the incarnation. At the heart of Franciscan theology stands Jesus, the incarnate Word of God. From the goodness of God the Creator flows the entire created world. The crowning glory of creation is the Word, and the whole created world is modeled on it. Each being—living and nonliving—in some way resembles the model, but humans bear the divine image (*imago Dei*). The incarnate Word, Jesus of Nazareth, is the pattern or "image of the invisible God" (Col 1:15) through whom the entire universe was created. These amazing realities have led Franciscan scholars and mystics to develop theological reflections on Christ's centrality. Indeed, "Christ became the answer to the philosophical question, 'Why is there something and not nothing?' "[5] According to Short, the early Franciscan theologians provided additional insights into how christocentric theology and spirituality is rooted in the New Testament and is relevant to Christian life. Our challenge today is to make St. Francis's teaching concrete in our daily life and to stop romanticizing about keeping him as a lifeless, cute garden statue! As we will see, like St. Francis, our Christian life needs to focus on the goodness of God; Christ, the Image of God; the christocentric universe; the imitation of Christ; and love.

---

[3] Leonardo Boff, *Cry of the Earth, Cry of the Poor*, trans. Phillip Berryman (Maryknoll, NY: Orbis Books, 1997), 213–16.

[4] See William Short, "The Franciscan Spirit," in *Franciscan Theology of the Environment*, ed. Nothwehr, 111–27.

[5] Ibid., 118.

The radical desire to live the *full Gospel* marks the distinctive Franciscan way (charism) of living the Christian life. Living the full Gospel stresses the challenge to balance the active and the contemplative aspects of life. Such a balance enables us to hold a nonutilitarian attitude toward all of creation, to respect, reverence, and care for it, and to seek the optimal conditions of justice and mutual relationship among all creatures in the world and the cosmos. This attitude is all but absent from the dominant cultures in the modern world, particularly in the West. Many scholars of both science and religion hold that it is the absence of an *attitude of reverence* for creation in relationship with the human that is at the heart of the current ecological crisis.[6]

For St. Francis and for us, it is in prayer that we meet the Poor Christ who deified (made whole and holy) us and the material world by becoming part of it, and it is in the activity of daily living that we meet Christ in our neighbors. It is Christ, not humans and their desires for power or wealth, who stands at the center of the universe. Both contemplative action and active contemplation that is engaged with the realities of the world (modeled exquisitely by St. Clare) are necessary for just and mutual relationships among the human family and for their relationships with all of creation.

St. Francis would certainly be the first to admit that it was through God's work of conversion in him that he was able to move beyond the false promises of wealth and power that were within his grasp as the son of an upwardly mobile cloth merchant of the early twelfth century. We are left to wonder what it was exactly that allowed St. Francis to be open to such a conversion. According to theologian Thomas Murtagh, St. Francis's capacity for fostering nature developed as a part of his growth in the love of the Lord Jesus. As one of his biographers explained, Francis embraced a life of penance as a pathway to coming to know the love of God.[7]

Francis was quite a literalist in that he readily personalized and gave religious definition to objects from the natural world around him, associating them with Scripture texts that spoke of those things or with liturgical and sacramental meanings associated with various objects or

---

[6] Boff, *Cry of the Earth, Cry of the Poor*, 1–34.

[7] *The Remembrance of the Desire of a Soul* by Thomas of Celano (1245–1247), IX, 14, in *Francis of Assisi: Early Documents*, vol. II, *The Founder*, trans. and ed. Regis J. Armstrong, J. A. Wayne Hellmann, and William J. Short (New York: New City Press, 2000), 253.

articles.[8] For example, water reminded Francis of the sacrament of baptism and, in turn, also of Christ. In addition, many have observed a mutual bond of trust and affection between animals and Francis. Proof positive that St. Francis was not a simple romantic or pietist is easily found in the early Franciscan sources. We can see evidence that Francis struggled with his human limitations in dealing with the natural world.[9] Like us, Francis, was at times annoyed by mice and flies; and Francis was *not* a vegetarian! Thus, though Francis sought God in all things, there is evidence that he too had his limits. And as for humans, Francis noted that though all creatures praise God, humans are particularly annoying in their refusal to praise God in a fitting way![10]

Poetry, Prayer, and Poverty

What made Francis so open to sympathy and synergy with all of creation? Brazilian theologian Leonardo Boff has suggested three main explanations.[11]

Poetic Sensitivity

First, Francis grew in his self-understanding as a poet who was able to grasp the essence and sacredness of all creation. As "the Troubadour of the Great King," he did not shy away from the erotic enchantment, wonder, fascination, and desire for and with all things in the universe.[12]

---

[8] "Mirror of Perfection," 118, in *St. Francis of Assisi: Writings and Early Biographies; English Omnibus of Sources for the Life of St. Francis*, ed. Marion A. Habig (Chicago: Franciscan Herald Press, 1983), 1256–57. See also, "A Mirror of Perfection of the *Status* of a Lesser Brother (Sabatier Edition, 1928)," 118, in *Francis of Assisi: Early Documents*, vol. III, *The Prophet*, trans. and ed. Regis J. Armstrong, J. A. Wayne Hellmann, and William J. Short (New York: New City Press, 2001), 366.

[9] Cf. "The Assisi Compilation" (1244–1260), 83, in FAED, vol. II, *The Founder*, 184–87. Also see Thomas of Celano, *The Remembrance of the Desire of a Soul* (1245–1247), 45, 75, in FAED, vol. II, *The Founder*, 297.

[10] Francis of Assisi, "The Undated Writings—The Admonitions," V, in Regis J. Armstrong, J. A. Wayne Hellmann, William J. Short, trans. and ed., *Francis of Assisi: Early Documents*, vol. I, *The Saint* (New York: New City Press, 1999), 131.

[11] Leonardo Boff, *Cry of the Earth, Cry of the Poor*, 213–16.

[12] Boff cites the *Legend of Perugia*, 64. See "The Assisi Compilation" (1244–1260), 99, in FAED, vol. II, *The Founder*, 202–3. See also "A Mirror of Perfection of the *Status* of a Lesser Brother" (Sabatier Edition, 1928), 121, in FAED, vol. III, *The Prophet*, 369–79.

Francis was captivated by the love of God seen in the incarnation, God become human in the person of Jesus, and demonstrated by Christ's death on the cross. God's profound and faithful love, shown from the stable to the cross, drew Francis first "to follow in the footprints of Jesus" and ultimately into union with the Crucified One.[13] That union with the crucified Jesus was most fully realized when Francis received the stigmata at Mount LaVerna.

Standing before the crucified Christ, Francis was keenly aware of his creaturely status with all of his imperfections. Nonetheless, in the "Fifth Admonition" Francis exhorts, "Consider . . . how excellent the Lord made you, for he created and formed you to the image of his beloved Son according to the body and to his own likeness according to the spirit."[14] The depth of such passionate love disposed Francis to be free of possessiveness and to extend himself in relation to all of creation because he saw Christ's presence in everything and everyone, especially the poor and the lepers. If, like Francis, you and I were to ourselves to wonder and desire for oneness with all creatures in creation, how would our lives be different?

Even a cursory reading of the early Franciscan sources reveals St. Francis's unique love affair with all of creation.[15] However, these passages, especially the Franciscan classic "Canticle of the Creatures,"[16] must never be read apart from Francis's profound personal insight into the significance of the incarnation. Indeed, the events immediately prior to the composition of the Canticle, recounted in the "Assisi Compilation," are important for our understanding.[17] Suffering from an eye disease

[13] Francis of Assisi, *The Earlier Rule* (The Rule without a Papal Seal) (1209/10–1221), I, 1, in FAED, vol. I, *The Saint*, 63–64.

[14] Francis of Assisi, "The Undated Writings—The Admonitions," V, in FAED, vol. I, *The Saint*, 131.

[15] See *The Life of St. Francis* by Thomas of Celano (1228–1229), bk. I, 21, 58–61, in FAED, vol. I, *The Saint*, 234–36. Also see *The Remembrance of the Desire of a Soul* (1245–1247), bk. II, 124, 165–66 and 168–71, in FAED, vol. II, *The Founder*, 353–57. See also "The Assisi Compilation (1244–1269)," 88 and 110, in FAED, vol. II, *The Founder*, 184–87; and *The Remembrance of the Desire of a Soul* (1245–1247), bk. II, 124, 165–66 and 168–71, in FAED, vol. II, *The Founder*, 192, 217–18.

[16] Francis of Assisi, "The Canticle of the Creatures" (1225), in FAED, vol. I, *The Saint*, 113–114. The canticle is more popularly known as the "Canticle of Brother Sun." See *St. Francis of Assisi: Writings and Early Biographies, English Omnibus of Sources*, ed. Habig, 128–29.

[17] "The Assisi Compilation" (1244–1269), 83, in FAED, vol. II, *The Founder*, 184–87. This document was formerly known as the *Legenda Perugina*, 43. See Ewert Cousins, *Christ of the 21st Century* (Rockport, MA: Element, Inc., 1992), 143–44.

that had left him blind and in excruciating pain, Francis lay in a mouse infested cell. There he had a vision in which he was offered a golden globe of the earth in exchange for his infirmities, and he was assured of eternal life. The alchemical symbolism of the earth changing to gold stood for Francis's conversion. That conversion was brought about by two critical experiences.[18]

THE FIRST EVENT

The first event was his renunciation of his father, Pietro Bernardone, before the bishop of Assisi. There Francis cast himself, in all his nakedness, totally into the care of his heavenly Father, saying, "Until now I have called you father here on earth, but now I can say without reserve, 'Our Father who art in heaven,' since I have placed all my treasure and all my hope in him."[19] Having embraced radical poverty, a rejection of the possession of anything in any form, Francis was also able to embrace the common source of all creation and thus know the radical relatedness of the entire cosmos as well. As Bonaventure writes in his biography of Francis, "From a reflection on the primary source of all things, filled with even more abundant piety, he would call creatures, no matter how small, by the name of 'brother' or 'sister,' because he knew they shared with him the same beginning."[20] Francis realized that humans stand among the other creatures.

In "A Salutation of the Virtues," Francis shows that the fitting relationship among all creatures is one of obedience, that is, carefully attending to the other: "[The person who possesses holy Obedience] is subject and submissive / to everyone in the world, / not only to people / but to every beast and wild animal as well / that they may do whatever they want with it / insofar as it *has been given* to them / *from above* by the Lord.[21]

---

[18] Zachary Hayes, "St. Francis of Assisi and Nature: A Model for a 21st Century Spirituality," unpublished manuscript, 8–16.

[19] Bonaventure of Bagnoregio, *The Major Legend of St. Francis* (1260–1263), II, 4, in FAED, vol. II, *The Founder*, 358.

[20] Ibid., VIII, 6, p. 590.

[21] Francis of Assisi, "The Undated Writings—A Salutation of the Virtues," 14, in FAED, vol. I, *The Saint*, 165.

THE SECOND EVENT

The second event toward Francis's conversion prior to writing the Canticle was his encounter with the Crucified One at San Domino. There he discovered that not only is God the glorious Creator, but God loves to the extent that "the Word of God became flesh" (John 1:14; Greek = *sarx*), part of the material universe. This realization served to deepen Francis's sense of the sacredness of creation, and he wrote: "Oh, how holy and how loving, gratifying, humbling, peace-giving, sweet, worthy of love, and, above all things, desirable: to have such a Brother and such a Son, our Lord Jesus Christ, Who laid down His life for His sheep" (cf. John 10:15).[22] Now, humans are not only sisters and brothers to one another; they are sisters and brothers of Jesus. And so, too, Jesus is related to the rocks and the worms. Thus, humans are sisters and brothers to rocks and worms as well. We read from *The Life of St. Francis* by Thomas of Celano (1228–1229), "He used to call all creatures / by the name 'brother' and 'sister' / and in a wonderful way, unknown to others, / he could discern the *secrets of the heart* of creatures / like someone who has already passed / *into the freedom of the glory of the children of God*."[23] Francis's union with nature is distinct from the parabolic *associations* of God with nature in the New Testament, the pantheistic *identification* of God and nature of the Renaissance, or the ecstatic joy *over* nature of the Greeks.[24] Francis's union was *with* God manifest *within* nature.

Experience of the Common Origin of Things

One day while at prayer, he had a religious experience that allowed him to understand the common origin of all things. This was the second aspect of Francis's self-understanding that gave him insight into his kinship with all of creation. That all in the world comes from the same Creator was not a dry dogmatic tenet for St. Francis. Rather, it was more like a love song that drew everything and everyone to "the heart of the

---

[22] Francis of Assisi, "The Earlier Exhortation to the Brothers and Sisters of Penance [The First Version of the Letter to the Faithful]" (1209–1215), I, 13, in FAED, vol. I, *The Saint*, 42.

[23] *The Life of St. Francis* by Thomas of Celano (1228–1229), 28, 81 in FAED, vol. I, *The Saint*, 251.

[24] Max Scheler, *The Nature of Sympathy*, trans. Peter Heath (Hamden, CT: The Shoestring Press, Inc., 1970), 90.

Father, through the Son in the enthusiasm of the Holy Spirit."[25] In light of this understanding, Leonardo Boff claims that it is more in the spirit of St. Francis to translate his famous *Deus meus et omnia* not as it is usually translated—"My God and my all"—but as "My God and all things."[26] Indeed, as Bonaventure recounts, Francis was most delighted to sing *with* the creatures: "Our Sisters Birds are praising their Creator; so we should go among them and chant the Lord's praises and the canonical hours."[27]

Radical Poverty

Francis's radical poverty is the third and final characteristic of his life that enabled him to be kin to all of creation. Not selfishly holding on to anything, but rather meeting life with open hands and heart, Francis was able to set aside usual human tendencies toward subordination or domination and meet everything and everyone as one utterly available and completely focused on the need of the other. As Bonaventure claims, Francis was able to return to the state of "primeval innocence," a place of full mutuality in relationship with God and all creatures.[28] Indeed, Francis saw himself as a son of the loving and generous Creator and Great King and as a brother to Jesus and the entire family created by God.

Francis came to *know* God and *know about* God through an integrated life of contemplation and action, choosing to live the Gospel and to follow in the footprints of Jesus. By doing so, he gave us both a *method* for theological reflection (seeking to understand our faith) and a *content* of theology (topics or subject matter) that are very "earth friendly." In the remainder of this chapter, we will first examine St. Francis's theological reflection process (method) and then highlight the content of what we might glean for a Franciscan ecotheology.

A Franciscan Theological Reflection Method

Just how did St. Francis go about trying to come to know God and the things God desires us to care about in creation? Regis J. Armstrong has

---

[25] Ibid.

[26] Boff, *Cry of the Earth, Cry of the Poor*, 66.

[27] See Bonaventure, *Major Legend of St. Francis* (1260–1263), VIII, 9, in FAED, vol. II, *The Founder*, 592–93.

[28] Ibid., VIII, 1, 586–87.

selected three starting points or ways that, when taken together, show us how St. Francis sought to know God and God's will—namely, penance, poverty, and prayer.[29]

Penance

The "Testament" of Francis bears witness to his call from God to do penance.[30] To do penance means to embrace a life of loving relationship with God, to see the world as an expression of the Creator's goodness, and to live in hope of the fulfillment of the reign of God. Francis shows us that a life of penance is a journey of faith that climaxes in conversion, a new way of knowing, and a greater sensitivity to the voice of God within ourselves and all of creation. Most importantly, this conversion leads to action.

In Francis's "Testament" (lines 1–2), he describes his experience of embracing a leper, a moment of true conversion in his life. In that moment, he became conscious of God's unconditional largess, and he responded by embracing the leper "with a heart sensitive to misery."[31] When Bonaventure tells of this experience of the leper, he also talks about Francis's encounter with a beggar and a poor knight, and he calls Francis's responses acts of *pietas*, acts "of devotion to God and of compassion."[32] Penance is a process of engaging in a spirit-filled life that draws one, in the fullest sense, into the very heart of God— the goal of all theology. Would we be in an ecological crisis today if you and I lived as Francis lived, "with a heart sensitive to misery?" Living the lifestyle of

---

[29] See Regis J. Armstrong, "Francis of Assisi and the Prisms of Theologizing," *Greyfriars Review* 10/2 (1996): 179–206. See also Giovanni Iammerrone, "Franciscan Theology Today: Its Possibility, Necessity, and Values," *Greyfriars Review* 8/1 (1994): 103–26.

[30] See Francis's "The Testament," 1–3, FAED, vol. I, *The Saint*, 124. See Clare's "Testament," 24–25, *Clare of Assisi: Early Documents*, rev. and expanded ed., trans. and ed. Regis J. Armstrong (St. Bonaventure, NY: The Franciscan Institute, 1994), 58. Sadly, not many works of Clare or records of the thought and action of other women of the Franciscan family exist. Thus, it is difficult to continue to illustrate their contribution to the development of Franciscan theology. An important explanation of this state of affairs is given in Margaret Carney, "Franciscan Women and the Theological Enterprise," in Kenan B. Osborne, ed., *The History of Franciscan Theology* (St. Bonaventure, NY: The Franciscan Institute, 1994), 331–45.

[31] Armstrong, "Francis of Assisi and the Prisms of Theologizing," 185.

[32] See Bonaventure, *The Major Legend of Saint Francis* (1260–1263), I, 5– 6, in FAED, vol. II, *The Founder*, 533–35.

a penitent (one who tries to conform her or his life to the ways of Christ) readily leads one to an attitude of poverty, which is Armstrong's second prism of a Franciscan theological method.

Poverty

Once one has caught a glimpse of the infinitely loving and gracious God, by contrast, one is confronted with one's human limitations of sin, arrogant self-centeredness, an unhealthy lack of self-confidence, or the deceptions of restrictive biases and prejudices. In this moment of recognizing that we humans are all weak and imperfect, it is possible to comprehend the necessity of choosing to face the world with open head, heart, and hands, not clinging to anything as exclusively one's own. *Our* power to control others and the natural world is often shortsighted and selfishly motivated. As Francis pointed out in his "Second Admonition,"[33] the Fall of humanity into sin had *everything* to do with the human desire to grasp things and use them in an arrogant and selfish manner. This grab for power and security is the injustice of appropriating for ourselves what is rightfully the Creator's.

Another aspect of poverty is material poverty. There is a sense in which material poverty is sacramental for Francis: "It is an outward sign of an inner reality, spiritual poverty, and, more importantly, an outward sign that leads to a deeper reality."[34] As we embrace material poverty more seriously, we are prompted to identify more honestly our other appropriations until, when we are bereft of everything, God alone becomes our treasure that we can both cherish and give away. What if the industrialists, corporate leaders, and entrepreneurs since the Industrial Revolution of the 1850s had had Francis's sense of material poverty? Would we be suffering an ecological crisis today? Typically, Francis insisted that the brothers attend to the prompting of the Spirit in all things. This kind of dependence comes through a consciousness of one's own poverty—sinfulness and limitations—and utter reliance on God's ever-abiding love and goodness.

---

[33] Francis of Assisi, "The Undated Writings—The Admonitions," II, 1–2, in FAED, vol. I, *The Saint*, 129.

[34] Armstrong, "Francis of Assisi and the Prisms of Theologizing," 189.

Prayer

Prayer, Armstrong's third prism of the Franciscan theological reflection method, can be described as the process of attending to one's relationship with God. Francis reminds us that we are empowered to see, know, and believe by the same Holy Spirit that animates the very life of the triune God. Indeed, it is the Holy Spirit who enables Christians to recognize the human Jesus as the Christ and the bread and wine of the Eucharist as the Body and Blood of Our Lord Jesus Christ. Beyond the Eucharist, the Spirit enables one to perceive *ordinary earthly things* as reflections of God, not as objects of one's egotistical, self-aggrandizing grasp for power.[35]

When describing Francis's capacity to grasp and know things beyond what he could see, Bonaventure uses an interesting and unusual Latin verb, *contuere*. When one knows something through the Holy Spirit, one "co-intuits" (*conituita*) both the contingent particulars (for example, the size, shape, color, and smell of a rose) and the eternal reasons in those particulars (the love of God the Creator imaged in the beauty of the rose). So, Bonaventure explains, concerning Francis's perception of the world,

> in beautiful things he [St. Francis] contuited Beauty itself
> and through the footprints impressed in things
> he followed his Beloved everywhere,
> out of them all making himself *a ladder*
> through which he could climb up to lay a hold of him
> *who is utterly desirable.*
> With an intensity of unheard devotion
> he savored
> in each and every creature
> —as in so many rivulets—
> that fontal Goodness,
> and discerned
> an almost celestial choir
> in the chords of power and activity
> given to them by God,
> and, like the prophet David,
> he sweetly encouraged them to praise the Lord.[36]

---

[35] See Francis of Assisi, "The Undated Writings—The Admonitions," VI, in FAED, vol. I, *The Saint*, 131.

[36] Bonaventure, *The Major Legend of Saint Francis* (1260–1263), IX, 1, in FAED, vol. II, *The Founder*, 596–97.

The more deeply Francis lived in the life of the Spirit, the more he grew in his capacity as a "contuitive," delighting in the world as a revelation of the divine. Indeed, "prayer, then, a principal activity of the Spirit, must be the starting point of our theologizing, but it must also be its culmination. For the contuitive person, one who gazes upon the world with the eyes of the Spirit, every moment becomes, to borrow Thomas Merton's words, 'a seed of contemplation.' "[37]

Three Elements of Content for a Franciscan Ecotheology

Having briefly reviewed Armstrong's three prisms for a Franciscan theological method—penance, poverty, and prayer—we now turn to the content (topics or subject matter) of Franciscan theology to see what we can glean for a Franciscan ecotheology.

The World Is Good

[handwritten: World is good — + will provide for every authentic human need.]

The first insight we find is St. Francis's strong intuition that the world is good and will provide for every authentic human need. The vast variety and abundance in creation is, for Francis, ample evidence of the nature of God. His usual ways of identifying God in superlative terms show he understood God to be both powerful and profoundly intimate, loving, and generous. One of many examples of his naming God this way may be found in *The Earlier Rule*, chapter 23:

> Therefore,
> let us desire nothing else,
> let us want nothing else,
> let nothing else please us and cause us delight
> except our Creator, Redeemer and Savior,
> the only true God,
> Who is the fullness of good,
> all good, every good,
> the true and supreme good,
> *Who alone is good,*
> merciful, gentle, delightful, and sweet,
> Who alone is holy,

---

[37] Armstrong, "Francis of Assisi and the Prisms of Theologizing," 199.

just, true, holy, and upright,
Who alone is kind, innocent, clean,
from Whom, *through Whom* and in Whom
is all pardon, all grace, all glory
of all penitents and just ones,
of all the blessed rejoicing together in heaven.[38]

And Francis goes on and on naming God in superlative terms! What if *our* response to God's love was as total and as spirited as Francis's response? Would we destroy the exquisite fertile soils or pollute the ground waters of our farmlands for the sake of earning more money?

The Incarnation Deifies Creation

A second insight for the content of a Franciscan ecotheology concerns the meaning of the human Christ. This insight both flows from and suggests a positive worldview. Francis's understanding of creation was that creation manifests Christ.[39] Everything—flowers, lambs, worms, lepers, poor women—is recognized in the incarnate Christ, the human "babe from Bethlehem," portrayed at Greccio.[40] Clearly, because Christ chose a human form and the limits of time and space of *this* world, the goodness of this world is affirmed. Indeed, as humans and as followers of this Christ, our place, too, is in *this* world. We don't have to escape this world to be in the presence of Christ. What if we really believed that all creation is deified, sacramental, imaging Christ? Would we tolerate the destruction of the vast biodiversity of the Amazon Rainforest or allow urban sprawl to encroach on what is left of the natural beauty of our forests and mountains?

---

[38] Francis of Assisi, *The Earlier Rule* (1209/10–1221), XXIII, in FAED, vol. I *The Saint*, 81–86, at 85.

[39] *The Life of Saint Francis* by Thomas of Celano (1228–1229), bk. I, 28, 77, in FAED, vol. I, *The Saint*, 248.

[40] Ibid., bk. I, 30, 84, in FAED, vol. I, *The Saint*, 254–57. It is an understatement to say that Francis was deeply moved by the great love of God who came to this world as a meek human child, Jesus. Christmas was for Francis the most important day of the year. In order to make clear what it meant for God to come to us in the form of a baby, Francis gathered people in the Italian city of Greccio to enact the nativity of Our Lord. Today this tradition lives on in the numerous Christmas plays and crib displays around the globe.

Authentic Humanness Requires Relationship with Christ

The third intuition that reveals Francis of Assisi's theology is found in Thomas of Celano's account of Francis receiving the stigmata.[41] When the Crucified One gave Francis "a kind and gracious look," Francis was frightened because he also saw the pain and suffering of Christ. From this experience Francis drew insight into the meaning of the human person. People are fragile, limited, and vulnerable. Yet it is this very condition of fragility, limitedness, and vulnerability that reveals human creatureliness and the wondrous love of God. *Authentic humanness is revealed in relationship with Christ.*

For our purposes in understanding the content of a Franciscan eco-theology, we see that Francis's insights about how we *know* God and what we *know about* God in creation form a pattern of conversion, action, and contemplation. Through that threefold pattern, we can be transformed and converted and then repeatedly recycled through the process, moving ever more deeply into the heart of God. This is the pattern of Francis—living the Gospel and following in the footprints of Jesus.

Thomas of Celano and the first generations of Franciscan theologians understood St. Francis and St. Clare to be the embodiment of this theology. This theology understood God as a compassionate lover made manifest in the incarnation and revealed in all of creation. Though marred by sin and finitude, the world is a good place. As God, in Christ, looks lovingly upon humanity in its vulnerability, so too must humans reach out to the lepers of our day—the poor, the oppressed and forgotten, the polluted environment, and threatened species. We must value the entire cosmos and cherish its every member, in its particularity and for its own sake, insofar as each reveals something of God who is good, the highest good!

Thus far, we have seen that Francis was open to sympathy and synergy with all things because he had a poetic heart, he experienced God as the common origin of all creation, and he embraced radical poverty. We have seen how Francis discovered his *relationship with* and *knowledge of* God by actively practicing the virtues of *penance* and *poverty* and by engaging in a vibrantly active life of *prayer*. Through all of this activity, Francis gained three important insights; namely, God is good, the highest good; because of the incarnation, all of creation is deified, made holy and sacramental;

---

[41] *The Life of Saint Francis* by Thomas of Celano (1228–1229), bk. II, 3, 94, in FAED, vol. I, *The Saint*, 263–64.

and a relationship with Christ is necessary for the most authentic human living. With this background in mind, we now turn to an examination of what is certainly the best-known work of St. Francis of Assisi, his "Canticle of the Creatures" (1225).

From the Writings of St. Francis

"The Canticle of the Creatures" (1225)[42]

Most High, all-powerful, good Lord,
　　Yours are *the praises, the glory,* and *the honor,* and all *blessing.*
To You alone, Most High, do they belong,
　　And no human is worthy to mention Your name.
Praised be You, my Lord, with all *Your creatures,*
　　Especially Sir Brother Sun,
　　Who is the day and through whom You give us light.
And he is beautiful and radiant with great splendor;
　　and bears a likeness of You, Most High One.
Praised be You, my Lord, through Sister *Moon* and the *stars,*
　　in heaven You formed them clear and precious and beautiful.
Praised be You, my Lord, through Brother Wind,
　　and through the air, cloudy and serene, and every kind of weather,
　　through whom You give sustenance to Your creatures.
Praised be You, my Lord, through Sister *Water,*
　　who is very useful and humble and precious and chaste.
Praised be You, my Lord, through Brother *Fire,*
　　through whom *You light the night,*
　　and he is beautiful and playful and robust and strong.
Praised be You, my Lord, through our Sister Mother *Earth,*
　　who sustains and governs us,
　　and who produces various *fruit* with colored flowers and *herbs.*

Praised be You, my Lord, through those who give pardon for Your love,
　　and bear infirmity and tribulation.
　　Blessed are those who endure in peace
　　　　for by You, Most High, they shall be crowned.

Praised be You, my Lord, through our Sister Bodily Death,
　　from whom no one living can escape.

[42] See text in FAED, vol. I, *The Saint,* 113–14.

Woe to those who die in mortal sin.
Blessed are those whom death will find in Your most holy will,
For *the second death* will do them no harm.

Praise and *bless* my *Lord* and give Him thanks
and serve Him with great humility.

Reflection and Application

Without a doubt, the best-known written work of St. Francis is his "Canticle of the Creatures."[43] Contrary to the popular conception of this work as a fanciful, lyrical poem that tritely romanticizes the natural environment, scholarly study has shown it is packed with profound meaning. From the wide repertoire of creatures named in his other works, Francis includes only a few in the Canticle. The fact that the Canticle is built around the four classical elements—earth, air, water, and fire—is of major significance.

The circumstances of three different occasions for which Francis wrote the various parts of the Canticle are also important for understanding its full impact. When Francis wrote verses 1–9 of the Canticle, he had received the gift of the stigmata, a sign of the profound intimacy of his identification with Jesus. He had recently been able to let go of his deep attachment to determining the future of the Order of the Friars Minor, realizing that it was not he but God who would determine that. Verses 10 and 11 were written for the brothers to sing in the presence of the quarreling civil and religious authorities of Assisi as part of a peacemaking strategy. And though verse 14 is thought to be the refrain to be sung after each verse, verses 12 and 13 were composed near the end of Francis's life, when he was weak and suffering from a painful eye disease that left him sensitive to light and almost blind. Given this background, one is led to wonder how anyone who was suffering so much could compose such limpid, lyrical lines. More will be said about this later in this chapter.

Clearly, Francis's relationship with God was the governing factor for understanding his relationship with all creatures. There is little evidence

---

[43] See "The Canticle of the Creatures" (1225), in FAED, vol. I, *The Saint*, 113.

that Francis had any unusual scientific understanding of the natural world. Yet his insight into the three-dimensional relationship of humans and God, God and creatures, and creatures and humans was unique. The common relationship of both humans and creatures with God makes humans and all other creatures sisters and brothers—and that makes all the difference!

The dynamics of Francis's journey toward this conversion is more than hinted at in the Canticle.[44] Franciscan theologian Eric Doyle calls the Canticle the work of St. Francis the poet-mystic. Poets use words in ways that point beyond the usual meanings assigned them. In the Canticle we have beautiful poetic praise of the God of all creation, as well as an "expression of the authentic Christian attitude toward creation which is to accept and love the creatures as they are."[45] As such, creatures are not reflections of us or objects over which we can claim power or control. Rather, creatures, like us, are the expression of the goodness and love of God; in our creaturehood, we are equal with all other creatures. As we have seen (in chapters 1 and 2), in the covenant, God purposefully established a relationship with humans, but also with *every living creature* (Gen 9:12-13). Each creature is a unique reflection of God and God's goodness. As God loves each creature uniquely, so too must we. Francis could know this way of the divine only because he first entered into a contemplative union with God; he knew God in and through all other beings and elements of creation. In union with God and all creatures, Francis found his uniqueness as one ever more original.

The realization of his uniqueness among the creatures, yet of his likeness to them as a recipient of the love of God, was in turn a source of his great love of God's creation. To reflect on this immersion in love is to encounter Mystery, "the never-the-last-wordness" of our existence.[46] We are always seeking and searching for something more, yet every human attempt to satisfy the "more" ends in more seeking. Francis's "heart sight" told him he had found the "more" in God and that God was ever present in the here and now and was all around him.

[44] See Eric Doyle, *St. Francis and the Song of Brotherhood and Sisterhood* (St. Bonaventure, NY: The Franciscan Institute, 1997; reprint of *The Song of Brotherhood* [New York: Seabury Press, 1981]).

[45] Eric Doyle, "'The Canticle of Brother Sun' and the Value of Creation," in *Franciscan Theology of the Environment*, ed. Nothwehr, 158.

[46] Doyle, *St. Francis and the Song of Brotherhood and Sisterhood*, 47.

The words of the Canticle express the depth of Francis's spiritual integration and the inner reaches of his soul. As Doyle holds, "All beautiful words and music come from the mystery of personhood, welling up from the inner depths. It is not so remarkable that Francis, though blind, was able to write a song about the beauty and unity of creation. He was already one with himself and with the world, and the world was one in him."[47] This integration provided Francis with an inner confidence and a cure for alienation from any and all "others" that could pose a threat to him in any way. The path to such integration for Francis was a path of prayer that began with the first step of self-surrender.

The biographies of Francis tell the story of his struggle toward embracing poverty as a way of opening himself in freedom to God and all of creation. Through his relationship with God in prayer, he learned to love *as* and *what* God loves. To love authentically is to love and accept other humans and all creatures on their own terms. It is particularly significant for our ecologically threatened world that Francis was able to find himself, and true peace and harmony, not in warfare or wealth but through spiritual means. In our own time when we are experiencing a spiritual malaise, prayer and spiritual practices are necessary to assist us in reversing the devastation of the planet.[48] This is a call not to escapism but rather to a move to the depths of our being, to confront the deepest truth of being human, namely, that we are creatures who stand in relationship with both God and our fellow earth creatures. When we realize we are not alone but rather surrounded with wondrous manifestations of God's love and care, personal integration can take place and alienation vanishes.

To understand one's relationship to all of creation through prayer and contemplation is also a political act. To be in a love relationship with all of creation is to risk being motivated to act in defense and protection of those we love. We cannot tolerate injustice or abuse of the environment, because everything in creation is our "sister" or our "brother." When one is motivated to defend another, one's focus shifts from self to the other. It is often risky to be so motivated; it is a move toward poverty, indeed perhaps the ultimate poverty of losing one's own life for the sake of another. Quite significantly, Francis even called death "sister," for he understood death as integral to life. Indeed, death is the ultimate journey

---

[47] Ibid., 49.
[48] Boff, *Cry of the Earth, Cry of the Poor*, 187–202.

into poverty, a letting go of all possessions, including life itself. Having given his life completely to Christ, he had nothing to fear from death. Death was for Francis a passage into the fullness of life with Christ. In our day when fear of the "small deaths" of life, such as personal limitations or the inability to achieve wealth or position, are frequently the cause of discord, abuse, or other kinds of violence, we can learn much from Francis's embrace of "Sister Death" as a friend who opens the way to new life beyond imagination.

Cosmic Elements and the Human Person

Franciscan ethicist Thomas A. Nairn holds that St. Francis of Assisi's "Canticle of the Creatures" is an exercise of the moral imagination and a call to moral conversion.[49] According to the expositor of medieval popular culture Aron Gurevich, the Canticle's four cosmic elements—earth, air, water, and fire—had great significance in their historical context. Human beings were not merely part of the larger world but rather a "microcosm" reflecting the larger "macrocosm" and revealing a parallelism between the person and the world. People of the Middle Ages understood the heavenly objects of the sun, moon, stars as powers that affected human destiny. Indeed, they believed that the four elements affected a person's very identity. The goal of both medicine and natural philosophy was to restore disease or temperamental problems caused by an imbalance among the four elements. With this in mind, Nairn engages us in an exercise of moral imagination.

Moral Imagination for the Future

Focusing on the verses that name the four elements, Nairn notes that this section differs from the rest of the Canticle. In each strophe there is both a movement toward God and a movement toward humanity. Francis shows the earth elements relating to God but also serving humanity. Nairn offers that perhaps Francis wished to show us that when confronted with the cosmic elements, we must remember that they are *merely* creatures of God. Further, Nairn suggests, the terms "brother" and "sister" not only show the relationship of the elements to God and humans

---

[49] Thomas A. Nairn, "St. Francis of Assisi's *Canticle of the Creatures* as an Exercise of the Moral Imagination," in *Franciscan Theology of the Environment*, ed. Nothwehr, 175–87.

but are intended to serve "a relativizing function as well."[50] In the medieval context, then, Francis's use of the four elements brought "the cosmic elements, understood as elements which influence humanity, down to a human level."[51]

In the medieval context, nature was valuable insofar as it contributed to humanity's knowledge of God and drew humans to God. It was evil if it hindered humanity's quest for God. If the elements do not move humans to praise God, they are misused. "If the proper role of the elements points humanity to God, then God and not the elements is the true influencer of humanity. . . . But as humanity accepts its place in the microcosm of this universe it must also appreciate its own vocation in serving God. It is in this calling that humanity finds true freedom."[52] Francis's Canticle, understood in this way, becomes a call to conversion to a freedom found only in God.

Such freedom in God broadens our human vision and imagination to see the world as God sees it and challenges us to act in proper relationship to all of creation as God acts. In this way, the moral imagination is stimulated by and converted to the very mind of God. What a challenge the Canticle presents for environmental theology and ethics today! I believe that the "relativizing" challenge the four elements present to us today is huge and important, though somewhat different from its meaning in St. Francis's day.

While today science and technology have given humans some control of the elements, such control is in fact illusionary. Human abuse of the natural environment has pushed vast bioregions of the world to their breaking point and increasingly past any reasonable measure of their carrying capacities. In fact, some contend that the carrying capacity of the earth was breached already in 1986.[53] And we continue to reap the results.

---

[50] Ibid., 183.

[51] Ibid.

[52] Ibid.

[53] See Tim Flannery, *The Weather Makers: How We Are Changing the Climate*, 246, cited in Sallie McFague, *A New Climate for Theology: God, the World, and Global Warming* (Minneapolis: Fortress Press, 2008), 20: "In effect, 1986 marks the year that humans reached Earth's carrying capacity, and ever since we have been running the environmental equivalent of a deficit budget, which is only sustained by plundering our capital base. The plundering takes the form of overexploiting fisheries, overgrazing pasture until it becomes desert, destroying forests, and polluting our oceans and

Implications for Praxis

Our habitat, this earth, this *oikos*, which is our home, is a closed space; sunlight is the only life form that comes to it from outside. Thus, for better or for worse, everyone and everything are permanently united in one household (*eco-*). Earth beings are one family who must find the laws or rules (*nomos*) that will make possible the surviving and thriving of the entire family, *if indeed* any *one* being would live to its fullest. This twenty-first-century observation finds common voice with Francis of Assisi's notion of the kinship of creation.

As Guy Beney has shown, it is no longer possible to flee to yet another place to escape the closed nature that is our *oikos* (earth home).[54] We have been living in a false reality! The long pattern of neglecting limits and disrespecting the cyclical patterns through which the natural world renews itself is reaching its breaking point. We are now in an ecological crisis! We have violated the goodness of God and the integrity of creation that requires that we recognize each member as having intrinsic value and, thus, moral status. We now are reaping the results: "Between 1500 and 1850 *one* species was eliminated every *ten years*. By the year 2000 *one* species [vanished] *every hour*."[55]

According to the International Union for Conservation of Nature (IUCN), many species are in danger of extinction. One out of eight birds, one out of four mammals, one out of four conifers, one out of three amphibians, and six out of seven marine turtles are threatened with extinction. Furthermore, 75 percent of genetic diversity of agricultural crops has been lost; 75 percent of the world's fisheries are fully or overexploited; up to 70 percent of the world's known species risk extinction if the global temperatures rise by more than 3.5°C; one-third of reef-build-

---

atmosphere, which in turn leads to the large numbers of environmental issues we face. In the end, though, the environmental budget is the only one that really counts."

[54] Guy Beney, in *Global Ecology*, ed. Wolfgang Sachs (London: Zed Books, 1993), 181–82, cited in Larry Rasmussen, *Earth Community, Earth Ethics* (Maryknoll, NY: Orbis Books, 1996), 91–92.

[55] Worldwatch Institute, cited in Leonardo Boff, *Ecology and Liberation: A New Paradigm* (Maryknoll, NY: Orbis Books, 1995), 15. Also see more recent findings that show both the difficulty of studying species extinctions and the reality that significant threats are still trending upward: Brian Handwerk, "Global Extinction Rates May Have Been Overestimated by as Much as 160 Percent, According to a New Analysis," *National Geographic News*, May 18, 2011, http://news.nationalgeographic.com /news/2011/05/110518-species-extinctions-habitats-science-animals, accessed September 25, 2011.

ing corals around the world are threatened with extinction; and over 350 million people suffer from severe water scarcity.[56]

Clearly, the human species is not excluded from this disturbing picture. At the start of this millennium, according to the United Nations Development Program, if the world population was divided into quintiles according to income, the *richest fifth* of the population received *82 percent* of the total income, while the *poorest fifth* received *1.4 percent* of the total income.[57] Globalization became a potent force of exploitation, and among the most threatened are now the human poor, especially indigenous peoples. As of this writing, at least 80 percent of humanity lives on less than ten dollars per day.[58] More than 80 percent of the world's population lives in countries where income differentials are widening.[59] The poorest 40 percent of the world's population accounts for only 5 percent of global income. The richest 20 percent of the world's population accounts for 75 percent of the world's income.[60]

To be human—as Francis knew humans to be created in God's image and likeness, loved and redeemed by the Lord Jesus—and to be poor is an oxymoron. In the case of many indigenous peoples today (and in the recent past), to be poor is to be absolutely powerless in the face of government and corporate collusion to exploit the only home they know; food, clothing, shelter, land, and their entire way of life are taken by a bulldozer, a drill, or the pollution of industry and technology.

Theologian Leonardo Boff experienced this kind of poverty among the indigenous peoples of the Brazilian Amazon region. His insights can help us understand the relationship between issues of economic poverty and ecological issues. Following his Franciscan roots, he argues that

[56] Anup Shah, "Loss of Biodiversity and Extinctions," *Global Issues*, http://www.globalissues.org/article/171/loss-of-biodiversity-and-extinctions, accessed September 25, 2011; page last updated Wednesday, April 6, 2011.

[57] The United Nations Development Project, cited in Daniel C. Maguire, *Sacred Energies* (Minneapolis: Augsburg Fortress, 2000), 27.

[58] Anup Shah, "Poverty Facts and Stats," *Global Issues*, http://www.globalissues.org/article/26/poverty-facts-and-stats, accessed September 25, 2011; page last updated Monday, September 20, 2010. See Shaohua Chen and Martin Ravallion, *The Developing World Is Poorer Than We Thought, But No Less Successful in the Fight Against Poverty*, World Bank, August 2008, http://papers.ssrn.com/sol3/papers.cfm?abstract_id=1259575, accessed August 12, 2012.

[59] See United Nations Development Program, *2007 Human Development Report* (HDR), November 27, 2007, 25.

[60] Ibid.

liberation theology and ecology must become partners in light of the current state of affairs of the poor.

After Ernest Haeckel first formulated the notion of ecology in 1866, ecology was soon understood as the unity of three ecologies: environmental ecology, social ecology, and mental ecology.[61] *Environmental ecology* is concerned with the relations that various societies and individual human beings have with the environment. *Social ecology* explores the reality that humans are both earth creatures and social beings. Depending on how humans organize themselves, there will be exploitation, collaboration, or respect and reverence for the natural world. "Hence social justice, the right relationship with persons, roles, and institutions, implies some achievement of ecological justice, which is the right relationship with nature, easy access to its resources, and assurance of quality of life."[62] *Mental ecology* starts from the recognition that nature is *within* human beings—in their minds, in the form of psychic energy, symbols, archetypes, and behavior patterns that embody attitudes of aggression or of respect and acceptance of nature.

As classical liberation theologies claim, people stand in need of a threefold liberation: first, as an integral human person; second, as a social being who participates in political, economic, and social relations; and third, as a spiritual person in need of redemption from sin. Notice how the three levels of liberation align well with the three ecologies. They also find a correlative in the threefold Franciscan method of doing theological reflection by engaging in penance, poverty, and prayer. Human persons thrive when they are at home, in a place where they are at peace, in right relationship with God and neighbor, and respectful of the integrity of creation. Boff rightly contends that when any of these relationships are broken, we *also* see the emergence of dehumanizing poverty, oppression, and injustice of all sorts.

What works to hold all of these relationships together is a sense of the sacredness of nature like that held by St. Francis. If humanity, indeed the planet, is to live through the third millennium, we must face the reality that *science* taken to its depths brings us to *mystery*, and *mystery* brought to intelligibility moves to *concreteness*. Indeed, our Sister, Mother Earth, nourishes and sustains all. So, too, in the modern world of work, which has removed itself from the earth into concrete jungles and cy-

---

[61] F. Guattari, *As Três Ecologias* (Campinas: Papirus, 1988).
[62] Leonardo Boff, *Cry of the Earth, Cry of the Poor*, 105.

berspace, we must find ways to touch the earth from which we came—
attuning body, mind, and spirit to the rhythms of this earth that reveal
God the good Creator—so that we also will come home to the heart of
God.

Questions for Reflection and Discussion

1. St. Francis was moved and motivated by the fact of the incarnation,
   and nature became holy to him. What difference does the fact of the
   incarnation make in how you deal with environmental issues?

2. Describe Francis's understanding of "poverty." How does his understanding connect with your own understanding of poverty? In what
   ways can Francis's understanding impact how we regard the earth,
   people, and our environment?

3. What have you learned about the spirituality of St. Francis and St.
   Clare? What do you find appealing in their spiritualities? To which
   of these spiritualities do you most naturally relate? Why?

4. Franciscan theologian William Short defines "sin" in Franciscan terms
   as "the will to possess." Is this understanding helpful in thinking
   about the environmental crisis? Explain.

5. How do you see Haeckel's three dimensions of ecology operative in
   your own daily life?

Suggestions for Action

Today we stand at a crossroads. We must make a radical turn to the
earth, choosing to do penance as Francis did and be converted to live
with nature, not *from* nature.[63] This will require that we take seriously
the foundational moral experience that Francis knew so well: reverence
for persons and their environment. Such a conversion is the only real
choice if indeed we are to avoid the fate of the dinosaurs. To that end, I

---

[63] Ibid., 128.

suggest there are five lessons and four learning exercises that can assist us on the path toward conversion.

1. Daily we must recall that we are daughters and sons of the earth; we are the earth itself become self-aware, animated by the very breath of the Spirit of God!

2. We must become aware of the vastness of the universe, from deep space to the smallest fractal—dimensions that boggle the mind and place us humans in relationship with all other powers and forces.

3. Frequently, we must reflect on the 13.7 billion years of the evolution of the universe and the sacred wonder of our own existence. How astonishing it is that we exist at all!

4. Humans must recognize themselves as members of the species *Homo sapiens*, in communion and solidarity with other species that make up the community of living beings.

5. We humans must become aware of our role in the dynamics of the universe. Perhaps now, more than at any time in the history of the universe, what we do matters. Yet we are latecomers to the earth—it existed before us, and it likely can exist without us!

Now those are some major assignments! So here are some actions to help us learn those lessons.

1. On every sunny day, take eight minutes to experience the sun. Feel the sun's rays touch your body. Then imagine—sunlight is the only life form that comes to us from the outside. Now hold your hand up so as to block the sun from your view. Let yourself become conscious that it takes each ray of sunlight, traveling at 186,000 miles per second, eight minutes to reach you! Such are the dimensions of the universe!

2. Go outside on clear nights. Lie on the ground and look *down and out* into space. Let yourself become conscious of gravity—like the arms of Sister Mother Earth gently holding you to herself, thus preventing you from falling or flying off into space.

3. Find a spot in nature that you can return to at least once a week. This might be a tree, a hillside, a garden, or even a particular rock. As often as you can, go to your spot. Spend at least fifteen minutes in quiet there, and let that tree, hillside, garden, or rock speak to you. See if

what it has to tell you relates to anything we've heard from St. Francis of Assisi. You will be amazed at what you can learn!

4. Write your own "Canticle of the Creatures."

Prayer

"Creation," by John VanderPhoeg[64]

He flung the world out into space,
    And set the planets spinning.
He ordered the paths of the stars,
    In grandiose time of beginning.
He tinted the rosette sunrise,
    Enkindled the lightning flashes,
And with His omnipotent hand
    He turned the rocks to ashes.
He guided the colorful sunset,
    Directed the rolling thunder.
He prompted the rain and the rivers,
    And rent the heavens asunder.
He fashioned the frail woodland lily,
    Brought forth the clear gushing fountain,
Made pigments and colored the desert,
    And sculptured the loftiest mountain.
He garnished the colorless prairies,
    Created the hills and lakes.
He planted the majestic redwoods,
    And wafted down glistening snowflakes.
He took of that he made,
    A likeness of self He did mold,
With infinite love gave it breath
    And the future of man[kind] did mold.
He wrought all of this and much more,
    No mortal man had a part.
I cry out in awesome wonder, *Almighty God, how great Thou art!*

---

[64] The original source of the poem is unknown. It was found in a typewritten manuscript of prayers and poems that was edited and locally published by Beata E. Nothwehr, entitled *Book of Prayers and Devotional Thoughts of American Legion Post 206*, Windom, MN, 1976.

Sources for Further Study

Secondary Sources

Bodo, Murray. *Francis: The Journey and the Dream.* 40th anniversary ed. Cincinnati, OH: St. Anthony Press, 2011.

Boff, Leonardo. *Cry of the Earth, Cry of the Poor.* Ecology and Justice Series. Maryknoll, NY: Orbis Books, 1997.

Doyle, Eric. *St. Francis and the Song of Brotherhood and Sisterhood.* St. Bonaventure, NY: The Franciscan Institute, 1997. (Reprint of *St. Francis and the Song of Brotherhood.* New York: Seabury Press, 1981.)

Sorrell, Roger D. *St. Francis of Assisi and Nature: Tradition and Innovation in Western Christian Attitudes toward the Environment.* New York: Oxford University Press, 1988.

Primary Sources in English Translation

Armstrong, Regis J., ed. and trans. *The Lady—Clare of Assisi: Early Documents.* Rev. ed. St. Bonaventure, NY: Franciscan Institute Publications, 1993.

Armstrong, Regis J., J. A. Wayne Hellmann, and William J. Short, trans. and eds. *Francis of Assisi: Early Documents.* Vol. I, *The Saint.* New York: New City Press, 1999.

Armstrong, Regis J., J. A. Wayne Hellmann, and William J. Short, trans. and eds., *Francis of Assisi: Early Documents.* Vol. II, *The Founder.* New York: New City Press, 2000.

Armstrong, Regis J., J. A. Wayne Hellmann, and William J. Short, trans. and eds., *Francis of Assisi: Early Documents.* Vol. III, *The Prophet.* New York: New City Press, 2001.

Part 3

St. Bonaventure of Bagnoregio: Creator, Christ, Creatures, Cosmos

Chapter 5

Who Is God?
Christ in the Middle of a Love Triangle

Introduction: The Seraphic Doctor

Born in 1217 at Bagnoregio, a small town in between Viterbo and Ovieto in the Papal States, St. Bonaventure was baptized Giovanni (John) di Fidanza (after his father, who was a physician). Between the ages of seven and fourteen he was dedicated to St. Francis[1] by his mother, Maria di Retellio.[2] Bonaventure attended classes at the Faculty of Arts at the University of Paris in 1236–42.[3] In 1243 he began his theological studies as a novice of the Franciscan Order in Paris.[4] He was licensed as a bachelor of Scripture and also made his profession of perpetual vows in 1248. Franciscan scholar Alexander of Hales was his "father and

---

[1] J. Guy Bourgerol, *Introduction to the Works of Bonaventure* (Patterson, NJ: St. Anthony Guild Press, 1964), 3. Legend holds that he was healed of some illness by St. Francis of Assisi. However, that is not probable because at the age to which Bonaventure assigns his dedication appears to be *pueritia*, a date after the death of Francis (October 3, 1226).

[2] Ewert Cousins, *Bonaventure*, ed. Richard J. Payne, The Classics of Western Spirituality (New York: Paulist Press, 1978), 4.

[3] The dating of the life chronology of Bonaventure depends on the date established for his election as minister general of the Franciscan Order. I follow John Quinn's study. See John F. Quinn, "Chronology of St. Bonaventure (1217–1274)," *Franciscan Studies* 32 (1972): 173.

[4] Bourgerol, *Introduction to the Works of Bonaventure*, 5–10.

master."[5] He was educated according to the usual academic curriculum of the thirteenth century. In late 1250 or early 1251 he began to read the *Sentences* (Peter Lombard) as a *baccalarius sententiarius*, and he simultaneously received training in preaching from 1252 to 1253. He finished reading the *Sentences* in Advent of 1252. In late November of 1253 he became a master of theology and began to teach exclusively at the Franciscan School. He was finally incorporated into the College of Regent Masters in 1254.[6] As a doctor of theology he was regent master of the Franciscan School with official recognition by the university from 1254 until 1257. While still acting as regent master, he was elected minister general of the Franciscan Order on February 2, 1257.

Bonaventure's academic career was truncated because the office of minister general is a full-time administrative position concerned with the governance of the entire Franciscan order. That was a mixed blessing that profoundly shaped the maturing of his theology.[7] Though he maintained his speculative theological scholarship, as minister general he was compelled to focus on Franciscan spirituality in ways he may not have otherwise. The result was his integration of a carefully crafted theology and a powerful spirituality that gives Bonaventure's work great promise for our time.[8] During his seventeen years as minister general,

---

[5] Ibid., 4.

[6] John F. Quinn, "Chronology of Bonaventure's Sermons," *Archivum Franciscanium Historicum* 67 (1974): 151–52.

[7] See Zachary Hayes, "The Life and the Christological Thought of St. Bonaventure," in *Franciscan Christology: Selected Texts, Translations and Introductory Essays*, ed. Damian McElrath, Franciscan Sources, no. 1 (St. Bonaventure, NY: The Franciscan Institute, 1980), 62–63: "While the Christology developed by Bonaventure is clearly incomplete, yet that which he has accomplished is a powerful presentation that unites in a coherent manner the multiple dimensions of Christology already present in Scripture and often over-looked in contemporary Christologies. . . . The work of Bonaventure reflects the same concern [as in the New Testament], for it is a Christology that is at one level profoundly personal, but which shows how personal meaning is embedded in communal and indeed in cosmic meaning. Hence the Christian understanding of the moral life of man is not one way among many possible ways, but truly the obligatory way for man as such. The actual living out of this ethic is the personalization of the structural law of reality. And yet at another level, the Christology of Bonaventure is profoundly mystical, for personal reflection and contemplation are the indispensable tools for the personalization of the Christ-meaning which then issues in the living practice of this vision."

[8] See *Aeterni Patris*, encyclical of Pope Leo XIII on the restoration of Christian philosophy (1879), no. 14, http://www.vatican.va/holy_father/leo_xiii/encyclicals/documents/hf_l-xiii_enc_04081879_aeterni-patris_en.html, accessed March 12, 2009.

role of personal reflection and contemplation in moral theology

he continued to teach at Paris as well as oversee the Order's business, making numerous trips to Spain, Germany, and Italy. He was appointed cardinal bishop of Albano by Pope Gregory X, and he played a major role in the reforms of the Council of Lyons. Bonaventure died at the Council of Lyons in 1274.

Yet without St. Francis of Assisi, there would be no Bonaventure as we know him today. Significantly, Francis asserted the life-sustaining virtue of mutual obedience among all creatures. As Francis put it, the obedient one is "subject and submissive / to everyone in the world, not only to people, / but to every beast and wild animal as well / that they may do whatever they want with [that person] / insofar as it *has been given* to them / *from above* by the Lord."[9] Further, Francis denounced abusive relationships that humans create with others.[10] Humans use other creatures to meet daily survival needs, yet they are ungrateful to these "sisters and brothers," failing to recognize the Creator of such gifts and blessings. These teachings of St. Francis, as we shall see, sing in harmony with Bonaventure's highly relational worldview and trinitarian creation theology.

The philosophical and theological synthesis or teachings of Bonaventure included, but went beyond, the mystical experience and spiritual reflection of the Poverello. The influence of Francis is seen primarily in Bonaventure's interpretation of St. Francis's religious experience and in his Christ-centered theology, which provides an explanation of the Poverello's profound reverence for Christ.[11] For example, he followed

---

This encyclical nearly destroyed Franciscan theology. Even though Pope Leo XIII named Bonaventure one of the preeminent theologians of the church, Leo's personal preference for and active promotion of Thomism caused the gross neglect and near loss of other orthodox theologies of the church. See Gerald A. McCool, *From Unity to Pluralism: The Internal Evolution of Thomism* (New York: Fordham University Press, 1989), 163, 171–72, 190, 196–97.

[9] Francis of Assisi, "A Salutation of the Virtues," 14–18, in *Francis of Assisi: Early Documents*, vol. I, *The Saint*, trans. and ed. Regis J. Armstrong, J. A. Wayne Hellmann, William J. Short (New York: New City Press, 1999), 165.

[10] "A Mirror of Perfection of the *Status* of a Lesser Brother" (Sabatier Edition, 1928), in *Francis of Assisi: Early Documents*, vol. III, *The Prophet*, trans. and ed. Regis J. Armstrong, J. A. Wayne Hellmann, William J. Short (New York: New City Press, 2001), 278–86.

[11] Zachary Hayes, "Bonaventure: Mystery of the Triune God," in *The History of Franciscan Theology*, ed. Kenan B. Osborne (St. Bonaventure, NY: Franciscan Institute, 1994), 45. See also Regis J. Armstrong, "Francis of Assisi and the Prisms of Theologizing," *Greyfriars Review* 10/2 (1996): 196–98.

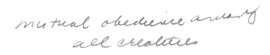

mutual obedience among all creatures

St. Francis in frequently naming God the "supreme good." But Bonaventure also drew upon the work of the theologian Pseudo-Dionysius,[12] who wrote about the idea that "goodness is self-diffusive."[13] Thus, Bonaventure called God *fontalis plenitude* (font of all goodness). Bonaventure developed these linkages between Christ, creation, creatures, and humans, solidifying an inseparable connection between Franciscan theology, spirituality, and ethics.[14]

Though the poetic and aesthetic (artistic) vision of Francis, the nature mystic, is far from absent in the work of Bonaventure, the Seraphic Doctor gave the spirituality of the Little Poor Man of Assisi a philosophical and theological framework. The insights of Bonaventure recorded in the thirteenth century still serve to deepen our understanding of the relationship of God, the cosmos, and human identity in relation to God and the cosmos. In this chapter, we examine St. Bonaventure's work to discover how his understanding of Christ in relation to the Trinity finds a place in his Franciscan creation theology, and we bring forward the insights that holds for our ecotheology. In Bonaventure's work we find grounds not only for the sacredness of creation in general but for the value of each cosmic element in particular.

---

[12] See Ilia Delio, *Simply Bonaventure: An Introduction to His Life, Thought, and Writings* (Hyde Park, NY: New City Press, 2001), 51n6: "Pseudo-Dionysius was a monastic writer who probably lived in Syria around the year 500 C.E. . . . For a summary of the Pseudo-Dionysius's writings and thought see Bernard McGinn, *The Foundations of Mysticism*, vol. 1, *The Presence of God: A History of Western Christian Mysticism* (New York: Crossroad, 1991), 157–82."

"Dionysius, or Pseudo-Dionysius, as he has come to be known in the contemporary world, was a Christian Neoplatonist who wrote in the late fifth or early sixth century CE and who transposed in a thoroughly original way the whole of Pagan Neoplatonism from Plotinus to Proclus, but especially that of Proclus and the Platonic Academy in Athens, into a distinctively new Christian context." *Stanford Encyclopedia of Philosophy*, http://plato.stanford.edu/entries/pseudo-dionysius-areopagite, accessed July 8, 2011.

[13] The basic idea is that goodness tends to inspire more goodness. If something good happens to a person, it is rare that she or he would tell no one else about it; in fact; they may tell everyone who will listen! In more technical terms, according to Ilia Delio, "To say that the Father is 'self-diffusive goodness' is to say that the 'self' of the Father is identified by the nature of the good to 'diffuse' or communicate itself to another. Therefore, that which the Father *is*, is self-diffusive goodness—and nothing other!" See Delio, *Simply Bonaventure*, 44–45.

[14] Zachary Hayes, "Christ, Word of God and Exemplar of Humanity," *The Cord* 46 (1996): 6.

Pseudo-Dionysius → @ 500

Especially important for us is that Bonaventure also gives us a vision of the created world and the need to place that vision in conversation with the science of our day in order that the story of creation be told and understood in its various forms and dimensions. Just as Bonaventure engaged theology and philosophy with the science of his day, we must engage in an interdisciplinary conversation today.[15] To leave the story of creation to either science or theology alone would be to neglect the fuller truth provided by consideration of both dimensions. Where science can tell us how creation takes place, theology can help us understand what it means for us—why there is something and not nothing.

Something about St. Bonaventure's Thought

In order to understand Bonaventure, one must be aware of the many dimensions of his thought and the two kinds of language he employs.[16] He uses both the language of the imagination and the language of metaphysics.[17] It is important to note that Bonaventure sees imagination and metaphysics as interconnected and understands that they impact one another. As the preeminent Bonaventure scholar of the English-speaking world, Zachary Hayes, shows, at the core of Bonaventure's theology is the doctrine of the Trinity.[18] Bonaventure understands the Trinity (using the philosophy of neoplatonism) as divine exemplarity—that is, as the immense fecundity of the goodness of God expressed in the emanation (outward movement) of the Three Persons and flowing outward into the created cosmos.

---

[15] In his study on creation, Bonaventure acknowledges that there are many kinds of wisdom that assist us in knowing about God's creation. See Zachary Hayes, "The Cosmos: A Symbol of the Divine," in *Franciscan Theology of the Environment: An Introductory Reader*, ed. Dawn M. Nothwehr (Quincy, IL: Franciscan Press, 2002), 255–56, 266nn9–12, where Hayes cites Bonaventure's *Collations in Haexemeron*, 2, 20 (V, 339–40), and 12, 15–16 (V, 386).

[16] Hayes, "The Cosmos," 250–52.

[17] See *St. Mary's Press Glossary of Theological Terms*, ed. John T. Ford, Essentials of Catholic Theology Series (Winona, MN: St. Mary's Press, 2006), 120, s.v. "Metaphysics": "This word (from the Greek *metaphysika*, which literally means "after physics") was originally used by editors to describe the section of the works of Aristotle that came after the section on physics. Because this section addresses the *nature of being*, 'metaphysics' has come to mean the philosophical study of being in terms of its most foundational aspects, such as *matter* and *form*."

[18] Hayes, "Bonaventure: Mystery of the Triune God," 53–60.

At the level of the imagination, the world outside ourselves impacts our consciousness through our senses—touch, taste, smell, sound, and sight—and we make judgments about what we experience. Bonaventure holds that because God created all things, we can know something about God by experiencing the created world.[19] However, our intellect is also involved in knowing. As we reflect on the information given us by our senses, we raise the metaphysical questions of interpretation and meaning. We move to the ontological[20] level of finding the nature of the One (God) reflected in the encounters brought to our awareness through our senses. Here we see Bonaventure's use of Plato's philosophy to show that the nature of the created order is influenced by the nature of the Creator, and all created reality is therefore grounded (i.e., it originates) in God.

Bonaventure explains that the existence of the created world is the result of the tremendous creative productivity of the goodness of God. Bonaventure addresses divine exemplarity by building on Pseudo-Dionysus's neoplatonic[21] principle that goodness is necessarily self-diffusive and on Richard of St. Victor's[22] understanding of ecstatic love.[23] The concept of "exemplarity" for Bonaventure expresses the fundamental claim that all created reality is grounded in God and therefore manifests something of the mysteries of God in the created world. The triune God expresses a dynamic, creative love within the Godhead that is the "emanation" (giving out) of the Three Persons. The divine life of the Godhead flows outward and is reflected in the created cosmos. The created world is therefore "theophanic":[24] it images and reveals God in varying degrees. As we will

---

[19] In chap. 2 of *The Journey of the Soul into God*, Bonaventure shows how the senses bring us in contact with God.

[20] See *St. Mary's Press Glossary*, 133, s.v. "Ontology": "This word (from the Greek *onta* meaning 'things that exist,' and *logos* meaning 'word') refers to the branch of philosophy that considers *being* and *existence*."

[21] "Neoplatonism is a modern term used to designate the period of Platonic philosophy beginning with the work of Plotinus and ending with the closing of the Platonic Academy by the Emperor Justinian in 529 CE." *Internet Encyclopedia of Philosophy*, http://www.iep.utm.edu/neoplato, accessed October 1, 2011.

[22] See *New Catholic Encyclopedia*. vol. 12, 2nd ed. (Detroit: Gale, 2003), 234–35. Richard of St. Victor was a theologian and mystical writer who died March 10, 1173. He was a regular canon of the Abbey of St. Victor, Paris. He was a superior, and later he was elected prior in 1161.

[23] Hayes, "Bonaventure: Mystery of the Triune God," 56. See also chap. 2 of the present text for an explanation.

[24] This word comes from the Greek words *theos*, meaning "God," and *phaneia*, meaning "appearance."

see, the theophanic nature of creation is at the heart of a Franciscan ecotheology.

All created things image God in some way.[25] As Franciscan philosopher Phil Hoebing explains, "All living things are vestiges (footprints) of God whereas man who represents God closely and distinctly is an image of God. The man conformed to God by grace is a similitude [necessary likeness] because such a person represents God most closely."[26] Divine exemplarity is most perfectly found in the figure of Christ, who is also the incarnation of the divine Word—the Art of the Father—in which the divine exemplarity is most concentrated. Creation is brought to transformative fullness in union with God in the conjunction of the divine archetype and the microcosm of creation.[27] "So, when the divine exemplarity is focused so sharply in the self-expressive Word, when that Word enters into the most profound relationship to creation in the humanity of Jesus, this conjunction of the divine archetype and what Bonaventure calls the "macrocosm" (because something of all creation is in human nature)—when that comes together, this is the synthesis of all that makes up the created cosmos. It is at that conjunction when the divine aim for all creation is brought to fruition."[28]

This is *why* God created—so that through love, the creation can be brought into transforming fullness in union with the divine.[29] Put simply, God desires to express divine love. And this happens first and to the fullest extent in Jesus. Given this vision, we could say that the world of

---

[25] See Bonaventure, *Breviloquium* 2.12 [5:230], cited in Zachary Hayes, *Bonaventure: Mystical Writings*, Spiritual Legacy Series (New York: Crossroad Publishing Company, 1999), 90. Note that all citations Hayes gives in this work are his translations from *Doctoris Seriphici S. Bonaventurae Opera Omnia*, 10 vols. (Quaracchari: Collegium S. Bonaventurae, 1882–1902). The first two numerals indicate the section of the text, the bracketed numerals indicate the volume and the page in that volume.

[26] Phil Hoebing, "St. Bonaventure and Ecology," in *Franciscan Theology of the Environment,* ed. Nothwehr, 276. Note that Hoebing's use of "man" is intended to include both female and male human beings.

[27] Bonaventure, *Collations on the Six Days of Creation*, 1.13 [5:332], cited in Hayes, "Bonaventure: Mystery of the Triune God," 74.

[28] My transcription of Zachary Hayes, "Of God's Fullness We Have All Received: The Teachings of St. Bonaventure on Creation," lecture, June 12, 1997, at The National Franciscan Forum, "Franciscans Doing Theology," Franciscan Center, Colorado Springs, CO. The videocassette of the lecture is included in Mary C. Gurley, "An Independent Study Program to Accompany *The History of Franciscan Theology*," ed. Kenan Osborne (St. Bonaventure, NY: The Franciscan Institute, 1999).

[29] See Hayes, "Bonaventure: Mystery of the Triune God," 63–64.

All things are footprints of God
(√. God's fengerprints)

creation has its own truth and beauty.[30] However, there is much more to this story. "Beyond this, each creature in itself and all creation is in its truest reality, an expressive sign of the glory, truth, and beauty of God. Only when it is seen in these terms is it seen in its most profound significance."[31] Here is the basis upon which we can hold that each element of creation has intrinsic value in itself.

Bonaventure's metaphysics grounds a whole series of metaphors about how the cosmos reveals things about God, and these metaphors express his understanding of creation. The Seraphic Doctor employs metaphorical language to show the relationship between God and the cosmos. Zachary Hayes has selected seven of Bonaventure's many metaphors— "circle, water, song, book, window, micro/macrocosm, and the cross"— to further illustrate the Seraphic Doctor's vision of the created world and how it reveals God.[32] God is like an intelligible circle whose center is everywhere and whose circumference is nowhere.[33] God, as Trinity, is like a gushing fountain—that is, the source from which the river of all reality flows and to which it ultimately returns. Again, God is like the water of an overflowing fountain, generously showering all of creation with love. Or, God is like the expansive deep oceans that are like the vast depth of God's faithful love.[34] Like a song—where all of the notes in a carefully crafted order must be heard for the song to be known—so too, in its wide diversity, the various dynamic cosmic elements make up the interrelated cosmos.[35] God's self-revelation is like a book: it is first "written" within the consciousness of God in the form of the divine Word (cf. Plato's divine ideas) and then becomes the book "written without" as the whole creation—all created things are the expression of the divine Artist.[36] Or, the Book of Creation is God's primeval revelation to which people become blinded through the Fall; the Scriptures are given to sinful humanity to guide and enlighten them and entice them away from sin; and the Book of Life is the revelation of the fullness of God in Christ.[37]

---

[30] Bonaventure, *The Collations on the Six Days of Creation*, 3.8 [5:344], cited in Hayes, *Bonaventure: Mystical Writings*, 73.

[31] Hayes, "The Cosmos," 252–53.

[32] Ibid., 253–58.

[33] Ibid., 253.

[34] Ibid., 253–54.

[35] Ibid., 254.

[36] Ibid., 254–55.

[37] Ibid., 255.

Then there is Bonaventure's window metaphor. Each element of creation reveals something of the Creator like the array of colored glass in a stained-glass pane, which flashes with dynamic hues as sunlight passes through it, setting up an orgy of color.[38] Finally, there is the metaphor of the macro/microcosm. The medievals believed that the macrocosm was made up of the four elements—earth, air, water, fire—and the spiritual order beyond them. Each human is a microcosm made up of the four elements, and each has a spiritual dimension as well. Bonaventure believed that through the resurrection of the incarnate Christ, the transfiguration of the entire cosmos began.[39]

Bonaventure's vision of the world of creation given at the level of metaphor and symbol is summarized by Hayes in this way:

> For Bonaventure, the relationship between creation and God can be expressed in two words: manifestation and participation. All things in the cosmos exist so as to manifest something of the mystery of God. And all things exist by virtue of some degree of participation in the mystery of being that flows from the absolute mystery of the creative love of God. An appropriate reading of the book of the cosmos, therefore, gives us some sense of the divine goodness and fecundity; of the divine wisdom and beauty; of the divine intelligence and freedom; and of the relational character of the divine mystery of the trinity in which all of creation is grounded. It gives us some sense of the pain and tragedy of existence in a fallen condition.[40]

But the good news for us is that Bonaventure's integrated understanding of God's creation also holds important clues toward our ecological conversion and sustainable living in our ecologically threatened world. We turn now to Bonaventure's Christ-centered theology to find those clues.

Christ "the Firstborn of All Creation" in the Middle of a Love Triangle

Situating Bonaventure's Christology in the Franciscan Theological Tradition

Franciscan theology is characterized by a particular set of core values and beliefs, namely, conversion, peacemaking, the emphasis on divine

---

[38] Ibid., 256.
[39] Ibid., 257.
[40] Ibid., 258. See also Hayes, "Bonaventure: Mystery of the Triune God," 65.

love and freedom, the primacy of Christ, the centrality of the incarnation, Christ crucified, the sacramentality of creation, the goodness of the world, the human person in the image of God, the emphasis on poverty and humility, and the development of *affectus* (goodwill, emotion, disposition of mind).[41] The "common thread" sustaining the Franciscan theological tradition across time is the person and witness of Francis of Assisi, "the patron of ecology."[42] St. Francis's theological authority originated in the gift of his graced experience of God (*ex beneficio*, not *ex officio*),[43] and so he became known as a "vernacular theologian."[44] Three major themes in Francis's vernacular theology irrevocably link Franciscan spirituality and Franciscan theology: the humanity of Christ, the mystery of God as generous love, and the sense of creation as family.[45] Bonaventure develops these linkages between Christ, creation, creatures, and humans, solidifying an inseparable connection among Franciscan theology, spirituality, and ethics.[46]

St. Bonaventure's Christology and Creation

SOME KEY SOURCES

As we saw in chapter 2, Bonaventure of Bagnoregio stands as the founder of the Franciscan theological tradition[47] and the clearest inter-

---

[41] See Ilia Delio, "The Franciscan Intellectual Tradition: Contemporary Concerns," in Elise Saggau, ed., *The Franciscan Intellectual Tradition: Tracing Its Origins*, The Franciscan Heritage Series, vol. 1, Washington Theological Union Symposium Papers, 2001 (St. Bonaventure, NY: The Franciscan Institute, 2002), 1–19.

[42] On, November 29, 1979, John Paul II proclaimed Francis of Assisi the patron saint of ecology. See Ioannes Paulus Pp. II, Litterae Apostolicae, *Inter Sanctos, Franciscus Assisiensis Caelestis Patronus Oecologiae Cultorum Eligitur*, http://www.vatican.va/holy_father/john_paul_ii/apost_letters/1979/documents/hf_jp-ii_apl_19791129_inter-sanctos_lt.html, accessed March 18, 2009.

[43] See Congregation for the Doctrine of the Faith, "Instruction on the Ecclesial Vocation of the Theologian," *Origins* 20/8 (July 5, 1990): 119. Also see United States Conference of Catholic Bishops, Doctrinal Responsibilities: Approaches to Promoting Cooperation and Resolving Misunderstandings between Bishops and Theologians, *Origins* 19/7 (June 29, 1989): 101.

[44] Bernard McGinn, *Meister Eckhart and the Beguine Mystics* (New York, Continuum, 1983), 6–7, and *The Flowering of Mysticism: Men and Women in the New Mysticism, 1200–1350* (New York: Crossroad, 1998), 21.

[45] See John 14:6-9 and St. Francis, *Admonition* I, 1–4, in Regis Armstrong and Ignatius Brady, *Francis and Clare* (Mahwah, NJ: Paulist Press, 1982), 25–26.

[46] Zachary Hayes, "Christ, Word of God and Exemplar of Humanity," 6.

[47] See Osborne, ed., *The History of Franciscan Theology*, vii–ix. See Zachary Hayes, "The Life and the Christological Thought of St. Bonaventure," in *Franciscan Christol-*

pretive christological voice of St. Francis of Assisi.[48] Other important
sources in Bonaventure's thought include Augustine, Pseudo-Dionysius,
and Richard of St. Victor.[49] These ground and support an evangelical
theological synthesis that is faithful to the intuitions of Francis and a
rigorous intellectual structure and method.[50] Bonaventure's integration
of a rigorous theology and a powerful spirituality gives his work great
promise for our time.[51] The three themes of St. Francis's christocentric
and connected spiritual vision run deep in the speculative theology of
Bonaventure.[52]

BONAVENTURE'S CHRISTOLOGY: CREATION AND THE INCARNATION

While clearly we cannot simply dust off Bonaventure's theology and
then impose it on our current ethical challenges of human-caused climate
change or the loss of biodiversity, for example, Bonaventure's Christology significantly opens a horizon to a renewed image of God intimately
concerned with creation, of the human person, and of "earth-friendly"
moral living. Bonaventure's theological insights provide the basis for a
moral normativity (values, standards, or principles) of mutual relations
that compel us to take seriously God's mandate to care for creation and
to live sustainably.

Bonaventure begins his christological discussion with the faith claim
that "the Word became flesh" (John 1:14), and he asks, "Why?" He then
proceeds to probe this question from the God side (God's perspective)
and from the human side (human perspective).[53] Bonaventure finds the
answer rooted in the ways God reveals Godself. The incarnation (union

ogy: Selected Texts, Translations and Introductory Essays, ed. McElrath, 62–64.

[48] See Timothy Johnson, "Lost in Sacred Space: Textual Hermeneutics, Liturgical
Worship, and Celano's *Legenda ad usum chori*" (unpublished paper presented at the
Thirty-Sixth International Congress of Medieval Studies, May 3, 2001, Kalamazoo,
MI), 12. See E. R. Daniel, *The Franciscan Concept of Mission in the High Middle Ages*
(New York: The Franciscan Institute, 1975), 48.

[49] See J. Guy Bougerol, *Introduction to the Works of Bonaventure*, vol. 1, trans. José
de Vinck (Patterson, NJ: St. Anthony Guild Press, 1964), especially 23–49.

[50] Delio, "The Franciscan Intellectual Tradition," 8. See Ilia Delio *Crucified Love:
Bonaventure's Mysticism of the Crucified Christ* (Quincy, IL: Franciscan Press, 1998).

[51] See Leo XIII, *Aeterni Patris*. See also McCool, *From Unity to Pluralism*, 163, 171–72,
190, 196–97.

[52] See chap. 2 of the present work for discussion of Bonaventure's method and
metaphysics, trinitarian theology, and doctrine of creation.

[53] Hayes, "Bonaventure: Mystery of the Triune God," 87.

of human and divine natures) is grounded in the possibility of God as the Creator. God created out of self-diffusive and self-communicative love. God's self-revelation is given in its broadest sense in all of creation. The Divine is revealed more specifically in human nature (*imago Dei*). But, beyond that, the most complete revelation of God is in the human-and-divine, Jesus Christ.[54]

As we have said, in Bonaventure's Logos-centered (Word-centered, Christ-centered) theology, the Word, God's revelation, is given in the entirety of the universe. Also, within creation God's revelation is found in humans as the *imago Dei*. Recall that in Bonaventure's trinitarian theology the Son is also known as the Image. "Thus, in the mystery of the incarnation, the created image is filled with the eternal exemplary Image. In this way humanity reaches its fullest participation in the divine archetype and thus, the deepest fulfillment of its potential."[55] Humans are unique among the creatures (as is each creature) in that by virtue of their spiritual dimension, they have an inner ordering to immediacy with God. When this capacity is brought into act by divine initiative, "the created order finds its highest form of fulfillment. This is what Bonaventure understands the hypostatic union to involve."[56]

Zachary Hayes recaps all of this (above), showing the relationship of the incarnation and creation: "In this sense, when God comes into the world, God comes into his own (John 1:11). This coming is not a change of physical place. It is, rather, a matter of spiritual presence to that which, by virtue of the act of creation, was formed as a potential recipient of the divine. In such a world, an incarnation is not an unwelcome intrusion of a foreign God. It is, in fact, but the fullest realization of the most noble potential in the created order."[57] Here we see in Bonaventure a kind of evolutionary worldview that later theologians would name "Christogenesis."[58]

---

[54] Ibid., 83.

[55] Ibid., 86. See *St. Mary's Press Glossary of Theological Terms*, 94, s.v. "Hypostatic Union": "This term (from the Greek *hypostasis*, meaning 'what lies beneath,' and the Latin *unio*, meaning 'oneness,' or 'unity') refers to the union of the divine and the human natures in the one divine person of Jesus Christ, the Son of God. (See CCC 494–469.)"

[56] Hayes, "Bonaventure: Mystery of the Triune God," 87.

[57] Ibid., 88.

[58] Leonardo Boff, *Cry of the Earth, Cry of the Poor*, Ecology and Justice Series (Maryknoll, NY: Orbis Books, 1997), 174–86, especially 185. Christogenesis in the thought of Teilhard de Chardin is the notion that Christ would be the start and the end of

BONAVENTURE'S CHRISTOLOGY: COSMIC DIMENSIONS

Following the long tradition of the Franciscan school, Bonaventure does not limit his discussion of the meaning of Christ to the reality of the cross. Rather, he "perceive[s] the possible relations between the story of Jesus and the larger picture of the world."[59] The incarnation must be thought of as God's intent from the very moment of creation; it was not an afterthought, subject to human sin. Rather, the meaning of the cross is situated within the context of the broader cosmic vision.

Bonaventure's Franciscan cosmic Christology provides a framework for a hope-filled rediscovery of the fact that in Jesus we find the divine clue to the structure and meaning not only of humanity but of the entire universe. Central to Bonaventure's understanding of Jesus is its intimate and necessary integration with an incarnational spirituality. Through the divine-human person, Jesus, our relationship with God, one another, and all of creation forms an interconnected whole. This understanding of Jesus Christ is helpful as we face the moral and spiritual malaise that undergirds the human-caused ecological problems of our day[60]

Bonaventure came to understand the incarnation of Jesus Christ not as an isolated event but as integral to the possibility of creation itself. Christ is not an accident or an intrusion in creation. As Franciscan theologians put it, "A world without Christ is an incomplete world, that is, the whole world is structured Christologically."[61] Three New Testament texts gave Bonaventure insights for an understanding of Jesus Christ and the relationship of creation and incarnation. This understanding can assist us in our moral choices about ecological issues and sustainable living.

COLOSSIANS 1:15-20

The first text is the early christological creation hymn in Colossians 1:15-20. Here, Christ is God's preeminent and supreme agent in creation. This hymn has its roots in Genesis 1 and Proverbs 8. Franciscan Scripture scholar Robert J. Karris reflects, "Yes, Colossians 1:15-20 invites us, challenges

---

evolution, its Alpha and Omega. All the energies of the universe would be continuously rising to some superior level that would be a movement toward Christ.

[59] Hayes, "Christ, Word of God and Exemplar of Humanity," 6.

[60] See ibid., 16–17. Also see Ilia Delio, *Christ in Evolution* (Maryknoll, NY: Orbis Books, 2008), especially chaps. 3 and 7.

[61] Hayes, "Christ, Word of God and Exemplar of Humanity," 6.

us to take flight in our religious imagination back to the beginning, nay, before the beginning, and to see Christ thoroughly enjoying creating and longing to become human to express tangibly God's unconditional love for all human and nonhuman creation."[62]

Jesus is also the mediator of redemption: "Through him God was pleased to reconcile to himself all things, whether on earth or in heaven, by making peace through the blood of his cross" (Col 1:20). The whole cosmos—all things on earth and in heaven—finds reconciliation and peace in Jesus Christ. The saving activity of God in Jesus is the unfolding of God's purpose in creation and the beginning of its transformation in, as the passage continues, "his fleshly body" (v. 22). As Australian theologian Denis Edwards explains,

> Here the cosmic Christ is celebrated as both the *source* of creation and its *goal*: all things have been *created* in Christ and all things are *reconciled* in him. The words "all things" are repeated like a refrain. All things are created in Christ, who is the image (*icon*) of the invisible God. As in the wisdom literature *Sophia* is with God in creation and continually sustains all things, so in Colossians the risen Christ is the one in whom all things are created and in whom all things hold together. The Colossians hymn goes further, asserting that in Christ and Christ's cross, God has reconciled all things to God's self. Everything in creation is created in Christ, sustained in him, and reconciled in him.[63]

Throughout the Colossians 1:15-20 text, it is repeatedly made clear that Christ has a truly universal role. As Karris points out, in the ancient context the "principalities and powers" are initially good but have fallen and are now in need of reconciliation.[64] But even the cosmic powers, "whether thrones or dominions or rulers or powers," are subject to Christ's rule (Col 1:16-18). This would have been reassuring to the Pauline community, who lived in what Karris terms an "age of anxiety" in which angelic beings were thought of as controlling earth, air, water, and fire, as well as the movements of the sun, the moon, and the stars.[65] But

---

[62] Robert J. Karris, "Colossians 1:15-20—Jesus Christ as Cosmic Lord and Peacemaker," in *Franciscan Theology of the Environment*, ed. Nothwehr, 86.

[63] Denis Edwards, *Ecology at the Heart of Faith* (Maryknoll, NY: Orbis Books, 2006), 56.

[64] Karris, "Colossians 1:15-20," 90.

[65] Ibid., 75.

"in him" all cosmic forces are taken up and transformed in the power of the cross and resurrection. The entire universe is to be transfigured in Christ, "who is the image of the invisible God" (Col 1:15). In Colossians, Christ's death and resurrection are understood as the beginning of the transformation of the whole of creation. This is possible because of "the primacy of Christ"—the belief or faith claim that insists on the absolute priority of God's will and grace and the secondary role of human sin. This concept comes through in six different ways, according to Scripture scholar Jean-Noël Aletti, as follows:[66]

- Eminence—"image" (1:5a), "firstborn" (1:15b), "preeminent" (1:18).

- Universality—"all things" is mentioned eight times in 1:15-20.

- Uniqueness—it is solely and uniquely Jesus Christ who does what the hymn says.

- Totality—on all levels of creation, in every level of being, all is reconciled for Christ and through Christ.

- Priority—"firstborn" (1:15b), "before all things" (1:17), "the beginning" (1:18b), "firstborn from the dead" (1:18b).

- Definitive accomplishment—the hymn celebrates what Christ has already accomplished.

This leaves us with great hope, but also with the equally profound challenge to participate with Christ as cocreators and coredeemers of the cosmos.

DEEP INCARNATION—JOHN 1:1-14

Already as a student Bonaventure had an affinity for the Gospel of John. As we saw in chapter 2, the Prologue of John presents us with the amazing reality of the incarnation. For Bonaventure, this is not only a central belief of the Christian faith but also the link uniting the doctrines of creation and redemption. Indeed, the great theologians of the first centuries of Christianity, such as Irenaeus and Athanasius, taught that in the Word made flesh, God became human so that the whole of humanity might be healed, taken up into God, and deified—that is made whole

---

[66] See ibid., 81–83.

and holy—in God. The meaning of the incarnation, of becoming flesh, includes the whole interconnected material world in some way.

Further, Australian theologian Duncan Reid suggests that God's embrace of humanity in the incarnation must be understood in context of the wider claim in John's gospel that the Word has become flesh.[67] The Greek term *sarx*, often translated as "flesh," also points beyond the humanity of Jesus and us to the world of biological life, and it calls forth the entire interwoven web of life that God sustains and embraces in divine love.

New Zealand theologian Neil Darragh builds on Reid's thought: "To say that God became flesh is not only to say that God became human, but to say also that God became an Earth creature, that God became a sentient being, that God became a living being (in common with all other living beings), that God became a complex Earth unit of minerals in the carbon and nitrogen cycles."[68] Edwards elaborates, "In Jesus of Nazareth, God becomes a vital part of an ecosystem and a part of the interconnected systems that support life on Earth. Danish theologian Niels Henrik Gregersen calls this the idea of *deep incarnation*."[69] Gregersen explains further that, "in Christ, God enters into biological life in a new way and is now with evolving creation in a radically new way."[70] Christ's suffering on the cross is not only a redemptive act for humans. Rather, it is also God's act of suffering with the limitations of all life forms in creation—God's identification with all of creation in all of its complexity, struggle, and pain.

Gregersen writes: "In this context, the incarnation of God in Christ can be understood as a radical or 'deep' incarnation, that is, an incarnation into the very tissue of biological existence and system of nature. Understood this way, the death of Christ becomes an icon of God's redemptive co-suffering with all sentient life as well as with the victims of social competition. God bears the cost of evolution, the price involved in the

---

[67] Duncan Reid, "Enfleshing the Human," in *Earth Revealing—Earth Healing: Ecology and Christian Theology*, ed. Denis Edwards (Collegeville, MN: Liturgical Press, 2000), 69–83.

[68] Neil Darragh, *At Home in the Earth* (Aukland: Accent Publications, 2000), 124. See discussion of "deep incarnation" in Denis Edwards, *Ecology at the Heart of Faith* (Maryknoll, NY: Orbis Books, 2006), 58–60.

[69] Edwards, *Ecology at the Heart of Faith*, 59. See Neils Henrik Gregersen, "The Cross of Christ in an Evolutionary World," *Dialog: A Journal of Theology* 40 (2001): 205.

[70] Edwards, *Ecology at the Heart of Faith*, 59.

hardship of natural selection."[71] All of these insights concerning "deep incarnation" are faithful to the Christian tradition. These insights provide a timely understanding of what St. Paul claims in Rom 8:19-23, that the whole creation waits with "eager longing" for its liberation from "bondage to decay" and for "the freedom of the glory of the children of God."

ROMANS 8:18-27

Anne M. Clifford rightly points out that in Romans 5:12-21 Paul recalls Genesis 2–3 and discusses the justification of human beings in Christ, whom he calls the "New Adam."[72] In Romans 8, he presents a vision of the future of the earth as intimately bound to the future of humanity. Paul reflects on a theme found in Genesis 6–9, Hosea, and Jeremiah, and he describes how "the creation waits with eager longing for the revealing of the children of God; for the creation was subjected to futility, not of its own will but by the will of the one who subjected it, in hope" (Rom 8:19-20). Because of human sin, the created world became subject to a kind of fruitlessness that results in decay (v. 21). St. Paul states: "We know that the whole creation has been groaning in labor pains until now; and not only the creation, but we ourselves, who have the first fruits of the Spirit, groan inwardly while we wait for adoption, the redemption of our bodies" (8:22-23). But Paul gives us a glimpse of God's generous, creative compassion when he writes that it is not only creation that groans, but "likewise the Spirit helps us in our weakness; for we do not know how to pray as we ought, but that very Spirit intercedes with sighs too deep for words" (8:26). Not only do humans groan inwardly in longing for redemption, but creation as a whole does as well. There is great hope in the midst of the groaning of creation: the Spirit gives life in an outpouring of compassion that extends to all of creation.

Bonaventure clearly understands that the entire world was transformed at the moment of the incarnation—when the divine became part of the material world. Just how widely and deeply are the various elements of creation related to one another? Bonaventure replies: "All things are said to be transformed in the transfiguration of Christ. For as a human being, Christ has something in common with all creatures. With the stone

---

[71] Ibid.

[72] "Foundations for a Catholic Ecotheology of God," in *"And God Saw It Was Good": Catholic Theology and the Environment*, eds. Drew Christiansen and Walter Grazer (Washington, DC: United States Conference of Catholic Bishops, Inc., 1996), 36.

he shares existence; with plants he shares life; with animals he shares sensation; and with the angels he shares intelligence. Therefore, all things are said to be transformed in Christ since—in his human nature—he embraces something of every creature."[73]

From the Writings of St. Bonaventure

Collations on the Six Days of Creation, *1.10–11 [5:330–31]*[74]

It is necessary to begin with the center, that is, with Christ. For He is the Mediator between God and humanity, holding the central position in all things, as will become clear. Therefore, it is necessary to begin with Him if a person wishes to reach Christian wisdom. . . . Our intention is to show that in Christ are "hidden all the treasures of wisdom and knowledge," and that He Himself is the central point of all knowledge. He is the center point in a sevenfold sense: namely, He is the center of essence, nature, distance, doctrine, moderation, justice, and concord. . . . Christ is the first center in His eternal generation, the second in His incarnation, the third in His passion, the fourth in His resurrection, the fifth in His ascension, the sixth in the judgment to come, and the seventh in the eternal retribution or beatitude.

The Journey of the Soul into God, *1.15 [5:299]*[75]

Open your eyes, alert your spiritual ears, unseal your lips, and apply your heart so that in all creatures you may see, hear, praise, love, serve, glorify and honor God, lest the whole world rise up against you. For the "universe shall wage war against the foolish." On the contrary, it will be a matter of glory for the wise who can say with the prophet: "For you have given me, O Lord, a delight in your deeds, and I will rejoice in the work of your hands. How great are your works, O Lord! You have made all things in wisdom. The earth is filled with your creatures."

---

[73] Bonaventure, *Sermo I, Dom II*, in Quad. IX, 215–19, quoted in Hayes, "Christ, Word of God and Exemplar of Humanity," 13.

[74] Bonaventure, *Collations on the Six Days of Creation*, 1.10–11 [5:330–31], in Hayes, *Bonaventure: Mystical Writings*, 116.

[75] Bonaventure, *The Journey of the Soul into God*, 1.15 [5:299], in Hayes, *Bonaventure: Mystical Writings*, 77.

Reflection and Application

Though after the Fall (Gen 3) the human view of God's self-revelation in creation was obscured, it was not lost. Biblical and historical revelation supplements and clarifies what we see in nature and enables us to read the cosmic revelation with greater accuracy. The story of the love of God expressed in creation is elaborated in the Scriptures and modeled most perfectly in the person, life, and ministry of Jesus. In the end, there is little excuse for those who do not heed the call to return to the fountain source of all goodness.

Now it is one thing to speak about creation this way in a medieval setting where Christian theology and belief formed and contextualized the daily life for the vast majority. How does this fit with the contentions of some who claim that science and religion have nothing to say to each other? As part of a burgeoning conversation between science and religion, already in the 1990s Franciscan theologian Zachary Hayes challenged Timothy Ferris and others of a similar opinion who maintained that cosmology can tell us nothing about God.[76] Hayes carefully argued that the real focus of concern is what questions we expect religion and science, respectively, to answer. Science and religion each rightfully address a different set of questions. Science: How? Religion: Why? The danger comes when either science or religion makes exclusive claims to have the entire truth and to be able to interpret all levels of meaning. Just as Bonaventure utilized and conversed with knowledge that the science of his day made available as a way to begin to grasp the wonders of creation, we need to be conversant with the information made accessible to us through sophisticated methodologies such as quantum physics, astrophysics, or ecology and to use that data as the subject of our theological reflection.

Franciscan philosopher Phil Hoebing points out that one early example of a successful conversation between science and theology has already been significant. Scientists such as J. Baird Callicott hold that if we are to change the way we treat the natural world (and indeed, in our ecologically threatened world we must), then we need to find ways to recognize the intrinsic value of the created world, not only its instrumental value.[77] Certainly, Bonaventure's vision of the Creator and the world of creation offers reasons for Christians of today to assign intrinsic value to all in

---

[76] See Hayes, "The Cosmos," 258–65.
[77] Hoebing, "Bonaventure and Ecology," 270.

the created world. Hoebing shows how this assessment can be made by grounding one's reasoning in Bonaventure's philosophy and theology. As Bonaventure so eloquently stated,

> The entire world is a shadow, a road, a vestige, and it is also a book written without (Ex 2:8; Ap 5:1). For in every creature there is a shining forth of the divine exemplar, but mixed with the darkness. Hence creatures are a kind of darkness mixed with light. Also they are a road leading to the exemplar. Just as you see a ray of light entering through a window is colored in different ways according to the colors of the various parts, so the divine ray shines forth in each and every creature in different ways and in different properties; it is said in Wisdom: *In her ways she shows herself* (Wis 6:17). Also creatures are a vestige of the wisdom of God. Hence creatures are a kind of representation and statue of the wisdom of God. And in view of all of this, they are a kind of book written without.[78]

In our ecologically threatened world, may we be wise enough to follow Bonaventure's vision. Bonaventure's vision of creation includes a particular role for humans and an ethical system to guide them in that role. In the next chapter, we will take up those two considerations.

Questions for Reflection and Discussion

1. How do you understand the incarnation? What is the relationship between the incarnation and creation?

2. After thinking about Bonaventure's understanding of the "theophanic nature" of creation, list some of the ways that creation tells you something about God.

3. Bonaventure calls Christ the "Art of the Father." Explain what you understand about this and how thinking about Christ in this way can influence how you value the created world.

4. Read Colossians 1:15-20. How do you see Christ's work of redemption to be helpful in your efforts to live sustainably?

---

[78] Bonaventure, *Hexaemeron*, XII, 14, quoted in Ewert Cousins, *Christ of the 21st Century* (Rockport, MA: Element, Inc., 1992), 152.

5. In what ways do you consider science a source for theological reflection or prayerful contemplation?

Suggestions for Action

1. Visit a science museum. When you return home, reflect on what you learned. What new insights about Christ come to mind?

2. Bonaventure found the use of metaphors helpful in understanding God and God's acts. List some metaphors that describe how humans violate God's marvelous creation. Allow these images to motivate you to live sustainably.

3. Bonaventure held that because Christ became incarnate, the entire material world was deified. Walk through you neighborhood. How does what you see, hear, smell, touch, or taste reflect the value people place on creation? List ways you can act to improve the care for creation.

4. Do an Internet search on sustainable living. Pick one way to change your lifestyle to express your care for the earth.

5. Buy fair-trade beverages, food, and household items that are produced using sustainable methods.

6. Read and reflect on Romans 8:18-27. List ways that Christ incarnate suffers with the polluted, abused, and ravaged earth in your region of the world. What will you do to be a coredeemer with Christ in this state of affairs?

7. Expand your "earth literacy quotient." Study composting, pollution of various kinds, the life cycle of butterflies, or the hydrocycle in your region. Act on what you learn.

Prayer

Give praise to God along with thirteenth-century Franciscan poet Jacopone Da Todi.[79]

"How the Soul Finds God in All Creatures by Means of the Senses," *Lauda LXXXII*, by Jacopone Da Todi

O Love Divine and Great,
   Why dost thou still besiege my heart?
  Of me infatuate thou art,
     From me thou canst not rest!

My five engirdling battlements
   Are all besieged by Thee;
The Ear, the Eye, Taste, Smell, and Touch,
   By Love, mine Enemy:
   If I come forth I cannot flee,
     Nor hide me from Thy quest.

If I come forth by way of Sight,
   Love, Love is all around;
In radiance painted on the skies.
   In colour on the ground:
   They plead with me, in beauty drowned,
     To take Thee to my breast

If I come forth by Hearing's gate,
   O what is this I hear?
What is this woven mist of sound
   That breaks upon mine ear?
   Here's no escape! Thy voice is clear,—
     'Tis Love, in music drest.

If I come forth by way of Taste,
   In savours Thou art set;
That Love Divine, Who craves for me,
   And snares me in His net,

---

[79] Jacopone Da Todi, "How the Soul Finds God in All Creatures by Means of the Senses," *Lauda LXXXII*, in Evelyn Underhill, *Jacopone Da Todi: Poet and Mystic, 1228–1306; A Spiritual Biography*, Italian text translated into English verse by Mrs. Theodore Beck (London, Toronto: J. M. Dent & Sons Ltd.; New York, E. P. Dutton & Co., 1919), 443–45, available at *Internet Archive*, http://www.archive.org/details/jacoponedatodipo00underich, accessed October 2, 2011 (this work is in the public domain).

Prisons me close, and closer yet.
    To be His child and guest.

If I come forth by way of Smell,
    Thine odours sweet and fine
In every creature I perceive.
    And every one divine;
    Thy spears they are, to make me Thine,
      They wound at Thy behest.

If I come forth by way of Touch,
    On every creature fair
In sacred awe I lay my hands.
    For Thou art sculptured there;
    'Twere madness, Love, this way to dare
      Escape Thy sweet conquest.

O Love, why do I flee from Thee?
    Why should I fear to yield?
Because Thou wouldst re-make my heart,
    In fires of love annealed?
    No more myself, in Thee concealed,
      And by Thy love possessed.

I, if I see another moved
    The downward step to make,
I am made partner of his loss,
    I suffer for his sake:
    Whom, Love Unmeasured, dost *Thou* take
      To Thy compassion blest?

Lead me to Christ, Who died for me,
    Draw me from sea to shore:
And make me mourn in penitence
    The wounds and griefs He bore:
    Why did He suffer pains so sore?
      That I might be at rest.

Sources for Further Study

Cirino, Andre, and Joseph Raischl. *The Journey into God: A Forty-Day Retreat with Bonaventure, Francis, and Clare*. Cincinnati, OH: St. Anthony Messenger Press, 2002.

Delio, Ilia. *Simply Bonaventure: An Introduction to His Life, Thought, and Writings*. New York: New City Press, 2001.

Hayes, Zachary. *Bonaventure: Mystical Writings*. A Spiritual Legacy Book. New York: Crossroad Publishing Company, 1999.

Hayes. Zachary. *The Hidden Center: Spirituality and Speculative Christology in St. Bonaventure*. St. Bonaventure, NY: The Franciscan Institute, 1992.

Part 4

Blessed John Duns Scotus:
One in a Million

Chapter 6

Sacred Subtle Thoughts Concerning Creation

Introduction: The Subtle Doctor[1]

John Duns Scotus was born in 1265 at Duns, Berkwickshire, Scotland. Named after St. John the evangelist, he was raised in a devout Christian family, frequenting the Abbey of Melrose for catechism classes. In 1280 he completed the novitiate of the Franciscan Friars Minor at Dumfries, Scotland. Following his ordination to the priesthood in 1291 by the bishop of Lincoln, England, he studied philosophy at Cambridge and then at Oxford. He lectured on the *Sentences* of Peter Lombard at Oxford until 1302, then traveled to Paris for further study. In June of 1303 he was banished from France because he objected to an appeal by King Philip IV to oppose Pope Boniface VIII. He was likely at Oxford until April of 1304. The banishment did not hold, however, and he returned to Paris and was named regent master in theology in 1305. He lectured in Paris until his relocation to Cologne, Germany, in 1307 to take charge of the Franciscan House of Studies. On November 8, 1308, John Duns Scotus died in Cologne at the young age of forty-two.

---

[1] Large portions of this chapter previously appeared in my book *The Franciscan View of the Human Person: Some Central Elements*, The Franciscan Heritage Series, vol. 3 (St. Bonaventure, NY: The Franciscan Institute, 2005), 45–62, and are published here with permission.

Something about Blessed John Duns Scotus's Thought

Scotus: True Son of St. Francis

Because of the precise and subtle philosophical distinctions that define his work, John Duns Scotus became known as the "Subtle Doctor." His thought frequently combined philosophical ideas and theological notions, integrating them to form a new understanding. Yet he is a true son of St. Francis and St. Clare. As English Scotus scholar Séamus Mulholland puts it, John Duns Scotus might be called "the metaphysical wing of St. Francis."[2] Indeed, any careful reading of John's work readily reveals that love dominates. His conclusions are colored with Franciscan spirituality, expressed in metaphysical terms. Scotus is a person who is in love with Love, and his ultimate purpose in his thinking and writing is union with God. Scotus is not an emotionless, sterile thinker but rather one utterly amazed at the intensity of God's love revealed in creation, the Scriptures, theology, and ultimately in Christ. He indeed had a beautiful mind that enabled him to express truths about God, creatures, creation, and the cosmos in the language of metaphysics with the same passion and brilliance as we find in the poetic and mystical language of St. Francis or St. Bonaventure.

Scotus: Metaphysician

Metaphysics is a specialized area of the study of philosophy.[3] The term "philosophy" literally means "love of knowledge" or "love of wisdom" (from the Greek *philosophia*). So, philosophy is the investigation of the nature, causes, and principles of human existence. In their pursuit of knowledge, philosophers use logical reasoning rather than empirical investigation (learning from either sensory or internal experiences). The term "metaphysics" is a word that was originally used by editors to describe a section of the writings of the Greek philosopher Aristotle (384–22 BCE). The editors called that chapter *Metaphysika* because it came before his chapter on the science of physics. The Greek word *metaphysika* literally means "after physics." Since Aristotle's *Metaphysika* addressed

---

[2] See "Christ: The *Haecceitas* of God; The Spirituality of John Duns Scotus' Doctrine of *Haecceitas* and the Primacy of Christ," in *Franciscan Theology of the Environment: An Introductory Reader*, ed. Dawn M. Nothwehr (Quincy, IL: Franciscan Press, 2002), 307.

[3] See John T. Ford, ed., *St. Mary's Press Glossary of Theological Terms*, Essentials of Catholic Theology Series (Winona, MN: St. Mary's Press, 2006), 118, 120, 144.

the *nature of being*, that specialty area of philosophy became known as metaphysics. Metaphysics deals with *the study of being* in its most foundational aspects of *matter* and *form* (*matter* = the stuff out of which an object is made; *form* = the way in which an object is made). Metaphysicians understand *matter* to be the potential or underlying reality, while *form* is what individualizes or actualizes matter.

In this chapter we will encounter many words that describe God, creatures, creation, and the cosmos in philosophical, particularly metaphysical, terms. In this sense, reading this chapter may take a little extra effort. However, every effort will be made to assist readers by defining and explaining the more technical words as they appear in the remainder of this chapter. This effort will be well worthwhile, however, because Franciscan metaphysician John Duns Scotus has important ideas for ecotheology for today. Like Francis and Bonaventure before him, he recognized God as the creator of all and therefore saw creation as a source of God's self-revelation. Yet Scotus came to that understanding in his own unique way, and his reflections provide distinct insights that can assist us as we wrestle with our current ecological crisis.

Scotus: Realist

GOD AS FIRST PRINCIPLE

In order to comprehend how John Duns Scotus saw the created world (including humans) we need first to understand his view of God's relationship to creation, the value placed on the created world in general, and the dignity of creation overall. As Franciscan theologian Kenan B. Osborne explains, Scotus was a Christian realist who understood that everything in the created world somehow had its source in God.[4] Scotus began his reflections with empirical (experiential) observation of the created world in its totality, trying to find what he could discover through observation and experience. He accepted that reality includes the natural environment—its physical nature, its vegetative and animal life—as well as good and evil, virtue and sin, the angelic and the demonic. He then asked what kind of a credible God would allow this wildly diverse reality to exist. What does all of this tell us about God?

---

[4] Kenan B. Osborne, "Incarnation, Individuality, and Diversity," in *Franciscan Theology of the Environment*, ed. Nothwehr, 296–97.

As a Christian, he realized that there was *nothing* that remained forever and that *everything* was ultimately dependent on God for its life and existence. He expressed this insight in the metaphysical notion of *contingency*, that is, the reality that things or situations don't have to exist *at all*, nor do they need to exist *as* they exist; they *are utterly dependent on something else or someone* else to bring them to life or make them happen. For example, a rose could be red, yellow, or pink. If the gardener does not water the rosebush, it will die; or the gardener may care for the rose so well that it wins a prize at a garden show. On the other hand, there is only so much the gardener can do to make a rose grow in a particular way; all else depends on its God-given capacity to live and grow. Scotus reasoned that *if* something *exists* (e.g., a stone), that means that it is somehow *possible* for it *to* exist if the conditions are right (e.g., lava cools and becomes obsidian). He traced backward through a series of causes that could make something exist or happen until he reached the ultimate point of origin where a Being existed, but it had no cause, yet it had the potential to cause other things, and he ended up with *only* God. For Scotus, the only being that is *not contingent* but uncaused and *necessary* is God.

God is *necessary* simply because there is *nothing* that could bring about God or "make God happen." The Divine exists because God *chooses* to exist, and the creation exists because God artistically, freely, and lovingly calls it into being in the act of creation. That God is *love* is most important for Scotus, and for us.[5] Because God is absolutely free, God is absolutely loving and this love is absolutely immanent (present, here with us). As long as anything exists, God is present to sustain it.

God is not known only through empirical observation (human experience) but also through divine revelation (e.g., Sacred Scripture). The vast diversity of creation leads Scotus to a wonderful conclusion, namely, that the God revealed in such a creation is the First Principle and is absolutely *necessary*,[6] yet utterly *free*, and the created world is equally utterly *contingent*.[7] Such an utterly free God did not *have* to do anything! Just think of it—everything we have ever known and loved did not have

Only, God is not contingent —

[5] Ibid., 299.

[6] Something that is *necessary* is characterized by the impossibility of it being otherwise.

[7] Something that is *contingent* is something that is liable to happen but not certain to happen; it could happen or not depending on the circumstances. The *contingent* includes all those things that are not necessary and that are not impossible.

contingency
Way do I exist rather than not being alive at all?

to be created, including you and me! In fact, the entire created world is pure grace and gift! This stands in contrast with the watchmaker or machine models of the origins of the universe proposed by the Enlightenment philosophers or Deists of the past.

GOD IS THE LOVING CREATOR

Further, as Osborne points out, Scotus holds that God has primacy in three ways: efficiency, finality, and eminence.[8] God is *necessary* simply because there is *nothing* that could bring about God or "make God happen." However, what is most important for Scotus (and for us) is that God is more than the "uncaused cause" of created things; God is *love*.[9] Because God is absolutely free, God absolutely loves and this love is absolutely eminent. For our purposes, this insight speaks loudly to the kind of attitude we need to have in relation to the created world. If the entire creation (ourselves included) is God's free gift of love, how dare we abuse it? If in absolute divine freedom God generously provides such vast diversity and abundance in creation, how dare we withhold what is needed for the flourishing of our human sisters and brothers *and* of entire ecosystems? At present, many of the world's economic systems operate on the presupposition of scarcity with an eye only toward satisfying the greed of a few human elites who profit from the mining or harvesting of particular elements of the earth's wealth.

GOD CREATED TO MAKE HIS GLORY KNOWN

Scotus explains the kind of power that God has and discusses how that power was used to bring about the creation. God's power is manifested in two ways: first, *potentia absoluta* allows God to act with indifference (not be influenced by anyone or anything) toward creation. This power could seem threatening and not typical of someone who loves. However, because God *is always* loving and rational, the exercise of

---

[8] Osborne, "Incarnation, Individuality, and Diversity," 298. John Duns Scotus understands God as the "First Principle." This means that God is the cause of all that is (efficiency), the purpose and ultimate end for everything that exists (finality), and the first or best in the order of relative perfection (eminence).

[9] Ibid., 299. Aristotle's "uncaused cause" was abstract and characterized as eternal, self-sufficient, self-moving, one, completely actualized, immaterial, good, unchanging, immutable, Divine Mind.

God's absolute freedom is expressed in God's absolute freedom + love —

divine power *is always* rational and loving and never arbitrary. *Potentia ordinata* refers to what God has chosen to do or has in fact done, and so it requires conformity to rules predetermined by divine wisdom or motivated by the divine will.[10] To be sure, things work the way God created them to work, and God respects the requirements of this world because they express the divine creative intent. This consistency in God and in God's actions serves as an affirmation of humanity that inspires trust, fidelity, and orderliness, making possible a loving human-divine relationship. Divine revelation and personal accounts of salvation history witness to the fact that God *is loving and faithful* through all times and circumstances. So in short, God chose to create to make his glory known (Eph 1:3-10). Such an utterly free God did not *have* to do anything. Indeed, the entire created world is pure grace and gift given out of love and to express love.

HAECCEITAS

There is one very important aspect of creation that is the focus of Scotus's attention and that profoundly reveals the great dignity of God's creation. The Subtle Doctor claims that in order for one subject (person, thing, or idea) to be related to another, it must *first* be known and understood for what it is *in itself*. Scotus's principle of *haecceitas*[11] (individuation or "thisness") provides the philosophical foundation for everything in created reality to be specified (identified as specific entities). As Osborne points out, "Scotus makes the claim that individuation must be based in the very substance of a thing or a person, not in some acci-

---

[10] John Duns Scotus, *Ordinatio*, III.37, trans. Allan B. Wolter, *Duns Scotus on the Will and Morality* (Washington, DC: Catholic University of America Press, 1986), 269. See also John Dun Scotus, *Tractatus de primo principio*, 4.15, in *John Duns Scotus: A Treatise on God as First Principle*, 2nd ed., trans. Allan B. Wolter (Chicago: Franciscan Herald Press, 1981), 82; and John Duns Scotus, *Ordinatio*, I.4, 4 trans. Wolter, *Will and Morality*, 255.

[11] *John Duns Scotus: God and Creatures, The Quodlibetal Questions*, paperback ed., trans., Felix Alluntis and Allan B. Wolter (Washington, DC: Catholic University of America Press, 1981), "Glossary," 511: "*Haecceitas* (from the Latin *haec*, this): The term means literally, 'thisness.' It designates the unique formal principle of individuation that makes the nature, which all individuals of the same species have in common, to be just this or that individual and no other. Scotus regards it as a distinct positive formality over and above the common nature of the individual (*natura communis*)."

dental aspect of a thing or person."[12] *Haecceitas* makes a singular thing what it is and differentiates it from all other things (of common nature) to which it may be compared (because of its commonality).[13]

For example, the principle of *haecceitas* holds that if I have a bouquet of twenty-two flowers (items of a common nature) made up of roses and daisies, I not only have a bouquet (things of a common nature), roses (that can be compared because of their commonality), and daisies (that can be compared because of their commonality), but I have *twelve distinct individual flowers* (that we judge to be enough alike as to call them roses) and *ten distinct individual flowers* (that we judge to be enough alike as to call them daisies). In Scotus's thought a rose is a rose, and not a daisy; and each rose or each daisy is distinct from every other rose and every other daisy! So too it is with all of creation, including human beings. Each person (or thing or idea) is unique in all time and eternity; there never has been nor will there ever be another human being identical to you or me—no, not even a clone! A human person's identity cannot be reduced to her or his physical makeup or current embodied existence. As Mary Beth Ingham so aptly puts it:

> *Haecceitas* points to the ineffable within each being. The sacredness of each person, indeed of each being is philosophically expressed in this Latin term. According to Scotus, the created order is not best understood as a transparent medium through which divine light shines (as Aquinas taught), but is itself endowed with an inner light that shines forth from within. The difference between these two great scholars can be compared to the difference between a window (Aquinas) and a lamp (Scotus). Both give light, but the source of light for

---

[12] Osborne, "Incarnation, Individuality, and Diversity," 301. The *substance* of a thing is the real essence of that thing, without which that thing would not exist and would not be what it is. The *accidental aspect* of a thing is the quality of a thing that is not essential to a thing's true nature, is not needed by the thing in order to be what it is, and cannot be inferred from the essential nature of that thing—for example, the red color of an apple.

[13] Eric Doyle, "Duns Scotus and Ecumenism," in *De Doctrina Ioannis Duns Scoti*, vol. III of *Acta Congressus Scotistici Internationalis Oxonii et Edimburgi*, September 11–17, 1966, celebrati, ed. Camille Bérubé (Roma: Cura Commissionis Scotisticae, 1968), 460: "The uniqueness, the unrepeatable something of all things, is what gives them their intrinsic and eternal value. There is about everything, every person, an originality that gives new insight into reality, another aspect that has never been seen before. Each person enters into a new enriching relationship of knowledge and love with every new person met, with every new thing encountered."

> Scotus has already been given to the being by the creator. Each being
> within the created order already possesses an immanent dignity; it
> is already gifted by the loving Creator with sanctity beyond our
> ability to understand.[14]

Not only does the entire creation have dignity because of its vastness
and diversity; it is profoundly valued for its particularity—each being
in itself. Thus, from observing creation and from divine revelation Scotus
uncovers a Creator who is powerful, artistically free, loving, and who
sustains creation in general and in particular in an ordered, absolutely
loving way. Most important for our purposes is that *haecceitas* makes it
possible for each person, plant, animal, and earth or cosmic element (or
idea) to be distinct from one another. Without individuation, in which
there are at least two distinct entities, no authentic relationships—inter-
personal or otherwise—are possible.

The implications that *haecceitas* holds for ecology and environmental
ethics are vast; consider biodiversity issues, for example.[15] *Haecceitas*
potentially affects human relating in general because it affects how we
understand contingent reality as thoroughly laced with God's absolutely
free and loving intent. Humans are created by God with freedom to
choose good or evil, right or wrong, yet are unconditionally loved by
God. Humans are not loved by God simply as a species, but each is loved
in her or his person—in her or his individual essence. Just as human
value is enhanced by such intimate regard, so too the value of all elements of the cosmos is revered. Not only is each element of the cosmos
different in its accidental characteristics, but each is distinct in its very
essence. If this is the case, then for Christians, issues of biodiversity must
be considered in this light. Not only are entire species of great worth;
each particular being is valued in particular for its own sake.

INTENDED BEFORE ALL TIME:
THE INCARNATION AS GOD'S MASTERPIECE

But Scotus's insights draw us into an understanding of God that is
deeper still. The reality of the humanity of Jesus as revealed in Scripture

---

[14] Mary Beth Ingham, *Scotus for Dunces: An Introduction to the Subtle Doctor* (St.
Bonaventure, NY: The Franciscan Institute, 2003), 55.

[15] For an excellent discussion on biodiversity and Christian ethics, see Kevin J.
O'Brien, *An Ethics of Biodiversity: Christianity, Ecology, and the Variety of Life* (Washington, DC: Georgetown University Press, 2010).

is also included in the reality with which Scotus dealt. Without a doubt, the most profound and perfect self-revelation of God took place in the incarnation. God, the divine Artist, conceived of the best way in which the fullness of divine glory could be shared. Before the beginning of time, and like a diligent artist who envisions a gorgeous landscape and then begins to execute the design by creating the background that will support the whole of the work, so too, before the beginning of time, Scotus contends, God freely planned the incarnation.[16] This teaching is known as the primacy and predestination of Christ (Eph 1:3-10; Col 1:15-18). In a sense we can say that Jesus Christ is "the *haecceitas* of God"—God's Masterpiece!

Simply stated, according to Scotus, the reason for the incarnation, in the first place, was God's free and eternal decision to have (outside himself) someone who could love him perfectly. Through the humanity of Jesus, God expressed the absolutely free divine desire to communicate divine love in a contingent and finite world.

And so it was that the world was created through the Word (John 1:1-18). Humans were created as those having the capacity to respond freely to God's invitation and who are capable of entering into a personal relationship with God and one another. As Scotus sees it, humans were not only created in the image and likeness of God (*imago Dei*); they were also created in the image of the incarnate Son (*imago Christi*). Just as Bonaventure taught, Scotus also sees Christ as the pattern after which all creation is fashioned. Like the Seraphic Doctor, Bonaventure, the Subtle Doctor holds that progress in the spiritual life is a process of *christification* as well as *deification*; the more Christ-like one becomes, the more God-like one is. Indeed, human union with God is mediated (made possible) through the incarnation.

The Subtle Doctor joins a long line of Franciscan scholars in maintaining that the Word would have become incarnate even if *Adam* had not sinned.[17] *Adam*'s sin was not the sine qua non for the incarnation. In

[16] Scotus's position on the incarnation is articulated in his *Reportatio* and *Ordinatio*, III.7.3. See Allan B. Wolter, "John Duns Scotus on the Primacy and Personality of Christ," in *Franciscan Christology: Selected Texts, Translations and Essays*, ed. Damian McElrath, Franciscan Sources, no. 1 (St. Bonaventure, NY: Franciscan Institute Publications, 1980), 147–55. See also Antonio Aranda, "La Cuestión Teológica de la Encarnatión del Verbo: Relectura de Tres Posiciones Características," *Scripta Theologica* 25 (1993): 49–94.

[17] See Robert North, "The Scotist Cosmic Christ," in *De Doctrina Ioannis Duns Scoti*, vol. III, 194–98. The following are positions of key Franciscans concerning the reason

Scotus's view, the incarnation was not necessitated by human choice to sin, for that would effectively subject God (who is absolutely free) to the permission of sin. Also, if the incarnation had been the result of sin, contrary to charity, humans would have reason to rejoice at the sinfulness of others.[18]

Rather, the incarnation represents the manifestation of God's eternal glory and God's intent to raise human nature to the highest point of glory by uniting it with divine nature. Understood in this way, the incarnation is a paradigm for divine-human mutuality. As Mary Elizabeth Ingham stresses, "Mutuality between God and humanity was foreseen from eternity, begun in the Incarnation and is to be fully realized in the future when Christ will be 'all in all.' The summit of creation is the communion of all persons with one another and with God. . . . Christ is the very person in whom the human and divine achieve mutuality."[19] Christ embodies the divine message that human actions are pleasing to God, human persons are pleasing to God, and humans are loved by God. The fact that, according to Scotus, God's freedom and liberality inspired the incarnation provides a positive enhancement of human nature that is not possible in a sin-centric understanding of the doctrine. God, in Scotus's view, is a creative artist who selected the human nature as the "material" most fitting to receive the highest glory of subsisting in the person of the Word.[20] But humans are not the only elements of creation

---

for the incarnation: Alexander of Hales (1200)—it would have been suitable had there been no sin; Matthew of Aquasparta (1282)—it was supposed for the perfection of the natural order; Raymond of Lull (1289)—its primary aim was to show forth the love of God; Roger Marston and William of Ware both believed it would have taken place "apart from sin"; Bonaventure affirmed that either position was orthodox, but he opted for the traditional Anselmian solution that held sin as the cause.

[18] John Duns Scotus, *Ordinatio*, III, d. 7, in *Four Questions on Mary*, 25, cited in Ingham, *Scotus for Dunces*, 77.

[19] Mary Elizabeth Ingham, "Integrated Vision," in *The History of Franciscan Theology*, ed., Kenan B. Osborne (St. Bonaventure, NY: The Franciscan Institute, 1994), 222.

[20] John Duns Scotus, *Ordinatio*, III.7, q. 3, trans. Wolter, "On the Primacy," 151: "Now the sequence in which the creative artist evolves his plan is the very opposite of the way he puts it into execution. One can say, however, that in the order of execution, God's union with a human nature is really prior to his granting it the greatest grace and glory. We could presume, then, that it was in the reverse order that he intended them, so that God would first intend that some nature, not the highest, should receive the highest glory, as he bestowed natural perfection. Then secondly, as it were, he willed that this nature should subsist in the Person of the Word, so that the angel might not be subject to a [mere] man."

that are positively affected. Because Jesus Christ became part of this material created universe, the entire cosmos is divinely affirmed. Understood in this way, the incarnation is a paradigm for human beings and all of created reality as partners with God in the ongoing cocreation and coredemption of the world.

One strong implication for ecology suggested by this understanding of the incarnation is that humans have a particularly Christ-like role to play in the cosmos. That role is to love God and everything in the entire cosmos, which is God's self-expression. Because the entire cosmos in some way resembles Christ, the "first born of all creation" (Col 1:15-20), we must cherish creation with reverent care, just as we reverence Christ. This is the finest example of authentic church teaching known as *panentheism.*[21]

From the Writings of John Duns Scotus

De primo principio [A Treatise on God as First Principle], *I, 1.1–2*[22]

1.1   May the First Principle of things grant me to believe, to understand and to reveal what may please his majesty and may raise our minds to contemplate him.

1.2   O Lord our God, true teacher that you are, when Moses your servant asked you for your name that he might proclaim it to the children of Israel, you, knowing what the mind of mortals could grasp of you, replied: "I am who am," thus disclosing your blessed name. You are truly what it means to be, you are the whole of what it means to exist. This, if it be possible for me, I should like to know by way of demonstration. Help me then, O Lord, as I investigate how much our natural reason can learn about that true being which you have predicated of yourself.

[21] Panentheism is the belief that all things are imbued with God's being in the sense that all things are *in* God. God is more than all that is and is a consciousness and the highest unity possible.

[22] John Duns Scotus, *John Duns Scotus: A Treatise on God as First Principle*, trans. Wolter, 3.

Reflection and Application

A Spirituality of Haecceitas

Scotus scholar Séamus Mulholland claims that Scotus's doctrine of *haecceitas*, the primacy and predestination of Christ, and Scotus's other teachings bear implications for Christian spirituality. This is particularly significant because, as we have suggested, much of the ecological crisis has roots in the spiritual malaise of our time. At the heart of each of these understandings is God, who is love. Mulholland states, "They [the teachings] are the conclusions of a man of prayer and deep spiritual serenity, for in Scotus, the ultimate aim of all theology is union with God and this is also the ultimate aim of spirituality."[23]

In absolute freedom "God's will is that he be loved outside himself by someone who can love perfectly. He foresees the intensity of the union between Christ and himself who loves him *as* he loves himself. Christ therefore, one concludes from this, is the center of all creation, all of which has its beginning, source, and end in the love God has for himself in Christ most perfectly."[24] This activity unfolds a story of love, intimacy, union, redemption, acceptance, gratitude, goodness, and creation. Creation, Christ, and the human family are formed in love and drawn toward the end of ultimate union with God.

But it is to a very specific and individual intimacy that we are drawn. Scotus's *haecceitas* "concerns itself . . . with the absolute unique individual distinction of originality that is the result of God's free loving creative activity and effects every animate and inanimate thing."[25] It is in this utter uniqueness that God loves each and every thing for its own sake in and of itself. There is no insignificant being! A spirituality based on "thisness" calls forth a profound regard for life, hope, and respect for the uniqueness of God's creation and the ever-present love of God.

It is this spiritual celebration of *God's freely expressed love in creation* and the primacy of Christ that Franciscan theologian William Short finds in

---

[23] Séamus Mulholland, "Christ: the *Haecceitas* of God; The Spirituality of John Duns Scotus' Doctrine of *Haecceitas* and the Primacy of Christ," in *Franciscan Theology of the Environment*, ed. Nothwehr, 307.

[24] Ibid., 309. See Scotus's full teaching on the predestination of Christ in John Duns Scotus, *Opera Omnia*, editio nova, 26 vols. (Parisiis: L. Vivès, 1895; Farnborough, England: Gregg International Publishers, 1969). See especially *Ordinatio*, III, d. 7 (Vivès edition, XIV, 348–49, 354–55) and *Reportatio Parisiensis*, III, d. 7, q. 4 (Vivès edition, XXIII, 301–4).

[25] See *Reportatio Parisiensis*, III, d. 7, q. 4 (Vivès edition, XXIII, 310–11).

the poetry of Gerard Manley Hopkins: "The world is charged with the grandeur of God."[26] As the firstborn of all creation, Christ is the model after which all the created world is fashioned. The materiality of Jesus and the materiality of all of creation alike are the result of the absolutely free, loving expression of God. As Short points out, as each distinct created thing or person lives, each enacts itself. In the process of each being enacting itself into existence, each thing or person is simultaneously enacting or manifesting something of Christ (in his human materiality).[27]

Scotus's understanding of nature stands in contrast to other scholastics, such as Thomas Aquinas, whose "theory of the analogy of being . . . held that true being exists only in God and all other being is derivative, pointing toward true being, but only weakly and indirectly."[28] Scotus's *theory of the univocity of being* holds that each created being in its own singular manner expresses the total image of the Creator.[29] So when we observe the natural world or other persons, we see "things are/do themselves. That doing/being themselves is their doing/being Christ."[30]

In contrast to Thomas Aquinas's view that things have two components, matter and form, Scotus claims everything has a third component: "this" (*haec*).[31] "Here is the corollary of the incarnation—God became *this* Jewish carpenter: this unique, unrepeatable, specific creature is the incarnate Creator. From this belief one can conclude that things are God-like in their specificity. Things deserve the respect of our attention, for whatever *is* is because of Christ."[32]

[26] William Short, "Pied Beauty: Gerard Manley Hopkins and the Scotistic View of Nature," in *Franciscan Theology of the Environment*, ed. Nothwehr, 316. Short quotes from "God's Grandeur, #8," in *Poems and Prose of Gerard Manley Hopkins*, ed. W. H. Gardner (New York: Penguin Books, 1985). Hopkins was greatly influenced by the theology and philosophy of John Duns Scotus.

[27] Short, "Pied Beauty," 317.

[28] Ibid.

[29] See Ingham, *Scotus for Dunces*, at 320–21: "Univocity of being—The concept being (*ens*) is univocal according to Scotus. This refers to the common, indistinct concept of which the mind is aware in knowing anything at all. *Being* is the most basic and virtual aspect of anything known; it is the *not-nothing*. Scotus affirms that were being not univocal in this way, the human mind would have no natural knowledge of God, nor would Theology have any claim to scientific status."

[30] Ibid., 319.

[31] Ibid., 320.

[32] Ibid.

Essential Order: Human and Divine Relationship Made Possible

As Scotus sees it, both in creation and through salvation history God sets out a design for human life to be lived in relationship with the Divine and with others. In fact, Scotus's principle of *essential order* gives an explanation of this design, using the language of metaphysics. Another way to talk about this relational design is to use the language of *natural law*. Reasoning human beings can observe a kind of order in the created world without any kind of special divine revelation. People can see cycles in nature, or they might observe that treating human beings in a disrespectful manner lowers their self-esteem, perhaps even leading them to a psychotic break.

However, Scotus explains that the Scriptures (revelation) fine-tune what we can know from the natural law about relationships with God and with other creatures and place it in the context of God's love for humanity. Thus, there is a qualitative difference in how we live. In light of God's love for us, we need to consider not only whether an action is reasonable (rational judgment) but also whether the act is motivated by love (affective motivation). For example, at Christmastime, Person A may donate to the Boys and Girls Club because she genuinely cares about the quality of life children have, especially poor children. This is a reasonably good thing to do. In another instance, Person B, who is a caring person, wants to make life better for poor children. However, she knows some of the children because she meets them on her way to work every day. She has grown attached to them, and though she can't afford to give each child what she or he might need, she knows they all participate in the Boys and Girls Club. Thus, she can help all of them by giving to the club. In either scenario, a good deed was done. However, the deed in the second scenario is qualitatively (subjectively) distinct from the first because Person B has a relationship with the children.

When Scotus discusses the summary of God's covenant with the people of Israel, given in the Ten Commandments, he explains that the first table (commandments 1–3) deals with our relationship with God, while the second table (commandments 4–10) deals with relationships between neighbors. The Franciscan claims that the meaning of the first three commandments is obvious to anyone who recognizes that God is the highest most perfect being—namely, that God is to be loved unconditionally (*Deus diligendus est*).[33] Significantly, the commandments of the second table could be known through the natural law. Yet if they are

---

[33] See *Ordinatio*, IV, d. 46, q. 1, n. 10.

understood in light of the first table, one can see that the reason we are to act lovingly toward our neighbors (including our other-than-human neighbors) is not because we are models of generosity or great humanitarians but rather because God deeply loves us and desires that we love one another. In this light, the Ten Commandments are no longer chapters of a legal code but themes of a love song about our relationship to God, neighbors, and all creatures.

Scotistic Ethics

HUMAN FREE WILL AND AFFECTIONS

A central notion of John Duns Scotus's ethical thought is that human persons are created by God and have free will. According to Scotus, our human will has two affections or orientations. The first, the affection for possession or happiness (*affectio commodi*), is directed inward at a healthy kind of self-preservation or happiness. This is not "selfishness" but rather a healthy kind of self-interest.[34] It is a mature self-esteem that enables and requires a person to grow in personal integrity and to place himself or herself in perspective with others, while not permitting disrespect or abuse.[35] The second, affection for justice (*affectio iustitiae*), is directed outward toward others and seeks what is just and to love each individual according to his or her worth (what is rightly due to them).[36] Right living requires that we balance these two affections when making choices about things that we do or things that will shape our character. If we do follow our affection for justice, Ingham states, "the result is a dynamic of mutual love and expanding inclusivity."[37] Such a stance would also enable us to live into the right relationships characteristic of the reign of God. This,

[34] See Ingham, *Scotus for Dunces*, 226: "*Affection for possessions/happiness (affectio commodi)*—Also from Anselm, this represents the natural disposition toward self-protection and perfection in every living being. In the will, this is the disposition whereby the will is drawn to love goods that bring pleasure and enjoyment to the self. It is the self-directed disposition that is perfected by hope."

[35] John Duns Scotus, *Ordinatio*, II, d. 6., q. 2., n. 8 (Vivès edition, 12:353), trans. Wolter, *Will and Morality*, 463.

[36] See Ingham, *Scotus for Dunces*, 225–26: "*Affection for justice (affectio iustitiae)*—Originally from Anselm, this represents the highest moral disposition whereby the will is drawn to love the good because of its intrinsic value . . . and not because of any personal gain. For Scotus, this affection constitutes the will's native freedom or innate liberty; it was not lost after the Fall. This disposition is perfected by charity."

[37] Mary Elizabeth Ingham, "A Certain Affection for Justice," *The Cord* 45/3 (1995): 15.

according to Ingham, would require each of us to develop *a self-reflexive stance* toward our own lives, *a critical awareness of injustice* around us, and the *courage to act as quickly as possible* on behalf of justice.[38]

HUMAN WILL AND FREEDOM OF CHOICE

In Scotus's ethical thought, the focus is on the human person. The objective of ethics (moral science) is the perfection of the moral person.[39] For Scotus, the *will* is the sole rational faculty capable of self-determination and self-movement. The *will* is a term for the human person's capacity for desires, loves, and choices.[40] It can will, nil, or refrain (affirm, renounce, or not make a choice) from passing judgment on any object.[41] The *intellect* is the term for the human cognitive capacity to know and to understand. While these faculties (powers) are formally distinct, they work together in the human process of choosing. Like a host who introduces a speaker to an audience, the *intellect* presents an idea or an object (that it has attained through either abstract or intuitive knowledge) to the *will*. The *will* then considers the possibilities and makes a choice. The significant point here is that the *will* also has access to the *intellect* in the process of choice making. Thus, we are able to place any one particular choice in perspective with other factors and choose intelligently and wisely. Scotus was clear that nothing outside of the *will* determines its choice. This means that even though humans can be forced to act against their *will*, each person is responsible for the choices he or she makes. Human freedom then is set in the context of moral rationality in the form of self-control and self-determination according to the light of reflection.[42]

---

[38] Ibid. Also see Mary Beth Ingham, "Presence, Poise, and Praxis: The Three-Fold Challenge for Reconcilers Today," *The Cord* 53/6 (2003): 303–14.

[39] *Ordinatio*, prol. 5, q. 1–2, n. 262 (Vatican I, 177.11–12).

[40] Ingham, *Scotus for Dunces*, 94. Ingham defines will and intellect in the context of faculty psychology.

[41] John Duns Scotus, *Quaestiones metaphysicam*, IX, q. 15, trans. Wolter, *Will and Morality*, 145–47. See also *Ordinatio*, IV.49.1.10, n. 10 (Vivès edition, 21:333b). Wolter views this position in light of self-determination or rational self-direction, which ideates the will from potency to act. See his essay "Native Freedom of the Will Key to the Ethics of Scotus," in Marilyn McCord Adams, ed., *The Philosophical Theology of John Duns Scotus* (Ithaca, NY: Cornell University Press, 1990), 152.

[42] Ingham, *Scotus for Dunces*, 96.

The morally good act and its circumstances are determined by the virtues of right reason or prudence and must be suitable to the agent, have a suitable object, and be performed under suitable circumstances (end, manner, time, and place).[43] Love for God is, for Scotus, the self-evident first principle of praxis (acting). He demonstrates in *De primo principio* that God is infinite being and therefore also infinite goodness.[44] Then he restates the Aristotelian/Stoic maxim "Good is to be pursued, evil avoided," as the theological principle *Deus diligendus est*—that God is to be loved is necessarily true because God is infinite goodness and as such is worthy of all love.

THE TRIUNE GOD:
A BASIS FOR ALL REALITY AND RELATIONSHIPS

For Scotus all of reality is better understood if we think about it in light of the Christian doctrine of the Trinity. He gives particular attention to the likenesses and differences between the activity of the Trinity *ad intra* and *ad extra*. The life of the Trinity *ad intra* is the internal aspect of trinitarian life (the necessary relationship of the Father, Son, and Holy Spirit with and among each other). The life of the Trinity *ad extra* is that aspect whereby the Trinity expresses its divine will, freely choosing to enact the creation, incarnation, and *acceptatio*.[45] Scotus asserts that the essence of God involves both aspects of trinitarian life, however.[46]

In Scotus's view, the basis for the relationship among the three persons reveals an important aspect of God's essence. Not only are there three

---

[43] John Duns Scotus, *Quodlibet*, 18.1.n.3–18.8 trans. Alluntis/Wolter, 400.

[44] John Duns Scotus, *Tractatus de primo principio*, 4.87–94, trans. Wolter, *First Principle*, 146–51. See also *Ordinatio*, III, suppl. d. 27, trans. Wolter, *Will and Morality*, 425: "As for the first, I say that to love God above all is an act conformed to natural right reason, which dictates that what is best must be loved most; and hence such an act is right in itself; indeed, as a first practical principle of action, this is something known *per se*, and hence its rectitude is self-evident. For something must be loved most of all, and it is none other than the highest good, even as this good is recognized by the intellect as that to which we must adhere the most."

[45] *Acceptatio* is the acceptance of a human act by God as a meritorious act.

[46] Of the two dimensions, the incommunicable (internal) dimension is seen as the logical *suppositum* that is necessary for the *ad extra* relationship. For a definition of the term *suppositum*, see Ingham, *Scotus for Dunces*, 230: "A general name for a *per se* being which has its ultimate actuality. In the case of a rational or intellectual nature, such a being is called a person. This term is a translation of *hypostasis*, the Greek term used to refer to the persons of the Trinity." See also her example at 110.

distinct persons in the Godhead, but the very interaction of those persons forms and shapes one another and actively gives each other life.[47] Scotus holds that each of the persons and the relationship or communion of the three persons are essential to the divine life.[48] There can be no relationship without at least two terms joined in interaction.[49] In his discussion in the fourth of the *Quodlibetal Questions*, Scotus is most clear about how God's essence is also communion.[50]

Scotus's discussion of the Trinity is significant for understanding that *mutuality* is fundamental to human relationship for several reasons. First, the Trinity can be understood as a model for human relations—all members of the Godhead are distinct and of equal value, but they share a mutually life-giving life with one another. Second, the individuality Scotus claims for each person of the Trinity provides the metaphysical basis for mutuality; the persons of the Trinity are constituted *as persons* through the relationship (*ad intra*) of mutuality. Insofar as the Trinity is a communion of persons that models the goal for human community, the Trinity exemplifies the relationship of mutuality as the ideal and goal of all human activity.[51]

SCOTISTIC WISDOM FOR SUSTAINABLE ECONOMIC LIFE

Scotus's understanding of trinitarian life is the basis for his understanding of the love of neighbor. While each person of the Trinity is distinct, each is constituted in relation to one another. This is also the case with human relationships: we become the persons we are because of the influences that shape us in relationship with one another, with God, and with the cosmos.

---

[47] In the *Lectura* discussion of *Ordinatio*, I.26 on the constitution of the Divine Persons, Scotus argues for some kind of constitutive cause for each person of the Trinity. By insisting on the integrity of each person of the Trinity in the absolute sense, he designates the basis upon which he can later assert that God's essence is also communion.

[48] Mary Elizabeth Ingham, "John Duns Scotus: An Integrated Vision," 213. Ingham cites *Lectura*, n. 54.

[49] Ingham, "Integrated Vision," 214. Ingham cites *Quodlibet*, 1, n. 3 (Alluntis 1:5–6), trans. Alluntis/Wolter, 6–7.

[50] Ingham, "Integrated Vision," 217. Ingham cites *Quodlibet*, 4, n. 28 (Alluntis 4:61), trans. Alluntis/Wolter, 103–4.

[51] Ingham, "Integrated Vision," 218.

At the heart of human relationships with God and one another is love—not a possessive, domineering, or jealous love but rather a dynamic, reciprocal love that empowers and enhances life. This love is expressive and inclusive.[52] Since the nature of the love of God requires that the lover seeks only what enhances the well-being of the beloved, we find that Scotus's understanding of love is not a minimalistic concern for the other. It is rather a radical, generous, overflowing identification with the needs of the other (including any beings or things considered of a lesser status) by the lover.

Now Scotus did not write a systematic treatise on society, politics, or economics. However, we find an interesting discussion in his treatise on the sacrament of penance. There he responds to the question of whether or not restitution is necessary prior to receiving the sacrament. Within this discussion, we also find his treatment of the origins of civil authority and of the use and ownership of property.[53] Scotus insists that the best form of government is a form in which the people who are the subjects of governance participate in determining its structure and give it authority over them.[54]

In the realm of economic life, Scotus's assumptions are that "the earth is the LORD's and all that is in it" (Ps 24:1) and that it is only human law that allows the existence of the concept of "mine" in the human vocabulary.[55] True to Francis of Assisi, who admonished that we live in the world as strangers and guests (see Lev 25:23), Scotus does not identify "use" with "ownership," even in the case of fungibles.[56] According to

---

[52] *Ordinatio* III.suppl.d.37.10, trans., Wolter, *Will and Morality*, 283: "Hence it follows that if God is to be loved perfectly and orderly, then the one loving God must will that his neighbor love God; but in so willing, he is loving his neighbor."

[53] *Ordinatio* IV, in *Duns Scotus' Political and Economic Philosophy: Latin Text and English Translation*, with introduction and notes by Allan B. Wolter (St. Bonaventure, NY: The Franciscan Institute, 2001).

[54] *Ordinatio* IV.1, trans. Wolter, *Duns Scotus' Political and Economic Philosophy*, 39.

[55] *Ordinatio* I, trans. Wolter, *Duns Scotus' Political and Economic Philosophy*, 35.

[56] *Ordinatio* IV.1, trans. Wolter, *Duns Scotus' Political and Economic Philosophy*, 51. Also see ibid., 105nn5–6. Also see St. Francis of Assisi, *Regula bulata* (1223), chaps. 5–6, trans. Regis J. Armstrong and Ignatius C. Brady, in *Francis and Clare: Complete Works*, The Classics of Western Spirituality (New York: Paulist Press, 1982), 140–41. Also see "Fungibility" in Wikipedia: "Fungibility is the property of a good or a commodity whose individual units are capable of mutual substitution, such as crude oil, wheat, precious metals, or currencies. For example, if someone lends another person a $10 bill, it does not matter if they are given back the same $10 bill or a different one, since currency is fungible; if someone lends another person their car, however, they

Scotus, money is to be viewed as a fungible because by its nature it is essentially a medium of exchange and is "consumed" in the process of exchange for other goods. Scotus also joined in the condemnation of usury.

While Scotus's approach to economics is simple, and seemingly even naïve for such a great thinker, in practice if his very basic principles were followed, they could radically and positively impact the quality of political and economic life. The participation of the governed in a context where there is no absolute ownership and where material wealth and goods are considered the generous bequest of God, the Gracious Host, suggests a radical contrast to our present-day political and economic reality. In Scotus we find acknowledgement of the contingent nature of wealth and a radical recognition of the sole purpose of material goods, namely, the divinely ordained well-being of the entire cosmos. Both political and economic decisions must be made through participation of the community, with the common good of the whole as the first and foremost criterion.

Also, at the heart of the economic and political philosophy of this Franciscan is the common good and a special consideration of the poor that acknowledges the interrelationship between ecology and economics. Because all humans are but caretakers and borrowers of a common creation—a generous gift from God—to use material goods unjustly is to effectively steal, especially from the poor. As current economic data bears out, the poor suffer the repercussions of injustice disproportionately. Thus, it is the poor who require repayment when circumstances prevent the person who has been wronged from being repaid directly.[57]

These very fundamental considerations that Scotus set forth are still basically true today. On October 24, 2011, The Pontifical Council for Justice and Peace issued a document entitled Towards Reforming the International Finance and Monetary Systems in the Context of Global and Public Authority.[58] In order for all the nations of the world to have

---

would not expect to be given back a different car, even of the same make and model, as cars are not fungible. It refers only to the equivalence of each unit of a commodity with other units of the same commodity. Fungibility does not describe or relate to any exchange of one commodity for some other, different commodity" (http:// en.wikipedia.org/wiki/Fungibility, accessed October 20, 2011).

[57] *Oridinatio* IV.4, trans. Wolter, *Duns Scotus' Political and Economic Philosophy*, 79–87.

[58] See the English translation of the document on the Vatican Radio web site: http://www.news.va/en/news/full-text-note-on-financial-reform-from-the-pontif, accessed November 6, 2011.

their fair share of the goods of creation, there needs to be a just distribution of wealth among the people across the globe. According to the council, this requires an ethic of solidarity:

> Recognizing the primacy of being over having and of ethics over the economy, the world's peoples ought to adopt an ethic of solidarity as the animating core of their action. This implies abandoning all forms of petty selfishness and embracing the logic of the global common good which transcends merely contingent, particular interests. In a word, they ought to have a keen sense of belonging to the human family which means sharing the common dignity of all human beings: "Even prior to the logic of a fair exchange of goods and the forms of justice appropriate to it, there exists something which is due to man because he is man, by reason of his lofty dignity."[59]

This ethic, along with the time-honored principle of subsidiarity that requires participation and involvement of people at the local level, enables adopting policies that care for the earth while providing sufficient goods for the health and well-being of all.

Importance of Scotistic Theology and Philosophy for Ecotheology

As we have already suggested, Mary Elizabeth Ingham proposes that Scotus is relevant for our day on several counts. His moral vision is rooted in an optimistic view of the human capacity to be morally active in the world. Our will for self-preservation and our affection for justice can work together to respond rationally to the command to love God, neighbor, and self. Scotus is also optimistic about creation. The created world has the all-powerful, free, generous love as its source. Thus, all reality is good and beautiful. The moral life involves everything that is in our environment and all our efforts to strengthen and enhance our mutual relations with it. Scotus's view is both organic and dynamic. All reality progresses through the present toward a future that potentially includes greater integration and awareness. Ingham concludes: "If relationship and mutuality are appropriate human goods, then they are

---

[59] Ibid., 5.

moral goals. Accordingly, all persons have a right to share equally in the resources of the earth."[60]

We can sum up the significance of John Duns Scotus's philosophy and theology for ecotheology and ethics as follows: God created the world in absolute freedom. But, more, God is love. Out of a desire to be loved perfectly, God chose the human form as the material in which to express the Masterpiece of creation, Jesus Christ. Each particular being in creation is an expression of God in its own right. The created world and all that is in it is good, and thus there is great hope for humans and the entire cosmos. In our ecologically threatened world, humans need to follow their affection for justice and inclination to live in mutual relation with all of creation. If we do this, we, like St. Francis, will be following in the footprints of Jesus as we find them in our world today.

Questions for Reflection and Discussion

1. According to Scotus, we know God through the univocity of being. How might this belief influence your understanding of creation?

2. Scotus held that God is both "absolutely necessary" and also "absolutely free." Discuss the implications of this belief for how we understand the created world.

3. How would Scotus answer the question "Why did God create?" Does our belief about the origin and reason for the existence of the created world make a difference in our treatment of the environment?

4. Recall Scotus's notion of *haeccietas* ("thisness"). Discuss your understanding of this principle and its relation to present-day issues of biodiversity.

5. What difference does Scotus's understanding of economics make in your approach to environmental issues?

[60] Ingham, "A Certain Affection for Justice," 18.

Suggestions for Action

1. Explore the Internet for the most recent data on biodiversity and extinction of species.

2. Explore the meaning of "common good" in Catholic social teaching. For example, see the web site of Catholics in Alliance for the Common Good, http://www.catholicsinalliance.org/whatisthecommongood.html.

3. Reflect on the ways you are drawn to more self-preserving actions and ways you are drawn to actions that serve others. How might God be calling you to further conversion of heart?

4. Make a list of plants, animals, and earth elements. Reflect on the reality that Scotus pointed out—each one originates in God.

5. Reflect on the power relationships in your life. How might you act to engage your personal power to influence others in a way that invites them into a mutual relationship (rather than exerting only power over them)?

Prayer[61]

O Lord, our God! You are one in nature. You are one in number. Truly have you said that besides you there is no God. For though many may be called gods or thought to be gods, you alone are by nature God. You are the true God from whom, in whom, and through whom all things are; you are blessed forever! Amen!

Sources for Further Study

Secondary Sources

Cross, Richard. *Duns Scotus*. New York: Oxford University Press, 1999.

---

[61] This prayer by John Duns Scotus appears at the end of his *De primo principio*, 4.94. See John Duns Scotus, *John Duns Scotus: A Treatise on God as First Principle*, trans. Wolter, 150.

————. *The Physics of Duns Scotus: The Scientific Context of a Theological Vision.* New York: Oxford University Press, 1998.

Ingham, Mary Beth. *The Harmony of Goodness: Mutuality and Moral Living According to John Duns Scotus.* Quincy, IL: Franciscan Press, 1996.

————. *Scotus for Dunces: An Introduction to the Subtle Doctor.* St. Bonaventure, NY: Franciscan Institute Publications, 2003.

Ingham, Mary Elizabeth. "John Duns Scotus: An Integrated Vision," in *The History of Franciscan Theology,* ed. Kenan B. Osborne. St. Bonaventure, NY: The Franciscan Institute, 1994.

Shannon, Thomas A. *The Ethical Theory of John Duns Scotus: A Dialogue with Medieval and Modern Thought.* Quincy, IL: Franciscan Press, 1995.

Shannon, Thomas A., and Mary Beth Ingham. "The Ethical Method of John Duns Scotus." *Spirit and Life* 3 (1993): 1–99.

Wolter, Allan Bernard, and Marilyn McCord Adams, eds. *The Philosophical Theology of John Duns Scotus.* Ithaca, NY: Cornell University Press, 1990.

Primary Sources in English Translation

John Duns Scotus. *John Duns Scotus: God and Creatures; The Quodlibetal Questions.* Paperback ed. Translated by Felix Alluntis and Allan B. Wolter. Washington, DC: Catholic University of America Press, 1981.

————. *John Duns Scotus: Political and Economic Philosophy.* Translated by Allan B. Wolter. St. Bonaventure, NY: The Franciscan Institute, 2001.

————. *John Duns Scotus: A Treatise on God as First Principle.* 2nd ed. Translated by Allan B. Wolter. Chicago: Franciscan Herald Press, 1981.

————. *John Duns Scotus on Divine Love: Texts and Commentary on Goodness, Freedom, God and Humans.* Edited by A. Voss, H. Veldhuis, E. Dekker, N. W. den Bok, J. A. Beck. Aldershot, England: Ashgate Publishing Limited, 2003.

Part 5

What Is Ours to Do: Urgent Issues

Chapter 7

Human-Caused Global Warming:
A Leper Awaiting Our Embrace

Introduction: Embracing a Leper

In St. Francis's day, lepers and leprosy presented complex and daunting public health issues that were not properly understood, even by experts. Therefore, lepers were feared, outcast, and denied their full dignity as human persons. Such anxiety-based hostile behavior insulted God's gift of the divine image that is found in each person and that is at the root of our human dignity. It was through St. Francis's actual encounter and embrace of a leper that he found his salvation and his true Christian identity. I believe that we are being called to make a similar embrace today. Just as through embracing the leper Francis learned the truth about that person, which enabled him to reverence the dignity of lepers and love them into life, we need to embrace the truth concerning our suffering planet Earth so that we can radically change our treatment of God's creation. We must stop abusing the delicate atmosphere and all the complex earth systems that are damaged when we continue to pour greenhouse gases (GHGs) into them with impunity. Just as Francis's entire life was changed by his embrace of the leper, so too must our lives be converted. Our conversion needs to be internal and spiritual, shifting our dispositions and attitudes, as well as external and moral, changing our behaviors and practices in daily life. We already know what needs to change. The question is, when will you and I make this embrace?

This chapter will no doubt be disturbing, but take courage and read on! Many would argue that "a gloom and doom approach" to the moral challenges of human-caused global warming is merely disempowering. But to this I reply that to see global climate change through "rose-colored glasses" is not only delusional—it is spiritually dangerous! It is to toy with sacrilege, to insult God and blaspheme God's gift of creation.

Facing the Raw Data of Human-Caused Global Warming

Human-induced global warming is occurring even as you read this sentence. Ninety-seven percent of climate scientists[1] agree that global warming is taking place and that it is largely caused by human activities and industries (4.85 out of 5 = 97 percent). Unfortunately, over the past several years, some well-funded and often self-interested people have denied any validity to the scientific data. "Disinformation" campaigns have been a major factor in developing public apathy in the face of this serious planetary crisis.[2] Ironically, that same public would buy mouthwash that claims to be recommended by four out of five (80 percent) dentists, or spend thousands of dollars on policies that insure against possible tragic events that are by far less likely to take place than human-caused climate change—which is already in progress!

Climate change is not "mad science."[3] Increasingly, even those "climate doubters" are admitting that the best science and the 97 percent of the world's climatologists are correct.[4] The critical story is told in the

---

[1] Climate is distinct from, though related to, weather. Climate is the long-term weather pattern of an area, including temperature, precipitation, and wind. For an explanation of the difference between weather and climate, see NASA, "What's the Difference between Weather and Climate?" http://www.nasa.gov/mission_pages /noaa-n/climate/climate_weather.html, accessed November 28, 2011.

[2] For examples of this disinformation, see the following: Rowan Hooper, "'Oil Giants' Money Fuels a Climate of Suspicion," *New Scientist*, 193/2586 (January 13, 2007): 14; Joseph Romm, "Big Oil Keeps Blowing Smoke," *U.S. News & World Report*, 147/4 (April 2010): 24; Rupert Murdoch, "The Disinformer," *Rolling Stone*, 1096 (January 21, 2010): 36; and "How ExxonMobil Manufactures Dissent," *Star Tribune* (Minneapolis, MN), January13, 2007.

[3] For a basic discussion of the fundamentals of global warming and climate change, see "Global Warming," http://en.wikipedia.org/wiki/Global_warming, accessed November 27, 2011.

[4] See Richard A. Muller of the Berkeley Earth Surface Temperature Organization at http://berkeleyearth.org/faq, accessed June 25, 2012.

Fourth Assessment Report of 2007 published by the United Nations Inter-governmental Panel on Climate Change (IPCC).[5]

Evidence of global warming is "unequivocal," with a more than 90 percent probability that humans are largely responsible. The main culprit is greenhouse gas from fossil fuels, which traps solar heat in the atmosphere, warming Earth's surface.

Levels of carbon dioxide (CO_2) have risen by about one-third since preindustrial times and are now at their highest in 650,000 years. They surged by 2.3 parts per million (ppm) between 2009 and 2010, according to the World Meteorological Organization (WMO). This was higher than the average in the 1990s (1.5 ppm) and in the past decade (2.0 ppm).

Between 1990 and 2010, there has been a 29 percent increase in "radiative forcing," meaning the warming effect on our climate system, the WMO says. CO_2 in the atmosphere will linger for decades to come, adding to warming even if all emissions stopped tomorrow.

Since 1900, the sea level has risen by ten to twenty centimeters (four to eight inches). Global average surface temperature has risen by 0.8°C (1.44°F). Average temperatures above land have risen far faster, by 0.91°C (1.64°F) since the mid-20th century, according to the Berkeley Earth Surface Temperature Project.[6]

Climate change is already visible in sea-level rise, loss of alpine glaciers and snow cover, shrinking Arctic summer sea ice, thawing permafrost, and poleward migration of many animals and plants toward cooler habitats.

By 2100, best estimates for the rise in global average surface temperatures run from 2.4–4.0°C (4.3–7.8°F), depending on fossil-fuel use. These figures also mask big variations, according to region and country.

In 2007 the IPCC projected sea levels will rise by at least eighteen centimeters (7.2 inches) by 2100. Since then, many studies point to the risk of melt-off from the Greenland and West Antarctic ice sheets. Most experts now say that, overall a one-meter (thirty-nine-inch) increase is plausible.[7]

---

[5] IPCC, *Climate Change 2007: Synthesis Report Summary for Policymakers,* http://www.ipcc.ch/publications_and_data/ar4/syr/en/spm.html, accessed November 27, 2011. Data below is taken from this report, unless indicated otherwise.

[6] See the report at the Berkeley Earth Surface Temperature Project, http://berkeleyearth.org/resources.php, accessed November 27, 2011.

[7] See, for example, the Pontifical Academy of Sciences report "Fate of Mountain Glaciers in the Anthropocene," May 11, 2011, http://www.vatican.va/roman_curia

Twenty to thirty percent of plant and animal species are threatened with extinction if average global temperatures increase by 1.5–2.5°C (2.7–4.5°F) compared to the average temperature during the two last decades of the twentieth century.

In Africa, by 2020 up to 75 to 250 million people will be exposed to increased water stress. Yields from rain-fed agriculture in some African countries could be reduced by up to 50 percent. Desert-like areas could expand by 5–8 percent by 2080.

In Asia, available fresh water will decrease by mid-century. Coastal megadeltas will be at risk from flooding due to rising seas. Mortality due to diseases associated with floods and droughts will increase.

Extreme weather events such as heat waves, droughts, and rainstorms are likely to become more frequent and/or intensive, according to an IPCC special report published on November 18, 2011.[8]

Stabilizing emissions at 445–535 ppm of CO_2 equivalent would limit the overall rise in global warming since preindustrial times to 2.0–2.8°C (3.6–5.0°F). Concentrations are currently 389 ppm. A level of 450 ppm corresponds roughly to the target of 2.0°C (3.6°F) embraced at the UN climate talks in Cancun in 2010.

Countries have to close a CO_2 "gigatonne gap" to meet the 2.0°C (3.6°F) target. Researchers at the Institute for Atmospheric and Climate Science at ETH Zurich calculate emissions would have to fall by 8.5 percent by 2020 compared to 2010 and then continue to decline.

So why should Christians care, and what can we do about it even if we do care? The short answer is this: we must act out of love for the poor and for the preservation of God's planet. For example, in Malawi, which is now experiencing more frequent droughts at unprecedented rates and less rainfall, a poor woman now needs to choose between already inadequate nutrition (food) and her children not going to school. And in Haiti or the Mekong Delta stronger and more frequent hurricanes deluge and destroy the meager existence people have been able to scrape together since the previous storm.

Those in more sophisticated and industrialized regions of the world are able to "adapt" by building reinforced houses or turning the ther-

---

/pontifical_academies/acdscien/2011/PAS_Glacier_110511_final.pdf, accessed June 25, 2012.

[8] Intergovernmental Panel on Climate Change, Working Group II, "Managing the Risks of Extreme Events and Disasters to Advance Climate Change Adaptation (SREX)," http://ipcc-wg2.gov/SREX, accessed June 25, 2012.

mostat up or down depending on the conditions, and life goes on relatively untouched! For the moment, we in North America have the luxury of being able to ignore climate change and the *real impact* that *our* pollution—and that of generations before us—causes to our precious atmosphere. That pollution affects what life is like across the globe. Compared to the devastation experienced by our sisters and brothers all over the world, we in the United States (and Europe) have had only a wee taste of what unchecked changing climate can bring about, through Hurricane Katrina or the wildfires that scorched the southwestern states in the summer of 2011 and the dust storms that continue to occur there.

As anyone who ever needed to evacuate a home or region due to a storm, drought, flood, or fire can testify, people in such conditions justly assert their human right to survive. But when there is no help in sight, the struggle for survival can turn into desperation, becoming vicious and violent. And, of course, those who do reach safe havens will put additional pressure on the available resources of the locale in which they find refuge. Thus, beyond the abuse of God's creation, human-caused global warming and climate change has a human face; and these are moral matters of justice. Indeed, these are spiritual matters for Christians that affect our journey toward salvation (see Matt 25:31-46). But how do we bring all of this to practical action? Let me begin with a story.

A Story

Susan Strauss tells of Gerry, who was walking with a Native American friend during the ruckus of a busy lunch hour in Washington, DC. The traffic—engines roaring, horns honking, and crowds bustling—made it difficult to hear anything else. In the middle of the traffic, Gerry's friend stopped and said, "Hey, a cricket!" "What?" said Gerry. "Yeah, a cricket," said his friend. "Here, look," and he pulled aside some bushes that separated the sidewalk from the government buildings. There in the shade was a cricket chirping away. "Wow," said Gerry, "How did you hear that with all this noise and traffic?" "Oh," said the native man. "It was the way I was raised . . . what I was taught to listen for. Here, I'll show you something." The native man reached into his pocket and pulled out a handful of coins—nickels, quarters, dimes—and dropped them on the sidewalk. Everyone who was rushing by stopped—to "listen."[9]

---

[9] Susan Strauss, *The Passionate Fact* (Golden, CO: North American Press, 1996), 9.

Our listening to the drone of the dominant, economistic, Western culture has deafened us to cricket chirps—to say nothing of the cries of our human sisters and brothers across the globe! Continuing to attend to the same old things in the same old ways will not enable us to adequately and ethically halt global warming! We must learn to value and attend to things differently.[10]

Ecological Conversion: From Carbon Footprints to "Footprints of Jesus"

Church teaching is clear about the immorality of damaging the environment and destroying the earth's ecosystems. The Vatican is exemplary as the only "carbon neutral" state on the planet! Remarkably, on March 10, 2008, Archbishop Girotti of the Vatican Office of the Apostolic Penitentiary listed "ecological offences" among the "new forms of social sin."[11] In their 2001 statement Global Climate Change: A Plea for Dialogue, Prudence, and the Common Good, the US bishops declare that people in the United States must make *significant* life changes toward halting global warming and do it now![12] All of this points directly to *ecological conversion* and a life of *Christian simplicity*. In fact, in 2001 the late Pope John Paul II called for "ecological conversion," a return to a relational vision and way of living.[13]

In light of all of this, first, we must admit our limitations and that—wittingly or not—we are complicit in ecological destruction. Then, when we pray for forgiveness—"for what I have *done* and what I have *failed to do*"—we need to consciously confess our "ecological offenses." Yet compounding and wallowing in our guilt alone will not resolve our dilemma. What *will* help us is to first come to better understand our spiritual, cultural, and intellectual resistances to paying attention to human-induced global warming, and then to take it seriously enough to make the necessary personal changes. Our moral disposition, attitude, and concrete daily

---

[10] Barbara Brandt, *Whole Life Economics* (Gabriola Island, BC: New Society, 1995). Economisim prizes money, work, and possessions.

[11] See Philip Pullella, "Vatican Lists 'New Sins,' Including Pollution," Reuters, Vatican City, March 10, 2008, http://www.reuters.com/article/2008/03/10/us-pope-sins-idUSL109602320080310, accessed November 27, 2011.

[12] See the full text of this document at http://www.usccb.org/issues-and-action/human-life-and-dignity/environment/global-climate-change-a-plea-for-dialogue-prudence-and-the-common-good.cfm, accessed November 27, 2011.

[13] Pope John Paul II, general audience address, January 17, 2001, http://www.vatican.va/holy_father/john_paul_ii/audiences/2001/documents/hf_ip-ii_aud_20010117_en.html, accessed May 26, 2009.

activities *do matter*, especially when taken cumulatively. But beyond that, it is up to us—yes, you and me, the generation that is capable of reading this text—to literally make all the difference in the world! How much do we have to change? Oh, about a 360-degree reversal might do! After all, we are talking about *conversion*. In a word, we need to stop making carbon footprints and start following in the footprints of Jesus!

Why Do We Resist Dealing with Human-Induced Global Warming and Climate Change?

Human-Induced Global Warming: From Denial to Ethical Engagement

Denial takes various forms when people perceive there is a serious threat to the status quo that may threaten their way of life.[14] For example, in April of 2009 the leaders of the G-20 held a world summit. Rather than focusing on ways to make a transition to an economic system that relies on truly sustainable forms of commerce and on low-carbon technologies, they chose to simply reconfigure the same old global economic system, which is arguably at the root of the current crisis.[15] This response is typical of *the illusionary frame of mind* that fails to confront the size and scale of the heating global climate and its complexity. As we shall see, such responses that frame global warming as a problem requiring *only* scientific and technological fixes fail to deal with the deeper human ethical issues that have been ignored but have resulted in the current state of affairs.[16]

---

[14] Tom Pyszczynski, "Terror," in *International Encyclopedia of the Social Sciences*, ed. William A. Darity Jr., 2nd ed., vol. 8 (Detroit: Macmillan Reference USA, 2008), 326–27. *Gale Virtual Reference Library.* http://go.galegroup.com/ps/i.do?id=GALE%7CCX3045302728&v=2.1&u=chic95518&it=r&p=GVRL&sw=w, accessed November 28, 2011, at 326: "To effectively protect against existential terror, cultural worldviews and self-esteem requires ongoing validation by others. Those who share one's worldview and believe in one's value increase faith in the worldview and self-esteem, whereas those who disagree with one's worldview or one's value undermine this faith. To maintain the anxiety-buffering effectiveness of these structures, people exert great effort to keep their self-esteem and faith in their worldview strong and to ward off any threats to these beliefs that might arise."

[15] See David Adam, "Scientists Fear Worst on Global Warming," *Guardian* (April 14, 2009): 14.

[16] See Alastair McIntosh, *Hell and High Water: Climate Change, Hope, and the Human Condition* (London: Birlinn, 2008).

A disturbing reality is the denial of global warming on the part of the more industrialized nations in North America and Europe. Equally problematic is their refusal to take moral responsibility for the injustice that has resulted from ever-increasing levels of air, water, and soil pollution from the 1850s Industrial Revolution to the present. The effects of this pollution are now manifested as global warming and an ever-increasing threat to and devastation and destruction of human populations in clearly less industrialized nations (typically in the global South).[17]

While there are increasing numbers of people who do openly acknowledge the importance of combating global warming and climate change, even they often remain infected with a serious "doublethink syndrome." They continue to engage in rampant consumerism, are frequent fliers, and drive SUVs—practices that have been proven to be among the most egregious sources of CO_2 emissions.[18] Beyond that, this kind of thinking makes possible a kind of "political gamesmanship." Those "doublethinkers" become the constituents who support candidates who publically proclaim their support of stringent CO_2 emission–reduction targets, when in fact those candidates (if elected) would allow day-to-day business to go on as usual! Then, when their "reduction efforts" fail, they often ultimately remain unconcerned, because as the well-known political adage holds, "Nobody ever rioted for the cause of austerity!"[19]

Yet others succor their conscience by buying carbon offsets before flying, purchasing green products, or supporting carbon trading. But while all of these things *do* have *some small* effect and cumulatively can have some influence on global warming, Jess Worth says that "it's like finding out that you've got cancer, but then delaying going to the doctor for treatment for a few months because you want to paint your house."[20] Efforts that take on human-induced global warming at its roots are what is ultimately needed. We must shift from focusing on only science and technology to wrestling with *ethical issues* of climate injustice and ecocide. This will require that we move from stressing personal behavior changes to stressing *spiritual transformation*. It will require that we face the terrific

[17] See Sunita Narain, "A Million Mutinies," *New Internationalist* 419 (January–February 2009): 10–11. Also see Vandana Shiva, *Soil Not Oil: Climate Change, Peak Oil and Food Insecurity* (London: Zed Books, 2008), 9–47.

[18] See McIntosh, *Hell and High Water*, 88.

[19] Ibid., 208.

[20] Jess Worth, "Is the Economic Crisis Going to Be the End of Green?" *New Internationalist* 419 (January–February 2009): 1.

and all-encompassing nature of the problem and draw deeply from our most profound spiritual treasures.

The Status Quo:
Human Limitations in Facing Human-Caused Global Warming

When dealing with any problem, the solution one finds will depend in part on how the problem is defined. In the case of human-induced global warming, many experts have presumed that if the vast majority of people simply become "environmentally literate," they will automatically change their behaviors sufficiently, the atmosphere will become pure, and the climate will stop changing, and all will be well. Clearly, this presumption already has been proven false. According to climate change educators, past approaches to "environmental literacy" have been ineffective because the problem has been defined too simplistically.[21] It is important to keep in mind that authentic "environmental literacy [is] the acquisition of information about the environment [that] rests on a political substrate, as well as critical social practices, linked to the concept of citizenship."[22] In light of this understanding, the content of environmental education needs to include mentoring in spiritual practices that can equip people to restore the relationships of the web of life that have been destroyed through past actions, and revolutionizing social, political, and economic structures that have all but ignored the totality of ecological interdependence. This will require engaging ethics content, not merely questions of science and technology.

But it is not only climate change educators that have contributed to the simplistic presentation of the problem of human-caused global warming. The complex and sobering realities of climate change are not thoroughly or adequately explained in media sound bites. Nor are they likely to be conveyed by messengers such as politicians or commercialized news media, who are dependent upon popular approval for survival in

[21] See Edgar González-Gaudiano, *Educación ambiental: Tragectorias, rasgos y escnarios* [Environmental education: Paths, features, and settings] (Mexico: Plaza y Valdés-UANL / Instituto de Investigacionses Sociales, 2007). Even the UNESCO and UNEP educational materials treat climate change in a "business as usual" manner as part of a formal educational curriculum.

[22] Edgar González-Gaudiano and Pablo Meira-Cartea, "Climate Change Education and Communication: A Critical Perspective on Obstacles and Resistances," in Fumiyo Kagawa and David Selby, ed., *Education and Climate Change: Living in Interesting Times* (New York: Routledge, 2010), 14.

rival markets. Thus, most popular information concerning human-induced global warming continues to be delivered to the public with a "feel good" spin that distorts the stark facts.

Again, if we were to believe (as many do) what popular sources tell us, climate change could be resolved by a minimal effort on the part of everyone to do individual acts on a purely voluntary basis, such as re-cycling, buying hybrid or electric cars, or switching from incandescent light bulbs to halogens, light-emitting diodes (LEDs), or compact fluo-rescent lamps (CFLs). Notably, these changes require only a minimum effort against the status quo, while continuing to reinforce a consumer mentality that presumes we (notably those in rich industrialized nations) can buy enough technological fixes to save the planet!

The reality is that such minimal token efforts only leave people with the illusion that now that we've "gone green" to "save green," we can spend "what we've saved" on other stuff! The *net cost* to the earth's at-mosphere *actually increases*! What even the most well-intended among us accept as scientific knowledge concerning human-caused global warming thus runs up against the dominant economic model of devel-opment that *still* is ultimately kept in place by *fossil fuel consumption*. The point is that the roots of the problem go deeper to our Western consump-tive lifestyle that continues (in one form or another) to unjustly suck life and sustenance from our sisters and brothers across the globe. The eco-logical reality is that carbon emissions from coal-burning power plants in Chicago contribute to droughts and food insecurity in sub-Saharan Africa!

Difficulties Complexity Poses

Perhaps what is most difficult for ordinary people to comprehend is the reality that human-caused global warming takes place as the result of an *aggregate effect*. This means that it is difficult to predict the effect of any *one* human action *by itself*, beyond the immediate moment. Many people find this discouraging and confusing. However, there is vast scientific certainty that the combined cumulative effect of emissions of greenhouse gasses (GHGs) from billions of people across the globe and over the centuries has altered, and still is substantially altering, the earth's climate system.

Further, climate change is differentiated in time and space. This means that if we consider the natural evolution of climate, compared to the human-induced changes in the atmosphere, then over the last decades, changes have been extremely rapid—especially after the Industrial Revolution and post–World War II industrial expansion and globalization. On the other hand, if we look *only* at the human scale, from the 1850s to the present the change has been rather slow. This is because there is a lag time between the actual emission of GHGs and their differentiated or cumulative effect of changing the surface air temperature and causing global warming. Thus, it is hard for people to imagine that the emissions from "Coal-Fired Power Plant A" are responsible for a rise in the surface air temperature on the other side of the globe, or that even if "Plant A" were shut down today, its past emissions would still continue to contribute to global warming for years to come.

There is also the reality that the global warming effects of GHG emissions do not take place in linear time. Rather, crucial changes take place as "threshold effects." This means that the effects of day-to-day progressive additions of GHGs into the atmosphere are often barely perceivable. Yet any one addition of more GHG may suddenly cause a sharp shift in the established equilibrium of the atmosphere, causing surface air temperature warming across the globe. These patterns do not grab headlines or the attention of ordinary citizens in daily living, yet they are of vital importance. The consequences of not paying attention are deadly. Like a frog basking in a pot of water sitting on a fire that fails to detect the gradual increases in temperature until the water boils, we humans ignore these important realities to our peril!

People—even in sophisticated developed nations—fail to grasp the interconnected nature of global air, water, and soil systems or the basic chemistry of GHGs. Thus, in their denial, people fail to act to reduce GHG emissions; and in their failing to act, they further decrease the possibility of negating the devastation of the biophysical environment and human communities. Further disincentives accrue because what science can document as overall trends in the climatic systems as a whole does not always manifest that way in the *local scene*. For example, human-induced global warming has caused climate changes that have reduced the total fresh potable water that is available on the planet, especially in sub-Saharan Africa. However, people that experience flooding in Chicago will find that reality difficult to believe.

Among the most misunderstood dimensions of the global warming and climate changes discussion is what scientists mean when they use the term "uncertainty." It is vital that people clearly understand that for scientists, the word "certainty" is a technical term that is distinct from the word "risk." While "risk" involves *what is known*, or what is a reliably estimable probability, "uncertainty" arises when such probabilities are not available. Thus, to say that there is scientific "uncertainty" surrounding global warming is to simply claim that we do not know and cannot reliably estimate the probability that climate change will occur, nor its extent if it does occur.

In light of this clarification, then, it is of major significance that, beginning already in their *Third Assessment Report: Climate Change 2001*, the IPCC *did assign probabilities* to its main climate predictions, making the situation one of *risk*, rather than of *uncertainty*. Furthermore, those probabilities are of *considerable magnitude*. For example, the IPCC says that: "it is 'very likely' that in the 21st century there will be higher maximum temperatures and more hot days over nearly all land areas."[23] By this they mean a *probability of 90–99 percent*! We fly on airplanes and drive our cars with less certainty in knowing that we will return home alive. As stated in the first page of this chapter, the 2007 IPCC report reconfirmed this probability, but with much more supportive data than ever before.[24]

Moral Issues: Navigating the Terrain

Most comprehendible perhaps, is the reality that the greatest amounts of GHGs were emitted for over two centuries by the world's most industrialized nations, which represent only one-fifth of the world's population. Those same nations account for the greatest levels of fossil fuel consumption. Moreover, the emissions coming from less industrialized nations were arguably in large part produced via industrial processes that met the needs and desires of the "first world." Today nations trying to catch up technologically to highly industrialized nations continue to bear the burden of needing to choose between becoming polluters (using often less expensive old GHG-emitting technologies) or postponing economic development. (Some small-scale, truly sustainable efforts are in process, but they are still at risk of being crushed by globalized enter-

---

[23] IPCC, *Third Assessment Report: Climate Change 2001*, 162, http://www.ipcc.ch/publications_and_data/publications_and_data_reports.shtml, accessed November 28, 2011.

[24] See the scientific evidence submitted to the United Nations Conference of Parties (COP 17) conference held in Durban, South Africa, November 28–December 9, 2011. United Nations Framework Convention on Climate Change, "Feeling the Heat: Climate Science and the Basis of the Convention," http://unfccc.int/essential_background/the_science/items/6064.php, accessed December 24, 2011.

prises.) The tragic irony remains that the world's poorest nations are already suffering most severely from the results of toxic emissions, though they are not responsible for producing them. But further, those same nations still have economies that are dependent upon the extraction and export of natural resources, which requires technologies—all of which most severely affect ecological balance (e.g., forestry, mining, or monocrop agriculture). In their poverty, these nations are ill equipped to mitigate the impacts on general safety, water supplies, new diseases, economic breakdown, or food security.

Out of Sight and Out of Mind

In highly industrialized nations, ordinary citizens frequently do not make the effort to understand the sources of the energy that is piped or wired into their homes or businesses, powering the many and various appliances they use daily. Most have no idea that the coal that fires the power plant comes from blown-up mountaintops of Appalachia or that the oil for a proposed pipeline requires destruction of thousands of acres of carbon-absorbing ancient boreal forest in Canada.[25] Energy prices do not reflect the real costs of extraction and use in terms of environmental damage, or even the actual cost to locals or the society at the extraction sites. For example, how many people in the United States are aware of the federal subsidies that are paid to the petroleum industry? Most of the fossil fuel consumed in the United States is quite invisible in that it is taken for granted and thus unnoticed. For example, what is the real cost in environmental terms of the beef roast for tonight's dinner? What is the cost in terms of the emission of greenhouse gasses to bring it from the pasture to your table?

When considering the history of major world civilizations, we in the United States seem to have a very short memory. The fact is that numerous highly sophisticated and technologically developed civilizations across the globe met their demise over ecological disasters that overwhelmed

[25] On mountaintop removal, see the West Virginia Catholic Conference, http://www.catholicconferencewv.org/discussionVideos.htm, accessed December 24, 2011. On Canadian oil, see Luc Bouchard, bishop of St. Paul in Alberta, The Integrity of Creation and the Athabasca Oil Sands: A Pastoral Letter to the Faithful of the Diocese of St. Paul on the Occasion of the Jubilee Year in Honour of St. Paul, January 25, 2009, http://www.dioceseofstpaul.ca/index.php?option=com_docman&task=cat_view&gid=15&lang=en, accessed December 24, 2011.

their technologies and "progress."[26] It seems that we too have joined the same kind of a "cult of progress" as we quite unquestioningly worship the gods of science and technology, trusting that innovations will continue to liberate us from any need to change the status quo or to leave our opulent comfort zone. This mentality makes us vulnerable to even allowing ourselves to seriously ask (the truly delusional question) whether it would actually be better if the climatic zones of the world *would* shift, opening shipping lanes across the polar icecaps and giving Chicago a Mediterranean climate! Such fantasy blatantly ignores two facts current science shows us: (a) a variety of climatic regions must exist on the planet in order for any one region to have such "ideal" conditions; and (b) it is just impossible to continue "business as usual"—emitting the same (or greater) levels of GHGs—and to sustain the required conditions for human life on earth.[27]

Psychological and Cognitive Limits

Human sensate capacities are not designed to perceive long-term temperature rise that occurs in highly significant increments that are quantifiable only in tenths of degrees per decade. Thus, anyone who accepts the incremental changes that are reported by scientists is primarily predisposed to overall trust of empirical science. Many individuals have little understanding of the climate patterns of their region (as opposed to the local weather), and so in the popular mind, extreme short-term changes—warmer or colder—are readily interpreted as "proof" for or against the existence of human-caused global warming.

To further complicate matters, many people have difficulty perceiving the complexity of the composition of the earth's atmosphere itself. To many people, the atmosphere is simply empty space into which anything, including toxic emissions, can randomly be pumped, so that the winds can just mysteriously blow it all "away." By contrast, scientists understand the atmosphere to be a comparatively thin, fragile, multilayered system that changes in composition and dynamics over planetary history. There

---

[26] See Jared Diamond, *Collapse: How Societies Choose to Fail or Succeed* (New York: Viking-Penguin, 2005). Also see Morris Berman, *Dark Ages in America: The Final Phase of Empire* (New York: Norton, 2007).

[27] For a powerful study that illustrates what life would be like on the planet with global heating of 1–6°F, see Mark Lynas, *Six Degrees: Our Future on a Hotter Planet* (London: Fourth Estate, 2007).

is no "away" to take toxic gasses, because there is only one atmosphere for the entire planet. No matter where one lives, whatever is forced into the atmosphere by humans affects *all* of us—plants, animals, and earth systems—and all of us depend on the atmosphere for existence!

It is certain that our very *denial and resistance* to human-caused global warming *itself* brings with it a self-fulfilling prophecy. People often imagine that the scale of change that is being asked of them is far too large—"a return to the lifestyle of the caveman." This engaged anticipation of the loss of security results in inaction, the problem of harmful emissions of GHGs continues to grow, and the global heating increases. The price, in terms of scale and size of retraction on harmful emissions that is then needed, only grows. Then the gap between the lifestyle changes required for halting global warming also increases. In this scenario, the reality is that individuals readily pass on their responsibilities to industry, governments, pressure groups, politicians, or international organizations. This loss of accountability results in the "tragedy of the commons."[28]

In the case of global warming, the nations of the world are aware that any emission of GHGs is harmful to all nations on the planet. To drastically reduce GHG emissions will require sacrifice on the part of all nations (though justice demands different kinds of sacrifices from each). In recent years of economic crisis across the globe, there is a greater overall insecurity, especially among traditionally stable societies of North America and Europe. Many people clearly turned inward to their personal survival needs, and they have lost track of their common interest in halting global warming. The issue of global warming appears to be

---

[28] González-Gaudiano and Meira-Cartea, "Climate Change Education and Communication," 28. See Garrett Hardin, "The Tragedy of the Commons," *Science* 162 (1968): 1243–48. Also see Stephen M. Gardiner, "A Perfect Moral Storm: Climate Change, Intergenerational Ethics, and the Problem of Corruption," in Stephen M. Gardiner, Simon Caney, Dale Jamieson, and Henry Shue, eds., *Climate Ethics: Essential Readings* (New York: Oxford University Press, 2010), 88–89. Gardiner explains what philosopher and game theorist Garrett Hardin calls "the tragedy of the commons." Gardiner's purpose is to show how humans' tendency to serve only their own self-interest corrupts their ability to serve the *common good*, which is also *their own ultimate good*. In a given case, it is clear that everyone would benefit the most if everyone would make a sacrifice that would allow everyone to participate in an ultimate good. All of the stakeholders in the scenario agree to a specific way each will sacrifice something (that is agreed upon in advance by all parties). However, lack of trust that each and all will fulfill their pledge emerges, and in the end each stakeholder chooses not to sacrifice and instead to follow his or her own self-interest. The end result is that the ultimate good cannot be reached because not everyone fulfills his or her promise.

distant and of a low priority. Yet if we look at global warming in light of psychologist Abraham Maslow's hierarchy of needs,[29] this issue is foundational to meeting the most important survival needs. If we allow the business of emitting GHGs to continue unchecked, ultimately we will most certainly not have access to air, water, and food—essentials for human life at the base of Maslow's hierarchy. This is a moral challenge of the highest order, and it promises to remain so well into the future.

The difficulty of even achieving a basic agreement on legally binding and enforceable GHG standards is enormous. Yet some progress is being made. As of this writing, the most recent attempt at agreement was the seventeenth session of the United Nations Conference of Parties (COP 17), convened in Durban, South Africa, November 28–December 9, 2011.[30] The good news is that 194 nations slaved overtime seeking all possible ways to achieve the best and most just limits to and drawback of GHG emissions across the globe. They sought a more progressive treaty that would take the place of the Kyoto Protocol (1997–2012) that legally bound only the emission-reduction targets of industrialized countries. However, after working nearly two full days beyond their scheduled meeting time, "the 194-party conference agreed to start negotiations on a new accord that would put all countries under the same legal regime enforcing commitments to control greenhouse gases. It would take effect by 2020 at the latest. The deal also set up the bodies that will collect, govern and distribute tens of billions of dollars a year to poor countries to help them adapt to changing climate conditions and to move toward low-carbon economic growth."[31]

---

[29] See Abraham H. Maslow, "A Theory of Human Motivation," *Psychological Review* 50/4 (1943): 370–96. Maslow holds that humans have five sets of needs that are required for a fully developed human life. At the very base are physiological needs (food, water, shelter, sex, and sleep), followed by safety needs, love needs, esteem needs, and self-actualization needs. If humans are unable to meet their most basic needs, they cannot satisfy the others and their development is stunted. Clearly, global warming threatens all of us. See also Kelly Dye, s.v. "Abraham Maslow," *International Encyclopedia of the Social Sciences*, ed. William A. Darity Jr., vol. 5, 2nd ed. (Detroit: Macmillan Reference USA, 2008), 11–12.

[30] See the web site of the United Nations Framework Convention on Climate Change at http://unfccc.int/meetings/durban_nov_2011/meeting/6245.php, accessed November 28, 2011.

[31] See "UNEP press release: Climate Talks End with Hope for a New More Comprehensive Legally-Binding Agreement," December 11, 2011, http://cop17insouth africa.wordpress.com, accessed June 25, 2012.

Lessons from the Leper: Embracing True Sustainability

From Intoxication to Sustainability

In 1987 the UN-sponsored Brundtland Commission published a book called *Our Common Future*.[32] That commission defined sustainable development as "development that meets the needs of the present without compromising the ability of future generations to meet their needs."[33] The commission presumed that "sustainable development" meant raising productivity, accumulation of goods, and technological innovations.[34] But that kind of thinking caused them to fail to address key sources of poverty: the exploitation of workers and the pillaging of nature. Brundtland's notion of "sustainable development" is an oxymoron because its real focus was economic growth for its own sake, and the primary goal was profit making. This thinking has permeated the globalization of world markets through the present day.

By contrast, "sustainability" as it is defined in biology and ecology is "the trend of ecosystems toward equilibrium, sustained in the web of interdependencies and complementarities flourishing in ecosystems."[35] Genuine sustainability requires social and economic structures that support *social justice*—the right relationship between persons, roles, and institutions—and *ecological justice*, which is the right relationship with nature, sufficient access to resources, and assurance of quality of life.[36]

A renewed vision of community is essential for interdependent sustainability.[37] Such a vision is found in early Christian sources, utilizing the rich meanings gleaned from the Greek root *oikos*. The habitability of the earth is the central reality that links economy, ecology, and ecumenicity. "Economy in its Greek-root meaning is the ordering of the household for the sustenance of its members."[38] The contrast between this Christian

[32] The World Commission on Environment and Development, *Our Common Future* (New York: Oxford University Press, 1987).

[33] Ibid., 43.

[34] James B. Martin-Schramm and Robert L. Stivers, *Christian Environmental Ethics: A Case Study Method Approach* (Maryknoll, NY: Orbis Books, 2003), 90.

[35] Leonardo Boff, *Cry of the Earth, Cry of the Poor* (Maryknoll, NY: Orbis Books, 1997), 66.

[36] Ibid., 105.

[37] See World Council of Churches (WCC), *Accelerated Climate Change: Sign of Peril, Test of Faith* (Geneva: WCC Publications, 1994).

[38] Ibid., cited in Larry L. Rasmussen, *Earth Community, Earth Ethics* (Maryknoll, NY: Orbis Books, 1996), 144.

understanding of sustainability and that of the Brundtland Commission is remarkable. This contrast is but one indication of how deeply a consumer mentality has permeated all of life in the highly industrialized world.

Sue McGregor explains this reality well: "People behave as they do in a consumer society because they are so indoctrinated into the logic of the market that they cannot 'see' anything wrong with what they are doing. Because they do not critically challenge the market ideology, and what it means to live in a consumer society, they actually contribute to their own oppression. . . . Consumerism [is] a way to self-development, self-realization, and self-fulfillment. In a consumer society, an individual's identity is tied to what she or he consumes."[39]

Quantum physicist David Bohm adds his voice to those challenging consumerism. He compares our uncritical adherence to growth and treating everything other than human as mere "natural resources" or "natural capital" to a man in a Sufi story who lost the key to his house: "He was found to be looking under the light. He looked and looked, and he couldn't find it. Finally, someone asked where he had lost the key. Pointing to another area of his yard, he said, 'Over there.' And when asked why he had not looked 'over there,' the man responded, 'Well, it's dark over there, but there's light here for me to look.'"[40]

Quantum theologian Diarmuid O'Murchu speaks of "cultural intoxication," or the addiction of the Western world to material acquisition that drowns out an alienation from the life-and-death realities of the world and thus maintains the illusion of power and control.[41] But the raw truth is that this addiction simply signals a desperation and a deep denial of its opposite.

The Way Out Is the Way Through

According to ecophilosopher Joanna Macy, many in the industrialized West live in a state of what she calls "apathy," noting that the word etymologically comes from the Greek *apatheia*, meaning "the refusal to ex-

---

[39] See Sue McGregor, "Consumerism as a Source of Structural Violence," 2003, http://www.kon.org/hswp/archive/consumerism.pdf, accessed December 5, 2011.

[40] David Bohm and Mark Edwards, *Changing Consciousness: Exploring the Hidden Source of Social, Political and Environmental Crises Facing Our World* (San Francisco: Harper, 1991), 17.

[41] See his *Quantum Theology: Spiritual Implications of the New Physics* (New York: Crossroads, 2004), 139–40.

perience pain."[42] Macy has shown that when Westerners face the facts of global warming, they tend to become paralyzed or move to denial and inaction.[43] Macy asserts that people of the developed world have lost many of the values, attitudes, and skills required to resolve global warming. Westerners repress the overwhelming pain of ecocide and gaiacide because, culturally, expressing pain is thought dysfunctional! We ignore the complexities of global warming because we fear our intellectual inadequacy for developing solutions to the problem—so we "leave it to the experts." We in the United States live in opulence, disproportionately consuming the world's goods. And we don't know how to cope with the guilt, whether personal or collective.

Macy contends that the way out of our paralysis is to realize that the guilt and pain are not only real but healthy. Because we are sufficiently aware of global warming, there is renewed hope within our experience of pain. By acknowledging pain, facing fears, and choosing to live within limits, we break the isolation and begin the healing, restoration, and renewal for ourselves and the earth. This awakening provides opportunities to live out humility, poverty, obedience, and love through a life of Christian simplicity.

Toward Christian Simplicity: Insights from Social Sciences

ENVIRONMENTAL EDUCATION

Environmental educator David Selby suggests that we look to "education for contraction" as a systematic and organic way of transforming human living to less exploitative and more harmonious ways of being.[44] He believes that the key to such a shift is ecological awareness, frugal consumption, and personal spiritual growth. As early as 1981, Duane Elgin submitted that rather than material progress, our goal in life needs to focus on achieving a balance of the material with the spiritual.[45] We

---

[42] Joanna Macy, "The Greatest Danger: *Apatheia,* the Deadening of Mind and Heart," in *Coming Back to Life: Practices to Reconnect Our Lives, Our World,* Joanna Macy and Molly Young Brown (Gabriola Island, BC: New Society, 1998), 26.

[43] Ibid., 23–38.

[44] David Selby, "As the Heating Happens: Education for Sustainable Development of Education for Sustainable Contraction," *International Journal of Innovation and Sustainable Development* 2, 3/4 (2007): 258.

[45] See Duane Elgin, *Voluntary Simplicity: Toward a Way of Life That Is Outwardly Simple and Inwardly Rich* (New York: William Morrow, 1981), 40.

must stress conservation, need-limit frugality, and living life in cooperation with others. Our personal identity needs to flow from our interper-
sonal relationships and from living with all other-than-human creatures
and earth elements. While each person is uniquely an individual, she or
he is ultimately inseparable from the whole of humanity. Rather than
viewing the cosmos as a storehouse awaiting looting and exploitation,
it must be seen as a precious living organism with its own integrity. Our
personal behavior needs to include only a sufficient amount of self-
sustaining activity to remain healthy, rather than excessive self-serving
activity exclusively focused on maximum material acquisition. We thrive
better living in connected communities than as highly mobile autono-
mous individuals.

MOTIVATIONAL STUDIES

More insights come from recent motivational studies on the empowerment of people to act toward halting global warming.[46] There are four
common characteristics that contribute to and motivate a moral stance
of ecological responsibility and action: (1) people develop emotional
connections with nature that are expressed in caring for the earth and
all creatures; (2) people find mutual support from social groups; (3)
people become ecologically literate and understand God as incarnational;
and (4) people develop a sense of the ability to make a difference, con-
tending that creative ideas and strategies can be realized.[47]

---

[46] Noreen Allossery-Walsh, "Christian Ecological Responsibility: Intimations of
Prophetic Witness for the Church in the New Millennium," (unpublished Doctor of
Ministry thesis, Catholic Theological Union, May 14, 2009). I am grateful to Allossery-
Walsh for the references to the other three studies that I report here. See "Motivating
and Sustaining Pro-Environmental Behaviors: A Review of the Literature," http://
www-personal.umich.edu/~sarhaus/courses/NRE530_F1998/kjlawren/motivate.
html, accessed May 25, 2009; Kaman Lee, "Factors Promoting Effective Environmental Communication to Adolescents: A Study of Hong Kong," *China Media Research*
4/3 (July 2008): 28–36; and Elizabeth Ann Bragg, "Ecological Self: An Invitation on
a Shamanic Journey," paper presented at the cameo session of "Environment Stream—
'Thinking Like a Mountain,'" World Futures Studies Federation XV World Conference,
University of Queensland, Brisbane, Australia, September 28–October 3, 1997, http://
www.rainforestinfo.org.au/deep-eco/shaman.htm, accessed May 25, 2009.

[47] Allossery-Walsh, "Christian Ecological Responsibility," 99. Additional significant
factors motivating ecological responsibility include people having visions of future
possibilities, making verbal commitments, and cultivating a sense of individual responsibility and competence in bringing about change. Significantly, Allossery-Walsh

Through her research on Catholic Lay Earth Ministers, Noreen Allossery-Walsh found that key to ecological responsibility is the emergence of the "ecological self."[48] This is a kind of self-understanding that expands beyond individualism to embrace human communities, the rest of the natural world, our evolutionary past, and the distant future, and it is a positive ongoing source of motivation.[49] Two major motivating factors were uncovered by Allossery-Walsh that lead to ecological responsibility and action. First, Earth Ministers found cognitive dissonance in attempting to maintain an individualistic self-identity.[50] Second, Earth Ministers found motivation through avoiding the internal conflict produced by attempting to sustain a utilitarian conception of the earth. That conflict led the Earth Ministers to a "consciousness of a deep ecology. Deep ecology is a vision of life which holds that we cannot deal with, transform, [or] solve ecological conflict by an endless series of *ad hoc* remedies to each catastrophe."[51]

From all of this, Allossery-Walsh concludes: "Ultimately then, ecological responsibility motivated by . . . [the] Christian tradition is determined by consciousness of the ecological self, where the expansion of the self acknowledges the centrality of relationship with the Creator [and] where caring for all Creation is understood as a call to participate communally in the divine life where justice flourishes."[52] I submit that these studies only confirm what St. Francis knew in his own time, namely, that we live in an interdependent, connected world and that we humans need to care for it in ways that respect the interrelationship of everything. St. Francis's entire life and ministry stands as the supreme example of Christian simplicity. In light of all of this, we need to shift our course—and act now!

---

found guilt and fear to be the least effective motivators; in fact, they deterred people from becoming proactive.

[48] Ibid., 100: "The Christian tradition does . . . offer tangible motivation for ecological responsibility in the case of lay leaders."

[49] Ibid.

[50] Ibid., 101–2. See also Robert A. Ludwig, *Reconstructing Catholicism for a New Generation* (New York: Crossroad Publishing Company, 1995), 192; and Robert C. Fuller, *Ecology of Care: The Interdisciplinary Analysis of the Self and Moral Obligation* (Louisville: Westminster John Knox Press, 1992), 32.

[51] Allossery-Walsh, "Christian Ecological Responsibility," 102.

[52] Ibid., 103.

From the Writings of St. Francis

"The Testament" (1226), 1–3[53]

The Lord gave me, Brother Francis, thus to begin doing penance in this way: for when I was in sin, it seemed too bitter for me to see lepers. And the Lord Himself led me among them and I showed mercy to them. And when I left them, what had seemed bitter to me was turned to sweetness of soul and body.

Reflection and Application

Embracing the leper was a life-changing move for St. Francis. In the moment of that embrace, many things shifted in his life and person. In a small but vitally healthy way, at that moment a part of him died. It was that part that clung to the status quo of his former life as a rather spoiled, upwardly mobile son of one of the newly wealthy mercantile class of his day. There in his embrace of the leper, he began to see what the source of wealth in life *truly* is, namely, the mercy of God and the healing that love of God and neighbor can bring into the world. As we saw in earlier chapters of this book, St. Francis was able to care deeply for creation because he saw in each creature the one common source of life. His care for the poor was motivated by his deep desire to follow in the footprints of the Poor Christ, who had lived and died for the love of the poor—those overcome by sin, personal weaknesses, or economic destitution.

Today we are called to a similar kind of dying and conversion. We must admit to devastation that results from our drive to material wealth and that continues to inflict disproportionate suffering on the poor. Particularly, the "American Dream" has become the "Global Nightmare." The toxins spewing from our cars, homes, and industries and our raping of ecosystems, destroying their capacity to function to absorb and filter greenhouse gasses, have all caused atmospheric changes that bring destruction and death far from our shores. We must acknowledge that (as was discussed above) the denial of our complicity often drives us into

---

[53] St. Francis. "The Testament," in *Francis of Assisi: Early Documents*, vol. I, *The Saint*, trans. and ed. Regis J. Armstrong, J. A. Wayne Hellmann, and William J. Short (New York: New City Press, 1999), 124.

even deeper delusional negation of our responsibility and to inflicting even more destruction. *Now is the time* to let go of our false securities and allow God's mercy to touch and heal us! Quantum theologian O'Murchu says it well: "We are compelled to assert what seems initially to be an outrageous claim: a radically new future demands the destruction and death of the old reality. It is from dying seeds that new life sprouts forth. Destruction becomes a precondition for resurrection: denigration undergirds regeneration.[54]

Confronting Spiritual Malaise

Many experts in science and religion have long held that the environmental crisis that now imminently threatens human extinction is the result of unfettered materialism and consumerism that has plagued the industrialized world and has roots in a deep spiritual malaise.[55] Conveniences, unspeakable variety, and abundance overshadow, blind, satiate, and pacify us against the deeper longings of the human spirit. Then, in our self-inflicted ignorance, we nonsensically send ourselves into yet one more cycle of denial and consumption that only aggravates our threatened condition—especially that of the poor. What is needed is a renewed moral and spiritual formation concerning limits, the acceptance of death as part of life, and a vision of the common good.

Moral Formation and Death Acceptance: Francis of Assisi as Model

One model of conversion worthy of our attention is St. Francis of Assisi, the patron saint of ecology. To know the life of St. Francis is to see that he, like us, often wrestled with his inner "angels and demons." He had his moments of doubt, of being overwhelmed and discouraged (Pathos). Yet Francis modeled what Freud called the true dynamic of life—"desire," or Eros. Eros is the dynamic force of life within us that calls out to life and invites us to live forever. This is the drive to totality. Brazilian theologian Leonardo Boff tells us that "by their very nature, Eros and Pathos—because they constitute the basic energy of human life—expand in all

---

[54] O'Murchu, *Quantum Theology*, 190–93.

[55] See National Religious Partnership for the Environment, "The Joint Appeal in Religion and Science: Statement by Religious Leaders at the Summit on Environment," June 3, 1991, in New York City, http://fore.research.yale.edu/publications/statements /joint_appeal.html, accessed December 24, 2011.

directions. Because of this, we must always recognize that, as a force, they lend themselves as much to constructive as to destructive purposes."[56] We can see this reality in the current threat of global warming. We have known for over thirty years that consumerism drives massive uncontrolled pollution of GHGs into the atmosphere, and that exacerbates climate change. Yet we have done precious little to change our ways.

Fortunately, the human capacity for reasoning and making meaning (Logos) allows us to direct our God-given energies toward the good. In St. Francis's case we see this (Logos) in action in his gentleness, compassion, and care for all of creation that characterized his holiness. Notably, Francis did not deny or ignore his "demons"; he embraced them. As Boff puts it, "The accepted negativity loses its virulence and behaves like a house pet."[57] Francis's capacity to embrace the negativity in his life was also his source of great joy.

Deep Joy and the Mercy of God

Today what our Western industrialized culture has lost track of is that genuine quality of joy. In our misguided spiritual striving, we try to "create" our security, happiness, and pleasure by buying and consuming ever more "stuff," material things, which in turn drives more pollution. Yet just as the black text on a white page would be impossible to read without the black/white contrast, so too genuine joy can never be known without also knowing and experiencing the contrast of its opposite—sadness, grief, sorrow, and gloom. We see that St. Francis allowed himself to know and experience such things. Francis chose to confront, embrace, and integrate negative experiences as part of life. Like Jesus before him, Francis took his hard, overwhelming, or painful experiences to God in prayer and to his brothers in community. He spent time reflecting on what he might learn from the limits he faced. Indeed, the key to St. Francis's joy was his profound experience of the mercy of God.[58] And as

---

[56] Leonardo Boff, *St. Francis: A Model for Human Liberation*, trans. John W. Diercksmeier (New York: Crossroad Publishing Company, 1982), 131.

[57] Ibid., 133.

[58] See Margaret A. Farley, *Compassionate Respect: A Feminist Approach to Medical Ethics and Other Questions*, Madeleva Lecture in Spirituality (New York: Paulist Press, 2002). Farley reminds us that Jesus is the model of mercy and compassion for Christians (John 15:9, 12). She provides a rich exposé of the meaning of mercy using a word study of various Latin roots that have given this term meaning. Her key examples of Jesus' practice of mercy are in relationship with doubting Thomas (John 20:24-29),

we see in the accounts of the suffering and death of St. Francis, when his ultimate limits were reached, he surrounded himself with the love of brothers and sisters who accompanied him with compassionate care.[59]

If we are to reach human maturity, each of us needs to accept the reality that there is a certain amount of suffering, misunderstanding, and absurdity that is inherent in human life, and we will never have control over it. In our human reality there are definite limits to our drive to totality (Eros). In daily activity we are also frequently confronted with "small deaths"—frustrated desire, the need to deny ourselves something, the obligation to accept something else, or facing a situation we must overcome. "A sign of human and religious maturity is to integrate the trauma of death in the context of life. Then death is dethroned from its status as lord of life and ultimate reality. Eros triumphs over Thanatos and desire wins the game. But there is a price to pay for this immortality: the acceptance of the mortality of life. The acceptance of death, the frustrating empirical and superficial desire that demands eternal life, is the condition by which desire achieves its truth of living forever, in absolute triumph."[60] We find this process of acceptance of death, in a marvelous manner, in the life of St. Francis. Two dimensions illuminate St. Francis's reconciliation with death: (1) acceptance of death as part of life and (2) his identification with the source of life.

ACCEPTANCE OF DEATH AS PART OF LIFE

When we look at creation from an evolutionary point of view, we readily see that the structure of creation includes (and indeed requires) death

---

where Jesus' response to Thomas was to reveal healed wounds, and with James and John (Mark 10:35-45), where Jesus' response to James and John was to offer the cup of covenant love and mercy. Summing up the church's teaching on mercy, she cites Thomas Aquinas's words: "In every work of God, viewed at its primary source, there appears mercy. In all that follows, the power of mercy remains, and works indeed with even greater force" (*Summa Theologiae* I, q. 21, a. 4). Divine mercy is creative and redemptive, and it is significantly a concrete response of the Lover to the reality of the beloved.

[59] *The Life of St. Francis* by Thomas of Celano (1228–1229), bk. II, chap. VIII, 109–11, in *Francis of Assisi: Early Documents*, vol. II, *The Founder*, trans. and ed. Regis J. Armstrong, J. A. Wayne Hellmann, and William J. Short (New York: New City Press, 2000), 277–79.

[60] Boff, *St. Francis: A Model for Human Liberation*, 146.

and mortality because God made it so.[61] Though we rarely allow ourselves to think this thought, from the moment we are born, we begin to die! Contrary to popular understanding, mortality did not arise with sin. As Boff rightly points out, from a Christian viewpoint, within the mortality of life humans walk toward eternal life. What sin introduced to human-kind was "the closing off of understanding, shuttering off a vision of mortal life, making life and death enemies."[62] Death then became the negation of life. Humanity clung to life so that it could escape death. Frequently, fear of death blossoms and desperation rises at the first hint of death's proximity. Key to dealing with acceptance of death is how we deal with its signs—for example, limitations, illness, ignorance, corporal or spiritual weakness, or loss of power, prestige, and status.

IDENTIFICATION WITH THE SOURCE OF LIFE

Francis's genuine joy developed over the course of his lifetime. His joy had a deep source. His link with life, nature, and all people was so radical that it reached the root of what gives life to all, the source from which comes all that exists and all that moves—God, who is loving, just, and merciful. Gabriel Marcel characterizes such a relationship thus: "If you love me, I know it, I will never die."[63] Can we Christians come to such a place on our spiritual journey that we can genuinely entrust our lives to our loving, merciful God in this way? Did Christ not promise us the constant sustaining presence of the life-giving and communion-building Holy Spirit? How much simpler life could be if our focus moved from our own self-preservation to the common good of the planet and care for our sisters and brothers—human and otherkind. Those who come to integrate death with life in this way certainly achieve their fulfillment in the reign of God. Nothing can threaten them any more because they have no enemies. Our true joy is in sustaining loving relationships with God, our neighbors (human and otherkind), ourselves, and the cosmos.

As we saw in his "Canticle of the Creatures," for Francis, death became a sister—a fellow creature, named in the life-giving female gender. She is the necessary *transitus* toward a new and definitive birth. A shift to

---

[61] Evolutionary sciences show us that some species reach their limits and then simply become extinct, while others adapt and exist for many more generations.

[62] Boff, *St. Francis: A Model for Human Liberation*, 151.

[63] Cited in ibid., 153.

this stance of accepting death as part of life was a profound conversion for Francis, and indeed that stance can be ours as well. In our time, we are being called to a similar kind of conversion. Such change can be painful, as is all birth, but it makes possible a new advent with life—now with God in a different way.

Called to Be and to Do New Things

Pope Benedict XVI has been consistent in his call to Catholics and to all people of good will to protect the environment and act to halt human-induced global warming. In his encyclical, *Caritas in Veritate* he states, "The protection of the environment, of resources, and of the climate obliges all international leaders to act jointly and to show a readiness to work in good faith, respecting the law and promoting solidarity with the weakest regions of the planet."[64] Also, in his World Day of Peace Message in 2010, he insists, "To protect the environment, and to safeguard natural resources and the climate, there is a need to act in accordance with clearly-defined rules . . . while at the same time taking into due account the solidarity we owe to those living in the poorer areas of our world and to future generations."[65]

Further, the United States Catholic bishops have promoted prudent action to halt global warming, which is based on solid scientific evidence, while placing the needs of the poor and vulnerable at the center of climate legislation. Such action is to be guided by their 2001 statement Global Climate Change: A Plea for Dialogue, Prudence, and the Common Good and by other principles of Catholic social teaching. In 2011, in a letter to Congress, the bishops and the National Religious Partnership for the Environment outlined broad agreement on four key principles:

- The principle of prudence requires us to act to protect the common good by addressing climate change.

- The consequences of climate change will be borne by the world's most vulnerable people, and inaction will only worsen their suffering.

[64] Pope Benedict XVI, *Caritas in Veritate*, no. 50, http://www.vatican.va/holy_father/benedict_xvi/encyclicals/documents/hf_ben-xvi_enc_20090629_caritas-in-veritate_en.html, accessed December 24, 2011.

[65] Pope Benedict XVI, If You Want to Cultivate Peace, Protect Creation, World Day of Peace Message, 2010, no. 7, http://www.vatican.va/holy_father/benedict_xvi/messages/peace/documents/hf_ben-xvi_mes_20091208_xliii-world-day-peace_en.html, accessed December 24, 2011.

- Policies addressing global climate change should enhance rather than diminish the economic situation of people in poverty.

- Policies should help vulnerable populations, here and abroad, adapt to climate impacts and actively participate in these efforts.[66]

The USCCB then suggested actions we can take to support making their position concrete in policies to halt global climate change. A priority toward that end is that Catholics and people of good will contact members of Congress and urge greater US leadership to address climate change, especially its disproportionate impact on poor and vulnerable people here and abroad.

The strong Catholic intellectual tradition enables us to see that the science is clear and the hard evidence is true. Human-caused global warming is threatening life on our planet—even the demise of its major life-giving systems. We dare not take a "business as usual" attitude to our bishops' call for action.

We are blessed to live in a nation where the public has an enormous amount of power when it makes its voice heard en masse. On Saturday, March 14, 2009, it was reported that American International Group, Inc. (AIG) awarded $165 million in bonuses to its employees, including those who had caused the near collapse of the finance system![67] Outraged citizens flooded the Congressional phone lines, e-mails, faxes, and tweets, demanding action against that injustice. By March 17 Congressional leaders had a plan to get the bonus money returned to the United States Treasury; and on March 19 the House overwhelmingly voted a 90 percent tax on AIG's bonuses and any others like them. Dear brothers and sisters, the damage of global warming is nearly irreversible! Should we not be at least equally outraged? Should we not be demanding an equally rapid and thorough response from ourselves, our industries, our institutions, and our governments?

---

[66] United States Conference of Catholic Bishops, Department of Justice, Peace, and Human Development, Office of Domestic Human Development, "Global Climate Change," February 2011, http://catholicclimatecovenant.org/wp-content/uploads/2011/02/Global-Climate-Change-backgrounder-2011-FINAL.pdf, accessed July 7, 2012.

[67] See Richard W. Miller, "Global Climate Disruption and Social Justice: The State of the Problem," in *God, Creation, and Climate Change: A Catholic Response to the Environmental Crisis*, ed. Richard W. Miller (Maryknoll, NY: Orbis Books, 2010), 22.

Questions for Reflection and Discussion

1. Do you know how much greenhouse gas (GHG) emissions your daily activities contribute to global warming? Go to the United States Environmental Protection Agency web site. Use their Household Carbon Footprint Calculator at http://www.epa.gov/climatechange/emissions/ind_calculator.html.

2. Were you surprised by the results of your household carbon footprint? How does it fit with the "footprints of Jesus" as he walked with the poor and the marginalized of his day?

3. Whom do you know that is considered to be prudent? Talk with that person and see if she or he fits the description of the virtue of prudence given by the US bishops in the 2001 pastoral.[68]

4. How can you become more prudent in consuming less?

5. Find out what scientists are saying about the effect of global warming on your region of the world. Do you understand the earth cycles and climatic systems that are being disrupted? Go to your public library or surf the Internet and learn more.

6. What biblical texts or stories of saints or heroes and heroines of faith can help you confront the "small deaths" that can free you from denial to accept God's mercy and a life of Christian simplicity?

Suggestions for Action

1. Reduce, reuse, and recycle *everything*.

2. Insulate your home and be thrifty with heating and cooling.

3. Leave your car at home; use public transportation.

---

[68] See United States Conference of Catholic Bishops, Global Climate Change: A Plea for Dialogue, Prudence, and the Common Good, June 15, 2001, http://www.usccb.org/issues-and-action/human-life-and-dignity/environment/global-climate-change-a-plea-for-dialogue-prudence-and-the-common-good.cfm, accessed December 24, 2011.

4. Lower the temperature on your water heater; do laundry in cold water; air-dry your dishes.

5. Urge your utility company to use renewable energy sources.

6. Buy energy-efficient products.

7. Join the Catholic Coalition on Climate Change at http://catholic-climatecovenant.org.

Prayer

"Search . . ." by Eileen Haugh, OSF[69]

Many Frail people we are,
vulnerable,
needing to reinvent the bluegreen relationship,
the human/earth, we've desecrated.

All of us are stricken
with a sickness incurable,
We raise up walls, hire dogs
to keep us safe (or am I the enemy)?

All of me is stricken
with a sickness incurable
because I refuse to divide what I have.

The rims of my house are broken,
the ground of my farm infected;
I can't make space by stretching a boundary.

There's forgiveness needed—
not sure where it begins—
but one of us has to start.

Maybe we'll know it when water is gone,
our planet a quilt of dry patches—

---

[69] Unpublished poem, used with permission of the Sisters of St. Francis, Rochester, MN. In loving memory of Sr. Eileen Haugh, OSF (November 3, 1928, to May 23, 2011), member of the Sisters of St. Francis, Rochester, MN, cherished teacher and gifted poet.

and anyone who still remembers wet
is pretty old. Tie that all into peace:
the need for us to talk, to listen, to accept,
to understand. That's it. That's the word.

Take this mosaic of broken peace,
give it burial in a green shroud,
under a mountaintop removed to a valley.

As icebergs turn to water, raw hunger begins,
people who know how to starve
will have it easier; for us, it will be hard

because we've never missed a meal
and don't think we'll have the courage to start now.
Our stash of snacks will be long gone.

I'm afraid of this global climate change.
A coward, I want to hide in yesterday.
Let's have things the way they used to be,
enemies over there somewhere,
beyond enough so I'll never see them;
yes, let's go back to then.
I know about beauty: about northern lights,
babies, ancient wrinkles, soulmates,
English apple orchards in the spring, in the spring

And snow, whitely untouched, untracked,
music to fill the night's vast cavern
and silence to swallow up the soul.

children singing bright colors,
faithfulness, and rain. I can't name them all—
but living them is throwing off cowardice.

Peace is a mirage some say;
that's because it has to start with us.
We make the first move.

If the world is a vast pothole
that swallows the good, is it my fault?
As earth-voice says,

Well, turn up the lights
and get a more animated, upbeat hold on the reins!
Your own opinion really does count,
is worth some sunshine, and could bring in and spread
love earth healing Spirit
winds of change,
fires of promise;
but it takes all of us—loving healing earthing Spirit—
to consecrate us whole again.

Sources for Further Study

De Flon, Nancy, and James A. Wallace, eds. *All Your Waves Swept Over Me: Looking for God in Natural Disasters.* New York: Paulist Press, 2007.

Delio, Ilia, Keith Douglas Warner, and Pamela Wood. *Care for Creation: A Franciscan Spirituality of the Earth.* Cincinnati, OH; St. Anthony Messenger Press, 2008.

Miller, Richard W., ed. *God, Creation, and Climate Change: A Catholic Response to the Environmental Crisis.* Maryknoll, NY: Orbis Books, 2011.

Parker, Cindy L., and Steven M. Shapiro. *Climate Chaos: Your Health at Risk; What You Can Do to Protect Yourself and Your Family.* Public Health Series. Westport, CT: Praeger Publishers, 2008.

Schaefer, Jame, ed. *Confronting the Climate Crisis: Catholic Theological Perspectives.* Milwaukee, WI: Marquette University Press, 2011.

Chapter 8

Flowing Water for Life:
A Human Right

Introduction: Morally Significant Facts

Who among us has not had the experience of working or playing on a hot summer day and then—"dying of thirst"—running indoors and heading straight to the refrigerator for an icy cold glass of water to quench our thirst? Water is indeed a life giver and a life saver!

Now imagine that same scenario, only this time transport yourself and your thirst to sub-Saharan Africa. There you would find it impossible to casually take a drink of water! But why, you may ask. Consider these facts concerning the status of water and its use across the globe today.[1] The minimum daily requirement each person needs for water (including drinking, cooking, bathing, and sanitation) is thirteen US gallons. The average person in the United States uses sixty-five to one hundred gallons of water per day! By contrast, the average African person uses twelve gallons at home each day. In Africa at least 314 million people lack access to safe drinking water, and 437 million lack access to adequate sanitation. According to the United Nations, women and girls in sub-Saharan Africa spend forty billion hours per year collecting water,

---

[1] See United Nations, *Water for Life Decade: 2005–2015* (New York: United Nations Department of Public Information, 2005). Also see charts and data updates at http://www.unwater.org/statistics.html, accessed January 1, 2012.

the same amount of time that the total workforce of France spends working each year. The time collecting water is one of the primary reasons African girls cannot attend school.

Lest we be tempted to brush off this data as an extreme example or simply an "African problem," also consider the following.[2] One billion people worldwide do not have *any* water within a fifteen-minute walk of their homes. There is no more water on the earth than there was two thousand years ago. The world population sharing the planet's finite freshwater supply back then was about two hundred million. Today, nearly seven billion people depend on that same finite water supply. Between 1900 and 2000, global water consumption rose sevenfold—that is more than double the population growth! Regions of the world that are pumping out ground water faster than aquifers can be replenished include the western United States, northern China, northern and western India, and northern and western Africa. One-third of US rivers, one-half of US estuaries, and more than one-half of US lakes are not fit for fishing and swimming, let alone drinking.

Nearly 40 percent of the world's populations live alongside international rivers. Two billion people depend on international cooperation to ensure an adequate water supply.

It is common knowledge that there is no life as we know it without water: The human newborn is 91 percent water; the human adult is about 75 percent water, while the human brain alone is 75 percent water. A drop in body water of a mere 2 percent brings fuzzy short-term memory, trouble doing basic math, or difficulty focusing on a computer screen. As the Pontifical Justice and Peace Council asserted in its 2003 statement, "Water is an essential element for life."[3]

The Hydrologic Cycle: Basic Facts

What has gotten us into the environmental crisis is that we lost track of the interrelatedness of our entire world. This is glaringly the case when we consider the world's water supply. The tides, currents, and weather

[2] See *National Geographic*, special issue, "Water: Our Thirsty World" (April 2010): 112–13 and passim.

[3] Pontifical Council for Justice and Peace, Water: An Essential Element for Life, http://www.vatican.va/roman_curia/pontifical_councils/justpeace/documents/rc_pc_justpeace_doc_20030322_kyoto-water_en.html, accessed June 25, 2012.

patterns that sustain the water supply in any one part of the globe are intimately connected to all other parts. And we cannot separate the quality of the air or the soils from the quality of the water. For example, the coal-generating power plants of Chicago spew mercury into the air.[4] The mercury filters down into Lake Michigan and enters the food supply of small fish and plants eaten by humans and other fishes. The toxic effect of mercury bioaccumulates with other toxins, and eventually the remaining plants in the lake can no longer filter out the biological waste contained in the runoff—especially after rains—flowing into the lake from the surrounding rivers, streams, and agricultural lands. The waters become contaminated, making fishing, swimming, and drinking this water hazardous to humans and other living beings.

Like all of the systems that keep our planet and us alive, the hydrologic system is tremendously complex and interconnected with every other earth system.[5] At the risk of oversimplification, we can say that the hydrologic system has six interrelated processes that keep water falling and flowing in any part of the earth (see chart at the end of this chapter). These include the *solar energy* radiated by the sun that keeps the never-ending cycle moving (creating various degrees of warmth in the atmosphere, land, other beings, and earth elements). The *evaporation* process is the way the liquid water (H_2O) in rivers, lakes, or streams is heated by the sun (or by human interventions) and breaks apart into its gaseous components—two hydrogen atoms and one oxygen atom per molecule of liquid. Vapor is also created by trees and plants that give off moisture through their living process, and this is called *transpiration*. *Condensation* takes place when tiny droplets of water form as water vapor rises into the air and cools. *Precipitation* then takes place as moisture is released when clouds become heavy and form rain, snow, or hail (depending on atmospheric temperatures). Depending on the altitude of the land on which this moisture comes to rest, as well as the kind of surface on which it lands, the rain, snow, or hail begins the *percolation* process. *Percolation* is the movement of water over, through, or into the ground. This dynamic six-step cycle, if left unimpeded by human-built obstructions, pollutions, or toxins, has the ability to interact freely with other earth systems to sustain any given ecosystem on Earth—all the genius of the God of

[4] See Clean the Air, "Illinois' Dirty Power Plants," http://www.csu.edu/cerc/documents/IllinoisDirtyPowerPlantsFactSheet.pdf, accessed June 25, 2012.

[5] See Frank B. Golley, *A Primer for Environmental Literacy* (New Haven: Yale University Press, 1998), especially chaps. 4–13.

creation, and not of human making! So what is the problem? Simply put, water is (often wastefully and carelessly) being consumed and retained faster than the hydrologic cycle can process it in a world where the human population is now poised to exceed seven billion—thus, the crisis exists.

The Global Water Crisis: An Exposé

The amount of water on Earth has not changed; the water the dinosaurs drank millions of years ago is the same water that falls as rain today! If all of Earth's water (liquid, ice, freshwater, saline) were put into a sphere, it would be about 860 miles (about 1,385 kilometers) in diameter (about the distance from Salt Lake City, Utah, to Topeka, Kansas).[6] In volume that amounts to a mind-boggling 1,338,000,000 cubic kilometers, or 321,000,000 cubic miles.[7] Nearly 70 percent of the world's freshwater is locked in ice. Most of the rest of it is locked in aquifers that we're draining faster than the natural recharge rate (the ability of the hydrologic cycle to replenish it). Two-thirds of our water is used to grow food. With approximately eighty-three million more people being born on Earth each year, water demand will keep going up, unless we change how we use this most precious of God's gifts. Arguably, there are three distinct yet interconnected dimensions that require our attention, namely, the access to safe drinking water; pollution and climate change (byproducts of the use of natural resources); and scarcity and depletion of water sources.[8]

Access to Water: For Whom?

Numerous factors contribute to the problems of access to water, but chief among them are lack of adequate and affordable technologies, and institutional and political obstacles such as the ability to raise and sustain

[6] See United States Geological Survey, "How Much Water Is There on, in, and above the Earth?" http://ga.water.usgs.gov/edu/earthhowmuch.html, accessed January 2, 2012.

[7] Peter H. Gleick, ed., *Water in Crisis: A Guide to the World's Fresh Water Resources* (New York: Oxford University Press, 1993), 13.

[8] This discussion closely follows Upmanu Lall and others, "Water in the 21st Century: Defining Elements of Global Crisis and Potential Solutions," *Journal of International Affairs* 61/2 (Spring/Summer 2008): 1–17.

the financial capacity to build reservoirs, treatment systems, or delivery systems to meet ever-growing needs.[9] Special attention to the access dimension of the crisis is given in the United Nation's Millennial Development Goals, with a target to "reduce by half the proportion of people without sustainable access to safe drinking water."[10] Even if generous donors can be tapped for loans or even for the outright donation of structures or technologies, often these efforts are not ultimately all that helpful. Interest to be paid on loans only adds to local financial burdens, and often the maintenance costs of such facilities alone outstrip the ability of remote or impoverished local governments or institutions to pay.

As Lall and others point out, there has recently been some progress toward assisting peoples across the globe with a variety of low-cost technologies, such as rainwater harvesting systems. There are also creative water purification techniques available—for example, the Purifier of Water, a powder developed by Pur and distributed by Population Services International. The powder inserted in a container of impure water causes metals, dirt, and parasites to clump together at the bottom of the container, leaving the water crystal clear and safe for drinking.[11] Another technique is the Swiss-pioneered solar disinfection process (SODIS) used in Nairobi's Kibera slum and elsewhere. In this process, plastic bottles (PET plastic works better than glass) are filled with water and left in the intense sun for six hours of full sunlight. The ultraviolet radiation will kill bacteria, viruses, and parasites in the water, making it potable.[12] In addition, there are several creative finance mechanisms that partner public and private resources for building adequate water supply systems. While these simple innovations certainly have some impact on local situations, they are but a small barrier holding a burgeoning complex of vastly larger industrial and corporate impacts at bay.[13]

---

[9] Lall and others, "Water in the 21st Century," 2. Also see Peter H. Gleick, "The Millennium Goals for Water: Crucial Objectives, Inadequate Commitments," in ed., Peter H. Gleick, *The World's Water, 2004–2005* (Washington, DC: Island Press, 2004), 1–15.

[10] Living Water International, "What Would It Take? How Much Money Would Solve the World Water Crisis?" http://www.water.cc/water-crisis/related-news, accessed June 25, 2012. See the goals at http://www.unmillenniumproject.org/goals/index.htm, accessed June 25, 2012.

[11] See *National Geographic*, "Water: Our Thirsty World," 112–13.

[12] Ibid., 36.

[13] See the World Health Organization database "Overview of Access to Safe Water and Basic Sanitation," http://www.wssinfo.org/guided-tours/introduction, accessed June 25, 2012.

Pollution: Can the Polluter Pay?

Even when otherwise adequate delivery and storage facilities exist for water in numerous locales, the water may not be safe for drinking due to pollution from industrial chemicals, toxins, microbes, and bacteria from improper sewage and agricultural sources. Most often corruption, collusion, the absence of enforcement of environmental regulations, and the lack of political will are the key to the lack of a sufficient potable water supply. This state of affairs is normally accompanied by extreme poverty, and the poorest suffer even though technologies exist that could remedy the problem.

Even when the political will to enforce regulations exists, the greatest problems involve "nonpoint source pollution," which includes organic and chemical runoff from farms and ranches with artificially fertilized fields and animal operations, or from industrial sites that spew toxins into the air with impunity. The pollutants are carried by air or water currents and combine to create "toxic soup." But if there is more than one emitter or possible source of the pollution, even highly skilled personnel with the most sophisticated monitoring find it nearly impossible to track down those responsible. Only over time (and often after the damage is done) do the effects of the poison gradually show up at various points in an ecosystem—in plants or animals of the food chain, in sludge in water pipes, or in damage to habitats—and thus it is very difficult or even impossible for enforcers to prosecute to recoup and restore pure water.[14]

Profit-focused industrial and commercial polluters usually oppose regulations that require them to spend money for filters necessary to cleanse their emissions. Similarly, farmers and ranchers hesitate to fence in cattle or plant buffer or cover crops that strain out pollutants. There are still those who would challenge the possible good effect such techniques produce for the water and overall environment. The weather is often sporadic and volatile, and pollutants are thus unevenly distributed over vast areas, having a more or less toxic effect in any one area. This makes it difficult to pin down the cause-and-effect relationship of nonpoint source polluters. One helpful solution may be to offer loans or tax breaks for emitters who

---

[14] Lall and others cite these examples: David Malakoff, "Death by Suffocation in the Gulf of Mexico," *Science* 281/5374 (1998): 190–92; Cavel Brown et al., "Re-Evaluation of the Relationship between *Pfiesteria* and Estuarine Fish Kills," *Ecosystems* 6/1 (2003): 1–10; and David Dudgeon, "Large-Scale Hydrological Changes in Tropical Asia: Prospects for Riverine Biodiversity," *BioScience* 50/9 (2000): 793–806.

voluntarily reduce pollution. Yet it is still possible for any one polluter to "catch a free ride" off the efforts of others.[15] The political, social, economic, and technological challenges presented by nonpoint pollution continue to be manifested across the globe. These challenges taken together are the very same political and profit-focused obstructions that stand behind inaction toward halting human-caused global warming. Because warm air holds more moisture than cooler air, the warming atmosphere, land surface, and water-body temperatures impede the natural workings of the hydrologic system. Though the causes of water pollution and human-caused global warming are both known to science, the lack of will to change individual behavior and the absence of political will to change the way we use water holds millions—including you and me, but especially the world's poorest—hostage to poisoned waters.

Water Scarcity

Water scarcity "refers to a situation when the water supply is inadequate in relation to the water demand for basic human and ecological necessities, including the production of food and other economic goods. . . . One-third of the developing world is expected to confront severe water shortages in this century due to increasing population size and changing climate conditions."[16] Increased numbers and duration of long-term droughts and increasing demands can render even the best-designed water supply systems useless. Such was the case in the drought suffered by metropolitan Atlanta, Georgia, from 2006 to 2011, resulting from the combination of extreme weather fluctuation and heavy

---

[15] Consider this scenario: Imagine a lake surrounded by ten factories. They each want to discharge wastewater containing 0.05 ppm (parts per million) of a toxin. Suppose, for the sake of argument, the lake could absorb one factory's worth of discharge; they will each argue that their discharge is not a risk and that they are providing necessary jobs for the local economy. If they convince the relevant legislators, then all will be discharging toxins into the lake, and the lake will be seriously poisoned. Once it is noticed that the fish and frogs are dying off and it is not safe to swim or boat on the lake anymore, the arguments will continue fast and furiously about how to solve the problem—which factories will be shut down? Who will pay for the costs of cleaning the discharge before it goes into the lake? While the arguments continue, the toxins will continue to build up and may even enter the groundwater supply, spreading the toxins far beyond the shores of the lake into the drinking water of many more people.

[16] Lall and others, "Water in the 21st Century," 6.

nonessential to opulent consumption of water; furthermore, large populations exacerbate water scarcity.[17] Similarly, in recent years the southwestern states in the Colorado River watershed have seen the levels of Lake Mead and Lake Powell drop to about 50 percent between 1999 and 2007. The summer of 2011 saw an unusual number of severe wildfires in Arizona and Texas due to drastic rainfall reduction in that region.

There is one solution to water scarcity that is "market driven": treating water as a "rare commodity." Proponents of such measures hold that if the price of water is high enough, people will cut back on their use. But with water—an essential for life—if such strategies are implemented outright, less wealthy and poor people will be harmed, as well as wildlife and ecosystems that can pay no price except their own death, no matter the monetary cost! Where such strategies are attempted, they are best done with price caps in place and within only a local and carefully limited sector. But in many contexts, while these limits help the overall local systemic water conservation efforts, other difficulties arise when, for example, farmers need to compete with other farmers whose water use is unrestricted.

Water pricing will likely not have much of an impact because it is generally accepted that water consumption in urban centers breaks down at 70 percent industrial, 20 percent institutional, and 6–10 percent domestic. Yet most of the discussions about water pricing are around individual water use. Large corporate users notoriously evade the cost of their water altogether.[18]

[17] See Michael Grunwald, "Did Georgia Bring the Drought on Itself?" *Time Magazine*, November 19, 2007, http://www.time.com/time/magazine/article/0,9171,1684513,00.html, accessed January 1, 2012; Andrew E. Knaak, Timothy K. Pojunas, and Michael F. Peck, "Extreme Drought to Extreme Floods: Summary of Hydrologic Conditions in Georgia, 2009," *Proceedings of the 2011 Georgia Water Resources Conference*, held April 11–13, 2011, at the University of Georgia, http://www.gawrc.org/2011paper_pdfs/2.6.1Knaak.pdf, accessed January 1, 2012; S. Heather Duncan, "Repeated Droughts Taking Toll on Midstate," *The Telegraph*, Sunday, September, 18, 2011, http://www.macon.com/2011/09/18/1707792/repeated-droughts-taking-toll.html, accessed January 1, 2012; and Shomial Ahmad, "Current Drought Conditions Projected to Worsen," broadcast transcript, November 15, 2011, http://www.publicbroadcasting.net/wabe/news.newsmain/article/2866/0/1875166/Atlanta.Morning.Edition/Current.drought.conditions.projected.to.worsen, accessed January 1, 2012.

[18] Maude Barlow, "Water as Commodity—the Wrong Prescription," *Backgrounder* 7/3 (Summer 2001), http://www.foodfirst.org/en/node/57, accessed January 3, 2012.

On a global scale, water pricing, combined with privatization, will seal water's fate as a commodity under the terms of international trade agreements supported by the World Trade Organization (WTO) and the North American Free Trade Agreement (NAFTA). Both the WTO and NAFTA consider water to be a tradable good, subject to the same rules as any other good.

WATER POLITICS, ENVIRONMENTAL JUSTICE, AND VIRTUAL WATER

As Lall and others point out, it is fair to say that most US citizens do not spend much energy thinking about the global water supply. However, the reality is that North India may soon deplete its groundwater supply; that China's Yellow River is so dry that it no longer reaches the sea; that an aquifer in Long Island, New York, is dry; and that Ethiopian women and children walk three hours each morning to eke out a day's supply from brackish mud holes that serve animals as well as humans.[19] US citizens and those of other traditionally "water-rich nations" have had the luxury until now of living in total oblivion concerning the fact that the world's climate is not exclusively a local thing. The hydrological cycle is affected by atmospheric conditions that are formed across the globe. Indeed, "the climate is a direct bridge between local rainfall or water availability and global processes."[20]

Further evidence of the interconnectedness of the world's water supply is seen when considering phenomena such as the El Niño Southern Oscillation that cause concurrent and persistent droughts in large areas of the world.[21] In wealthy nations the possibilities for water storage and

---

[19] Lall and others, "Water in the 21st Century," 8.

[20] Ibid.

[21] See "El Nino—and What Is the Southern Oscillation Anyway?!" http://kids .earth.nasa.gov/archive/nino/intro.html, accessed January 1, 2012: "El Nino, an abnormal warming of surface ocean waters in the eastern tropical Pacific, is one part of what's called the Southern Oscillation. The Southern Oscillation is the see-saw pattern of reversing surface air pressure between the eastern and western tropical Pacific; when the surface pressure is high in the eastern tropical Pacific it is low in the western tropical Pacific, and vice-versa. Because the ocean warming and pressure reversals are, for the most part, simultaneous, scientists call this phenomenon the El Nino/Southern Oscillation or ENSO for short. South American fisherman have given this phenomenon the name El Nino, which is Spanish for 'The Christ Child,' because it comes about the time of the celebration of the birth of the Christ Child—Christmas."

technological prowess that allow for ever more innovative access to water supplies from greater depths and distances have masked the realities of increased water depletion—often the result of wasteful uses. Those same peoples have relied on ever-greater amounts of grain—crops that demand high water usage—for food. Thus far, wealthy nations have been able to import foods from across the globe, making up for inadequate local water supplies. However, in the global equation, importation of foods—all of which require water to grow, harvest, and transport—effectively robs the water supplies of their places of origin. This "virtual transfer of water" is multiplied in spades when we consider the impact of other products that require the use of vast amounts of water in their production, transport, and arrival in our homes.

As Thomas M. Kostigan puts it, there is an "embedded water footprint of everything from boxers to bikinis."[22] Two-thirds of the world's freshwater is used to grow food.[23] It takes 123 gallons of water to grow one pound of oats, so the "virtual water count" for oats is 123 gallons. The US ships 30 percent of its freshwater overseas via agricultural exports. Of course, some of the virtual water is returned via imports of exports from nations such as Thailand, Canada, Australia, or Argentina, the world's top agricultural exporters. For each cup of coffee we drink, it takes thirty-seven gallons of water to grow and transport the coffee grounds to our kitchen. A hamburger costs 750 gallons of water from hoof to bun (a veggie burger costs less). While the import/export of virtual water via food supplies seems like a possible solution to the water crisis, it bears the constant threat of "price shocks"—the risk of soaring food prices, should there be crop failure or some other disruption in the patterns people become dependent on. One example of this has already occurred with the shift to the use of corn for the biofuel ethanol.[24]

---

[22] Thomas M. Kostigan, "Understanding Virtual Water to Conserve Water," Commentary, section 1, 21, *Chicago Tribune*, March 25, 2010. A definition of a water footprint has been standardized in recent years. Water Footprint Network, http://www .waterfootprint.org/?page=files/home, accessed January 2, 2012: "People use lots of water for drinking, cooking and washing, but even more for producing things such as food, paper, cotton clothes, etc. The water footprint is an indicator of water use that looks at both direct and indirect water use of a consumer or producer. The water footprint of an individual, community or business is defined as the total volume of freshwater that is used to produce the goods and services consumed by the individual or community or produced by the business."

[23] See *National Geographic*, "Water: Our Thirsty World," 52.

[24] More will be said about this in the next chapter on food security.

As for underwear, it takes 252 gallons to produce a pair of men's boxers and eighty-six gallons to make women's bikinis.[25] If I buy a T-shirt made from cotton grown in water-stressed Egypt, it will be the result of 100 percent irrigation of parched desert soil. To make a computer requires about forty-two thousand gallons to manufacture, while 50 percent of the freshwater in the United States is used to make electricity. Laptop computers require less water to make than a desktop. At this rate, the predictions of water scarcity are well underway to becoming reality. Kostigen helpfully illustrates the global interdependence of the hydrologic system: "The snow falling on New York City might once have been water at the bottom of Lake Superior, or rain runoff from someone's driveway in San Diego. Via evaporation, transpiration and precipitation, among other processes, water moves about. But when we use more here, it means less there. There are increasingly more people on the planet, and the things we do require water."[26]

From the Writings of St. Francis

"A Mirror of Perfection of the Status *of a Lesser Brother" (Sabatier Edition, 1928), Chapter 11, No. 118, "The Exceptional Love He Had for Water, Stones, Wood, and Flowers"*[27]

Next to the fire he had a singular love for water through which holy penance and tribulation is symbolized and by which the filth of the soul is washed clean and because of which the first cleansing of the soul takes place through the waters of Baptism.

Because of this, when he washed his hands, he chose a place where the water that fell to the ground would not be trampled underfoot.

---

[25] Kostigan, "Understanding Virtual Water to Conserve Water," 21.

[26] Ibid.

[27] See full text in *Francis of Assisi: Early Documents*, vol. III, *The Prophet*, trans. and ed. Regis J. Armstrong, J. A. Wayne Hellmann, and William J. Short (New York: New City Press, 2001), 366.

"The Canticle of the Creatures" (1225)[28]

Praised be You, my Lord, through Sister *Water*,
   who is very useful and humble and precious and chaste.

Reflection and Application

A Culture of Water: What Is It?

In contrast to taking water for granted, oblivious to the true value of water as God's precious gift, a "culture of water" requires of us an acute awareness of humans living within the limits of the hydrological cycle.[29] Like St. Francis, we need to understand the singular vitality of water and its essential role in sustaining our health in every moment of our existence, from the moment of our conception, during our nine-month swim within our mother's womb, and throughout our lifetime, as well as its role in receiving and recycling our bodies into the earth upon our death. A water culture requires that we care for the places where water is held—rivers, streams, lakes, oceans, reservoirs, aquifers, water tables, the atmosphere—as well as for the catchment forests, flowers, and fauna that require their own health to serve their role in recharging the gift of water. Water that flows freely is truly living water that can provide vitality for all. But this is not true for water that is confined to unlimited paved surfaces or to dams that restrict and imprison it, making it unable to return to the ground, leaving it only to stagnate or evaporate and to die.

There will be certain things we cannot do if we live in a water culture, as well as activities that we must do. We need to limit our use of water to what is necessary, rather than what we might desire. Indeed, we must conceive of our existence as sisters and brothers within the whole of creation. Not only humans but all plant, animal, and microbial life has a right to its share of water. Water does not comprehend the artificial constructs of "national boundaries" and massive engineering projects

---

[28] See full text in *Francis of Assisi: Early Documents*, vol. I, *The Saint*, trans. and ed. Regis J. Armstrong, J. A. Wayne Hellmann, and William J. Short (New York: New City Press), 113–14.

[29] See Andy Opel, "From Water Crisis to Water Culture: Dr. Vandana Shiva, an Interview by Andy Opel," *Cultural Studies* 22/3–4 (May–July 2008): 498–509.

that try to control it with impunity, but rather the economies of ecosystems, the smaller scale, the local that forms the web of life—human and otherkind.[30] Even with a global population of seven billion people, if we live with a conscious awareness and respect for water, we may not get all the water we want, but we can have the water we need.[31]

Illusions of Safety: Bottled Water and Water Privatization

THE CASE OF BOTTLED WATER

In the previous chapter we showed that one of the major weaknesses of much environmental education is that it focuses on individual action when the real solutions to most environmental problems also require systemic change. For example, it is known that the dry-cleaning solvent perchlorethylene is a common pollutant in drinking water, and it is a suspected carcinogen.[32] Rather than teaching people to demand that the government ban that chemical, we are encouraged to simply air out our freshly dry-cleaned clothing prior to hanging them in the closet! On other occasions, we are advised to rid ourselves of pollutions by purchasing the right gadget—air filters, water filters, bottled water, pesticide-removing

---

[30] See the vast array of evidence showing that the unprecedented disaster of Hurricane Katrina in 2005 in New Orleans, LA, was not a "natural disaster" but rather the result of engineering strategies based on a "knowledge-based worldview" model rather than an "ignorance-based worldview" model. See R. Eugene Turner, "Doubt and the Values of an Ignorance-Based World View for Restoration: Coastal Louisiana Wetlands," *Estuaries and Coasts* 32/6 (November 2009): 1054–68. Also see the web site of the documentary *The Big Uneasy*, directed and written by Harry Shearer, http://www.thebiguneasy.com/resources.html, accessed June 4, 2011. Note that this web site has links to official scientific and engineering studies and investigative reports that substantiate the claims made in the documentary.

[31] A couple of examples will serve to illustrate the wasteful opulence in the use of water that can be found across the globe. See *National Geographic*, "Water: Our Thirsty World," 30; a twenty-acre swimming hole that stretches half a mile, is 115 feet deep, and holds sixty-six million gallons of water was created at Chili's San Alfonso del Mar resort by the Chilean firm Crystal Lagoons, at the cost of $3.5 million. Plans are for an even larger facility in Egypt. See also *National Geographic*, "Water: Our Thirsty World," 150: Florida uses three thousand gallons to water grass for each golf game played; US swimming pools lose 150 billion gallons to evaporation each year.

[32] See Sandra Steingraber, "The Myth of Living Safely in a Toxic World, In These Times, April 30, 2001, http://www.inthesetimes.com/article/1491/the_myth_of_living_safely_in_a_toxic_world, accessed January 3, 2012.

soap to clean our vegetables, or antioxidant pills to supplement our lack of fresh produce.

The facts tell us a different story. No matter how hard we try, we cannot buy our way out of the hydrologic cycle and live to tell the story. In the case of bottled water, in the 1970s companies such as Coca-Cola, Nestle, Pepsi, or Suez noticed that their sale of soft drinks had peaked.[33] Indeed, there was a trend toward greater health and fitness afoot in the general public that exposed the unhealthy nature of soft drinks, potentially diminishing future sales. In light of this, these companies set out to manufacture a need for their new product, bottled water. Their advertising campaigns were designed to make people fearful of their local water supply—tap water. Bottled water was presented as the panacea against unsafe local water and fifty- to one-hundred-year-old water infrastructures and delivery systems that local governments had failed to properly maintain. At best, such appeals are half truths. What the ads did not tell the public is that the bottled water industry is unregulated, so there is no guarantee of the purity of what is in their bottles either! Further, random testing by independent sources has found trace carcinogens and bacteria in those bottles while local tap water was pure! What the ads did not tell consumers is that up to 40 percent of the water sold by the bottled water industry is local tap water. Nor did they mention that the annual cost of making the plastic bottles for the US market alone takes enough oil and energy to fuel a million cars, and that does not include fuel and costs for shipping the bottled water, often across the continent or the world.

Beyond that, it is more likely breathing polluted air rather than drinking water that exposes people to the most volatile chemicals. Pollution from chemicals in pesticides, solvents, or byproducts of chlorination in the water becomes airborne the minute the tap is turned on or the toilet is flushed. Therefore, filters are ineffective against those most common pollutants. Even if we could filter every drop of water that entered every household, about every three to six months people would still need to dispose of the filters, that is, throw them away. But exactly where is "away"? Throw dirty filters in the trash, and the chemicals leech back into the soil; incinerate them, and the chemicals go back into the air!

[33] Annie Leonard, "The Story of Bottled Water: Fear, Manufactured Demand and a $10,000 Sandwich," *Huffington Post*, March 22, 2010, http://www.huffingtonpost.com/annie-leonard/the-story-of-bottled-wate_b_507942.html, accessed January 3, 2012.

Either way, the hydrological cycle will be affected. Would it not be wiser to take on the structural questions of halting pollution in the first place? Would it not be better to demand the long-term solution of an updating and proper maintenance of municipal and rural water delivery systems and to require accountability and transparency to citizens and enforcement of regulations?

As Bill McKibben points out, though, it is encouraging to see that sales of bottled water dropped 3.5 percent in 2009, ironically there was also a boom in sales of filters for faucets and shower heads, as well as expensive filter dispensers like Aquaovo Ovopur's $650 "giant porcelain egg" or Design Within Reach's dispenser that sports "stones from the coast of the Sea of Japan and Binchotan charcoal for 'odor free water.'"[34] The tactics of fear mongering concerning tap water are still influencing people's behavior; indeed, safe drinking water is the number one environmental concern in the United States. But here is where we confront the larger issues of the privatization of access to water and of water delivery systems headlong.

PRIVATIZATION OF DRINKING WATER

It is true that the aging water systems in the United States are urgently in need of attention. In March of 2010 the *New York Times* reported that every hour there is a major water main break in some US city.[35] With rising populations and widespread citizen resistance to taxation to support the common good, it has become increasingly difficult for cities to maintain these infrastructures. Ironically, people are willing to spend thousands of dollars for bottled water and filters but nothing to safeguard the collective health of themselves and their neighbors. From a Christian view, such thinking smacks of moral and spiritual deficiency—something is terribly wrong here! Indeed, already back in 2005 the Global Concerns Committee of the Leadership Conference of Women Religious (LCWR) published a background paper in support of the LCWR's campaign against the privatization of water. It noted, "The private sector, especially

---

[34] Bill McKibben, "Water, Water, Everywhere," *Sojourners* (June 2010), http://www.sojo.net/magazine/2010/06/water-water-everywhere, accessed January 3, 2012. McKibben notes that $650 would pay for a decent well in a developing country!

[35] Charles Duhigg, "Saving U.S. Water and Sewer Systems Would Be Costly," Toxic Waters Series, *New York Times*, March 14, 2010, http://www.nytimes.com/2010/03/15/us/15water.html?pagewanted=print, accessed January 9, 2012.

privatization of water

a handful of transnational corporations, has recognized that water is the 'blue gold' of the 21st century."[36] Such thinking allows water to be treated exclusively as a commodity, and with impunity.

SIX KINDS OF WATER PRIVATIZATION

Over the decades six major approaches to water privatization have developed, each with its own commercial advantages and ethical challenges.[37] The first model is privatization of municipal services in urban areas. Here legislation and/or contracts "allow transnational corporations to appropriate municipal and regional purifying facilities and distribution networks."[38] The second model is the privatization of whole territories or bioregions. Private companies that trade in or bottle water require large amounts of water, contractually own all the water in an entire area, and often manage access to water for the region's population. In the third model, companies divert water from entire rivers or other sources from their natural courses into canals, waterways, or dams for their exclusive use in industry or agribusiness, removing any access from traditional users such as indigenous peoples or small farmers. The fourth model is frequently used by private mining, oil drilling, paper pulp manufacturing, electricity generation, and toxic agrochemical-intensive monocultures or operations. Companies pollute the water sources, rendering them too toxic for any others to use. A fifth approach used by transnational private companies is to bottle the water that they obtain in bulk "at extremely low cost (often from municipal water supplies, and often for much less per liter than households pay). The companies usually obtain state subsidies for building bottling plants and then bottle, export, and sell the water for a thousand times or more what they paid for it."[39] The sixth and final model is privatization by monopolizing technologies used to extract and purify water. In competitive markets

[36] Suzanne Golas, "Privatization of Water," *Resolutions to Action* 14/3 (June 2005): 1–2. See also S. Tully, "Water, Water, Everywhere," *Fortune* 141/10 (May 2000): 342–54. Tully states, "Water promises to be to the 21st century what oil was to the 20th century: the precious commodity that determines the wealth of nations."

[37] Christine E. Gudorf, "Water Privatization in Christianity and Islam," *Journal of the Society of Christian Ethics* 30/2 (2010): 20–21.

[38] Ibid.," 20.

[39] Ibid., 21. Gudorf also cites the case of Costa Rica's attempt to levy an export tax on such activities only to find that under the terms of the NAFTA treaty, nations could not discriminate according to product against global companies. See also Mara Flores-

and with stressed municipal and regional budgets, private companies can offer greater efficiency and purity in water extraction and delivery at a reasonable price (at least initially). Recent technologies allow private companies to go ever deeper into the hydrological cycle and bypass the extraction of water in its liquid form.[40] This presents yet other ethical challenges for the future.

Privatization has always been with us in some form, but on a vastly smaller scale and size. However, already back in 2000 at the Stockholm Water Symposium of world leaders and representatives from civil society, it was recognized that by 2025 two-thirds of the world's population would be living with water shortages or absolute water scarcity. This realization was coupled with the belief in a (then) new globalized economy where literally everything had its price and nothing was "off limits," including seeds, genes, cultural heritage, food, air, and water![41]

In more recent decades, these attitudes have become more pervasive, and more than 850 free-trade zones were developed across the globe in which environmental laws have been stripped of their clout or eliminated altogether, allowing for large-scale commercial exploitation of water and its criminal pollution. The door was left wide open for water to be marketed and managed—like any other economic resource, it is a commodity. As Barlow puts it, "Huge corporate factories are moving up the rivers of the Third World, sucking them dry as they go."[42] Setting aside any skepticism (risking naïveté), we acknowledge that the companies claim they provide services that are socially beneficial. Yet it is hard to trust their intent when corporate directors state, as did Mr. During of Suez Lyonnaise des Eaux, for example, "We are here to make money. Sooner or later the company that invests recoups its investment, which means the customer has to pay for it."[43] Additional doubt is raised when realizing the aggressive extent to which corporations go to make their profit. Global Water Corporation of Canada ships Alaskan glacier water by tanker to be bottled in a free-trade zone in China, bragging how clever

Estrada, "CAFTA Threatens to Turn Water into Merchandise," *Latinamerica Press* 20 (October 31, 2007): 6.

[40] McKibben, in "Water, Water, Everywhere," states, "Whatever pours out of the $1,595 'dehumidifier/purification system' from Atmospheric Water Systems that 'bypasses pipes altogether, pulling moisture from the air and sending it through a multi-step filtration process,' is not the living water we most need."

[41] Barlow, "Water as Commodity—the Wrong Prescription."

[42] Ibid.

[43] Ibid.

they are to exploit China's cheap labor and undercut other imported products. They attract investors with these words: "Water has moved from being an endless commodity that may be taken for granted to a rationed necessity that may be taken by force."[44] With privatization, water sustainability is not the top priority in commercial water management; rather, there is every incentive to encourage consumption for more profit. Moreover, the greater the scarcity of water, the more likely it is that complex technologies that disturb or destroy ecosystems (such as desalination, diversion, or export of water), rather than conservation, will be introduced.

Privatization severely limits or eliminates entirely involvement of ordinary citizens, and the transparency of the water systems' management moves out of public control. As we saw above, the World Bank has minimal disclosure requirements. As Maude Barlow points out, "A water corporation executive at the recent World Water Forum in The Hague said publicly that as long as water was coming out of the tap, the public had no right to any information as to how it got there. . . . To add insult to injury, the World Bank underwrites these giant corporations with public money, and often incurs the risk, while the companies reap the profit. And often, governments, who supposedly represent their people, have to assure a return to the shareholder. Chile had to guarantee a profit margin of 33 percent to Suez Lyonnaise des Eaux as a condition of the World Bank—regardless of performance."[45]

Beyond shifting citizen and local government control over water, public health and safety is also seen in a different light. In Ontario, Canada, it was well known that there was high risk for *E. coli* contamination in rural wells, and the government put the Drinking Water Surveillance Program (DWSP) in place with trained personnel who regularly tested those waters. After Ontario privatized its water system, the DWSP and its staff were cut from the budget. In June 2000, fourteen people, including a baby, died from drinking water in Walkerton, Ontario. As Maude Barlow tells it, "The town had subcontracted to a branch-plant of a private testing company from Tennessee. The lab, A&L Laboratories, discovered *E. coli* in the water, but failed to report the contamination to provincial authorities, an option it has under the new 'common sense' rules. In true corporate-speak, a lab spokesman said that the test results

[44] Ibid.
[45] Ibid.

were 'confidential intellectual property.' As such, they belonged only to the 'client'—the public officials of Walkerton who were not trained to deal with the tests."[46]

As already noted, commercial pricing of water is generally a bad idea. From the perspective of the poor, water pricing exacerbates the existing global inequality of access to water—those who can pay have access. Globally, water pricing by for-profit corporations will likely widen the North/South divide. Clearly, it is the rich (and water-rich) nations of the world, which constitute only 12 percent of the world's population, that use 85 percent of Earth's water.[47] The rich can afford safe and healthy alternatives. But, as in England, privatization will likely force millions to choose whether or not to wash their food, flush their toilets, or even bathe.[48]

Basic fairness dictates that the burden of proof must be on those who use water most and then remove the benefits of using this common good, this public trust, from the community in the form of profits, particularly in an age of mergers and transnationals. As we will elaborate below, business has no right to deprive anyone of his or her inalienable human rights; if that is the price of profit, the price is too high. And beyond that, if left unchecked, the "chickens will come home to roost" when the very ecosystems that create and sustain the hydrological cycle, but are not included in the corporate equation, lie in ruin. Simply put, if we lose public control of our water systems, there may be no one left with the ability to claim water—this life-giving source for *all*.

Toward a Way Forward

In order to responsibly deal with the present water crisis, we must first believe that water belongs to the earth and all species and is thus sacred to all life on the planet. All decisions about water must be based on genuinely sustainable ecosystem- and watershed-based management.[49] Second, water must be declared a basic human right and incorporated into the normative codes of law for meaningful enforcement. Third, such codes must hold water as a public trust to be guarded at all levels of government. No one has the right to appropriate it at another's

[46] Ibid.
[47] See *National Geographic*, "Water: Our Thirsty World," 22–23.
[48] Barlow, "Water as Commodity—Wrong Prescription."
[49] See the discussion of sustainability in chapter 7.

expense or for profit. Water must not be privatized, traded, or exported for commercial gain. Above all, we, as human beings, must change our behaviors to conserve God's precious gift of water.

WATER:
A HUMAN RIGHT WITH CHALLENGES FOR IMPLEMENTATION

On July 28, 2010, the United Nations General Assembly passed Resolution 64/292, "The Human Right to Water and Sanitation." It was introduced by Bolivia's permanent representative to the UN, Pablo Solon.[50] The vote was 122 members in support, and more than forty-one nations, including the United States, abstained.[51] As was widely reported, the significant portion of the resolution was contained in the last three points of the document.

> 1. [The General Assembly] *recognizes* the right to safe and clean drinking water and sanitation as a human right that is essential for the full enjoyment of life and all human rights;
> 2. *Calls upon* States and international organizations to provide financial resources, capacity-building and technology transfer, through international assistance and cooperation, in particular to developing countries, in order to scale up efforts to provide safe, clean, accessible and affordable drinking water and sanitation for all;
> 3. *Welcomes* the decision by the Human Rights Council to request that the independent expert on human rights obligations related to access to safe drinking water and sanitation submit an annual report to the General Assembly, and encourages her to continue working on all aspects of her mandate and, in consultation with all relevant United Nations agencies, funds and programmes, to include in her report to the Assembly, at its sixty-sixth session, the principal challenges related to the realization of the human right to safe and clean drinking water and sanitation and their impact on the achievement of the Millennium Development Goals.[52]

---

[50] Notably, Bolivia is a nation that has recently experienced severe droughts and whose major water supply from glaciers in immanently threatened by global warming.

[51] See the press release from the UN Department of Public Information, News and Media Division, New York, http://www.un.org/News/Press/docs/2010/ga10967 .doc.htm, accessed January 9, 2012.

[52] United Nations General Assembly, Resolution 64/292, "The Human Right to Water and Sanitation" (July 28, 2010), http://www.un.org/ga/search/view_doc .asp?symbol=A/RES/64/292, accessed January 9. 2012.

This resolution is not binding on member nations because it did not go through the UN's extensive procedures to make it so. In fact, the UN Human Rights Council was still in Geneva conducting discussions on water and sanitation, working to place the concerns reflected in Resolution 64/292 within the bounds of international law. Though many supporters of the resolution recognize the limitations it bears, they view it as a significant moral mandate and a starting point for incorporating the right to water and sanitation with equal weight of the 1948 Universal Declaration of Human Rights.[53] Thus, the language used in the resolution was highly intentional. Proponents rejected the phrase "access to water" in favor of "the human right to water and sanitation." The phrase "access to water" leaves the door open for governments to take a minimalistic approach and to circumvent the urgent concerns expressed in the resolution. That is, they could simply provide *access* to everyone, but then *charge unjust prices* directly or contract with commercial vendors who would do the same; alternatively, they could provide *inadequate services, supplies, or impure water*. Such possibilities would exclude many people, especially the poor and the vulnerable.

Nonetheless, if Resolution 64/292 is to become effective, just as with the 1948 Universal Declaration of Human Rights, this strong intent and language needs further clarification and integration into current international law.[54] Law Professor Bruce Pardy of Queens University, Kingston, Canada, criticizes the resolution on several counts, and his critique is typical.[55] He holds that the resolution is based on two conflicting premises: "The first is that governments cannot be trusted to make clean water available. Therefore, norms of international law must be brought to bear upon them. An international right is the means whereby national governments can be held accountable. The second premise is that only governments can be trusted to deal with water, and certainly the private sector cannot. The nature of the proposed rights implies that only governments may provide water, and therefore must do so in the form of water monopolies."[56]

---

[53] See the full text of the Universal Declaration of Human Rights (1948) at http://www.un.org/en/documents/udhr, accessed January 9, 2012.

[54] See Melvin Woodhouse and Malcolm Langford, "Crossfire: There Is No Human Right to Water for Livelihoods," *Waterlines* 28/1 (January 2009), http://www.jus.uio.no/smr/english/people/aca/malcolml/Human%20Right%20to%20Water%20and%20Livelihood%20Debate.pdf, accessed June 25, 2012.

[55] Bruce Pardy, "The Dark Irony of International Water Rights," *Rediscovering Sustainable Development Law*, 28/3 (Spring 2011): 907–20.

[56] Ibid., 907–8.

Pardy also presents three possible interpretations of the language of the resolution, which require clarification: "It could mean (a) that some countries can compel other countries to provide water and/or financial resources; (b) that individual citizens can require their own governments to provide water and sanitation; or (c) nothing in binding legal terms. These interpretations are vastly different but none of them protect against actual threats to clean water, and indeed may make them more acute."[57] He then elaborates various difficulties with each of the interpretations for achieving the goal of making adequate and sustainable water and sanitation a reality for the world's human population. He discusses the difficulty and impossibility of enforcing a positive right, pointing out that nearly all laws are written in terms of negative rights.[58] He is against commercial or government monopolies that control water. He concludes:

> The better approach is to not monopolize water. It may not be practical to build multiple sets of pipes underneath urban areas, but that does not mean that competition in treatment or delivery is not possible. Furthermore, where settlement is rural and people obtain their water via their own private or village wells, there is no rationale for monopoly.
>
> When water is captured, it becomes a private good. Before capture, it is a common resource, flowing underground and in surface bodies towards the ocean. Governments have a legitimate role to play, protecting both quality and quantity, so that there is clean water available for the taking. This role is as protector, not provider. All that is called for is to prevent pollution and depletion—not to actively provide water, but to protect the resource from interference from those who would impose environmental externalities upon it.
>
> Good water governance requires good governance, broadly conceived. International water rights do not achieve this objective, and are likely to threaten the enterprise of protecting water resources.[59]

A VIEW FROM CHRISTIAN ETHICS

Water is the most frequently named earth element in the entire Bible. The primary meaning is drawn from the physical reality of human existence—namely, that without water, humans and all living things die.

---

[57] Ibid., 908–9.
[58] Ibid., 912–17.
[59] Ibid., 919–20.

Both physically and spiritually, water, with its capacity for healing and purification as well as its biological life-giving qualities, is necessary for all of humanity, indeed for all life. A few familiar examples can serve to remind us. Psalm 51:2 reads, "Wash me thoroughly from my iniquity, and cleanse me from my sin." In John 13:5-6, Jesus "took off his outer robe, and tied a towel around himself. Then he poured water into a basin and began to wash the disciples' feet and to wipe them with the towel that was tied around him." In John 3:5, Jesus answers Nicodemus, "Very truly, I tell you, no one can enter the kingdom of God without being born of water and Spirit."

Yet we know that the earliest Christians were often in the minority in their communities, and there is evidence that they simply adopted the governance of the locales where they lived. Thus, there is really no explicit guidance from the Bible for today's water questions. However, there is a tradition of values that we can draw from the biblical material. Water has constantly been viewed as a free gift from God the Creator. From that, it is possible to conclude that it is idolatrous to presume absolute ownership, such as when a corporation lays claim to all water rights of a region or ecosystem. It is also a breach of fundamental human dignity when corporate ownership makes it impossible for legal recourse by people whose fundamental survival needs for water and whose life of dignity are violated.

Biblical discussions about water in the Hebrew Testament center on creation, stewardship, and hospitality. These themes are extended to the Christian Testament. Connected to the biblical material and philosophical ethics, natural law arguments have also been developed that make the basic access and use of water a matter of justice. Along with this, the ultimate test for the fulfillment of justice is how the poor and the vulnerable are treated and whether their fundamental needs for a life of dignity are met.

Bringing these notions to bear on the present-day privatization of water (treatment and delivery) or privatization by diversion (dams, canals, waterways), the test of justice still remains: the poor cannot be deprived of the access and use of water to meet their basic needs.[60] The central question is how justice is to be accomplished in the concrete case. In market economies, while the goal of justice for the poor remains, the

---

[60] See Christine E. Gudof, "Water Privatization in Christianity and Islam," *Journal of the Society of Christian Ethics* 30/2 (2010): 19–38.

demands of stewardship are particularly urgent given what we know of the realities and probabilities for water scarcity. Today there need to be ways to conserve as much water as possible. In most instances conservation implies some form of water pricing. Some party or parties need to bear the costs of extraction, treatment, storage, transportation, and recycling water in a closed-loop system—particularly in the urban areas where most of the world's people live. As Christine Gudorf points out, across the globe most urban water rates are typically only one-sixth of the full cost of providing clean, safe water to all.[61]

Gudorf helpfully suggests several models from different parts of the world that seem to meet the measure of justice for the poor and provide incentives for conservation, practical mechanisms for financial requirements, and provisions for legal recourse if violations against basic human water needs occur. She holds that models used in Saudi Arabia and Iran are such models. In Saudi Arabia, until 1994 water was provided to all for free. But thereafter near full pricing was introduced by the government "to acquaint its citizens with the cost of providing water services."[62]

It is widely recognized that thirty liters of water per person per day is a generous measure of water sufficient to meet the basic thirst of each person. Thus, the Iranian system provides that amount free to all domestic customers in urban areas. The full cost is then charged for additional liters, while commercial customers pay the full cost for all water used. Ecologically, everyone benefits: water is sufficient for all; it is conserved; everyone is also included in a separate sewer system; and leakage from pipes is all but eliminated.[63]

In Dhaka, Bangladesh, a local nongovernmental organization (NGO) called Dushtha Shasthya Kendra (DSK) and the international NGO WaterAid worked with the Dhaka Water Supply and Sewage Authority (DWSSA) to meet the moral right to water at a fair price for slum dwellers. DSK was the initial guarantor of the initial cost for installing the water faucets. The slum dwellers formed committees to maintain the faucets and insure everyone paid his or her bills. Eventually, the DWSSA turned control over to the slum dwellers, and DSK was no longer needed.[64] Again, everyone benefited. The slum dwellers got safe water, and illegal tapping into the municipal system ground to a halt.

[61] Ibid., 29.
[62] Ibid., 30.
[63] Ibid.
[64] Ibid., 34.

Generally, collective water faucets (with pressure shut-off valves for conservation) are a successful solution when they are strategically placed in a community through communal and collaborative efforts. Community committees are organized to collect money for the water at a reasonable price. Usually, the women and children extract the water from the faucets and carry it home. There is little waste and everyone has enough.

These models pool the resources of the community at the local level and ultimately reduce costs. As Gudorf shows, without intentionally organized community water supplies, poor people normally pay more than the full price (charged by municipalities) for water to meet their needs. In the informal market, street venders and truckers usually charge 75–100 percent or more above the municipal full cost. In Jordan, "unserved residents now pay $2 per cubic meter of water while served residents pay a maximum of $.50. The full-cost price is $1 per cubic meter."[65]

It is possible to control privatization, obtain justice for the poor, and conserve God's precious gift without sacrificing either sustainability or just access to and use of water to meet fundamental human needs. The Catholic Rural Life Conference of the United States recommends twelve excellent guiding principles that are most helpful in moral guidance for water resource management and decisions about resource distribution across the globe.

CONSIDERATIONS FOR DECISION MAKING

According to the Catholic Rural Life Conference, "Water management and resource distribution must be guided by considerations for the common good of the people of the world and the natural systems of the planet itself."[66]

1. Water has intrinsic value in itself, independent of its utilitarian and commercial value.

2. Access to enough safe, clean and affordable water for personal and domestic use is a basic human right.

---

[65] Ibid., 35.

[66] Catholic Rural Life Conference, "Pure Water: A Sacramental Commons for All," http://www.ncrlc.com/page.aspx?ID=80, accessed January 4, 2012.

3. Water should be held in the public domain, as a common good for all people. Governance decisions should not be based on profit, but should be made according to the criteria of equity and human dignity, sustainability of all life, and meaningful community participation.

4. If a government decides to shift the public responsibility for providing quality water to private entities, it should ensure the protection of the public interest so that the rights of poor and low-income people are not denied, and that principles of sustainability are protected.

5. Decision making should be characterized by openness, transparency, and strong public regulatory oversight. All local, national and international public institutions have responsibility to ensure these conditions.

6. Water must not be used as a tool of oppression. Political boundaries should not hinder access to water.

7. Water resource management should be based on the principle that water is an integral part of the ecosystem and on an understanding of the hydrologic cycle and the integrity of hydrographic basins.

8. Water is a social and cultural good. It has also become an economic good. Policies relating to the economics of water should ensure efficiency and the most beneficial uses as determined by all stakeholders.

9. When a community water supply becomes unsafe to drink or is in some other way interrupted, water must be provided at or below cost by public authorities.

10. Water should not be traded as a commodity. The sovereign right of each country to regulate its water resources and sanitation services should be reaffirmed.

11. Each person has the right to water for a basic livelihood. Marginalized and vulnerable social sectors should be given priority in terms of access to water and appropriate water technologies for subsistence.

12. In all policy decisions, always ensure the needs of poor and vulnerable people while meeting the goal of environmental sustainability.[67]

---

[67] Ibid.

We say again that water is a sacred gift, inspiring in people a response of gratitude. A spirituality of gratitude takes us beyond seeing water as only a physical or economic good, and even a social or cultural good: Water is a gift of the Creator and treated as a sacramental commons for its unique life-giving role in creation.[68]

Upon learning about the complex state of affairs concerning the water crisis, we can allow ourselves to become overwhelmed and paralyzed and to move into a state of denial and inaction. Or, as people of faith in the resurrected Christ, the one who is the Living Water of Life, we can move forward, analyze the problem, and act to make a difference.

CATHOLIC SOCIAL TEACHING AND WATER

Building on the life-giving and necessary nature of water, Catholic social teaching sets out a clear direction for our faith-filled choice to ensure that all people and all our fellow creatures have enough water to sustain life and health. "Water by its very nature cannot be treated as a mere commodity among other commodities. Catholic social thought has always stressed that the defense and preservation of certain common goods, such as the natural and human environments, cannot be safeguarded simply by market forces, since they touch on fundamental human needs which *escape market logic*."[69] Two foundational magisterial documents shape the basic outlines of Catholic belief and our call to act to bring water justice to all on our planet, namely, Water: An Essential Element for Life,[70] by the Pontifical Justice and Peace Council, and its update.[71] Both documents were presented to forums of the UN in 2003

---

[68] Ibid.

[69] Pontifical Council for Justice and Peace, Water: An Essential Element for Life, emphasis added. See also Pope John Paul II, *Centesimus Annus*, no. 40, http://www.vatican.va/holy_father/john_paul_ii/encyclicals/documents/hf_jp-ii_enc_01051991_centesimus-annus_en.html, accessed December 31, 2011. In this encyclical, the late Pope John Paul II admonished that there is an important role for governments in maintaining the common good.

[70] Pontifical Council for Justice and Peace, Water: An Essential Element for Life.

[71] Pontifical Council for Justice and Peace, Water: An Essential Element for Life; An Update, http://www.vatican.va/roman_curia/pontifical_councils/justpeace/documents/rc_pc_justpeace_doc_20060322_mexico-water_en.html, accessed December 31, 2011.

and 2006, respectively.[72] The teachings in these documents have been reaffirmed and elaborated in various contexts in subsequent years by the late Pope John Paul II and by Pope Benedict XVI, giving greater overall authority to their content while adapting them to current issues.

Safe drinking water is a necessity of life; people can survive only a few days without it. As we have indicated, the majority of the world faces enormous hardship daily, having neither sufficient nor safe water, and women disproportionately bear this burden. Certainly, water for the whole human family is a right-to-life issue.[73]

Equally important, "water is a major factor in each of the three pillars of sustainable development—economic, social, and environmental. In this framework, it is understood that water must meet the needs of the present population and those of future generations of all societies. This is not solely in the economic realm but in the sphere of integral human development. Water policy, to be sustainable, must promote the good of *every* person and of the *whole* person."[74]

Today the principle problem concerning water is one not of absolute scarcity but rather of distribution and resources. In recent years Catholic leaders have made strong arguments that the right to sufficient, free, and safe water is intimately linked to respect for the life and dignity of each human person.

Indeed, the foundational principle determining all Catholic morality, including the use of safe and sufficient water, is the invaluable worth and dignity of each person. Beyond this, given what the ecological sciences teach us about the interconnection of the web of life, we usually cannot have maximum human well-being without environmental integrity.[75]

Therefore, the Pontifical Justice and Peace Commission (PJPC) teaches: "The human person must be the central point of convergence of all issues pertaining to development, the environment, and water. . . . The first

---

[72] This section of the chapter utilizes the structure of the two documents by the Pontifical Justice and Peace Commission: Water: An Essential Element for Life and Water: An Essential Element for Life; An Update. This section is built from excerpts and paraphrases from the two Vatican documents.

[73] See Pontifical Council for Justice and Peace, Water: An Essential Element for Life.

[74] Ibid., emphasis added.

[75] Ibid.

priority of every country and the international community for sustainable water policy should be to provide access to safe water to those who are deprived of such access at present."[76]

According to the PJPC, a third pertinent principle of Catholic morality is the "*universal destination of the goods of creation* [which] confirms that people and countries, including future generations, have the *right* to fundamental access to those goods which are necessary for their development. Water is such a common good of humankind."[77] It is this principle that is the ground for giving priority to people living with water scarcity, especially those who are also poor. This principle also provides the basis for prohibitions against the powerful managing water supplies through policies that allow them to foul, waste, or manipulate water with impunity.

When addressing the bishops of Brazil in 2004, Pope John Paul II wrote, "As a gift from God, water is a vital element essential to survival; thus everyone has a right to it."[78] Indeed, water is a human right. In the words of the Pontifical Council for Justice and Peace, "A human right is generally protected by internationally guaranteed standards that ensure fundamental freedoms for individuals and communities. It principally concerns the relationship between the individual and the State."[79] In this regard, governments are obligated to respect, protect, and fulfill the human right to safe, drinkable water.

Even with the July 28, 2010, passage of the UN General Assembly Resolution 64/292, at present there is no single global organization mandated to coordinate and deal with water and its related issues among the community of nations. However, various international treaties and declarations legally support claims that the access to a regular supply of safe water clearly falls within the category of guarantees essential for securing an adequate standard of living.[80] All states who are parties to

[76] Ibid.

[77] Ibid., second emphasis added.

[78] Pope John Paul II, "Message of John Paul II for Brazil's Lenten 'Campaign of Fraternity 2004,'" http://www.vatican.va/holy_father/john_paul_ii/speeches/2004/february/documents/hf_jp-ii_spe_20040225_fraternita_en.html, accessed December 31, 2011.

[79] Pontifical Council for Justice and Peace, Water: An Essential Element for Life; An Update.

[80] See The Convention on the Rights of the Child, 1950, no. 24. See also UN Committee on Economic, Social, and Cultural Rights, Supervisory Body of the Covenant on Economic, Social, and Cultural Rights, "General Comment," 2002; International

such treaties and declarations have "an obligation to ensure that the minimum essential level of [the right to water] is realized."[81] This means that everyone, without discrimination, has access to enough water to prevent dehydration and disease.

The PJPC also asserts that *"people must become the 'active subjects' of safe water policies."* People have "the ability to perceive the needs of others and satisfy them. Water management should be based on a participatory approach, involving users, planners and policy makers at all levels. Both men and women should be involved and have equal voice in managing water resources and sharing of the benefits that come from sustainable water use."[82]

Yet another important principle the PJPC calls us to attend to is "solidarity." In the Catholic moral tradition, "solidarity is a firm and persevering determination to commit oneself to the common good, to the good of all and of each individual. It presupposes the effort for a more just social order and requires a preferential attention to the situation of the poor."[83] Both individuals and nations have the same duty of solidarity; advanced nations have the weightiest obligation to help developing people.[84]

Knowledge of local water supplies and their ecological functions and histories is normally best known by local people. In light of that, it is not only good common sense but also good moral practice to evoke the Catholic moral principle of "subsidiarity" when shaping policies pertaining to the human right to water. This principle "acknowledges that decisions and management responsibilities pertaining to water should take place at the lowest appropriate level."[85] As we can see from scientific explanations of the hydrocycle, water is not only a local matter but also a global one. What happens to any one water supply at the local level will effect changes across the planet. So it is important that the considerable wisdom about water be utilized through grassroots engagement of local peoples throughout any water program.

Covenant on Economic, Social, and Cultural Rights, article 2, no. 1; and the UN Committee Resolution on Economic, Social, and Cultural Rights, 2000.

[81] Pontifical Council for Justice and Peace, Water: An Essential Element for Life; An Update.

[82] Pontifical Council for Justice and Peace, Water: An Essential Element for Life.

[83] Ibid.

[84] Ibid.

[85] Ibid.

The PJPC also teaches that "while vital to humanity, water has a strong social content."[86] Its role is critical in establishing (1) agriculture and food security, (2) health and sanitation, (3) peace and conflict resolution, and (4) control of global warming and natural disasters.

Globally, agriculture is a key sector in all economies, but it cannot be sustained without sufficient water. Especially in developing countries, agriculture is a major source of livelihood and an essential dimension of local social cohesion and culture. Worldwide, agriculture accounts for 80 percent of the use of water and will continue to be necessary for food security.

Driven by necessity, rural poor people sometimes exploit beyond sustainable limits the little land they have at their disposal. Special training in water conservation techniques is needed to assist them in maximizing and conserving their precious water supplies. Also, the traditional forms of knowledge of indigenous people should be esteemed, and it can be vital and decisive in addressing and solving the question of water.[87]

In many places across the globe, damage from practices such as waterlogging and salinization has rendered land and water useless for human sustenance. In a world threatened by both water scarcity and food insecurity, it is vital that such lands and water sources be reclaimed. "Policies must encourage harnessing the wider potential of rainfed farming, incorporating water management for gardens and foods from common property resources."[88]

There is an intimate relationship between human health and the use of sufficient and safe water. So policymakers and local communities need to be concerned with issues of quantity—especially for water-poor countries; issues of the safe quality of water for growing populations; and issues stemming from waterborne diseases and chronic thirst.[89]

Management of water quantity can be carried out by (a) revising the allocation of water to different users; (b) better maintenance and repair of existing water systems; (c) implementing and enforcing water conservation methods such as rainwater harvesting, fog condensation, use of underground dams, stabilization ponds for wastewater, and treatment and use of that wastewater for irrigation.

---

[86] Ibid. In this section I am following the PCJP's structure throughout.
[87] Ibid.
[88] Ibid.
[89] Ibid.

Key solutions for maintaining and improving *water quality* include enforcing pollution controls at the main point sources, especially in urbanized areas in developing countries, and establishing sustainable and safe sanitation, garbage collection, and disposal systems.[90]

Because human and animal waste is the single largest source for waterborne disease and contamination, proper wastewater treatment throughout the entire world is the absolutely necessary solution toward eliminating water-transmitted illness.[91]

As the PJPC concludes, "Whether it relates to quantity, quality or disease, the trend away from centralized government agencies and toward empowering local governments and local communities to manage water supplies must be emphasized. This necessitates building community capacities, especially in the area of personnel, and the allocation of resources to the local level."[92]

Access to safe and sufficient water "is a strategic factor for the establishment and maintenance of peace in the world. Water is a dimension of what is referred to today as resource security. Conflicts have already occurred for control over water resources and others may come center stage the more water scarcity manifests its consequences on the lives of the human beings and their communities."[93] Global warming and climate change is exacerbating this development. Two glaring examples are the Horn of Africa and the Middle East. "Water scarcity can present a clear danger to the internal stability of countries" in entire regions.[94]

The good news is that there is also a long, and in many ways stronger, history of water-related cooperation. "Past experiences of such cooperation could represent an important road map or best practices framework for the promotion of a hydro-solidarity among countries and communities. The lasting foundations of water-related solidarity are economic, environmental and strategic factors but also require a strong ethical basis" that is key to preventing conflicts over this precarious resource.[95]

Beyond the usual devastation caused by water through natural disasters across the globe, the effects of global warming and climate change

---

[90] Ibid.

[91] Ibid.

[92] Ibid.

[93] Pontifical Council for Justice and Peace, Water: An Essential Element for Life: An Update.

[94] Ibid.

[95] Ibid.

pose substantial additional threats to areas of the globe that are already impoverished and poor in water. Predictions of the IPCC indicate that the wet places in the world will get wetter and dry places will become drier. Justice and solidarity now demand that we not only plan to assist people in the usual disasters but also make realistic strategic plans and provide life's necessities for climate refugees, who need to relocate and seek new livelihoods because of vast climatic shifts. As has been widely noted, these climatic changes are predicted to strike their most devastating harm on the world's most vulnerable poor, who are already in dire straits. "At the same time, it is of utmost importance to invest in the prevention of natural disasters" while respecting regional ecosystems.[96] The world's population should share equitably in the benefits of modern technological means for early disaster risk assessments. "Disaster risk assessment is an integral component of the development plans and poverty eradication programmes and ways need to be found to break the vicious circle between poverty, environmental degradation and lack of preparation that turns natural hazards into disasters that destroy development gains. Poor countries, especially, should be encouraged, with the help of the richer ones, to invest in mitigation measures to reduce the consequences of floods and droughts."[97]

The PJPC could not be clearer: A new "culture of water" is needed. "Water is central to life. However all too often water is not perceived as the luxury it really is, but is paradoxically wasted. This action of wasting water is morally unsustainable."[98] In many ways, the burden for making the change to this new attitude and dealing justly with water use is on the world's richest nations. Clearly, when one needs to walk miles to just get enough water to survive, one sees the real value of water differently. Yet even in wealthy nations, water-supply infrastructures are old and poorly maintained, allowing for the loss of millions of gallons of water. The effect of such waste is often visible in the water bills charged to the poor, who spend an extraordinary percentage of their income on this necessity of life. Water is not a commodity to be bought and sold for a profit; it is a gift for life. As the PJPC reminds us, "We must remember that all human beings are united by a common origin and the same supreme destiny. Water must therefore be considered a public good,

[96] Ibid.
[97] Ibid.
[98] Ibid.

need for a new culture of water

which all citizens should enjoy, but within the context of the duties, rights and responsibilities which accrue to each person."[99]

In facing the hard challenge posed by the water issue, there are many signs of hope. The United Nations has declared 2005–15 "The Water for Life Decade."[100] The issue of access to safe water and sanitation has become one of the top priorities of the international system. As Pope Paul VI declared years ago, "This hope in the Author of nature and of the human spirit, rightly understood, is capable of giving new and serene energy to all of us."[101]

Without neglecting profound reverence and regard for the natural environment, humans are at the center of the concern expressed in Catholic social teaching about water. Solutions for access to safe water and sanitation should express a preferential love and justice for the poor. The water issue is truly a right-to-life issue.

Wholly of Water and Holy Water

For Christians, baptism (often in "holy water") is the starting point for the life of faith. It is through the waters of baptism that we take on a new life in Christ and receive the power of the Holy Spirit for a life empowered by God's grace with hope for the future. But this empowerment comes with responsibilities and calls for commitment to follow in the footprints of Jesus. This means that the waters of baptism must remain "living waters" in our lives. We need to pass on the life that Christ and the Spirit offer through our practical actions of justice and mercy in relationship with our fellow humans, nonhuman creatures, and the earth itself. Indeed, as Jesus tells us, "Whoever gives even a cup of cold water to one of these little ones in the name of a disciple—truly I tell you, none of these will lose their reward" (Matt 10:42).

The Christian life is attuned to gratitude and praise for God's gifts of creation—such as Sister Water—and to a reverence that mandates careful use (never abuse) of such treasures. It is from a stance of gratitude that we most deeply appreciate God's generous love for the whole world, which is wholly dependent on water for life! But true worship is made credible through congruent actions. This necessity calls us to intentional

---

[99] Ibid.

[100] See http://www.un.org/waterforlifedecade, accessed January 9, 2012.

[101] Pope Paul VI, speech to the members of the Pontifical Academy of Sciences, April 19, 1975.

lives of prayer and reflection with an attitude of ongoing discernment about what God is inviting and requiring us to be and do. For many of us this will involve individual lifestyle changes. But the whole Christian community also needs to mobilize and act collaboratively through the justice and peace ministries of the churches in concerted efforts for water justice.

Making these changes is not impossible! The key to success is to make a plan to gradually add a new action every week—perhaps during Advent or Lent. All of this is possible. Each time you take action, be conscious of the sacredness of God's gift of water. Pray with St. Francis of Assisi, the patron of ecology: "*Praised* be You, my Lord, through Sister *Water,* / who is very useful and humble and precious and chaste."[102]

Questions for Reflection and Discussion

1. Do you know the source of the water piped into your home?

2. If you or your friends use commercial bottled water, what is the major reason for doing so?

3. What could motivate you to change to your local water supply?

4. Research the supply of water in your bioregion. How secure is the water supply in your area?

5. What can you do to conserve water?

Suggestions for Action

1. Your water company is legally obligated to tell you where your tap water comes from; where water goes after leaving your home or office; whether your water company is a subsidiarity of a larger (private) water company; and what the quality of your water is.

2. Eliminate use of bottled water in your home and institution; use "gray water" (water that has been used for washing but is not toxic) for watering gardens or crops.

[102] Francis of Assisi, "Canticle of the Creatures," in FAED, vol. I, *The Saint*, 114.

3. Place a weighted plastic bottle in the tank of your toilet and use less water for flushing.

4. Take a shower rather than a bath and use about one-third less water; when brushing your teeth, turn the tap off while brushing.

5. Eliminate chemical cleaners, fertilizers, and pesticides that require vast water use in their manufacture and that pollute waterways when disposed of; instead, use phosphate-free soaps and detergents.

6. Learn how trade agreements and policies of the World Bank, the International Monetary Fund (IMF), and the World Trade Organization (WTO) are influencing availability and delivery of water.

7. The United States agreed in 2000 to contribute to the Millennium Development Goal on water use and access. Ask the US ambassador to the UN, the White House, and your congressperson about US compliance with this commitment.

Prayer

"Sister Water," by Mary Goergen, OSF[103]

Praised be You, my Lord, through Sister Water,
who is useful and humble and precious
and chaste.
Sister Water
In my youth you came to me circuitously
Windmill pumping water to the cistern,
Iron pump bringing you in a white enamel pail,
Pail carrying you to the wash stand in the house,
Finally the long handled dipper bringing you to my lips.
I knew nothing of pollution.
Sister Water
Now you come streaming from a variety of faucets,
No longer pure, combined with chemicals,
Your purity has been defiled.

---

[103] Prayer poem is used with permission of the author. Sr. Mary Goergen, OSF, is a member of the Sisters of St. Francis, Rochester, MN, a beloved elementary school teacher, gardener, and ecological justice advocate.

Sister Water, beyond your control.
You are available to some, denied to others.
You are exploited in the name of progress, product, and profit.
You are polluted and unable to stop this danger from moving up
The food chain to settle in the cells of every living creature.
Sister Water,
You are still needed by earth and atmosphere.
You are refreshment and essential for all life.
You are used in sign and sacrament,
A life-giving source of God to all.
Sister Water
When will we put this all together in our minds and hearts
Recognizing that you are useful, humble, precious and chaste
For all, not just a few?

Sources for Further Study

Brown, Peter G., and Jeremy J. Schmidt. *Water Ethics: Foundational Readings for Students and Professionals*. Washington, DC: Island Press, 2010.

Catholic Rural Life Conference. "Water: A Sacramental Commons for All." http://www.ncrlc.com/page.aspx?ID=80.

National Geographic. Special issue, "Water: Our Thirsty World." April 2010.

Pontifical Council for Justice and Peace. Water: An Essential Element for Life (2003). http://www.vatican.va/roman_curia/pontifical_councils/justpeace/documents/rc_pc_justpeace_doc_20030322_kyoto-water_en.html.

Pontifical Council for Justice and Peace. Water: An Essential Element for Life; An Update (2006). http://www.vatican.va/roman_curia/pontifical_councils/justpeace/documents/rc_pc_justpeace_doc_20060322_mexico-water_en.html.

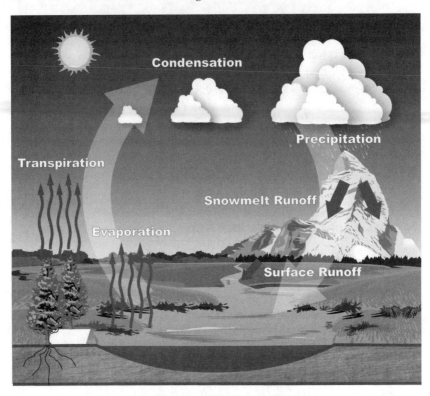

Source: National Weather Service, "The Hydrologic Cycle,"
http://www.srh.noaa.gov/srh/jetstream/atmos/hydro.htm.

Chapter 9

Food Access, "Foodprint," Food Security

Introduction

Do you know where your food comes from? Select one of the main items you had for your last meal. Where was that item grown? Who were the workers who labored to raise, harvest, clean, butcher, process and package, transport, shelve, and prepare it and put it on your plate? In the United States, most of us live far removed from rural life and agriculture, and we are illiterate concerning the land, waters and farming, ranching, or fishing processes that produce our daily fare. For many, the land is merely property and the waters are simply playgrounds, infrequently seen and less understood. We casually go to the supermarket and rarely think about our foods' sources or the people who brought it to us. Occasionally, we worry about the economic cost of groceries, but we rarely worry about the environmental or human costs involved.

Most of us are quite oblivious to the reality that our processed foods—full of salts, sugars, and fats—are among the world's worst for our health. Indeed we are often addicted to certain tastes and specific brands! Not surprisingly, obesity is our national scourge. According to the Centers for Disease Control, in 2008 only Colorado had a prevalence of obesity less than 20 percent. Thirty-two states had a higher than 25 percent obesity rate. And six of those states had an obesity rate of 30 percent or higher. Yet, according to the US Department of Agriculture, in November of 2009 approximately fifty million Americans, including a quarter of all children, went to bed hungry each night. In the United States 23.5 million people live in food deserts, and more than half of those (13.5 million) are low-income persons.[1]

Embarrassingly, in our nation's capital, Washington, DC, while there are forty-three full-service grocery stores, only two are located in Ward 3, only four are in Ward 7, and just three are in Ward 8. By contrast, Ward 3, the highest-income area of the district, has eleven full-service stores. And across the globe over a billion people lack access to sufficient food—not because the world has failed to produce plenty of it, but because it is not proportionately distributed and affordable.

This situation of the food crisis is difficult to consider. But this chapter is really about the *good news* behind the grim picture presented by our present reality. Things were not always so bleak, and there are many ways we can turn all of this around—if we *renew our knowledge* about what a truly sustainable food system is like and then *act* to change our lifestyle. St. Francis and St. Clare are great models for us because (in spite of the ascetic spirituality of their time) they understood the meaning of both feasting and fasting. As we shall see, we are called to hope and a life-filled moral consciousness of food, land, waters, plants, and animals and to action by following in the footprints of Jesus, who is also the Bread of Life.

In this chapter we will explore important information about the food system with particular attention to US involvement in it. We will then place that information in conversation with the moral vision concerning care for the land and food that is given us in Scripture and Catholic social teaching. In a pivotal passage, Leviticus 25:23, our Creator God summarily exhorts, "Land must not be sold in perpetuity, for the land belongs to me. And to me you are only strangers and guests."[2] Indeed, the food that the earth's land and waters bring forth is to be shared equitably as the Creator intended, because the earth is the Lord's and God is generous and just! Yet, domestically and globally, we have acted on far different premises. In recent decades, our attitude of taking food for granted has made us vulnerable and unconscious of a burgeoning globalized, industrialized food system that benefits a small elite group of agribusinesses while leaving most of the people in the world poorly served, malnourished, or starving, even with death imminent. The first step toward making a change is to learn how we got into this mess in the first place.

---

[1] See United States Department of Agriculture, http://apps.ams.usda.gov/food deserts/foodDeserts.aspx, accessed January16, 2012.

[2] This translation is mine.

Understanding Food Security

Most of us in the United States have never had to consider where our next meal is coming from. Indeed, we have little appreciation of how privileged we are among the millions across the globe whose *entire day* is *necessarily* consumed with seeking out food and water simply to survive another day. According to the United Nations Food and Agriculture Organization (FAO), "Food security exists when all people, at all times, have physical and economic access to sufficient, safe, and nutritious food that meets their dietary needs and food preferences for an active and healthy life."[3] There are four main dimensions to food security: (1) the physical ability to produce, stock, and trade for food; (2) economic and physical ability to access food; (3) food utilization (i.e., sufficient calorie and nutrient intake and good biological utilization of food consumed); and (4) stability of the other three dimensions over time. All four of these objectives need to be fulfilled simultaneously in order to have food security.

Food insecurity can be classified as either chronic or transitory. *Chronic food insecurity* is long term or persistent. It occurs when people are unable to meet their minimum food requirements over a sustained period of time. The results of this insecurity include extended periods of poverty, lack of assets, and inadequate access to productive or financial resources. This insecurity can be overcome by various measures such as education, access to productive resources, and financial credit. Initially, there may be a need to assist people by providing direct access to food to enable them to take advantage of other measures of recovery.

Transitory food insecurity is short term and temporary. It occurs when there is a sudden drop in the ability to produce enough food to maintain an adequate nutritional status. It results from short-term price shocks or fluctuations in the ability to access food, such as year-to-year variations in domestic food production, rising food prices, and reduction or loss of household incomes. This kind of food insecurity can be overcome by foresighted planning and programming. Such measures are best incorporated into the overall social health and safety policies of nations, states, regions, and individual families.[4]

---

[3] See Food and Agriculture Organization of the United Nations (FAO), "An Introduction to the Basic Concepts of Food Security," http://www.fao.org/docrep/013/al936e/al936e00.pdf, accessed January 16, 2012. The definition was drafted at the 1996 World Food Summit.

[4] See Kostas Stamoulis and Alberto Zezza, "A Conceptual Framework for National Agriculture, Rural Development, and Food Security Strategies and Policies," ESA

The severity of food insecurity involves a measure of the impact a food problem has on the overall food security and nutritional status of a population. This measure is used to determine the nature, extent, and urgency of the assistance that is needed. The definition the FAO uses to measure the severity of *undernourishment* is "the *proportion* of the population whose dietary energy consumption is less than a pre-determined threshold. This threshold is country specific and is measured in terms of the number of kilocalories required to conduct sedimentary or light activities."[5] For the food deprived, the *severity* of undernourishment indicates the extent to which their dietary consumption falls below the predetermined threshold.

Another important measure that the FAO uses is the Integrated Food Security Phase Classification (IPC). This measure is based on livelihood needs. It classifies food security crises into five categories: (1) generally food secure, (2) chronically food insecure, (3) acute food and livelihood crisis, (4) humanitarian emergency, and (5) famine / humanitarian catastrophe. Indicators for these classifications are any combination of the crude mortality rate, the prevalence of malnutrition, food access and / or availability, dietary diversity, water access and/or availability, coping strategies available, and livelihood assets.[6]

The final dimension of food security we need to understand is that of *vulnerability*. Here an assessment is made about a people's probable future insecurity. People's vulnerability to a particular outcome, a variety of risk factors, and their ability to manage those risks define their vulnerability. Even if people are not currently hungry, they can still be vulnerable to becoming so in the future. Two interventions are possible for reducing vulnerability, namely, reducing the degree of people's exposure to hazard(s) and increasing their ability to cope. Assessing food security vulnerability is vital for preparing effective food security policies and programs to maximize people's capacities to address future threats to their food security.

Clearly, "hunger" is more than a passing case of "the munchies" for millions in our world; indeed, what is scientifically classified as "hunger"

Working Paper No. 03-17, November 2003 (Rome: Agriculture and Development Economics Division), ftp://ftp.fao.org/docrep/fao/007/ae050e/ae050e00.pdf, accessed January 17, 2012.

[5] See FAO, "An Introduction to the Basic Concepts of Food Security."

[6] For more information, http://www.fews.net/ml/en/info/pages/scale.aspx, accessed August 13, 2012.

is very different. Hunger is the sensation that is caused by insufficient food-energy consumption, and it is more accurately called *food depriva-tion*. When people become hungry, any one of four interrelated factors is present, and often a vicious cycle of all factors quickly takes shape, threatening the lives of millions. These factors are: *poverty* (food insecu-rity, hunger, and malnutrition); *poor physical and cognitive development*; and *low productivity*, which in turn leads to an *intensification of poverty*, starting the spiral into ever more life-threatening states of affairs. What is needed to escape this spiral is sustainable income growth supported by direct nutrition interventions and investments in health, water, and education across the globe.[7] As we shall see, the current globalized industrialized food system does not adequately serve these needs for millions, and it increasingly threatens even the most food-secure nations, including the United States.

Background to the 2008 Access-to-Food Crisis

Early evidence of a burgeoning food crisis included riots and protests in 2007 over food prices in thirty countries across the globe.[8] In Haiti the prime minister was deposed over high food prices; in South Africa dozens of refugees and immigrants were scapegoated and killed; and even in the United States, leading food wholesalers, such as Sam's Club and Costco, limited the amount of rice sold per customer.

This volatile situation compelled UN Secretary-General Ban Ki-Moon to establish in 2008 a High-Level Task Force on the Global Food Security Crisis.[9] The task force brought together the heads of the UN specialized agencies, funds, and programs; the UN Secretariat; the World Bank; the International Monetary Fund; the Organization for Economic Cooperation and Development; and the World Trade Organization. The primary aim of the Task Force was to promote a comprehensive and unified response to the challenge of achieving global food security, to facilitate the creation of a prioritized plan of action, and to coordinate its implementation.

---

[7] See FAO, "An Introduction to the Basic Concepts of Food Security."

[8] Elizabeth Shelburn, "The Great Disruption," *The Atlantic* (September 2008): 28–29.

[9] See "The Secretary-General's High-Level Taskforce on the Global Food Security Crisis: Background Information," http://www.un.org/en/issues/food/taskforce /background.shtml, accessed January 16, 2012.

Causes Contributing to the Global Food Crisis

There were multiple, complex, and interlocking causes of the food crisis. Though space prohibits a thorough analysis of each, here we will indicate several factors. On the one hand, the globalized food market made better nutrition available to billions of people. However, the manner in which that was achieved was fraught with a lethal downside. What was happening to hungry people and farmers around the world? In 2001, 55 percent of all workers in developing countries[10] were employed in agriculture.[11] Over 840 million people worldwide were malnourished,[12] despite the fact that farmers globally produced enough food calories to adequately nourish everyone on the planet.[13] Thirty thousand children died of hunger and related causes daily.[14] Key factors contributing to the crisis included agriculture liberalization, changes in land use, global warming and climate change, fuel costs, the weak US dollar, export bans, and record profits by a tiny elite group of agribusinesses that monopolized key concentrated and vertically integrated markets. Our discussion first addresses the global scene. However, it is

[10] See United States Conference of Catholic Bishops, For I Was Hungry and You Gave Me Food: Catholic Reflections on Food, Farmers, and Farmworkers, November 18, 2003, http://www.usccb.org/issues-and-action/human-life-and-dignity /agriculture/for-i-was-hungry.cfm, accessed October 12, 2008, in the data box entitled "Global Agriculture: What Is Happening to Hungry People and Farmers around the World?" cites the Food and Agriculture Organization of the United Nations (FAO), *Mobilizing the Political Will and Resources to Banish World Hunger*, prepared for World Summit Plus Five (2002), 63. All technical data cited here and in citations of this USCCB document is found in the data boxes at http://www.usccb.org/issues-and -action/human-life-and-dignity/agriculture/for-i-was-hungry-data-boxes.cfm.

[11] USCCB, For I Was Hungry and You Gave Me Food, "Global Agriculture: What Is Happening to Hungry People and Farmers around the World?" cites FAO, *State of Food Insecurity in the World 2002*, 12. Seventy percent of the poor in developing countries live in rural areas and derive livelihoods from agriculture directly or indirectly.

[12] USCCB, For I Was Hungry and You Gave Me Food, "Global Agriculture: What Is Happening to Hungry People and Farmers around the World?" cites FAO, *State of Food Insecurity in the World 2001*.

[13] USCCB, For I Was Hungry and You Gave Me Food, "Global Agriculture: What Is Happening to Hungry People and Farmers around the World?" cites FAO, *World Agriculture: Towards 2015–2030* (2003). Sufficient nutrition requires 2,800 calories of food per person per day.

[14] USCCB, For I Was Hungry and You Gave Me Food, "Global Agriculture: What Is Happening to Hungry People and Farmers around the World?" cites *Mobilizing the Political Will*, no. 3.3. There are 1.2 billion people who live on less than $1 per day, 70 percent of whom are found in rural areas.

important to keep in mind that because the United States is such a powerful and central player in the global marketplace, US agribusinesses were usually "winners" in all the action, and US farmers were among the major "losers" along with others across the globe. A discussion of the US food security scene will then follow.

A Global Perspective

Agriculture liberalization began with the debt crisis of the 1980s when many governments in the global South were forced to borrow money from the International Monetary Fund, the World Bank, and other international sources.[15] These loan agreements required governments to eliminate all "barriers to trade"—state credit and subsidies for farmers, price supports, marketing boards, and extension services. Along with this, tariffs were lowered, so local markets of the borrowing nations were flooded with imported cheaper foods. In the case of Africa, a continent still in flux from decolonization in the 1960s, these conditions changed it from being a major exporter of food to an equally great importer. Africa had the greatest concentration of low income[16] and of food deficit countries that could not produce enough food to feed their populations and could not afford to import food.[17] In 2008, 70 percent of the nations in the global South imported more food than they grew.

Along with this, *major international financial institutions cut back their agricultural aid*, resulting in a drop of 54 percent from 1980 to 2005 (from $8 billion to $3.4 billion). In 2008 these same institutions gave less than 4 percent of their aid to agriculture, with even less going to small farmers. At the same time, grain reserves were decreased, with corn and rice stock cut in half by 2000, making those nations more vulnerable to crop failures and price fluctuations.

Changes in land use resulted from the liberalization of agriculture. Small farmers lost their land and their livelihoods, and less land grew food

[15] This section draws heavily on Maryknoll Office for Global Concerns, "Food Crisis 2008," *NewsNotes* 33/4 (July–August 2008): 14–15.

[16] USCCB, For I Was Hungry and You Gave Me Food, "Global Agriculture: What Is Happening to Hungry People and Farmers around the World?" cites FAO, *Gender and Food Security*. In sub-Saharan Africa, women produce up to 80 percent of basic food products.

[17] USCCB, For I Was Hungry and You Gave Me Food, "Global Agriculture: What Is Happening to Hungry People and Farmers around the World?" cites International Fund for Agricultural Development (IFAD), *Drylands: A Call to Action* (1998), 6.

70% of nations in global South import more food than they grow —

crops, while urbanization increased. Of great impact was the shift to *industrial-scale* farming practices, often growing a single cash crop on huge expanses of land for agrofuels (biofuels), the vast majority of which was for export. There was a shift from food crops to industrial mono-crops. From 2000 to 2008 cereals grown for food and animal feed increased by only 4–7 percent, while cereals grown for industrial purposes grew by 25 percent. "In the U.S., of the 48 million tons by which domestic consumption of maize increased in 2007, nearly 30 million were used exclusively for ethanol (agrofuel) production."[18]

Land use also changed drastically in this period *from raising plant crops* for direct human consumption *to raising feed crops* for massive industrial-sized animal feedlot operations. China and India experienced a growth in their middle class, and diets shifted to greater consumption of dairy and meat products. In China, meat consumption rose from forty-four pounds per person in 1980 to 110 pounds in 2008. This trend was dangerous on two counts. First, there was a loss of efficiency in food production generally, because it takes eight pounds of grain to produce one pound of beef, or two pounds of grain for one pound of chicken. Put another way, "While 100 million tons of grain [were] being diverted to make fuel [in 2008], over seven times as much (760 million tons) were be used to feed animals."[19] Secondly, animal waste produces large amounts of methane gas, one of the most lethal of the greenhouse gasses (GHGs). Cows are among the greatest producers of GHGs. In fact, "every cow produces more greenhouse gases in the form of methane per day than the average 4x4 on a 33-mile drive."[20]

As we saw in chapter 7, the food crisis is greatly affected by *climate change*. Due to human-induced climate change, Earth's dry regions are becoming drier—with longer droughts and more frequent and destructive fires—and Earth's wetter places are becoming wetter, causing flooding and crop loss.[21] In the summer of 2008, there was unusual flooding of the "breadbasket" of the United States (Iowa, Wisconsin, Illinois, In-

[18] Maryknoll Office for Global Concerns, "Food Crisis," 15. Also see Joshua Boak and Mike Haughlett, "Corn Bonanza Won't Cut Food Prices: A Fortunate Mix of Sunshine and Rain Is Helping Produce a Bumper Crop, but Much of the Grain Will Be Used to Make Ethanol," *Chicago Tribune*, August 13, 2008, section 3, pages 3–4.

[19] Maryknoll Office for Global Concerns, "Food Crisis," 15.

[20] Ibid.

[21] See Wulf Killmann and the Interdepartmental Working Group on Climate Change, *Climate Change and Food Security: A Framework Document* (2008), http://www.fao.org/docrep/010/k2595e/k2595e00.htm, accessed January 16, 2012.

diana, and Missouri) and record-setting fires in California. Australia's wheat belt experienced extreme drought, which sent grain prices spiraling upward.[22]

Fuel costs were another contributing factor to the food crisis. The entire global industrialized food system is highly dependent on fossil fuels. The Green Revolution of the 1970s introduced the use of tractors to mass produce crops (often monocrops) from preparing the soil, seeding, and spreading fertilizers and pesticides to harvesting. Not only are fossil fuels in the tractor gas tank, but the fertilizers and pesticides are fossil fuel based as well. Since most crops are mass produced for export, huge fossil fuel expenditures are also involved in the transport of produce to markets.

The onset of the food crisis of 2008 involved the *weakness of US dollar* as well. Because oil was sold in US dollars, with a weak dollar oil exporters needed to drive up the price of oil per barrel in order to keep their purchase power against other currencies that were maintaining or gaining value. Further, food commodities were also sold in US dollars, and so the global effect was the rise in food prices. Because of the weak dollar in this period, foreign investors did not invest much in the United States, for they could make greater profits elsewhere.

Prior to and during the onset of the 2008 food crisis, *more than forty countries banned exports of food* in order to keep their food supplies at home. This left a huge dent in the globalized industrialized food system. As the Maryknoll Office of Global Concerns explained in 2008, "China has banned rice and maize exports; India has banned milk powder exports; Bolivia has banned the export of soy oil to Chile, Colombia, Cuba, Ecuador, Peru, and Venezuela; Ethiopia has banned exports of major cereals; Argentina has temporarily stopped wheat exports; Brazil has suspended exports of government-owned rice; and numerous Asian countries have stopped rice exports."[23]

During this same crisis period, *a small number of agribusinesses were raking in profits at unprecedented rates.* Cargill, the world's largest grain trader, gained 86 percent in profits in the first quarter of 2008 from commodity trading; Bunge, a food trader, had a 77 percent increase in profits during the last quarter of 2007; Monsanto, the world's largest

---

[22] See Julie Ingwersen, "Farmers Scramble to Finish Harvest from Hell," *Reuters*, November 13, 2009, http://www.reuters.com/article/2009/11/13/us-usa-crops-harvest-idUSTRE5AC3BS20091113, accessed January 16, 2012.

[23] Maryknoll Office for Global Concerns, "Food Crisis," 15.

seed company, increased its profits by 108 percent between December 2007 and February 2008; Archer Daniels Midlands increased its profits by 42 percent; and Mosaic, one of the world's largest fertilizer companies, gained profits of 1,134 percent in the first quarter of 2008.

Years of underinvestment in agriculture productivity in developing countries was another contributing factor. While the food crisis seems to have appeared suddenly, the lack of investment in agriculture and market infrastructure, combined with other forces, created the crisis. According to Oxfam America's agriculture expert, Tim Mahoney, "There has been an underinvestment in smallholder agriculture for the last two to three decades. And now that agriculture production is down, the ability of small farmers to meet the increased demand is not there. They just don't have the capacity."[24] Ever since the Green Revolution that began in the 1960s, investment in agriculture supported those farmers who already had secure access to land, water, and markets. But more recently, when dealing with poorer quality soils and scarcity of water, which need expensive fossil-fuel–based fertilizers and high levels of technological knowledge to produce food, the resources simply have not been there.

One of the most insidious causes of the 2008 food crisis was brought on by a dramatic increase during the prior three to four years in *financial speculation in the commodity futures markets*, which resulted in artificially driving up prices for wheat, corn, and soybeans, as well as oil, gas, metals, and minerals. This became possible because of the several small changes in the commodities laws that were made under the Reagan administration. Key were the loopholes created by the Commodity Futures Trading Commission (CFTC) that allowed outside investors to invest unlimited amounts in commodities.

A bit of a history lesson here will help to understand what all this means.[25] Prior to the opening of the Chicago Board of Trade in 1848, each farmer sold grains to individual buyers. This process was risky and unregulated, and prices could vary widely. Once the board was orga-

---

[24] Tim Mahoney, "Understanding the Global Food Price Crisis," *Oxfam Exchange* 9/3 (Fall 2009): 6.

[25] Maryknoll Office for Global Concerns, "Speculation and World Food Prices," *NewsNotes* 33/4 (July–August 2008): 17. For an excellent short primer on commodities market speculation that also explains the continuing influence of this activity on current global food prices, see Stephen Suppan, "Commodities Market Speculation: The Risk to Food Security and Agriculture" (Minneapolis: Institute for Agriculture and Trade Policy, 2008), http://www.iatp.org/documents/commodities-market-speculation-the-risk-to-food-security-and-agriculture, accessed January 16, 2012.

nized, farmers and buyers agreed via contracts that grain would be delivered for a definite price and on a specific date ("forward"). These kinds of agreements, officially known as "forward contracts," were instated in 1865. A similar kind of contract was later initiated for the open (and indirect) exchange. These were traded on an open exchange called "the futures market," where many traders (including nonfarmers) can participate. Buyers on the futures market rarely, if ever, actually receive the physical product but are able to profit off changing commodity prices.

By the late 1800s, futures markets had been created for various products, with speculators betting on whether prices would rise or fall. But (similar to recent times) the numerous investors not actually involved in agriculture or food production became problematic. The market reeled under fraud, abuses, and the wide instability in investments, causing food prices to rise and fall unpredictably and unnecessarily. Finally, after the Great Depression, several regulatory laws, including the Commodities Exchange Act of 1936 (CEA), were passed to regulate markets in order to avoid another economic collapse. The CEA put limits on speculative investors to prevent them from manipulating commodity futures markets. "People directly involved in agriculture and food could still participate in the futures market in order to provide liquidity, but outside investors had severe limits placed on the manner and amount they could invest."[26]

The effect of the Reagan administration's deregulation policies in the 1980s again opened the door to multiple rounds of speculation that ultimately played havoc with food prices, first on energy (e.g., the Enron debacle), then on housing, and finally on commodities. As hedge-fund manager Michael Masters told Congress, even institutional investors (pension funds, university endowments, sovereign wealth funds, etc.) have increased their investments in commodity futures from $13 billion in 2003 to $260 billion in March 2008, and the price of twenty-five commodities has risen by an average of 183 percent in those five years.[27] Masters explained that "commodities futures prices are the benchmark for the prices of actual physical commodities, so when . . . speculators drive futures prices higher, the effects are felt immediately in . . . the real economy."[28] To grasp the great ability of commodities speculation to influence food prices, consider that in 2004 the total value of futures contracts

---

[26] Maryknoll Office for Global Concerns, "Speculation and World Food Prices," 17.
[27] Ibid.
[28] Ibid. The authors cite Masters's congressional testimony.

in twenty-five principal commodities was only $180 billion. But in the first fifty-five days of 2008, speculators placed $55 billion into these markets. These actions have had long-term effects that are still felt today.[29]

Agriculture in the United Sates and the Global Food Crisis[30]

What was happening to US farms and farmers? In 1930 there were 7 million farms in the United States.[31] By 1950 there were approximately 5.5 million farms in the United States.[32] There were only an estimated 2.16 million US farms by 2001,[33] and 10 percent of these farms accounted for nearly 70 percent of all agriculture production.[34] Not surprisingly, today there are fewer than 2 million farms. Of those remaining farms, only 565,000 are small family operations. It is estimated that the United States loses 330 farms every week.[35]

In 2001 in the United States, 1 in 5 of the approximate 41 million uninsured people (about 8 million people) lived in a rural area. They were older, poorer, and less healthy than people living in urban areas.[36] The 2002 occupational fatality rate was the second highest in agriculture: 22.7 per 100 thousand people employed.[37] Currently, the suicide rate among farmers throughout the world is higher than for the nonfarming

---

[29] Ibid.

[30] See USCCB, For I Was Hungry and You Gave Me Food.

[31] See Sustainable Table, "Family Farms," http://www.sustainabletable.org/issues/familyfarms, accessed January 16, 2012.

[32] USCCB, For I Was Hungry and You Gave Me Food, "U.S. Agriculture: What Is Happening to Farms and Farmers?" cites Bread for the World, *Agriculture in the Global Economy, Hunger 2003*, p. 36.

[33] USCCB, For I Was Hungry and You Gave Me Food, cites National Agriculture Statistics Service (NASS) (2002), 23.

[34] USCCB, For I Was Hungry and You Gave Me Food, cites "U.S. Agriculture: What Is Happening to Farms and Farmers?" US Department of Agriculture, *Food and Agricultural Policy: Taking Stock of the New Century* (September 2001), appendix 1, table A-1.

[35] See *Sustainable Table*, "Family Farms," http://www.sustainabletable.org/issues/familyfarms, accessed January 16, 2012.

[36] USCCB, For I Was Hungry and You Gave Me Food, "U.S. Agriculture: What Is Happening to Farms and Farmers?" cites The Kaiser Family Foundation, *Kaiser Commission on Key Facts* (April 2003).

[37] USCCB, For I Was Hungry and You Gave Me Food, "U.S. Agriculture: What Is Happening to Farms and Farmers?" cites US Department of Labor Statistics, *Census of Fatal Occupational Injuries* (2002). The rate was 12.2 in construction, 11.3 in transportation, and 23.5 in mining.

population. In the US Midwest, suicide rates among male farmers are twice that of the general population. The majority of these farmers are financially indebted.[38]

Concentration and Vertical Integration

What has been happening to our food from field to shelf? US food production has become concentrated and vertically integrated. In 1997 the top five food retailers held 24 percent of the US market; by 2000 that share increased to 42 percent of retail food sales.[39] Today only four giant firms process the majority of beef, pork, and broilers.[40] The four largest processors control the wheat and soybean market.[41] In 2009, 93 percent of soybeans and 80 percent of corn grown in the United States were grown from genetically engineered seeds patented by one company, Monsanto.[42] As the corporate concentration of farming inputs and distribution develops, farmers have fewer options for the inputs they have available to purchase; the prices they pay for machinery, seeds, fertilizers, and so forth; and the contracts, loans, and markets they have access to. The corporations are not only gaining greater influence on who grows what, and where, but they are increasingly putting ever-greater pressure

[38] See http://www.un.org/esa/sustdev/csd/csd16/PF/presentations/farmers_relief.pdf, accessed January 16, 2012.

[39] USCCB, For I Was Hungry and You Gave Me Food, "Concentration and Vertical Integration: What Is Happening to Our Food from Field to Shelf?" cites Mary Hendrickson, William Heffernan, Philip Howard, and Judith Heffernan, executive summary, report to National Farmers Union, *Consolidation in Food Retailing and Dairy: Implications for Farmers and Consumers in a Global Food System* (January 8, 2001).

[40] USCCB, For I Was Hungry and You Gave Me Food, "Concentration and Vertical Integration: What Is Happening to Our Food from Field to Shelf?" William Heffernan, *Multi-National Concentrated Food Processing and Marketing Systems and the Farm Crisis*, 7, a paper presented to the American Association for the Advancement of Science, February 14–19, 2002. Today the four largest beef firms process 81 percent of all the cattle; the four largest pork firms process 59 percent of pork; and four chicken firms process 50 percent of all broilers.

[41] USCCB, For I Was Hungry and You Gave Me Food, "Concentration and Vertical Integration: What Is Happening to Our Food from Field to Shelf?" cites Heffernan, *Multi-National Concentrated Food Processing*, 7. The four largest wheat processors have 61 percent of the market; the four largest soybean processors have 80 percent of the market.

[42] See Food & Water Watch, "Taking on Corporate Power in the Food Supply" (March 2011), http://bit.ly/nAyzm8, accessed January 16, 2012.

on governments at all levels to deregulate and legislate in favor of their corporate profit making. In 2010 agribusiness spent $121,335,788 on lobbying the federal government, for example.[43]

The United States was the largest exporter of agricultural goods[44] and the largest provider of food aid in the world.[45] But three companies control most corn and soybean exports, while four companies control over half of the grain terminals.[46] In 2001, developed countries (including the United States) gave six times as much in subsidies to their own farmers as they gave in total food aid to poor countries. These agricultural subsidies cause "direct harm to poor countries" because they lower the prices poor farmers would otherwise receive for their products.[47]

In summary, three significant factors emerge from this data. There has been an overall increase in production due to massive use of new technologies in agriculture. The concentration of farming and ranching in the United States and around the world is now controlled by a few huge and powerful agribusiness enterprises, where corporate executives make decisions that affect people and situations that are virtually unknown to them. And globalized agriculture has shifted the traditional purpose of farming and ranching from sustainable food production to production of commodities for maximum profits for an elite few.

[43] See the Center for Responsive Politics, "Lobbying Spending Database: Agribusiness, 2010," http://www.opensecrets.org/lobby/indus.php?id=A&year=2010, accessed January 16, 2012.

[44] USCCB, For I Was Hungry and You Gave Me Food, "Global Agriculture: What Is Happening to Hungry People and Farmers around the World?" cites US Department of Agriculture, Food and Agricultural Policy: Taking Stock of the New Century (September 2001), 40. Also, US global food aid in 2001 accounted for about 60 percent of all food donated worldwide.

[45] USCCB, For I Was Hungry and You Gave Me Food, "Global Agriculture: What Is Happening to Hungry People and Farmers around the World?" cites World Food Program, "Global Food Aid Flows," Food Aid Monitor (2001).

[46] USCCB, For I Was Hungry and You Gave Me Food, "Global Agriculture: What Is Happening to Hungry People and Farmers around the World?" cites William Heffernan, Multi-National Concentrated Food Processing and Marketing Systems and the Farm Crisis, 11, a paper presented to the American Association for the Advancement of Science, February 14–19, 2002. Three companies account for 81 percent of corn exports and 65 percent of soybeans; four companies account for 60 percent of the grain terminals.

[47] USCCB, For I Was Hungry and You Gave Me Food, "Global Agriculture: What Is Happening to Hungry People and Farmers around the World?" cites United Nations Development Report, Human Development Report (2003), 155–56.

Efforts toward Correction

G-8 and G-20[48]

Though publically and formally stating good future intentions to alleviate the global food crisis, at the G-8 Summit in Japan, July 7–9, 2008, the world's most powerful nations were unable to garner the political will to take the *necessarily stringent and enforceable* actions to make good on their prior commitment to the eight UN Millennium Development Goals to reduce world poverty by 2015.[49] The G-8 met again at L'Aquilla, Abruzzo, Italy, from July 8 to 10, 2009.[50] At the conclusion of their meeting, the G-8 published a joint statement that expressed their commitment "to take decisive action to free humankind from hunger and poverty through improving food security, nutrition and sustainable agriculture" and to work together to support country-led processes, ensure a comprehensive approach to food security, strategically coordinate assistance, support a strong role for multilateral institutions, and sustain a robust commitment of financial resources, including $20 billion in resources pledged at the G-8 Summit.[51] As of May 2011, ActionAid, a nongovernmental organization (NGO), found it difficult to assess the real progress toward fulfilling those goals because of the erratic and imprecise reporting by the various

[48] The G-8 nations include Canada, France, Germany, Italy, Japan, the United Kingdom, and the United States. The G-20 nations are Argentina, Bolivia, Brazil, Chile, China, Cuba, Ecuador, Egypt, Guatemala, India, Indonesia, Mexico, Pakistan, Paraguay, Peru, Philippines, South Africa, Tanzania, and Thailand. The G-20 nations make up 60 percent of the world's population, have 70 percent of the world's farmers, and produce 26 percent of the world's exports.

[49] The year 2008 marked the halfway point in reaching the eight Millennium Development Goals set by the UN General Assembly in September 2000. The aim is to halve the number of people in poverty, achieve universal primary education, and cut infant mortality by two-thirds by the end of 2015.

[50] See ONE, "Policy Brief: ONE's Analysis of the G8 L'Aquila Summit Statements," http://one.org/c/us/policybrief/2992, accessed January 14, 2012. The heads of the Roman Catholic bishops' conferences of the G-8 nations submitted a formal letter to the leaders of the Group of Eight Nations dated June 22, 2009. See the text of the letter at "Bishops' Letter to G-8 Leaders," http://www.zenit.org/article-26268?l=english, accessed January 14, 2012. Also, Pope Benedict XVI addressed a letter to Italy's President Silvio Berlusconi, challenging the G-8 to turn the crisis into "a model of global development." See "Crisis No Reason to Stop Aid, Says Benedict XVI," http://www.zenit.org/article-26373?l=english, accessed January 14, 2012.

[51] See ONE, "Agricultural Accountability: Holding Donors to Their L'Aquila Promises," http://www.one.org/c/international/hottopic/3929, accessed January 17, 2012.

countries. The goals remain largely unfulfilled in any case. One bright spot in ActionAid's report was that the United States had taken action and was well on the way to fulfilling its pledge of $3.5 billion in new money and was heavily investing in country-led agricultural development plans and has given substantial support to the Global Agricultural and Security Program.[52]

Though the G-20 nations signed on to the L'Aquila commitments, and in light of the fact that that group constitutes the major players on the world food and agriculture scene, they were egregiously slow to act to finance the pledges. Efforts to share necessary information concerning grain stocks; limiting over-the-counter derivatives and index-fund commodity futures trading; requiring all derivatives of food commodities to be subject to notification, clearing, and monitoring by making position information publicly available; and establishing a regulatory body similar to the US CFTC for European and other market futures trading—all actions that were pledged at L'Aquilla—are largely unfulfilled.[53] Also, yet to be seen are agricultural risk management tools and social safety nets.

World Summit on Food Security in Rome

From November 16 to18, 2009, about sixty heads of state met in Rome with the UN Food and Agriculture Organization. There, UN Secretary-General Ban Ki-Moon stated that "the food crisis is a wake-up call for tomorrow. By 2050 our planet may be the home of 9.1 billion people, over two billion more than today. . . . At a time when the global population is growing, our global climate is changing. By 2050 we will need to grow 70 percent more food, yet weather is becoming more extreme and unpredictable."[54]

At that conference, the FAO director general, Jacques Diouf, gave a clear picture of the crisis: "One billion hungry people, that is one of every

---

[52] See ActionAid, "Two Years On: Is the G8 Delivering on Its L'Aquila Hunger Pledge?" (May 2011), http://www.actionaid.org/sites/files/actionaid/g8-accountability-report-2011.pdf, accessed January 20, 2012.

[53] See ONE, "Why the G-8 and G-20 Need to Act on Agricultural and Food Price Volatility," http://one.org/c/us/policybrief/3975, accessed January 14, 2012.

[54] See Voice of America, "UN: Climate Change Deal Key to Fighting Hunger," http://www.voanews.com/english/news/a-13-2009-11-16-voa16-70423912.html, accessed January 17, 2012.

group of six persons in the world, 105 million more than in 2008, five children dying every 30 seconds. Beyond numbers this means suffering for each of these human beings."[55] Sadly, only one of the G-8 leaders, the Italian prime minister, was present at the summit. However, Latin American and African leaders turned out in large numbers. Among them were Zimbabwe's President Robert Mugabe and Libyan leader Moammar Gadhafi. In a poignant moment, Brazil's President Luiz Inacio Lula da Silva told the summit that hunger is the most devastating weapon of mass destruction on our planet; it kills not soldiers but innocent children.[56]

The Rome summit approved a final statement, *Declaration of the World Summit on Food Security*, in which countries pledged to substantially increase aid to agriculture in developing nations so that the world's hungry can become more self-sufficient.[57] They also committed to meet the UN Millennium Development Goal target to halve the number of hungry people by 2015.[58] But they did not commit to the $44 million per year for the amount of agricultural aid the FAO said would be necessary in the coming decades. The assembled states agreed that the path to achieve their strategic objectives for food security, commitments to agricultural aid, and other actions would be based on the Five Rome Principles for Sustainable Global Food Security enumerated in the *Declaration*.[59] Briefly, these principles are to (1) invest in country-owned plans; (2) foster strategic coordination at national, regional, and global levels; (3) strive for a strategic twin-track approach to food security that consists of (a) direct action to immediately tackle hunger for the most vulnerable and (b) medium- and long-term sustainable agriculture, food security, nutrition, and rural development programs to eliminate the root causes of hunger and poverty through the progressive realization of the right to adequate food; (4) ensure strong multilateral institutions; and (5) ensure sustained and substantial commitment by all partners to investment in agriculture, food security, and nutrition.

[55] Ibid.

[56] Ibid.

[57] See the full text of *Declaration of the World Summit on Food Security*, November 2009, at http://www.fao.org/fileadmin/templates/wsfs/Summit/Docs/Final_Declaration/WSFS09_Declaration.pdf, accessed January 20, 2012.

[58] For the complete list of the UN Millennial Development Goals, see http://www.un.org/millenniumgoals, accessed January 20, 2012.

[59] See *Declaration of the World Summit on Food Security*, 2–7.

hunger as the most devastating weapon of mass destruction

The Current Global Situation with a View toward 2015

Food prices came down slightly in 2009 since their peak in the summer of 2008, but they remained considerably higher than in 2006. The UN Food and Agriculture Organization's 2009 estimates showed that thirty-three countries still have critical food-supply shortfalls. Since 2007, there are forty-three million more undernourished human beings in the world, and 65 percent of them are living in India, Democratic Republic of the Congo, China, Bangladesh, Pakistan, and Ethiopia.[60] The global financial crisis impacted household income levels and intensified hunger issues. Global warming and climate change has continued to take its toll. And, there has been less government and donor support for agricultural infrastructure investment and research and for development of new sustainable agricultural technologies, thus paving the way for long-term food-supply shortages. Through the years it has been primarily the UN and numerous nongovernmental organizations (NGOs) such as churches, temples, and mosques that have cared for those most seriously affected by the food crisis.[61]

In its 2011 *State of Food Insecurity in the World* report, the FAO reported: "The Group of Twenty (G20) Finance Ministers and Central Bank Governors has become actively engaged in finding cost-effective ways to reduce price volatility and mitigate its effects when it does occur. By using previously unavailable data sources and studies, this report goes beyond the global-scale analyses to find out what happened on the domestic markets where poor people buy and sell their food in order to draw policy relevant lessons from the world food crisis of 2006–08."[62] The report addressed nine key lessons from the recent food crisis concerning how international price volatility affects domestic economies and food supplies and called for action to remedy them:

[60] UN World Food Programme, "Hunger Stats," http://www.wfp.org/hunger/stats, accessed January 20, 2012. See also Food and Agriculture Organization of the UN, "Hunger Declining but Still Unacceptably High," http://www.fao.org/docrep/012/al390e/al390e00.pdf, accessed January 20, 2012.

[61] See especially "Table 12.1: NGO Food Programs," in "NGOs and Food and Nutrition," chap. 12 of *A Guide to NGOs for the Military*, 121, at http://www.cdham.org/wp-content/uploads/2011/11/Chapter-12.-NGOs-and-Food-and-Nutrition.pdf, accessed January 20, 2012.

[62] See the executive summary of the 2011 *State of Food Insecurity in the World*, http://www.fao.org/docrep/014/i2330e/i2381e00.pdf, accessed January 14, 2012.

1. Small import-dependent countries, especially in Africa, were deeply affected by the food and economic crises.

2. High and volatile food prices are likely to continue.

3. Price volatility makes both smallholder farmers and poor consumers increasingly vulnerable to poverty.

4. Large short-term price changes can have long-term impacts on development.

5. High food prices worsen food insecurity in the short term.

6. High food prices present incentives for increased long-term investment in the agriculture sector, which can contribute to improved food security in the longer term.

7. Safety nets are crucial for alleviating food insecurity in the short term, as well as for providing a foundation for long-term development.

8. A food-security strategy that relies on a combination of increased productivity in agriculture, greater policy predictability, and general openness to trade will be more effective than other strategies.

9. Investment in agriculture remains critical to sustainable long-term food security.[63]

In light of these difficult and heart-rending realities, what is an ordinary person to do? Before suggesting some important ways we can all contribute to changing this state of affairs, let us briefly examine some central sources of values and moral principles our faith holds out to us for guidance. We turn first to Scripture and Catholic social teaching and then to some insights from St. Francis and current spiritual writers. We conclude by briefly examining some effective programs that are changing the unjust food system and by suggesting practical steps we can take to contribute to the cause.

---

[63] Ibid., "Key Messages of the Report."

Theology of the Land and the Moral Vision of Leviticus 25

The Theme of ʾEretz: "Land" and "Earth"

We rightly turn to Sacred Scripture for spiritual guidance, inspiration, and enrichment. But many biblical texts also hold practical and moral wisdom and are just as relevant for our time as for their original audiences. It is interesting to note that the Hebrew word ʾeretz or haʾaretz occurs 2,504 times in the Hebrew Bible (Old Testament).[64] The preponderance of this term in the Hebrew Bible signals the importance of the land for the Israelites and also for us. There are six related ways in which the land holds profound meaning for Israel: as a source of wealth; as a conditional grant from God; as lots distributed to families; as God's inheritance; as regulated to Sabbath laws; and as a host country for immigrants.[65]

Biblical scholar Walter Brueggemann has shown the social, political, and moral significance of how the term ʾeretz is translated throughout the Hebrew Bible.[66] He holds that while the earth is God's gift to humankind, it is also a creature intended for establishing fruitfulness and well-being.[67]

Brueggemann cautions translating ʾeretz as "earth" and suggests "two political ways under the guise of religion."[68] It can communicate an ideology that absolutizes as ontological the nature of the present distribution of land, or it can spiritualize and remove the passion that accompanies talk about those who are the dispossessed of the "land" (not the "earth") here and now. The term ʾeretz is properly translated as "earth" when it refers to the overall lordship of God that serves to relativize all

---

[64] See Kathleen Anne Farmer, "Land," in *The Westminster Theological Wordbook of the Bible*, ed., Donald E. Gowan (Louisville: Westminster John Knox Press, 2003), 281–84. "Land" in the singular occurs 1,961 times and an additional 165 times in its plural form. There are 2,126 occurrences where 'eretz is best translated as "land," but it is sometimes translated as "earth" or "ground."

[65] Ibid., 284. Farmer cites Norman C. Hable, *The Land Is Mine* (Minneapolis: Fortress Press, 1995).

[66] See Walter Brueggemann, "The Earth Is the Lord's: A Theology of Earth and Land," *Sojourners* (October 1986): 28–32.

[67] Translating 'eretz as "earth" is appropriate in Genesis 1–3, for example, because there is a nonhistorical quality that pervades those chapters. In other texts, such as in Genesis 12 where the promise of land is made to Abraham, the context is far more concrete. In order to make any sense of the ensuing conflictual situations, a more historical word is required, and thus 'eretz is best translated as "land." Indeed, rivalry and power clashes often accompany conversations about "land," but the same is not true about "earth" (see, e.g., Judg 2:11–3:6).

[68] Ibid., 30.

other claims to ownership of the "land" (see Ezek 29–30). If the "earth" is the Lord's, there is great power and freedom that accompanies the promises and interventions of God in the concrete lives of humankind. Then Exodus becomes a narrative of defiance and withdrawal from an oppressive "land" system (Gen 47), and it is the start of the grand experiment at play in our Leviticus text.

Brueggemann holds that throughout Israel's history, two ideologies about the land functioned (and continue to function for us today). First was the *royal ideology* that sought to keep the land without heeding the Torah. Such defiance resulted in loss of land and often in personal enslavement for Israel. Alternatively, the *prophetic* stance held that those who were dispossessed would receive land from God (e.g., 1 Sam 2:6-7). Indeed, at the heart of Israel's identity were the land and the belief that God provided the land for *all* people who live in holiness, because without land there is no food or livelihood or the accompanying social power to benefit from the land, and people cannot be fully human. With this in mind, we now turn to a closer look at Leviticus 25.

Leviticus 25 and Its Context

Leviticus (*wayyiqrʾ*) means "and he called," indicating that God called Moses to receive the revelation contained in this book. This instruction is a call to holiness understood as wholeness or a complete response to the mystery of God: "You shall be holy, for I the Lord your God am holy" (Lev 19:2; cf. 11:44-45; 20:7, 26). People need to attain proper ordering of their lives, reflecting the perfect oneness of the God who calls them. Leviticus is part of the Torah, which is the story of the birth of a people, the promises God made to the patriarchs, and the (New Testament) foregrounding for the fulfillment of those promises.[69] Our text is found in the Holiness Code (Lev 17–27), which provides instructions for maintaining and sustaining holiness that requires observance of the Sabbath, the Sabbatical Year, and the Jubilee Year.

---

[69] Scholars differ about the precise dating and division of the book. One common division shows four major sections of the book: (1) the Manual of Sacrifices (Lev 1–7), which depicts Israel at Mount Sinai receiving God's instructions mediated through Moses; (2) the Historical Narrative (Lev 8–10), which includes the ordination of the Aaronic priests and the beginning of sacrificial worship; (3) the Manual of Purity (Lev 11–16), which begins with the Jewish dietary laws and ends with a description of the observance of the Day of Atonement; and (4) the Holiness Code (Lev 17–27).

The God who speaks through Moses from Mount Sinai (v. 1) is also the Creator and the liberator of Israel from slavery in Egypt (vv. 38, 42, 55). It is significant that the first words of God in Leviticus 25 command rest—not only for *people*, but for the *land* (v. 2; cf. Exod 23:10-11; Deut 15:1-2). Every seventh year the land is to rest, to be left fallow. Why? "For the LORD" (vv. 2-4)! This is an act of worship, not a utilitarian strategy directed toward growing more produce for higher profits. Indeed, people who would be holy must honor God by doing what God does; namely, they must give intrinsic value to the land and allow it to rest. This sets the tone for a lifestyle that bears ecological responsibility and cares for the land. It brings to mind that the land itself is an integral part of the covenant and thus part of the redemption people seek.[70] High priority is given to rest for the land; it must occur every seventh year.

In the fiftieth year (following seven times seven Sabbatical Years) there is a grand celebration of Jubilee. Like the Sabbatical Year, the Jubilee Year is observed by all classes of people. And, notably, in the fallow years it is *God's providence*—not human ingenuity and effort—that supplies sufficient goods and produce to fill the needs of humans and animals. No hoarding is necessary (or allowed), and all share equally according to their needs.

The Jubilee Year was to start on the Day of Atonement (the tenth day of the seventh month), which is the most sacred day of the Israelite calendar (v. 9). Thus, a clear link is made between the spiritual life and economic slavery. Renewal of the land is thus connected to renewal of the human person; indeed, humans are inseparable from the land.

Further, the Jubilee Year reveals God's care not only for the land but also *for the poor* who cannot thrive because they are disconnected from the land. All humans without distinction (even today) must rely on the land and on community for their sustenance. The land distribution among Israel's tribes at the time of the conquest, according to the size of clans and families, signaled a concern for equity and fairness and, most importantly, acknowledged the inalienable character of the land. There is no hint of the absolute right to private property or of legitimating huge land grabs here! Restoration of property is clearly a free gift from God.

---

[70] See C. René Padilla, "The Relevance of the Jubilee in Today's World (Leviticus 25)," *Mission Studies* 13/1–2 (1996): 14. Padilla cites Christopher J. H. Wright, "God and Mammon: Biblical Perspectives on Economies in Conflict," *Mission Studies* 12/2 (1995): 147, when she writes that "of the 46 references to the promise from Genesis to Judges, only 7 do not mention the land, while 29 refer to it exclusively."

Holiness also required just and fair pricing in exchange of goods and the land (vv. 15-17). The wealthy and powerful were held to a standard of justice, not merely to a standard of generosity. Throughout the Holiness Code, there are a variety of mechanisms that protect the poor from exploitation, keeping them from becoming landless, on the one hand, while limiting the accumulation of exorbitant wealth, on the other (cf. Isa 5:8; Ezek 46:18). The singular reason for practicing justice is the fear of the Lord (v. 17). The reward for living justly is peace and security (v. 18). The fruitfulness of the land is a sign of the blessing of peace (v. 19), and this is especially true of the year prior to the Sabbatical Year (vv. 21-22).

It is in this broader context, then, that we read Leviticus 25:23: "Land must not be sold in perpetuity, for the land belongs to me, and to me you are only strangers and guests" (Jerusalem Bible translation). Here is the pivotal relativizing statement in Leviticus 25. In light of this, *if* God is the sole owner, *then* the only possible relationship of the people to the land is that of a steward/farmer. The steward cannot dispose of or use the land according to any whim but must fulfill the owner's instructions. The farmer is one who must nurture, care for, and tend to the needs of the land to sustain its fertility and fecundity.

Apart from the oppression of the poor by the rich, the text shows there are many ways people can become poor—illness, drought, and so forth.[71] However, three ways are set up for the redemption of land and property: one may buy back the land with the help of a relative (v. 25); one may save money and buy back one's land (vv. 26-27); and one may await the Jubilee Year when debts are relieved and land is returned (v. 28). What might elite agribusinesses learn from this today?

Special regulations were placed on those who lived in walled cities; the Levites (the priestly class) and Israelites were unable to pay a debt. Additional protections governed interest and loans (vv. 35-38) and enslavement due to unpaid debt (vv. 39-55). What might this say today about nonfarmers who speculate on the commodities market, driving up food prices?

Throughout the Jubilee Year mandates, especially in light of Leviticus 25:23, we see that the ecological well-being of the land is intimately tied to the spiritual and material well-being of the people of Israel. The God

---

[71] The Torah provides restorative mechanisms to deal with these events even beyond the Sabbatical and Jubilee years that enable all the people to have some access to their sustenance from the land—for example, gleaning (Lev 19:9; Deut 24:19-22), storage, and distribution of the triennial tithe (Deut 14:22-27; 26:12ff).

who owns the land is attentive to the needs of the poor and the need of the land for rest. The laws of holiness, when heeded, bring wholeness to human persons and all of creation.

The Jubilee Year is linked to the New Testament in Luke 4:18-19, where Jesus reads Isaiah 61:1-2 in the temple and then refers to Isaiah 58:6 (both texts point to the Jubilee Year). Here Jesus outlines his mission, and subsequently, through his ministry, he teaches his followers to engage in bringing about the kingdom of God. Such language hearkens back to the great prophetic promises and talk of the new covenant (Jer 31:31-34), the resurrection (Ezek 37:1-4), and the new creation (Isa 65:17-25).

Critique of US Land Use and the Food Crisis in Light of Leviticus 25

Today the moral vision of Leviticus 25 is as relevant as ever. The moral obligations revealed in this text still compel us to worship God and to live in loving and just relationship to self, neighbor, and the land.[72] Clearly, these norms stand against abusive power exerted toward humans and the food-producing land through greed for material wealth while the poor starve across the globe.

As the data on the global food crisis and on the state of the food system in the United States and across the globe indicates, much of the present maltreatment of the land is done by gigantic globalized industrialized monocrop operations that have evolved in recent decades, based on economic theories that presume scarcity (real or created) rather than an abundance of God's providence. They do not have moderate living, an adequate food supply, and the common good characterized by sufficiency as their primary goal. Instead, they exhaust the land by trying to maximize production and by using petrochemicals and exorbitant amounts of water, ultimately threatening the world's potable water supply and exacerbating the dire threat of climate change, while still failing to feed the hungry. Farm laborers also suffer from the demands of efficiency over just care and integrity for the land. There is no God in this scenario that requires Sabbath, Sabbatical, or Jubilee rest! The presumption is that material goods and prosperity result in happiness and goodness—though millions starve.

---

[72] See James Gustafson, "The Place of Scriptures in Christian Ethics: A Methodological Study," in *Theology and Christian Ethics* (Philadelphia: United Church Press, 1974), 121–45. The values revealed in this text fit his category of "general norms of revealed morality."

By stark contrast, and viewed as an agricultural system, the Jubilee Year requires and promotes values of sufficiency over superfluity, "the caring administration of what has been entrusted to us . . . , an economics of care, or an economics of enough."[73] Such a system requires and enables the maintenance of health and wholeness attained through a modest lifestyle that gives prime time to adequate rest and just relationships with God, neighbors, and the land.

Today the poor are often left as the "collateral damage" resulting from the impersonal activity of the "invisible hand" of the "free market" that industrializes and commodifies the land, farms, farmers, food, and food-processing workers. Often only when masses of the poor threaten violence (as in the food riots of 2007) is change or land reform offered—but it is offered out of fear and primarily as a tool of pacification rather than as an integral invitation to participate in the exercise of an intrinsic right. But the vision of Sacred Scripture and Catholic social teaching points to another way.

Catholic Social Teaching

Pope John Paul II, Homily at Living History Farms[74]

Already in the late 1970s, Catholic farmers sought out their bishops' guidance and analysis of issues concerning the "disturbing changes in rural America."[75] The US Midwest heartland bishops responded by engaging the farmers and their communities in dialogue and discussion. In affirmation of the work of these bishops, and in support of their rural communities, during his visit to the United States, Pope John Paul II stopped in the Diocese of Des Moines, Iowa, in early October 1979.

In his homily at Living History Farms on October 4, he addressed farmers, emphasizing their stewardship of God's creation: "The land is God's gift entrusted to humanity from the very beginning. The land is

---

[73] Padilla, "The Relevance of the Jubilee," 15, citing Bob Goudzwaard and Harry de Lange, *Beyond Poverty and Affluence: Toward an Economy of Care* (Grand Rapids, MI: Eerdmans Publishing Co., 1993).

[74] See the full text at http://www.vatican.va/holy_father/john_paul_ii/homilies /1979/documents/hf_jp-ii_hom_19791004_usa-des-moines_en.html, accessed January 20, 2012.

[75] Regional pastoral letter Strangers and Guests: Toward Community in the Heartland (1980), prologue, no. 1.

not only God's gift, it is also man's responsibility. . . . The land must be conserved with care since it is intended to be fruitful for generation upon generation. . . . You are stewards of some of the most important resources that God has entrusted to humanity. Therefore, conserve the land well, so that your children's children and generations after them will inherit an even richer land than was entrusted to you."[76]

Several principles for a Catholic land ethic are found here. Land is a *trust* that requires our attention as does any caring relationship. Those who own and manage the land must do so with tender care, for it is the human's role and *responsibility*. Because the land is an inheritance from God, there is an *intergenerational responsibility* for caring for it with intimacy as a subject with intrinsic value, not as just a material object or piece of real estate based on the cold calculation of profit margins. There is a human obligation to *conserve* the land and its goods. Farming is a vocation that involves *cooperation* with God, a valuable participation with God's creative action and Earth's rhythms, so that Earth might become ever more fruitful.

Strangers and Guests: Toward Community in the Heartland[77]

Following the pope's visit and as the result of consultation with the farming communities, the pastoral letter Strangers and Guests: Toward Community in the Heartland was promulgated on May 1, 1980, by all of the seventy-two active and retired bishops of a twelve-state area.

The bishops held that the earth is all too frequently "being subjected to harmful farming, mining and development practices" (no. 1). People's opportunity to live "a productive and rewarding life" is determined largely by their relationship to the land. That relationship should be one of "cooperative harmony, for the land, complemented in nature, by water and air. This relationship with the land is our most important and limited natural resource" (no. 7). This "resource" should be conserved with its goods and beauty "to benefit present and future generations at home and abroad" (no.7).

---

[76] Ibid., nos. 1–2.

[77] This regional pastoral letter was signed by seventy-one bishops of dioceses in the states of Colorado, Iowa, Illinois, Indiana, Kansas, Minnesota, Missouri Nebraska, North Dakota, South Dakota, Wisconsin, and Wyoming. It was originally published by the Heartland Project, 220 S. Prairie Ave., Sioux Falls, SD, 57104. It is currently out of print.

The bishops called for "the social reforms that are necessary to preserve our land, and the best of our heritage, and promote justice for our people" (no. 8). The primary focus in Strangers and Guests is placed on protecting and promoting the owner-operated family farm. With Leviticus 25 in the background, the bishops proposed ten "Principles of Land Stewardship" (no. 50) as a theological basis for care for God's creation. These are (1) the land is God's; (2) people are God's stewards of the land; (3) the land's benefits are for everyone; (4) the land should be distributed equitably; (5) the land should be conserved and restored; (6) land-use planning must consider social and environmental impacts; (7) land use should be appropriate to land quality; (8) the land should provide a moderate livelihood; (9) the land's workers should be able to become the land's owners; and (10) the land's mineral wealth should be shared. In these principles, we find a kind of land ethic that sings in harmony with the biblical theme of Leviticus 25! The bishops then applied each principle to the various forms of land abuse and other related moral violations.

Still building on the themes of Leviticus 25, the bishops stressed that God has "ultimate dominion" of the earth (no. 51); the earth is "entrusted to humanity's care" (no. 52); people are God's stewards (nos. 53-54) and are "co-creators with God in guiding the land's productive power and in conserving the land's natural gifts. As co-creators, God's stewards help the land fulfill the purpose for which God created it: to help satisfy the physical, social and spiritual needs of God's creatures" (no. 55). Thus, all of God's creatures, not just humans, are God's concern.

It is particularly noteworthy that the bishops of the US agricultural heartland advanced equitable distribution of the earth's goods in the human community; proposed widespread land ownership in the human community, including land distribution by means of a progressive land tax (no. 89); and supported struggles for justice by Native Americans (no. 103). These measures would consistently benefit a more just food system across the globe.

Voices and Choices: Forty-One Catholic Bishops of the US South[78]

As US farming operations shifted from family farms to industrial megafarms, many operations turned to the mass production of poultry,

---

[78] See the full text of Voices and Choices: A Pastoral Letter from the Catholic Bishops of the South, November 15, 2000, at http://www.americancatholic.org/news /poultrypastoral/english.asp, accessed January 15, 2012.

hogs, and cattle (factory farms). This was accompanied by rapid growth in gigantic meat processing plants that usually hired unskilled laborers, many of whom were people of color and/or recent immigrants. The US poultry processors and other food producing industries in the US economy became notorious for their egregiously abusive working conditions. On November 15, 2000, forty-one Catholic bishops of the southern United States issued a pastoral letter entitled Voices and Choices that challenged this state of affairs. The bishops were motivated by more than twenty years of experience and reception of testimony systematically gathered from hundreds of people and dozens of organizations representing poultry workers, poultry growers, processing workers, managers, diocesan officials, and bishops.

Voices and Choices details the high "price" poultry processing workers, poultry catchers, and poultry growers pay so that US consumers might enjoy plentiful and inexpensive poultry. That price includes serious injuries, disabling repetitive-motion trauma, disrespectful treatment, and inadequate pay. The bishops supported their criticism of the industry, citing several case studies gleaned from the hundreds of testimonies they had heard. The case of Maria Moñtez is one example. She is a senior citizen who has been in the United States for many years, and for the last five years she worked in poultry processing. She had numbness in her arms and hands and suffered from repetitive motion syndrome. The pain caused sleepless nights, and she had not seen a doctor because the company's insurance deductible outpriced her low wages. Her requests to be rotated to other tasks with different motions had been denied.

Maria's case is not uncommon. According to a 1997 US Department of Labor study, 60 percent of poultry companies surveyed were found in violation of the Fair Labor Standards Act.[79] Over 51 percent of the plants failed to pay workers for time spent on job-related tasks such as cleanup. Over 30 percent failed to pay for brief breaks during the day, such as restroom use. Over 54 percent deducted money from worker paychecks for protective gear for which the company is required to pay.

The bishops also viewed the issues from the perspective of managers such as John Stephens, a senior manager with a poultry company who needs to keep the operation profitable so that he and others have jobs.

[79] See, for example, United States Department of Labor, "Tyson Foods Found in Violation of Fair Labor Standards Act," http://www.dol.gov/opa/media/press/esa/esa20091232.htm, accessed January 15, 2012. All factual data included with these scenarios is found in Voices and Choices.

It is a competitive business and there are a lot of factors to consider. His single biggest problem is employee turnover, because "the work is very hard physically and repetitious—that's part of the problem." More and more, he must rely on immigrants, many with questionable documentation. He acknowledged, "We need to improve the way people are dealt with; the way we take care of their needs is most important."[80]

According to surveys conducted by the United Food and Commercial Workers International Union (UFCW), poultry workers are mostly African American and female, though Latinos are the fastest-growing segment of the workforce. The quality of supervision is a key to turnover and absenteeism. The higher the quality of just and fair supervisors, the better the work environment is. Supervisors must treat employees well. Workers must be trained to rotate through several jobs to relieve or prevent repetitive motion injuries.[81]

The bishops also considered issues from the perspective of poultry growers like Roy and Mary Stein. Roy explained that the company "can break [the contract] any time they want to; you can't, but they can." Mary said, "This is contract labor. You are not a partner." Growers are afraid to speak up because "everything they own is mortgaged."[82] Poultry growers often find themselves in unfair situations.

> The contract they sign with the poultry company is written to leave the major decisions in the hands of the *company*. The grower must spend large sums of money to build, and later update, the facilities where the birds will be raised. Such investments usually call for a mortgage on the family farm in the case of smaller growers. The antibiotics, feed and other supplies, including the chicks themselves, come from the *company*. The *company* weighs the feed and the finished chickens. The *company* also decides what the grower will be paid per pound of bird, once expenses for supplies are deducted. Unhealthy chicks, illness in the flock, weather problems, waste disposal and runoff problems are all risks for the *grower*, not the company. Current contracts are often written to specify arbitration as the only mode of redress, omitting the possibility of class action lawsuits which have been successful for some growers in the past.[83]

[80] Voices and Choices.
[81] Ibid.
[82] Ibid.
[83] Ibid., emphases added.

According to the Securities and Exchange Commission, poultry companies gain about 16 percent on their investment, while poultry growers gain about 4 percent. Of the Delmarva, Florida, poultry growers surveyed, 43 percent said they did not trust their company's feed delivery weights; 41 percent did not trust the figures on their pay statements; and 57 percent believe the company will retaliate if they raise concerns.[84]

The bishops were aware of the controversies that surround illegal immigration into the United States. Yet when seen from the perspective of the poor and those who have no other means to put food on the table for their families, moral questions need to be asked about a global economic system that makes Julio Lopez's case a common one.[85] His hand was seriously injured, requiring more than seventy stitches, when the line speed was increased. He had already been required to handle thirty birds per minute, making over twenty thousand cuts per shift. Weeks later the company doctor would not authorize his seeing a specialist. He was not compensated for the injury. He feared losing his current job. He was so desperate to feed his family in Mexico that he crossed the US border illegally. What would happen if he were to be sent back? He said it is safer to be silent.

The bishops teach:

> While the laws regarding immigration and immigrants must be respected, everything must be done to aid and protect this most vulnerable and exploitable group of brothers and sisters. . . . Whatever their country of origin, most are without a voice as they attempt to support themselves and their families by whatever means is available, no matter what the conditions. Their understandable reluctance to seek help from government authorities becomes another factor in the circumstances which many such people must face.
>
> Others involved in this industry have challenges as well, such as truck drivers, distribution employees and feed mill workers.[86]

The bishops highlight the necessity of recognizing the God-given dignity of each person, the need for a safe and just workplace, the special challenges of immigrant workers, and the essential priority of shared

---

[84] Ibid.

[85] For central magisterial teachings on immigration, see Justice for Immigrants, "Catholic Social Teaching and Migration," http://www.justiceforimmigrants.org/documents/immigration-and-catholic-social-teaching.pdf, accessed January 20, 2012.

[86] Voices and Choices.

responsibility and decision making—the "voices and choices"—in the workplace. The right of poultry workers to just employment is not based on the will of their employer. It is grounded in the reality that all are made in God's image and likeness. All Christians "are called to continuous growth in the awareness of God's presence in our daily lives . . ., such as [in] those who work to supply the food we place on our table." [87]

The bishops' pastoral was published in Spanish and English, reaching out to immigrant workers affected by the issues explored in the document. Like many Catholics who came to this country in the past, present-day immigrants are vulnerable and are often desperate for work. They rarely seek help from authorities when mistreated; they are the poor who require our special consideration.

In a globalized world the bishops could not neglect dealing with systemic injustices that characterize today's economy, such as "vertical integration" issues. Vertical integration is where the same company owns and/or controls every step of production, from the most basic components (such as feed grain) to the final product (such as boneless, skinless chicken breasts on grocery store shelves), and it has become a dominant force in the economy. According to the National Catholic Rural Life Conference, the ramifications of "'factory farming' impact prices, wages, natural resources, and the future of family farming, placing enormous power in the boardrooms of a few companies." [88]

The bishops called for legal and structural changes to address the intricate and interconnected web of environmental, technological, political, financial, and international issues involved. The forty-one southern US bishops challenged the Catholic community to live out the six basic principles of Catholic social teaching.[89] "We may not abdicate our concern and responsibilities for such matters to the anonymous group. The 'group' is made up of individuals. Structural change begins with the conversion of each heart." [90]

---

[87] Ibid.

[88] Ibid.

[89] Ibid. The six principles are (1) protection of human dignity (and the right to food); (2) the social nature of the human person (call to family, community, and participation); (3) option for the poor and the vulnerable; (4) dignity of work and the rights and duties of workers and owners; (5) solidarity; and (6) respect for creation.

[90] Ibid.

USCCB, *For I Was Hungry and You Gave Me Food to Eat: Catholic Reflection on Food, Farmers, and Farmworkers*[91]

In 2003 the United States Conference of Catholic Bishops revisited the status of land use and agriculture in the United States and the interrelated issues of poverty and food scarcity. They discovered that the problems cited in 1980 had only deepened and increased.[92] In their November 18, 2003, reflection, the bishops placed all of this in light of the imperative of the Last Judgment that we care for people in need (Matt 25:35) and in light of Leviticus 25:4-6.[93]

Based on these reflections, the bishops constructed a framework of six criteria against which policies concerning land use and agriculture must be measured:

1. *Overcoming Hunger and Poverty.* . . . A key measure of every agricultural program and legislative initiative is whether it helps the most vulnerable farmers, farmworkers, and their families and whether it contributes to a global food system that provides basic nutrition for all.

2. *Providing a Safe, Affordable, and Sustainable Food Supply.* . . . Caring for land and water resources, . . . farmers should expand the use of environmentally sustainable methods so that farmland in the United States can provide food for generations to come. We . . . continue to lose productive farm land for development . . . and transportation. . . . An important measure of international trade and agricultural policies should be how they promote safe and affordable food and sustainable, environmentally sound farming practices.

3. *Ensuring a Decent Life for Farmers and Farmworkers.* . . . Food can remain safe and affordable without sacrificing the incomes, health,

---

[91] See full text at www.michigancatholicrurallife.org/images/For_I_Was_Hungry .doc, accessed January 20, 2012. Subsequent citations of this pastoral letter use page numbers from this document.

[92] Hunger was more rampant across the globe, family farmers struggled to survive, and many more farms had been lost, while hundreds of farmworkers were denied a life of dignity. The new challenges converged around the growing concentration at every level of agriculture, increasingly making agricultural trade rather than an adequate food supply for the world the measure of economic vitality. Also, the corporate decision makers frequently only had a global market orientation that gave little or no consideration to the needs of small local farming communities, and thus they took advantage of relatively weak and powerless farmers and ranchers.

[93] USCCB, For I Was Hungry and You Gave Me Food, 6.

or lives of farmers and farmworkers. Catholic social teaching insists that all workers deserve wages and benefits sufficient to support a family and live a decent life.

4. *Sustaining and Strengthening Rural Communities.* . . . Public policies should encourage a wide variety of economic development strategies in rural areas.

5. *Protecting God's Creation.* . . . Care for God's creation is a central calling for believers. . . . . An essential measure of agricultural and food policies is whether they protect the environment and its diversity and promote sustainable agricultural practices in the United States and abroad.

6. *Expanding Participation.* . . . Truly effective policies will be developed when people who are most affected have adequate information, time, and opportunities for real contributions to legislation, regulations, programs, and trade agreements.[94]

The bishops conclude this statement with a "Catholic Agenda for Action: Pursuing a More Just Agricultural System." Concerning US farmers and farm policies, they challenge "the continuing concentration in the ownership of land and resources and in the marketing and distribution of food [that] leaves control in the hands of too few and diminishes effective participation."[95]

The most extensive set of actions called for addresses various issues of US agricultural workers. The bishops reiterate their call for just and living wages for these workers. They stress the need for worker participation in work-related decisions and in their communities, and they also stress the reality of the hazardous nature of the work and thus the need for adequate protection on the job. The bishops call for strict enforcement of the Fair Labor Standards Act and the Migrant and Seasonal Workers Protection Act to insure the dignity of workers. There remains a need to reform immigration laws and guest-worker programs to provide hardworking laborers the ability to obtain legal status and to avoid the breakup of families.

The section "International Trade, Aid, and Development" addresses the needs of small farmers and farmworkers in the United States and

---

[94] Ibid., 10–11.
[95] Ibid., 17.

abroad. There needs to be strong vigilance about the effect of major free-trade agreements on small farmers and their access to markets at home and abroad. These free-trade agreements must have appropriate flexibility to open just opportunities for the world's poorest and most desperate nations to keep food prices stable and accessible, while honoring just health and safety standards. "People have a basic human right to a sufficient amount of safe food to sustain life."[96] The bishops object to donors forcing genetically modified grains and other foods on needy peoples. They call for full disclosure when modified foods are brought into a country and also for efforts to be made to first supply the needy with locally produced produce.

The bishops encourage emerging technologies that contribute to opportunities for the world's poorest to move out of poverty and into food security. They particularly advocate increased public support for ongoing research to develop food crops that can grow in more arid and less fertile regions of the world. The bishops raise strong cautions about the development and use of genetically modified organisms (GMOs), especially for food: "We join the Holy See in raising two key concerns: the urgent need to focus new developments in agricultural technology on reducing poverty and hunger, and the importance of ensuring open discussion and participation in decision making regarding the development and use of genetically modified products."[97] The two fundamental moral questions raised by GMOs are "Who will decide about the use and availability of these new technologies? And who will benefit from them?"[98] Thus, the bishops firmly assert that the driving force behind GMOs needs to be "how hunger can be overcome, how poor farmers can be assisted, and how people participate in the debate and decisions."[99]

Stewardship of creation must be the goal of agricultural policies. Conservation and improvement of soils, water quality, wildlife, and biodiversity are important. In order to achieve those goals, the bishops strongly urge the use of alternative methods to even the minimal use of pesticides and chemicals, and they support the protection of farmwork-

[96] Ibid., 21.

[97] Ibid., 22. See Archbishop Renato R. Martino, address at the Ministerial Conference on Science and Technology in Agriculture, Sacramento, California, June 23–25, 2003, http://www.vatican.va/roman_curia/secretariat_state/2003/documents/rc_seg-st_20030625_gmo-martino_en.html, accessed January 21, 2012.

[98] USCCB, For I Was Hungry and You Gave Me Food, 22.

[99] Ibid.

ers from those toxins. Further, the bishops seriously question the practices of massive confined animal feeding operations and huge monocrop farms.

Pope Benedict XVI, Address to the World Summit on Food Security[100]

On November 16, 2009, for the first time ever, a pope visited the Rome headquarters of the UN Food and Agriculture Organization and addressed the opening session of the World Summit on Food Security. Pope Benedict XVI warned against the greed of speculators in cereal markets and criticized aid that gravely damages the agricultural sector. He noted that food insecurity was not a problem of global production capacity, but rather a problem of providing access to food. Referring to his encyclical letter *Caritas in Veritate* (CV), the pope noted that currently there is no international institution that can guarantee the adequate availability of food and water for all people. In the foreseeable future, especially in light of climate change, a long-term solution is needed. In Benedict XVI's view, the key solutions for addressing food security include eliminating structural causes and assisting poorer nations in establishing sustainable agriculture. The latter includes irrigation systems that do not waste water and better education about various agricultural technologies and the workings of modern markets. Most importantly, local human talents and natural resources must be utilized for greater overall efficiency and effectiveness for agricultural efforts.[101]

Benedict stressed that any adequate system providing access to food must work to fully integrate poor countries into the world's economic system. Citing CV, the pope held that the principle of subsidiarity must be honored and local peoples must be actively involved in determining solutions to their own problems. This kind of involvement honors integral human development as well. He challenged that the whole international community has a moral duty to act in solidarity with the poorer nations through being present to them and respectfully assisting them with supervision and training.[102]

---

[100] See full text of the address at http://www.vatican.va/holy_father/benedict_xvi /speeches/2009/november/documents/hf_ben-xvi_spe_20091116_fao_en.html, accessed January 20, 2012.

[101] Ibid., no. 2.

[102] Ibid., no. 3.

Benedict insisted that the food insecurity of lesser developed nations not merely be written off by wealthy nations as an inevitable structural consequence of their socioeconomic situation. He declared:

> It is not so, and it must never be so! To fight and conquer hunger it is essential to start *redefining the concepts and principles that have hitherto governed international relations*, in such a way as to answer the question: what can direct the attention and the consequent conduct of States towards the needs of the poorest? . . . Only in the name of common membership of the worldwide human family can every people and therefore every country be asked to practice solidarity, that is, to shoulder the burden of concrete responsibilities in meeting the needs of others, so as to favor the genuine sharing of goods, founded on love.[103]

The pope continued, making important distinctions between love, justice, and the moral and juridical obligations of Christians. In Christian ethics, love and justice always work hand in hand. We often speak of these virtues separately, but each virtue modifies the other. When it comes to giving to others, because everything each of us has was first God's gift to us, we need to remember that none of us ultimately owns anything. In light of this, when we give anything out of love, we first give the other person what is *justly* his or hers, but then we can be more generous and give out of love. The elimination of hunger requires changes in ethical behavior as well as changes in legal policies and economic structures. Such changes will require new levels of cooperation that respect the equal worth of all nations and peoples, no matter their level of sophistication in economic development.[104]

The pope cautioned that a huge error would be to continue to associate food production primarily with profit making. He was adamant that all people have a right to sufficient, healthy, and nutritious food and to safe and sufficient water. All analysis and actions for development and increased food security must safeguard the environment as a shared good.

The pope strongly maintained that individuals must change their habits of consumption and their perceptions of what is truly needed. He concluded:

---

[103] Ibid., no. 4.
[104] Ibid., no. 5.

Hunger is the most cruel and concrete sign of poverty. Opulence and waste are no longer acceptable when the tragedy of hunger is assuming ever greater proportions. . . . The Catholic Church . . . is committed to support, by word and deed, the action taken in solidarity—planned, responsible and regulated—to which all members of the international community are called to contribute. Such solidarity . . . must not exclude the religious dimension, with all the spiritual energy that it brings, and its promotion of the human person. Acknowledgment of the transcendental worth of every man and every woman is still the first step towards the conversion of heart that underpins the commitment to eradicate deprivation, hunger and poverty in all their forms.[105]

Whether we consider life in the global, national, or local community, food that is safe, sufficiently nutritious, accessible, and affordable is a common human need and indeed a human right.

From the Writings of St. Francis

"Fragments" (1209–23), 73[106]

Let all the brothers strive to follow the humility and poverty of our Lord Jesus Christ and remember that we should have nothing else in the whole world except, as the apostle says: *having food and clothing, we are content with those* [1 Tim. 6:8].

"Chronicle of Ernoul" (1227/29), 4[107]

The Sultan replied that he would gladly have them return safe and sound to the Christian camp. Furthermore, he brought great quantities of gold, silver, and silk garments and invited them to take whatever they wanted. They said they would not have taken anything once they saw they could not obtain his soul for the Lord God, for they considered this the most precious thing they could give to God, rather than precious and vast treasure. They said it would be sufficient if he would give them something

---

[105] Ibid., no. 10.

[106] See the full text in *Francis of Assisi: Early Documents*, vol. I, *The Saint*, trans. and ed. Regis J. Armstrong, J. A. Wayne Hellmann, and William J. Short (New York: New City Press, 1999), 91.

[107] See full text in ibid., 607.

to eat, and they would be on their way, since they could not accomplish anything else there. The Sultan gave them plenty of food to eat, whereupon they took their leave of him, and he had them escorted safely back to the Christian army.

A Mirror of Perfection, *Rule,* Profession, Life and True Calling of a Lesser Brother *(The Lemmens Edition), 24*[108]

Blessed Francis used to say: "My brothers, I say that each of you must consider his own constitution, because although one of you may be sustained with less food than another, I nevertheless want one who needs more food not to try imitating him on this. Rather, considering his constitution, he should provide his body with what it needs. Just as we must be aware of overindulgence in eating, which harms the body and soul, so we must be aware of excessive abstinence even more, because the Lord *desires mercy and not sacrifice*" [Hos 6:6].

The Deeds of Blessed Francis and His Companions, *XV, 8–16*[109]

St. Francis had the table prepared on the bare ground, as was his custom. And when it was time to eat, St. Francis and St. Clare sat down together, and one of his companions with St. Clare's companion, and all his other companions were grouped around that humble table. But at the first course St. Francis began to speak about God in such a sweet and holy

---

[108] See the full text in *Francis of Assisi: Early Documents*, vol. III, *The Prophet*, trans. and ed. Regis J. Armstrong, J. A. Wayne Hellmann, and William J. Short (New York: New City Press, 2001), 234.

[109] This adaptation is from "How St. Clare Ate a Meal with St. Francis," in Franciscan Pilgrimage Programs, *Pilgrim's Companion to Franciscan Places* (Assisi: Editrice Minerva Assisi, 2002), 323–25. The context for this passage is as follows: when Francis was staying in Assisi he often visited St. Clare and consoled her with his holy advice. And as she had a great desire to eat a meal with him once, she asked him several times to give her that consolation. But Francis always refused to grant her that favor. But his companions perceived St. Clare's desire and advised him that he should not be so rigid but should rather share a meal with her. After all, it was Francis's preaching that led her to give up everything to follow in the footprints of Jesus. Thus, on a given day Francis, Clare, and their companions met at St. Mary of the Angels, the place where Clare "was shorn and made a spouse of the Lord Jesus Christ." Then they ate together in the name of the Lord. See the full text in FAED, vol. III, *The Prophet*, 466–67.

and profound and divine and marvelous way that he himself and St. Clare and her companion and all the others who were at that poor little table were rapt in God by the overabundance of divine grace that descended upon them. . . . [To observers in Assisi and Bettona at this moment, it seemed that the forest and St. Mary of the Angels was set aflame. They came running to rescue the place.] Entering the place, they found St. Francis with St. Clare and all companions sitting around that very humble table, rapt in God by contemplation and invested with power from on high. . . . Later, after a long while, when St. Francis and St. Clare and the others came back to themselves, they so felt refreshed by spiritual food that they paid little attention to the material food. And when that blessed meal was over, St. Clare well accompanied went back to San Damiano.

Reflection and Application

Catholic social teaching principles clearly frame an ethics of eating. These principles originate in the Scriptures and in the key texts we have examined. The National Catholic Rural Life Conference has summarized the salient points this way.

Principles for Ethical Eaters[110]

For Human Dignity:
- Every person has a right to sufficient and nutritious food.
- Farmers, farm workers, and food workers deserve fair wages and safe working conditions.

For the Common Good:
- People around the world have a right to food security.
- Developing local food systems are more sound than depending on global trade mechanisms.

Preferential Option for the Poor:
- Poverty and hunger go hand-in-hand; we must eliminate poverty to end hunger.

[110] National Catholic Rural Life Conference, "Principles for Ethical Eaters," http://www.ncrlc.com/page.aspx?ID=49, accessed January 21, 2012.

- We must always concern ourselves first with the needs of those who go hungry.

For Integrity of Creation:

- Stewardship of the natural environment is essential for a future abundance of food.
- Animal production for human consumption must be carried out humanely.

For Subsidiarity:

- People around the world have a right to local control and food sovereignty.
- We affirm the consumer's preference for local food production.

For Solidarity:

- Enact fair trade provisions and uphold anti-trust enforcements.
- Respect farmers and producers worldwide as we would for our own farmers and producers.

Clearly, from all we have said thus far, for Catholics (and others) eating is a moral act that requires definitive changes in our food habits, especially for us who live in the United States.

Eating as a Moral Act: What's Your "Foodprint"?

A 2007 Cornell University study, conducted by Chris Peters and others, compared forty-two diets that had the same number of calories, the same core of grains, fruits, vegetables, and dairy products, but varying amounts of meat (from zero to 13.4 ounces daily) and fat (from 20 to 45 percent of calories) to determine each diet's "agricultural land foodprint" (footprint).[111] They found a fivefold difference between the two extremes. A person following a low-fat vegetarian diet will need less than half (0.44) an acre per person per year to produce his or her food, while a high-fat diet with a lot of meat, on the other hand, requires 2.11 acres. The reason for the difference in land use amounts is that fruits, vegetables, and grains must be grown on high-quality cropland, while meat

[111] Susan Lang, "Diet for Small Planet May Be Most Efficient If It Includes Dairy and a Little Meat, Cornell Researchers Report," *Chronicle OnLine*, October 4, 2007, http://www.news.cornell.edu/stories/oct07/diets.ag.footprint.sl.html, accessed January 14, 2012.

and dairy products from ruminant animals (which are hoofed and chew the cud) are supported by lower-quality, but more widely available, land that can support pasture and hay. Meat diets require increased land-use requirements; however, diets including modest amounts of meat can feed more people than some higher-fat vegetarian diets. So the "agricultural land foodprint" increases with the amount of meat that is included in the diet: 0 grams of meat / 0.5 acres of land; 63 grams of meat / 0.6 acres; 254 grams of meat / 13 acres; 381 grams of meat / 19 acres. So the overall proportion of "agricultural land foodprint" per gram of meat increases land use by only 0.1 acre.[112] What is significant for conserving land and other resources with our diets is limiting the amount of meat we eat and for farmers to rely more on grazing and forages to feed their livestock. Thus, it is important for consumers to realize that foods differ not only in their nutrient content but also in the amount of resources required to produce, process, package, and transport them.

Certainly, changes in lifestyle are not easy, but as the Cornell study shows, there are ways to still enjoy some of life's pleasures while still eating with a moral conscience. An additional consideration for moral eaters is to consider whether the food is grown and prepared in sustainable ways. Food needs to be grown in ways that are good for the earth. This means little or no use of chemical fertilizers, pesticides, or herbicides and keeping the soils fertile, the waters pure, and the air clean.[113] We need to consume foods that are good to grow. This means that the health and safety of all who handle the food from seed to table are sufficiently guarded. It also means that we view God's creatures (especially animals) not only as objects for our consumption but as sensate beings that require our respect and careful treatment. These principles rule out eating foods produced on most forms of industrial or factory farms.[114]

---

[112] Ibid. See the illustration by Steve Rokitka/University Communications that is included in Susan Lang's article. These proportions show "the area of agricultural land in New York state needed to feed the average person for one year."

[113] See Wes Jackson, "Farming in Nature's Image: Natural Systems of Agriculture," in Andrew Kimball, *Fatal Harvest* (Washington, DC: Island Press, 2003), 68.

[114] For an interesting and accessible discussion of this issue, see Jesse Ramirez, "Faith Seeking Food: Animals, Factory Farms, and Catholic Social Teaching," a paper presented on May 25, 2005, at Santa Clara University Student Research Ethics Conference, http://www.scu.edu/ethics/publications/submitted/Ramirez/FaithSeeking Food.html, accessed January 20, 2012. Also see the *Catechism of the Catholic Church*, nos. 2416–18, on the treatment of animals, http://www.vatican.va/archive/ccc_css /archive/catechism/p3s2c2a7.htm, accessed January 22, 2012.

The most central place where habits, values, and virtues around food are formed is in the home with family. As L. Shannon Jung points out, regularly shared meals are the place where children develop the understanding that mutual relationships are critical for life and ecological living.[115] Family meals are an early occasion for moving out of an individualism of tastes and priorities, for celebrating cultural traditions, and for learning the structure of conversations, enjoying jokes, telling stories, and sharing the concerns of each member's daily life. Children also need to learn through helping cook the meal, shopping, or working in the garden. While it takes work to be consistent with such practices, it is what is needed to reverse the value of the instant and fast food of the microwave and the "Mcfood" culture that demands the mass production of animals and monocrops to be maintained.

Eating lower on the food chain will positively impact our health, land use, water quality, and soil conservation. This requires reaching for whole foods and cooking from scratch. The fact is that whole foods require less energy to be produced and processed. Highly nutritious beans, rice, lentils, pasta, and vegetables are among the best items to start with. As the Cornell study shows, less meat is important, but chicken and wild-caught fish are among the most efficient when adding meat to the diet. Tasty recipes from the 1950s or earlier likely avoid the processed ingredients of more recent times. Also, the cuisine of Hispanic cultures, as well as of the Middle East and Asia, work very well for meatless meals.

Organically grown foods are the best because they use up to 35 percent less energy to produce while being good to the earth.[116] Another earth-friendly way to access food is to utilize "community-supported agriculture," a system where people buy a share in local farm production. Each week the family receives a basket of produce from the farm. The advantage is that food is locally grown and the source is known to the customer. Disadvantages include the limits on diversity of foods; at times the basket needs to be supplemented for proper nutrition for children. While ex-

---

[115] L. Shannon Jung, *Sharing Food: Christian Practices for Enjoyment* (Minneapolis: Fortress, 2006), 6.

[116] See the US Department of Agriculture for information on certified organic foods at http://www.usda.gov/wps/portal/usda/usdahome?navid=ORGANIC_CERTI FICATIO, accessed January 22, 2012. Generally, this means no use of chemical fertilizers, pesticides, herbicides, genetically modified organisms, antibiotics, or hormones. Practices include rotating crops, using cover crops to sustain soil quality and support biodiversity, and using waters that are not polluted.

penses vary concerning local food purchases, the key is the sustainable practices farmers use to produce foods.[117]

Feasting and Fasting in the Footprints of Jesus

Conversion: Feasting and Fasting

In his early life St. Francis, as a rather spoiled son of the burgeoning merchant class, was known for his carousing, opulence, and feasting.[118] Yet his joy in such festivities was soon found wanting, for they did not ever satisfy his deepest desires. It was when he embraced a simplified life, desiring to walk in the footprints of Jesus, that he really saw the Giver of all good gifts and the radical incarnational relatedness of everything and everyone.

In the Rule of 1221, he directed the order to fast from the feast of All Saints to Christmas and from Epiphany to Easter, as well as on every Friday.[119] He also disciplined his life by rarely eating cooked food, diluting it with cold water, or spreading ashes on it.[120] Yet when he was invited to feasts or fine dinners, he would eat some of what was placed before him (following Jesus' mandate in Luke 10:8). Following in the footprints of Jesus was to live at the margins with the poor and, as St. Paul instructed, to be content with having food and clothing (1 Tim 6:8). Any other material possessions—especially offers of silver, gold, or silk—held little attraction for him, for he knew from his past how empty of lasting value all such things are. Instead, what was important was the Giver of the gift of food and the relationships it symbolized.

Food was the occasion for realizing life's interdependency and contingency—we do not originate our own food, and we continually need to replenish it, lest we die. Indeed, we are dependent on the earth itself and on God's providence, and this dependency was also an opportunity

---

[117] See Julie Hanlon Rubio, "Toward a Just Way of Eating," in Tobias Winright, ed., *Green Discipleship: Catholic Theological Ethics and the Environment* (Winona, MN: Anselm Academic, Christian Brothers Publications, 2011), 360–78.

[118] *The Life of Saint Francis* by Thomas of Celano (1228–29), bk. I, chap. I, in FAED, vol. I, *The Saint*, 183–84.

[119] "Earlier Rule [Rule Without the Papal Seal] (1209/10-1221)," chap. III, in FAED, vol. I, *The Saint*, 65.

[120] *The Life of Saint Francis* by Thomas of Celano (1228–29), bk. I, chap. XIX, 51, in FAED, vol. I, *The Saint*, 227.

for the brothers to realize and respect the diversity among them. Not all brothers had the physical constitution for fasting, and one can only imagine the challenge to generosity and hospitality it was when some needed to eat while others fasted! But even St. Francis gave in to the needs of the hungry brothers as a gesture of hospitality.

For our postmodern sensibilities, St. Francis's feasting and fasting seem extreme. However, if we reflect on our experiences of fasting, there are many ways in which, as a spiritual practice, they can lead us to contemplate the ethics of eating and to seek justice, providing us with nourishment of a different kind. Catholics are called to fast on numerous occasions, such as on Fridays or during Lent. Through such practices, by feeling the real impact of the bodily stress of hunger, we can become clear about what it is like for millions who go hungry each day. Such experiences can teach us empathy and genuine compassion—not pity. But empathy compels us to move to action. Like the prophet Isaiah counseled, "The kind of fast I want is that you remove the chains of oppression and the yoke of injustice and let the oppressed go free, share your food with the hungry and open your homes to the poor" (Isa 58:6-7).

Another realization fasting can awaken is just how much and how often we eat and overeat—and the effects this has on our personal health. We need to question how money, time, and energy spent on excess food might be better and more justly spent on more healthy and earth-friendly whole foods or on projects of NGOs that assist the poor in changing the food system. Fasting can teach us about genuine self-denial for the sake of the well-being of others.

Further, fasting can teach us that "less is more." It can be a way to shift away from our dependencies on external things (nonessentials) to our real needs for love, intimate conversations, acceptance, and healthy self-confidence. Fasting from food, so dear to our physical existence, can demonstrate that we *can* live without much else. The other side of "less is more" is that we need to keep track of the value of those things we find we can indeed give up, such as money, time, or talent, and spend that capital on some action or project to bring about greater justice. As a wise rabbi once said, "God ignores fasting that does not result in greater compassion"—and greater just action, I would add.

The Eucharistic Feast

For Christians the finest meal is the Eucharist. At each Eucharist the fruit of the earth and the work of human hands, indeed all of creation, join together to feed us, giving us a foretaste of the eternal banquet to come. This same food empowers us to leave the Eucharistic table and to become "Eucharist"—the occasion of thanksgiving—for our world. It is the food that joins us in communion with other believers (as Francis and Clare did) to worship and bask in God's generous mercy and love. This is the food that makes it impossible to ignore the crying needs of the earth and the hungry and that compels us to make the right to food a reality in our world. As long as there is one hungry person in the world, we are in danger of celebrating the Eucharist to our detriment (see 1 Cor 11:21-29). Monika Hellwig concluded that the Eucharist should prompt Christians to support organizations that feed the hungry. This activity "is to become oneself in some measure bread for the life of the world . . . in tune with the life and Spirit of Jesus."[121]

Toward a Just Food System: A Hope-Filled Path Forward

On June 1, 2011, the highly regarded food aid and advocacy agency Oxfam International released a plan to tackle some of the most menacing and sizable factors perpetuating food insecurity and injustices across the globe.[122] Their document, *Growing a Better Future: Food Justice in a Resource-Constrained World* (GROW), did not mince words but stated plainly that population growth, overconsumption, and climate change will require any future food system to fit into the world's *resource limits.* "Nearly one billion people face hunger every day, while the unsustainable patterns of consumption and production from which they are excluded have placed us all on a collision course with our planet's ecological limits. The warning signs are clear. We have entered an age of crisis: of food price spikes and oil price hikes; of scrambles for land and water; of creeping, insidious climate change. . . . We now risk a wholesale reversal in human development."[123]

By 2050 the majority of population growth is expected to be in the financially poorest nations. Hunger responses that push increased production using the wares of globalized agribusinesses—especially fossil-

---

[121] Monika K. Hellwig, *The Eucharist and the Hunger of the World* (New York: Paulist Press, 1976), 39.

[122] See Oxfam, *Growing a Better Future Summary,* http://www.oxfam.org/sites/www.oxfam.org/files/cr-growing-better-future-170611-summ-en.pdf, accessed January 15, 2012.

[123] Ibid.

fuel–intensive inputs and genetically modified seeds—are simply counterproductive in the long run because they are neither healthy nor ecologically sustainable. Indeed, "growing better" requires "sharing better." In 2011 three companies—Archer Daniels Midland, Bunge, and Cargill—controlled an estimated 90 percent of the world's grain trade.[124] In the first quarter of 2008, when the food crisis peaked, Cargill's profits were up 86 percent; and in 2011, with food prices still rising and countries scrambling to ensure food security, Cargill was looking at its most profitable year yet.[125]

What is most urgent is change in food policies and programs so that food aid moneys are reallocated to small-scale producers in developing countries, where major gains in productivity, sustainable intensification, poverty reduction, and resilience can be achieved.[126] This sector holds the greatest potential for reducing hunger, renewing the earth's natural fertility, and sustaining food security within ecological limits. This means realizing the human right to water, increasing technical assistance, and achieving practical investment and credit, among other things. Equally urgent is to halt the "land grabs" of huge swaths of land in Africa and elsewhere at cheap prices, which do nothing for the economies or food security of local communities.

For those of us who live in the United States, since our nation is a major investor in agricultural aid, Oxfam urges that we require our government to take the lead on shifting resources to small producers.[127] The need to end speculation on agricultural commodities is urgent. We need to modernize food aid and stop giving huge subsidies for the corn-ethanol industry; and we need to regulate land and water grabbing. Our government has to "share better" in how food aid is accomplished. Currently, 75 percent of all food aid dollars must be sourced, bagged, fortified, and processed by US agribusiness firms with contracts with the US Department of Agriculture, thus insuring that the lion's share of US food dollars go to US agribusinesses. Food must also be transported by US companies on US-flagged vessels at taxpayer expense. Nearly 40 percent of total food costs are paid to US shipping companies.

---

[124] Ibid.

[125] See Cargill's 2012 earnings at http://www.cargill.com/company/financial/index.jsp, accessed June 26, 2012.

[126] Currently, the majority of public agricultural aid goes to agro-industrial farms in Northern countries.

[127] Oxfam, *Growing a Better Future Summary.*

As Oxfam states, "Oxfam's GROW Campaign has a simple message: another future is possible, and we can build it together. . . . But only if we stop our sleepwalk towards ecological disaster. This campaign is Oxfam's wake-up call."[128] They stress that we must simultaneously address the spiraling demand for food and the impending collision between ecological systems that sustain life and the economic systems that sustain wealth for only a few, making it impossible to protect the most vulnerable. They conclude their report by citing three powerful examples of how their proposals have already worked in three very diverse contexts. In Brazil twenty years of activism from civil society and social movements challenged elites and helped elect politicians with a new vision and moral purpose. Hunger fell by one-third in Brazil between 2000 and 2007. Similarly, Vietnam achieved the first Millennium Goal—to halve hunger—five years ahead of the 2015 deadline. This was achieved through investing in smallholder agriculture. In Canada a public campaign succeeded in untying Canada's food aid.[129] "As recently as 2007, more than half of Canadian food aid to developing countries had to be bought in Canada. This was known as tied aid, and it was neither cost effective nor efficient. Tied aid undermines the ability of developing countries to produce or buy goods for themselves and delays assistance from reaching the people who so desperately need it. In 2008, Canada fully untied its food aid, allocating 100 percent of its food aid budget to international procurement and supporting the purchase of food in developing countries."[130]

In this chapter we have explored the numerous intertwined and complex factors that have made food insecurity and hunger a crisis in our world. Our faith offers us a hope-filled vision, a set of values and principles, the examples of St. Francis and St. Clare, and also numerous church-related agencies that can assist us in creating a new and sustainable prosperity for all of our sisters and brothers across the globe. As St.

---

[128] Ibid. For additional discussion of the changes needed, see "Alternative Business and the Solidarity Economy," *Maryknoll NewsNotes* 36/5 (September–October): 13–14. Also see "Defining Climate Smart Agriculture," *Maryknoll NewsNotes* 37/1 (January–February 2012): 12–13. See also "Food Security: Principles for Partnership," *Maryknoll NewsNotes* 37/1 (January–February 2012): 13–14.

[129] Ibid.

[130] See Canadian International Development Agency, "Food Aid: Reducing World Hunger," http://www.acdi-cida.gc.ca/acdi-cida/acdi-cida.nsf/eng/JUD-24133116-PQL, accessed January 25, 2012.

Francis said, "I have done *what is mine; may Christ teach* you what is yours to do!"[131]

Questions for Reflection and Discussion

1. What feelings come to you when you hear there are millions of hungry people in the United States—even in your local community?

2. What do you know about the work and wages of farmers, ranchers, and food industry workers?

3. What do you know about the enforcement of labor, health, and safety laws and standards that govern farmworkers and food processing workers? Would you be willing to work under such conditions?

4. Which of the top four or five globalized agribusinesses produce your favorite foods? What do you know about their agricultural and employment practices?

5. What do you know about commodity futures? Do you, your employer, or your institution invest in them? If so, what alternatives can you find? Visit the Interfaith Center for Corporate Responsibility at http://www.iccr.org.

Suggestions for Action

1. Make hunger tangible by religious fasting and prayer for food justice. See the USCCB's "First Fridays for Food Security" web page and download monthly reflections at http://www.usccb.org/about/justice-peace-and-human-development/first-fridays-for-food-security.cfm.

2. Conscientiously purchase foods grown or produced within one hundred miles (or less) of home and demand that government nutrition program beneficiaries be able to purchase food at local farmers' mar-

---

[131] See *The Remembrance of the Desire of a Soul* by Thomas of Celano (1245–47), bk. II, CLXII, 214, "How in the End He Encouraged and Blessed the Brothers," in *Francis of Assisi: Early Documents*, vol. II, *The Founder*, trans. and ed. Regis J. Armstrong, J.A. Wayne Hellmann, and William J. Short (New York: New City Press, 2000), 386.

kets and retail stores. See http://www.sustainabletable.org/issues/eatlocal.

3. Advocate for stronger, innovative, community-based food programs such as community-supported agriculture initiatives.

4. Become an informed customer concerning fair trade practices that ensure farmers, artisans, and laborers receive fair wages.

5. Develop retail food markets, urban agriculture, and marketing networks in urban food deserts.

6. Learn about the US government's Farm Bill, the "comprehensive omnibus bill" passed by the US Congress every five years. This bill is the primary policy tool for the federal government's food and agricultural policies, domestic and global. Visit the National Catholic Rural Life Conference web site: http://www.ncrlc.com.

7. Support funding for child nutrition programs providing fruits, vegetables, and wellness and nutrition education in schools.

Prayer

Most high, glorious, and good God, Creator and Giver of all good gifts, fill us with gratitude. Through the power of your Holy Spirit, impassion us for justice and enable us to help our sisters and brothers in need. Give us wisdom and courage to confront the systemic injustices that cause millions to starve while other live in opulence. Forgive our complicity in the food insecurity that exists on our planet and enlighten and energize us to build anew so that everyone will have enough. As we eat each meal the food from your hand, may we grow in solidarity with those who hunger for food, for justice, and for you. We ask this in the name of Jesus, who is the Bread of Life and our Brother. Amen.

Sources for Further Study

Delio, Ilia, and Keith Douglas Werner and Pamela Wood. *Care for the Earth: A Franciscan Spirituality of the Earth*. Cincinnati, OH: St. Anthony Messenger Press, 2008.

Jung, L. Shannon. *Food for Life: A Spirituality and Ethics of Eating*. Minneapolis: Fortress Press, 2004.

Lappé, Anna. *Diet for a Hot Planet: The Climate Crisis at the End of Your Fork and What You Can Do About It*. New York: Bloomsbury USA, 2010.

National Catholic Rural Life Conference. *Food Security and Economic Justice: A Faith-Based Study Guide on Poverty and Hunger*. Des Moines, IA: National Catholic Rural Life Conference, 2011. Download from http://www.ncrlc .com/page.aspx?ID=126.

Roberts, Paul. *The End of Food*. New York: Houghton Mifflin Company, 2008.

Wirzba, Norman. *Food and Faith: A Theology of Eating*. New York: Cambridge University Press, 2011.

Chapter 10

Crisis of Peak Oil and Sustainable Energy

Introduction: Life without Oil?

It rarely, if ever, occurs to most of us that the day is coming when our oil-based lifestyle will no longer be a viable option. If we took all oil-based items out our homes or offices, very little would remain. Indeed, the once-disparaged theory (reality) of "peak oil" has gained great credibility in recent years.[1] "Peak oil" is the point at which global oil production reaches a maximum rate and thereafter steadily declines.[2] The basic principle is widely agreed upon, namely, that a finite, nonrenewable resource cannot expand endlessly. This has been demonstrated in practice at national levels all over the globe. The point not agreed upon is when exactly this juncture will be reached.

Indeed, experts who can hardly be called extremists, such as former energy secretary James Schlesinger and the US Army Corps of Engineers, have warned that we in the United States—indeed the world—need to prepare with some urgency for the gigantic economic, political, and security repercussions peak oil will bring about.[3] A most exhaustive

---

[1] Post Carbon Institute Energy Bulletin, "Peak Oil Primer," http://www.energy
bulletin.net/primer.php, accessed January 28, 2012.

[2] Ibid.

[3] See "Former Defense Secretary James Schlesinger: Peak Oil Is Here but Politicians Are Ignoring It," http://articles.businessinsider.com/2010-11-01/news/30001655_1_
peak-oil-oil-output-bromide#ixzz1knBJ1KwZ, accessed January 28, 2012. Also see US

study of peak oil was done in 2000 by the US Geological Survey. That study set the date for peak oil at between 2037 and 2044.[4]

According to the International Energy Agency, when discussing oil production we need to deal with several categories of oil sources: there is crude oil in currently producing fields, fields yet to be developed, and fields yet to be found; and crude oil can be taken from enhanced oil recovery processes, nonconventional oil or tar sands sources, and natural gas liquids.[5]

Those who challenge the theory of peak oil claim that future discoveries of new sources of oil will offset the economic threats of peak oil. They rely on projected production increases coming from fields yet to be developed, fields yet to be found, and nonconventional oil or tar sands sources.[6] Even if we could be certain these discoveries will occur, massive inputs of investment and new infrastructures will be needed. However, the rate of new discoveries since the 1960s has lagged behind consumption rates, and phenomenal and unprecedented rates of discovery would be needed, under the best conditions, if we continue to consume oil at current or higher rates.

What Are Some Moral Concerns about Peak Oil?

Generally, regardless of the precise date of peak oil, as we saw in chapter 7 and as it is convincingly argued by the International Energy Agency in their *World Energy Outlook 2009* report, there is a strong moral case to reduce and eliminate the use of fossil fuels. The greatest reasons for reduction in the use of fossil fuels are the long-known health hazards, to say nothing of the impacts continued use of oil will have on human-induced global warming and climate change.[7]

Army Corps of Engineers, Engineer Research and Development Center (ERDC), "Energy Trends and Their Implications for U.S. Army Installations," September 2005, http://www.karavans.com/EnergyTrendsUSArmySummary.pdf, accessed January 28, 2012.

[4] See Doug Craft, "Peak Oil and Our Future: How Energy Depletion Will Change Our Lives," http://resource.management6.com/How-Energy-Depletion-Will-Change-Our-Lives-download-w4196.pdf, accessed August 14, 2012.

[5] International Energy Agency, *World Energy Outlook 2011*, especially pages 122–23 and 225–26, http://www.eia.gov/forecasts/ieo/pdf/0484%282011%29.pdf, accessed August 14, 2012.

[6] We will discuss the tar sands oil supply later in this chapter.

[7] "Climate Change Is an Environmental Justice Issue, Experts Say," *Catholic Health World* 20/11 (November 15, 2011), http://www.chausa.org/Climate_change_is_an_environmental_justice_issue_experts_say.aspx, accessed January 28, 2012.

Most morally significant is the fact that peak oil directly challenges our gluttonous consumption of energy.[8] Though the United States represents only 5 percent of the world's population, we consume over 25 percent of the world's energy and emit 25 percent of the world's human-produced carbon dioxide (CO_2). As we saw in chapter 7, at a minimum the consumption and production of fossil fuels harms the global common good by polluting the air and contributing to global warming. By contrast, 80 percent of the world's population uses only 20 percent of the energy resources. At peak oil, the price of oil—and thus nearly everything else—will likely soar. At the very least, the gap that already exists between rich and poor nations could widen exponentially, causing massive human suffering.

The reality that the United States already imports upward of 55 percent of its oil raises yet different moral issues.[9] As oil increasingly becomes scarce, there is a real likelihood that oil-exporting nations would shift policies and hoard, or at least decrease, their exports so as to keep their oil at home. History that tells of numerous wars over scarce goods could well be repeated here. Given these possibilities, decreasing our consumption of oil not only becomes an issue of preserving the environmental common good of creation, but it also must be understood as a moral imperative for justice and world peace. Briefly put, each of us needs to decrease our use of fossil fuels—especially for transportation and home heating. Equally important is to use creative alternative technologies and to promote governmental and institutional policies and incentives for sustainable energy. In essence, unless we do this, we will increasingly confront the morally inadequate scenarios that have been developing at a growing rate across the globe.

In this chapter we will take a broad overview of the current US energy situation. With that in mind we will examine a set of moral criteria for evaluating alternative energy sources. Next we will look at how current energy options measure up to those ethical criteria. Then we will measure several viable alternative energy sources against those same criteria.

---

[8] Daniel Misleh "Don't Be Crude: End Our Oil Addiction," *U.S. Catholic,* March 18, 2011, http://www.uscatholic.org/oil, accessed January 28, 2012.

[9] See US Energy Information Agency, "Most of the Petroleum We Use Is Imported," http://www.eia.gov/energyexplained/index.cfm?page=oil_imports, accessed June 27, 2012: 52 percent comes from Western nations; 29 percent from Canada; 8 percent from Mexico; 14 percent from Saudi Arabia; 11 percent from Venezuela; and 10 percent from Nigeria. Put another way, 52 percent comes from the Western Hemisphere; 20 percent from Africa; 22 percent from the Persian Gulf; and 6 percent from other nations.

Here we include the criteria found in Catholic social teaching, especially in the US Catholic bishops' pastoral letters Renewing the Earth (1991) and Global Climate Change (2001). We will conclude with some suggestions for actions each of us can take.

An Ethical Framework for Assessing Energy Sources

Given the limited supply of oil and other fossil fuels, and the intimately related hazards of global warming, health, and safety, alternative energy sources have been developed in recent decades. We need to assess and judge those options in light of Christian ethics and Catholic social teaching. Several Christian denominations have developed ethical criteria and guiding principles for determining national and global energy policies. The most prominent actors have been the World Council of Churches (WCC), the Presbyterian Church in the Unites States (PCUSA), the Evangelical Lutheran Church in America (ELCA), and the United States Conference of Catholic Bishops (USCCB).[10]

Among these Christians the most widely agreed upon criteria have clear roots in the Bible. In chapters 1 and 2 of this book, we reviewed the fundamental themes that were found to undergird the four ecojustice norms the above Christian groups have raised up as essential criteria, namely, sustainability, sufficiency, participation, and solidarity. Ecojustice indicates a concern for other-than-human species and their habitats, as

[10] For an excellent discussion of these developments, see James B. Martin-Schramm, *Climate Justice: Ethics, Energy, and Public Policy* (Minneapolis: Fortress Press, 2010), 23–26. Also see WCC, *Study Encounter* 69, vol. 10, no. 4 (1974); WCC, *Accelerated Climate Change: Sign of Peril, Test of Faith* (Geneva: WCC Publications, 1994); PCUSA, *The Power to Speak Truth to Power*, 1981; PCUSA, *Restoring Creation for Ecology and Justice* (excerpts), http://gamc.pcusa.org/ministries/environment/pcusa-environ mental-policy, accessed June 27, 2012. Also see Renewing the Earth: An Invitation to Reflection and Action on Environment in Light of Catholic Social Teaching, a pastoral statement of the United States Catholic Conference, November 14, 1991, http:// www.usccb.org/issues-and-action/human-life-and-dignity/environment/renewing -the-earth.cfm, accessed January 30, 2012. See also Global Climate Change: A Plea for Dialogue, Prudence, and the Common Good, a statement of the United States Conference of Catholic Bishops, June 15, 2001, http://www.usccb.org/issues-and-action /human-life-and-dignity/environment/global-climate-change-a-plea-for-dialogue -prudence-and-the-common-good.cfm, accessed January 30, 2012.

well as for the ecosystems of the world. Justice is more centrally focused on human concerns, but it is intimately related to ecojustice.

Ecojustice

Justice has deep roots in the Hebrew Scriptures and is grounded in and qualified by God's covenant love. God is both loving and just, and all measures of those characteristics must be judged in light of who God is and how God acts. As we see in the Old Testament prophets and in Jesus' life and ministry, God's love and mercy sensitizes us to the needs of others and impassions us to seek justice, especially for the poor and vulnerable. Justice, then, is the work of love brought to the social and public realm, placing the needs and interests of all in proper balance for the common good.[11]

Sustainability

Contrary to definitions of sustainability that are based on economic theories that presume scarcity and the need for unbridled competition (e.g., the Brundtland Commission), a Christian view of sustainability is rooted in God's generosity and goodness—there is enough for all.[12] James B. Martin-Schramm defines sustainability as "the long-range supply of sufficient resources to meet basic human needs and the preservation of intact natural communities. It expresses a concern for future generations and the planet as a whole, and emphasizes that an acceptable quality of life for present generations must not jeopardize the prospects for future generations."[13]

The task for humans is to care for and nurture God's creation, and it is essential not to forget that God gave intrinsic value to each element of the creation and that we as humans have no right to harm creation in any way. As we explored in earlier chapters, the Psalms and God's

[11] Key biblical texts defining justice include Exod 22:21-24; Mic 6:8; Amos 2:6; 5:11; 8:4-8; Isa 10:1-2; Jer 22:13-17; Matt 5:1-14; Luke 4:16-20; 6:20-26; Acts 1–5; and Gal 3:28.

[12] The 1987 UN-sponsored Brundtland Commission presumed that "sustainable development" meant raising productivity, accumulation of goods, and technological innovations. See World Commission on Environment and Development, *Our Common Future* (New York: Oxford University Press, 1987), 8: sustainable development "meets the needs of the present without compromising the ability of future generations to meet their own needs."

[13] Martin-Schramm, *Climate Justice*, 28–29.

various covenants with humans, creatures, and the earth itself demonstrate this value and God's pledge to sustain them.[14]

Sufficiency

Sufficiency addresses the entitlement of each creature to an adequate share in the goods of creation. This norm prohibits unlimited consumption and wastefulness and supports frugality, humility, and generosity. As we saw in our study of Leviticus 25, the many ways God provided "enough" for Israel exemplifies the attitude we need to have toward creation. The biblical texts speak in terms of enough, care for the poor, rest, renewal, and need. But they also address fullness, abundance, gratitude, and appreciation. Wealth is to be gained justly and is to be limited—and preferably used to supply for the needs of others.

As we saw in the lives of St. Francis and St. Clare, throughout Christian history there have always been some who live in voluntary poverty, and these Christians serve as a reminder of the necessity to live in relationship to God and the poor with sensitivity to our other-than-human sisters and brothers. This wisdom is vital for achieving planetary sustainability in our day.

Participation

The norm of participation is hinted at insofar as from the moment of their creation, humans were partners with God. They were called to be the guardians of creation and God even invited Adam to name all creatures (Gen 2:16-17). In Jewish culture, giving a name to someone or something initiated a special intimacy with the one named. This kind of care is renewed in Jesus' notion of the kingdom of God (Mark 1:14-15).

In order for genuine relationships to form and thrive, there need to be limits on the size and scale of communities. When Jesus spoke of the reign of God, he spoke of small things—mustard seeds, for example— that draw their power from God's providence and/or close human bonds (Mark 4:30-32; Matt 13:31-32; Luke 13:18-19). When people are close to others they have greater confidence to participate, share their gifts, and

---

[14] Biblical texts addressing sustainability include Ps 104; 145; Gen 1:3-24; Gen 9 (the Noahic Covenant); Deut 30:16 (the Sinai Covenant); Exod 20–24; Luke 12:42; and Rom 8:18-25.

care for the needs of others. This is not the vision of today's globalized, industrialized, distant corporate management that dominates the poor.

In determining energy sources and technologies, the people affected need to have a voice in deciding what is best for them and for the common good of the planet. It includes "good faith" decision-making processes that use open and democratic means in government, institutions, and corporations. And significantly, it presumes major efforts to use environmental impact studies and other means to include the "voices" of the nonhuman environment in the process.

Solidarity

We saw in our discussion of St. Bonaventure that our trinitarian God models participation and solidarity. As equal persons in one divine being, God is one. Our radically relational God created a world that is relational to its core. Humans and the entire planet exist in reciprocal and mutual relationship with one another.[15] People are created for community (Gen 2:15), and when one suffers, all suffer (1 Cor 12:26). As bearers of the *imago Dei*, humans are at their best when they take on the character of God who extends to all creation overflowing goodness and mercy, offering to all eternal life itself through the birth, life, ministry, death, and resurrection of Jesus. People are recipients of such generosity and are called to pour out their lives for others—especially the wounded and suffering—including nonhuman creation (Rom 8; Matt 19:3; Phil 2:6-7). Indeed, our salvation—spiritual and material—depends on how our choices and actions fulfill that call to solidarity (Matt 25:31-45).

Energy Policy Guidelines

Various Christian denominations have developed different ways to incorporate the four norms into their ethical statements and policies. However, public policy discussions on energy issues require more particular guidelines, and these have been developed. Space prohibits a thorough discussion here; however, a general description of one excellent set of guidelines is summarized in the chart at the end of this chapter. The guidelines were originally developed by Christian ethicists James

---

[15] See especially Pope John Paul II, *Sollicitudo Rei Socialis*, no. 39, at http://www .vatican.va/holy_father/john_paul_ii/encyclicals/documents/hf_jp-ii_enc_30121987_ sollicitudo-rei-socialis_en.html, accessed February 4, 2012.

B. Martin-Schramm and Robert Stivers, and they were then further refined by Martin-Schramm to address explicitly the temporal, structural,
and procedural dimensions of policies dealing with global warming and
climate change.[16] Taken together, the four norms and the guidelines
provide important moral criteria for energy policy decisions, particularly
in light of global warming.

Catholic Social Teaching

From the Catholic perspective, there is a whole body of Catholic social
teaching documents issued by local bishops, the Vatican, and the pope
that stands behind the two major USCCB pastorals dealing with ecojustice and energy-related topics: Renewing the Earth (1991) and Global
Climate Change (2001).[17] While the USCCB has not endorsed particular
energy strategies or policies in these documents, in practice it asks church
agents, agencies, and parishes to utilize the criteria set forth in them.
These themes and criteria fully harmonize with the four norms and the
Martin-Schramm and Stivers guidelines.

Briefly, in Renewing the Earth, the US bishops outline seven themes
that frame developing and distinctive perspectives on environmental
ethics:

> The tradition of Catholic social teaching offers a developing and
> distinctive perspective on environmental issues. We believe that the
> following themes drawn from this tradition are integral dimensions
> of ecological responsibility:
>
> - *a God-centered and sacramental view of the universe,* which grounds
>   human accountability for the fate of the earth;
>
> - a consistent *respect for human life,* which extends to respect for
>   all creation;

---

[16] Martin-Schramm is professor of religion at Luther College, Decorah, IA, and
Stivers is professor emeritus of ethics at Pacific Lutheran University, Tacoma, WA.

[17] See the Pontifical Justice and Peace Council, Compendium of the Social Doctrine
of the Church, especially chap. 10, "Safeguarding the Environment," at http://www
.vatican.va/roman_curia/pontifical_councils/justpeace/documents/rc_pc_just
peace_doc_20060526_compendio-dott-soc_en.html, accessed January 30, 2012. See,
for example, John McCarthy, SJ, "Catholic Social Teaching and Ecology Fact Sheet,"
at ecojesuit.com/wp-content/uploads/2011/06/CST_ENG.pdf, accessed January
30, 2012.

- a worldview affirming the ethical significance of *global inter-dependence and the common good*;

- *an ethics of solidarity* promoting cooperation and a just structure of sharing in the world community;

- an understanding of *the universal purpose of created things*, which requires equitable use of the earth's resources;

- *an option for the poor*, which gives passion to the quest for an equitable and sustainable world;

- a conception of *authentic development*, which offers a direction for progress that respects human dignity and the limits of material growth.

Although Catholic social teaching does not offer a complete environmental ethic, we are confident that this developing tradition can serve as the basis for Catholic engagement and dialogue with science, the environmental movement, and other communities of faith and good will.[18]

The bishops further stress explicit criteria and concern about the relationship of consumption and population growth to environmental problems:

Consumption and Population

In public discussions, two areas are particularly cited as requiring greater care and judgment on the part of human beings. The first is *consumption of resources*. The second is *growth in world population*. Regrettably, advantaged groups often seem more intent on curbing Third-World births than on restraining the even more voracious consumerism of the developed world. We believe this compounds injustice and increases disrespect for the life of the weakest among us. . . .

Consumption in developed nations remains the single greatest source of global environmental destruction. . . . Advanced societies, and our own in particular, have barely begun to make efforts at reducing their consumption of resources and the enormous waste and pollution that result from it. We in the developed world, therefore, are obligated to address our own wasteful and destructive use of resources as a matter of top priority. . . .

---

[18] USCC, Renewing the Earth, section III, "Catholic Social Teaching and Environmental Ethics."

Technological fixes do not really work. Only when an economy distributes resources so as to allow the poor an equitable stake in society and some hope for the future do couples see responsible parenthood as good for their families. . . .

Respect for nature ought to encourage policies that promote natural family planning and true responsible parenthood rather than coercive population control programs or incentives for birth control that violate cultural and religious norms and Catholic teaching.[19]

The bishops do not see environmental issues apart from their relationship to other concerns within a web of life:

A Web of Life

These themes drawn from Catholic social teaching are linked to our efforts to share this teaching in other contexts, especially in our pastoral letters on peace and economic justice and in our statements on food and agriculture. Clearly, war represents a serious threat to the environment. . . . The pursuit of peace—lasting peace based on justice—ought to be an environmental priority because the earth itself bears the wounds and scars of war. Likewise, our efforts to defend the dignity and rights of the poor and of workers, to use the strength of our market economy to meet basic human needs, and to press for greater national and global economic justice are clearly linked to efforts to preserve and sustain the earth. These are not distinct and separate issues but complementary challenges. We need to help build bridges among the peace, justice, and environmental agendas and constituencies.[20]

There is no escaping the intimate relationship between fossil fuel use and global climate change. In their pastoral Global Climate Change the bishops explicitly accept the scientific consensus that global warming is real and dangerous, and thus they teach that the Christian virtue of prudence necessitates immediate action to halt and reverse it:

The virtue of prudence is paramount in addressing climate change. . . . Prudence is intelligence applied to our actions. It allows us to discern what constitutes the common good in a given situation. Prudence requires a deliberate and reflective process that aids in the

[19] Ibid.
[20] Ibid.

shaping of the community's conscience. Prudence not only helps us identify the principles at stake in a given issue, but also moves us to adopt courses of action to protect the common good. Prudence is not, as popularly thought, simply a cautious and safe approach to decisions. Rather, it is a thoughtful, deliberate, and reasoned basis for taking or avoiding action to achieve a moral good. . . .

In other words, if enough evidence indicates that the present course of action could jeopardize humankind's well-being, prudence dictates taking mitigating or preventative action.

This responsibility weighs more heavily upon those with the power to act because the threats are often greatest for those who lack similar power, namely, vulnerable poor populations, as well as future generations. According to reports of the IPCC [Intergovernmental Panel on Climate Change], significant delays in addressing climate change may compound the problem and make future remedies more difficult, painful, and costly. On the other hand, the impact of prudent actions today can potentially improve the situation over time, avoiding more sweeping action in the future.[21]

The bishops also stress four dimensions of the *universal common good* criteria that are found in Catholic social teaching:

Stewardship of God's Creation and the Right to Economic Initiative and Private Property

Stewardship—defined in this case as the ability to exercise moral responsibility to care for the environment—requires freedom to act. . . .

We believe economic freedom, initiative, and creativity are essential to help our nation find effective ways to address climate change. . . . In addition, the right to private property is matched by the responsibility to use what we own to serve the common good. Our Catholic tradition speaks of a "social mortgage" on property and, in this context, calls us to be good stewards of the earth. It also calls us to use the gifts we have been given to protect human life and dignity, and to exercise our care for God's creation.

True stewardship requires changes in human actions—both in moral behavior and technical advancement. Our religious tradition has always urged restraint and moderation in the use of material goods, so we must not allow our desire to possess more material

---

[21] USCCB, Global Climate Change.

things to overtake our concern for the basic needs of people and the environment. . . .

Protecting the Environment for Future Generations

The common good calls us to extend our concern to future generations. . . . As stewards of their heritage, we have an obligation to respect their dignity and to pass on their natural inheritance, so that their lives are protected and, if possible, made better than our own.

Population and Authentic Development

Population and climate change should be addressed from the broader perspective of a concern for protecting human life, caring for the environment, and respecting cultural norms and the religious faith and moral values of peoples. Population is not simply about statistics. Behind every demographic number is a precious and irreplaceable human life whose human dignity must be respected. . . .

A more responsible approach to population issues is the promotion of "authentic development," which represents a balanced view of human progress and includes respect for nature and social well-being. . . .

Caring for the Poor and Issues of Equity

Working for the common good requires us to promote the flourishing of all human life and all of God's creation. In a special way, the common good requires solidarity with the poor who are often without the resources to face many problems, including the potential impacts of climate change. Our obligations to the one human family stretch across space and time. . . .

No strategy to confront global climate change will succeed without the leadership and participation of the United States and other industrial nations. But any successful strategy must also reflect the genuine participation and concerns of those most affected and least able to bear the burdens. Developing and poorer nations must have a genuine place at the negotiating table. Genuine participation for those most affected is a moral and political necessity for advancing the common good. . . .

As an act of solidarity and in the interest of the common good, the United States should lead the developed nations in contributing to the sustainable economic development of poorer nations and help build their capacity to ease climate change.[22]

[22] Ibid.

Moral Problems and Fossil Fuels

In light of these ethical criteria and guidelines, we now examine some of the basic issues at stake in complying with the moral mandate to wean our planet from fossil fuel use. In the United States, energy comes primarily from coal, oil, natural gas, and nuclear power.[23] About half of the energy in the United States is used for generating electricity, and roughly 15–20 percent of it goes to transportation, industrial, residential, or commercial uses.

By contrast, globally, about one-third of the population lacks access to electricity. People depend on wood for cooking and other energy needs. According to Thomas Friedman, "addressing 'energy poverty' is one of the key factors in reducing all forms of poverty around the world."[24] Beyond poverty, the various social problems that result from fossil fuel use are legion—and so are health problems caused by polluted water, soil, and air. Illnesses ranging from lung cancer to asthma to cardiopulmonary disease, as well as low birth-weight infants, have ties to toxins emitted from burning fossil fuels.[25]

In addition to the problems discussed in the introduction of this chapter, the US dependency on large imports of oil leaves people vulnerable to price fluctuations. Those who depend on oil for home heating—especially the poor and those on fixed incomes or government assistance—are especially at risk. The United States spends $55–100 billion annually to militarily protect its oil interests across the globe, yet in lean economic times energy assistance for the poor is readily included in budget cuts.[26] Further, the oil industry is given subsidies and tax breaks by the federal government to the tune of $4 billion annually.[27]

Geopolitical concerns are always on the front burner. Simply put, the United States does a delicate balancing act between feeding its oil consumption habit and consistently supporting just and democratic governance across the globe. We buy oil from the likes of Nigeria, Iraq, Angola, and Kuwait, all of whom have questionable human rights records. Also,

[23] See Energy Justice Network, http://www.energyjustice.net/about, accessed January 29, 2012.

[24] Quoted in Martin-Schramm, *Climate Justice*, 6.

[25] Ibid., 7.

[26] Ibid., 9–10.

[27] John M. Broder, "Obama's Bid to End Oil Subsidies Revives Debate," *New York Times*, Environment, January 31, 2011, http://www.nytimes.com/2011/02/01/science/earth/01subsidy.html, accessed January 30, 2012.

1/3 of global population lacks access to electricity

address energy; reduce poverty

the oil we import must pass through risky bottlenecks and shipping routes such as the Suez Canal, the Bosporus, and the straits of Humuz and Malacca.

Fossil fuels enter domestic politics as well. In the case of coal, vast areas of Appalachia—one of the poorest regions of the United States—have been turned into a series of moonscapes that is visible from space.[28] The political power of major coal companies opened the way for the destruction of unique ecological systems but also the loss of the region's cultural heritage and the livelihoods of thousands and future generations.[29]

As we have seen, climate change looms in the background and is the consummation and problem child of what has been a long marriage of the industrialized world and fossil fuels. We now turn to a brief evaluation of energy options in light of the norms and guidelines presented above. Overall, our presumption is that prudence and justice require that an extensive transition away from greenhouse gas (GHG)-producing fossil fuel use be made as rapidly as possible in order to halt global warming and other toxic effects they produce. We begin by examining the four nonrenewable sources that produce 90 percent of the energy consumed in the United States: coal, oil, natural gas, and nuclear power.[30]

Coal

According to the US Energy Information Administration, 49 percent of the electricity generated in the United States in 2005 came from coal-powered plants.[31] The coal supply in the United States could support this rate of output for the next 250 years. An estimated 151 new plants are projected to be built and go on line to meet increasing electrical de-

---

[28] Jim Sciutto, "West Virginia Mountains Flattened to Retrieve Coal," ABC News, July 30, 2011, http://abcnews.go.com/US/community-rallies-mountaintop-removal -mining/story?id=13897050#.TycEuflZeWg, accessed January 30, 2012: "From the road, West Virginia's mountains look as pristine as ever, but from above, the landscape resembles more of a moonscape. From even higher up in space, entire swathes of countryside appear flattened. . . . Since the 1970s, 500 peaks and counting have been literally blown up for the coal that's deep underground."

[29] See Kyle T. Kramer, "Appalachia's Wounds: The Biblical Injustice of Mountaintop Removal," *America* 203/8, whole no. 4906 (October 4, 2010): 11–14.

[30] Here I follow the work of Martin-Schramm, incorporating the concerns of the USCCB into his excellent analysis and critique. I also utilize the insights from the Energy Justice Network, http://www.energyjustice.net, accessed January 30, 2012.

[31] Martin-Schramm, *Climate Justice*, 48.

2005

49% of electricity comes from coal powered plants —

mands. However, in April 2007, the Supreme Court ruled that the Environmental Protection Agency had the authority to control carbon dioxide (CO_2) emissions. According to Martin-Schramm, "These legal issues, combined with community opposition and financial uncertainty over carbon regulation in the future, are forcing electric utilities to reconsider major investments in coal-fired power plants."[32] No new coal-powered plant has gone live since 2008.

In view of the norms and guidelines on the plus side, coal is a reliable domestic energy source, neither requiring importation nor risking armed conflict. Large numbers of people are employed by the industry in extraction, transportation, and utility businesses, and it is priced at affordable rates. It can also be processed into liquid fuels and synthetic natural gas as well.

On the negative side, coal is not renewable and it is carbon intensive, accounting for 42 percent of US CO_2 emissions. It will negatively impact both present and current generations through mercury pollution, especially impacting people of color and pregnant women; acid rain; fly ash disposal; and the aesthetic destruction of mountaintop removal. All of this violates the norms of sustainability and solidarity.[33]

Coal companies claim to have developed "clean coal" technologies that increase coal energy-generation efficiency (from 38 percent to 50 percent). The companies also propose "carbon capture sequestration (CCS)" systems in which coal-generated CO_2 is pumped and stored underground.[34] Unfortunately CCS, is not a permanent solution because the CO_2 will eventually escape and cause further global warming. Deep ocean storage has also been proposed, but that would potentially acidify the water and damage the ecosystems of the ocean floor. CCS technology is far from perfect, judging by the three- to four-year delay and the billion-dollar cost overrun accrued by the FutureGas project in Mattoon, IL, that was to be completed and running by 2010.[35]

[32] Ibid., 49.

[33] See Dawn M. Nothwehr and Sylvia Hood Washington, *Struggles for Environmental Justice and Health in Chicago: An African American Perspective* (Chicago: The DePaul University John J. Eagan Urban Center, 2004).

[34] Martin-Schramm, *Climate Justice*, 51. Also see Annie Leonard, "The Story of Cap and Trade (2009)," http://www.youtube.com/watch?v=pA6FSy6EKrM, accessed January 30, 2012.

[35] Julie Wernau, "Ameren Casts Dark Cloud over Cleaner Coal Plant," *Chicago Tribune*, November 29, 2011, http://articles.chicagotribune.com/2011-11-29/business

The norms of sustainability and solidarity require that a moratorium be placed on new coal-fired power plant construction. Moneys would be better spent on reducing demand for electricity through conservation and renewable energy innovations.

Oil

As we have indicated, oil points to huge problems posed by our need to stop using it—simply because we are heavily addicted to it. The economic threats are profound. There is always a clear potential for economic disaster, as demonstrated in the British Petroleum (BP) oil spill in the Gulf of Mexico in April of 2010.[36] "If global oil production peaks in 2026 at approximately 42 billion barrels per year, the EIA [US Energy Information Administration] projects global oil production in 2050 to be approximately 6 billion barrels per year, which is a decline of approximately 85%. This rapid change in the availability of oil has the potential to spur inflation, plunge economies into recession and ignite conflict around the world."[37] Notably, every US administration since Truman has engaged in armed conflict over oil!

Needless to say, oil is an energy source that violates all four of the norms of ecojustice. It is nonrenewable and unsustainable. Oil places future generations in jeopardy through GHG accumulation and harms the health of current generations—all in violation of solidarity. Current uses of oil are largely inefficient and ecologically harmful to ecosystems and living beings, thus breaching the sufficiency criterion. Many exporters of oil with whom the US trades have shady human rights records and are not governed democratically, thus contravening the participation criterion. Therefore, there is every reason to stop using oil as quickly as possible and to redouble our efforts to develop and use alternative fuels.

Natural Gas

On the plus side, natural gas is about 50 percent less carbon intensive than either coal or oil. Natural gas has many uses and can be utilized

---

/ct-biz-1129-ameren-20111129_1_futuregen-alliance-futuregen-project-coal-plant, accessed January 30, 2012.

[36] See Earthjustice, "The Deepwater Horizon Spill: By the Numbers," http://earthjustice.org/sites/default/files/feature/2010/oilspill-ej-bythenumbers.gif, accessed January 31, 2012.

[37] Martin-Schramm, *Climate Justice*, 55.

efficiently in the production of electricity. Gas-fired power plants are less expensive to build, and production permits are easier to acquire.

On the negative side, more use of natural gas for electricity generation has forced a rise in prices for home heating and for commercial, industrial, and agricultural uses. Also problematic is the extraction technology commonly known as "fracking."[38] This horizontal drilling technique is being used to extract natural gas from coal shale beds. The process involves drilling a shaft and then fracturing the shale to release the natural gas. Huge amounts of water are required, as well as chemicals. Most controversial is the fact the 2005 Energy Policy Act exempted hydraulic fracturing from the Clean Water Act (1972), thus placing potable water supplies at risk.[39] Earthquakes, cave-ins, and the fouling of drinking water have occurred in areas near these extraction sites.[40]

Positively, natural gas is a flexible and efficient fuel resource that supplies about one-fourth of the US energy from domestic sources. It poses somewhat fewer risks to health, safety, and peace, and its extraction does less aesthetic damage than oil or coal. Yet it is an emitter of methane, a greenhouse gas. It is not renewable, and the global supply is expected to peak by 2050. Prices will likely spike, and thus the potential for global conflict will rise because the largest deposits are in the Middle East and in Russia.[41]

However, Martin-Schramm holds that the norms of sufficiency, sustainability, and solidarity require that we utilize natural gas wisely as a "bridge" to a future in which fossil fuels play a rapidly diminishing role. The transition to renewable energy is the driving imperative. Prudence also requires us to ask whether a false sense of security and a denial of the dangers even natural gas poses to global warming are created in our continuing to tolerate this evil. Natural gas is far from perfect, but it may help reach the goal of greater and total sustainability.[42] Prudence requires our greatest efforts to focus on developing renewable, not natural, gas.

---

[38] Mike Soraghan, "Baffled about Fracking? You're Not Alone," *New York Times*, Energy and Environment, May 13, 2011, http://www.nytimes.com/gwire/2011/05/13/13greenwire-baffled-about-fracking-youre-not-alone-44383.html?pagewanted=all, accessed January 30, 2012.

[39] See US Environmental Protection Agency, "Regulation of Hydraulic Fracturing under the Safe Drinking Water Act," http://water.epa.gov/type/groundwater/uic/class2/hydraulicfracturing/wells_hydroreg.cfm, accessed January 30, 2012.

[40] See Food and Water Watch, "Fracking: What Is Fracking and Why Should It Be Banned?" http://www.foodandwaterwatch.org/water/fracking, accessed January 30, 2012.

[41] Martin-Schramm, *Climate Justice*, 61.

[42] Ibid.

Nuclear Power

Even after the March 11, 2011, tsunami sent three reactors at Japan's Fukushima Dai-ichi plant into meltdowns in the worst nuclear crisis since Chernobyl in 1986, some still argue that the United States needs new nuclear power plants to reduce GHGs and to fill the growing demand for power. No new nuclear plants have been built in the United States since 1996, but subsidies were offered in the 2005 Energy Policy Act. In spite of the Three Mile Island catastrophe in 1979, the US Nuclear Regulatory Commission has recorded no deaths from the commercial operation of a nuclear power plant in the history of the US industry.[43]

Overriding all of the advantages is the very serious reality that to date there is no permanent disposal site for highly radioactive waste produced by reactors.[44] US law requires that the health and safety of citizens be insured against exposure to nuclear waste in perpetuity. But radioactive waste remains toxic for millions of years! The permanent disposal site authorized by Congress in 1987 to be constructed at Yucca Mountain in Nevada was scuttled after thirty years and billions of dollars without ever being opened for business. It was originally to be ready by 1998, but numerous technological and political problems plagued its construction.

Finally, President Obama's 2010 budget severely cut funds for the project, and he appointed a Blue Ribbon Commission to study new permanent disposal options. All this sparked interest in reprocessing nuclear waste.[45] On January 27, 2012, the commission released its report.[46] The panel's key finding was that "earning local consent at prospective

[43] US Nuclear Regulatory Commission, "Backgrounder on the Three Mile Island Accident," http://www.nrc.gov/reading-rm/doc-collections/fact-sheets/3mile-isle .html, accessed January 30, 2012. Also see Adi Narayan, "Comparing Nuclear Events at Fukushima, Chernobyl, Three Mile Island: Q&A," *Bloomberg*, March 17, 2011, http:// www.bloomberg.com/news/2011-03-16/comparing-nuclear-events-at-fukushima -chernobyl-three-mile-island-q-a.html, accessed January 30, 2012.

[44] Kristin Shrader-Frechette, "Five Myths about Nuclear Energy," *America* 198/20, whole no. 4819 (June 23–30, 2008): 12–16.

[45] See Union of Concerned Scientists, "Reprocessing and Nuclear Waste: Reprocessing Would Increase Total Volume of Radioactive Waste," http://www.ucsusa.org /nuclear_weapons_and_global_security/nuclear_terrorism/technical_issues /reprocessing-and-nuclear.html, accessed January 30, 2012.

[46] See Blue Ribbon Commission on America's Nuclear Future, *Report to the Secretary of Energy*, January 2012, http://brc.gov, accessed January 30, 2012.

nuclear waste disposal sites is critical."[47] It also proposed that "the federal government should relieve the DOE [US Department of Energy] of its oversight powers in nuclear waste disposal. The panel urged officials to create a federally chartered corporation whose sole duty would be to regulate and supervise the process."[48] In the meantime, more than sixty-five thousand metric tons of high-level nuclear waste sits in seventy sites across thirty-nine states awaiting permanent disposal.

Clearly, the norm of solidarity with current or future generations requires that the waste disposal issues be permanently resolved. The guideline of equality is not met. However, the norm of sustainability and the adequacy guideline allow that nuclear power does not imperil future generations with greenhouse gasses. While a far from perfect solution, it may be tolerated as a "bridge" solution while intently working to develop and use fully sustainable energy sources.[49] However, in light of prudence, it is ever more pressing to ask whether there are other ways to curb the need for nuclear energy other than to produce more highly radioactive waste, which we really cannot ensure will be kept safe for the future.[50]

A Review and Assessment of Key Alternative Energy Sources

Given the bleak moral assessment of the current energy sources utilized in the United States and beyond, the clear moral challenge and necessity is to change to renewable clean energy sources.[51] According to the EIA, in 2008 only 7 percent of the total energy used in the United States came from seven renewable sources: hydroelectric (34 percent), wood (28 percent), liquid biofuels (19 percent), wind (7 percent), municipal and agricultural waste (6 percent), geothermal (5 percent), and

[47] "Panel Urges Government to Establish 'Consent-Based' Approach to Nuclear Waste Disposal," *Knovel*, January 30, 2012, http://why.knovel.com/all-engineering-news/1237-panel-urges-government-to-establish-consent-based-approach-to-nuclear-waste-disposal.html, accessed January 30, 2012.

[48] Ibid.

[49] See Martin-Schramm, *Climate Justice*, 69.

[50] See Clean Edge News, "Renewables Now Provide 12 Percent of Domestic Energy," January 5, 2012, http://cleanedge.com/resources/news/Renewables-Now-Provide-12-Percent-of-Domestic-Energy-Up-14-Percent, accessed February 3, 2012.

[51] Richard J. Green and Wil Lepkowski, "Forestalling Disaster: Energy Policy for an Uncertain Age," *America*, 198/11, whole no. 4810 (March 31–April 7, 2008): 9–12.

solar (1 percent).[52] The plan for the future proposed in the American Recovery and Reinvestment Act of 2009 would increase renewable energy use to 16 percent by 2030.[53] One of the most important findings of several energy and environmental groups, as well as the US government, is that by 2030 the United States could get 50 percent of its energy from renewable sources, in large part by improving efficiency and conservation measures.[54] As Martin-Schramm rightly points out, the seven renewable energy sources clearly comply with the norm of sustainability and renewability.[55]

Energy Conservation and Increased Efficiency

The most immediate way to increase the energy supply in the United States is for everyone to simply use less energy and become efficient and less wasteful in their use. Government estimates reaching back into the 1990s projected that these measures alone could make the United States

[52] A quad is, "a unit of measure used to describe very large quantities of energy, such as the annual energy output of the United States. One quad is equal to one quadrillion—that is, one million billion, or 10^{15}—Btu." See The National Academy of Sciences, "Glossary," http://needtoknow.nas.edu/energy/glossary, accessed June 27, 2012. See full report of updated information on renewable energy in US Energy Information Administration, *Monthly Energy Review: January 2012,* http://www.eia .gov/totalenergy/data/monthly/archive/00351201.pdf, accessed June 27, 2012. See current and past report summaries at http://www.eia.gov/totalenergy/data /monthly/#summary. Of the 6.944 quads produced in the United States by renewable sources, 47.85 percent comes from biomass (wood, organic waste, and biofuels), 36 percent from hydroelectric, 12 percent from wind, 2.4 percent from geothermal, and 1.25 percent from solar (photovoltaic).

[53] See Martin-Schramm, *Climate Justice,* 71. Also see US Energy Information Administration, "EIA issues AEO2012 Early Release," January 23, 2012, http://www .eia.gov/todayinenergy/detail.cfm?id=4671, accessed January 31, 2012. See also Matthew Loveless, "A First Peek at Our Energy Future," January 23, 2012, http:// energy.gov/articles/first-peek-our-energy-future, accessed January 31, 2012.

[54] See Martin-Schramm, *Climate Justice,* 74. Also see John Schueler, "The Clean Energy Economy Is Not a Coming Attraction—It's Here," http://energy.gov/articles /clean-energy-economy-not-coming-attraction-its-here, accessed January 31, 2012. See also US Department of Energy, Building Energy Codes Program, "2012 IECC Final Action Hearings Deliver DOE's 30% Energy Savings Goals," http://www .energycodes.gov/status/2012_Final.stm, accessed January 31, 2012.

[55] See Martin-Schramm, *Climate Justice,* 75–76.

the global leader in cleaner energy generation.[56] Clearly, conservation is a hallmark of good stewardship and has the further advantage of making the United States less dependent on imports and the economic and conflict risks associated with them. Most use-reduction efforts will require public policy incentives in order to be effective. Such measures have been slow in being enacted and implemented. One glaring example is that US standards for gasoline mileage capabilities on cars and trucks has lagged far behind Japan (46 mpg), the European Union (EU; 37 mpg), and other nations.[57] In July of 2011, the Obama administration proposed a plan that would raise the total fleet fuel efficiency of new US cars and trucks to 54.5 mpg.[58] If approved, the plan could begin in the fall of 2012.

Conservation and efficiency measures adequately meet the norms of participation and sufficiency, as well as the norms of solidarity and the equity guideline.[59] Regulations and laws that incentivize or require conservation and increased efficiency clearly met the norm of sustainability and the cost guideline. Concerns about employment in the transition from heavy energy use will likely be offset by development of new technologies and products.

Solar Energy

The most powerful energy source by far is the earth's sun. The European Renewable Energy Council says that sunlight "provides 2,850 times more energy than human communities currently consume."[60] "There are several ways to use the sun's power to generate electricity. One of the most promising is called concentrating solar power [also called

---

[56] See Energy Justice Network, "Conservation and Efficiency," http://www.energy justice.net/solutions/c_and_e, accessed January 31, 2012: "Government [Office of Technology Assessment], industry, and independent analyses have shown that cost-effective energy improvements could reduce electricity use by 27% to 75% of total use within 10–20 years—without impacting quality of life or manufacturing output." Also see American Council for an Energy-Efficient Economy, "Energy Efficiency Programs," http://www.aceee.org/portal/programs, accessed January 31, 2012.

[57] See US Department of Energy, "2012 Most and Least Efficient Vehicles," http://www.fueleconomy.gov/feg/best-worst.shtml, accessed January 31, 2012. Also see Martin-Schramm, *Climate Justice*, 79–80.

[58] See Peter Valdes-Dapena "Cars Sold in U.S. Could Get 54.5 mpg by 2025," CNN Money, July 29, 2011, http://money.cnn.com/2011/07/29/autos/2025_fuel_economy _standards_obama/index.htm, accessed January 31, 2012.

[59] Martin-Schramm, *Climate Justice*, 82.

[60] Cited by ibid, 83.

concentrated solar thermal (CST)]. This involves using mirrors to reflect and focus the sun's rays, providing heat, which in turn helps power a generator. Another is photovoltaic panels [PV], such as the displays on the rooftops of homes and office buildings."[61] The US Department of Energy holds that solar power has the potential to provide 65–75 percent of home heating, hot water, dehumidifying, and cooling needs.[62]

Currently, the US solar industry needs to be heavily subsidized to compete with the lead producer, China. The political climate is tenuous given the financial failure of some projects—Solyndra of California, Evergreen Solar of Massachusetts, and SpectraWatt of New York—in 2011. Yet tax incentives sought by the solar industry require greater accountability and funding of only companies that already have a successful track record. "A one-year extension of the 1603 tax-grant program would create an additional 37,000 solar industry jobs in 2012, according to a report by EuPD Research."[63]

Clearly, there are some technological risks involved. There need to be efficient ways to supply energy during sunless times, so storage and backup sources are an issue. However, there continue to be improvements toward eliminating these difficulties. Major solar power (CST) facilities are under way in California, Arizona, and Florida. Washington and Wisconsin are working on a PV system that requires utilities to purchase power produced through solar technology at guaranteed long-term prices that are above market averages.[64] Prices are becoming more affordable and technologies are being perfected.

Solar power complies with all of the four ecojustice norms. Yet solar power systems remain more expensive than conventional forms of power and other forms of renewable power.[65] Subsidies are variable and dependent on the political will of those we elect to public office. Financial incentives are needed to cover expensive start-up costs. Solar power is not "dispatchable"—it is available only when the sun shines—so it fails the adequacy guideline. The clear advantages and potential for this

[61] See "Solar Energy," *New York Times*, Energy and Environment, January 27, 2012, updated on May 17, 2012, http://topics.nytimes.com/top/news/business/energy -environment/solar-energy/index.html, accessed January 31, 2012.

[62] Martin-Schramm, *Climate Justice*, 83.

[63] "Solar Energy," *New York Times*.

[64] Martin-Schramm, *Climate Justice*, 84–87.

[65] See Energy Justice Network, "Solar Power," http://www.energyjustice.net /solutions/solar, accessed January 31, 2012.

technology justifies continued and substantial investment in this vital and renewable source.[66]

Wind

Wind power technologies have contributed about 6,900 megawatts (MW) of new power to the US grid since 2008, making the United States a clear leader in wind-generated electricity.[67] There are plenty of windy environments across the United States ideal for wind-power generation, such as Texas, North Dakota, and Kansas.[68] Those states could potentially produce from wind power all the electric power they currently use.

Wind power has been heavily subsidized by federal and state programs. Central to these has been the Renewable Energy Production Tax Credit of 2008 and the American Recovery and Reinvestment Act of 2009.[69] About one half of the states have renewable portfolio standards (RPS) that require utilities to produce increasing amounts of electricity using renewable sources.

Obviously, the winds don't blow all the time, and the windiest times tend to be at night when demands are normally lower. Windy areas of the United States are at long distances from high-demand areas. Though Texas leads the United States in wind power, it is estimated that it would cost $3–6.4 billion to erect new transmission lines to places needing the power. Between twelve thousand and nineteen thousand miles of new high-power lines are needed to meet projected wind power needs.[70] Some resist increased power line installation because they fear the negative health effects of the electromagnetic fields that surround the wires.[71] Others are concerned about the aesthetic appearance of the large turbines across the landscape, and still others worry about harm done to birds when turbines are built along migratory flyways.

Wind power easily meets the test of all four ecojustice norms and the energy guidelines. Generally, the norm of sustainability is met, although the need for backup systems using natural gas is needed to maintain

[66] Ibid.

[67] Martin-Schramm, *Climate Justice*, 87–88.

[68] Ibid.

[69] Ibid., 89.

[70] Matthew Quirk, "Blowback: Is Wind the New Ethanol?" *The Atlantic* (October 2008): 30–31.

[71] Martin-Schramm, *Climate Justice*, 91.

transmission, and it is of concern. As the wind power industry has grown, electrical costs have decreased, while thousands of new jobs were created in construction and generation sectors. Wind turbines are easily installed, and they lack heavy security risks associated with nuclear power.[72] While there are some concerns, the ecojustice norms and energy guidelines support investment in wind energy.[73]

Biomass

Biomass energy has two major forms: biopower energy, which "is produced when agricultural and forestry residues are used to generate heat and power," and biofuels, which "are produced when crops and other plants are fermented into transportation fuels."[74] The most common products used for biopower are wood, crop residue, and switchgrass. These products can replace coal if power plants are properly retrofitted. Biomass from sewage, landfills, livestock waste, and organic matter emits methane, which can be used as fuel for heat or power.

What should not be used for biofuel is food crop residue, because that shrinks the amount of food available and drives prices higher. As Martin-Schramm stresses, "Recently, the United Nations Rapporteur on the Right to Food called a five-year moratorium on the production of first-generation biofuels made from food crops such as corn, wheat, palm oil, and rapeseed (the source of canola oil)."[75] Most promising for biofuel production is cellulose ethanol made from nonfood parts of plants, fast-growing trees, and switchgrass.[76] What is risky about production is that it can cost more in GHG emissions to create biofuel than is ever saved in GHGs by using it (when compared to gasoline). A recent discovery that holds promise as a source for biofuels is algae.[77] Also in experimental stages is a process for utilizing human sewage as a biofuel source.

---

[72] Ibid., 92.

[73] Ibid., 93.

[74] Ibid.

[75] Ibid., 95.

[76] Anna Austin, "A Study by a Group of Forest Scientists Confirms Forest-Derived Bioenergy Results in No Net Carbon Release" *Biomass Magazine*, January 25, 2012, http://biomassmagazine.com/articles/6122/words-from-the-wise, accessed January 31, 2012.

[77] See "Energy Resources: U.S. Energy Department Backs Plan to Produce AlgaeCrude Oil," http://www.upi.com/Business_News/Energy-Resources/2012/01/16/US

Currently, heavy use of corn in ethanol production, as well as other inefficiencies in the US biofuels industry, violates the norms of sufficiency and solidarity. The biofuels industry is also heavily dependent on government mandates and incentives, so close monitoring for genuine sustainability is necessary. However, biomass energy meets the sustainability standard of ecojustice norms as well as that of solidarity insofar as it is available domestically.[78] It is available worldwide, so the norms of sufficiency and participation are satisfied, as well as the energy guidelines for employment, appropriateness, and peace. Biomass energy thus deserves further development.

Hydropower

Hydropower accounts for about 6 percent of the electricity produced in the United States. Most of that power comes from dams across major US rivers. Most of the dams were highly subsidized by government at the time of their original construction. These facilities are flexible in their capacity to adjust their output of electricity according to demand by adjusting water flow through the turbines connected to the dam.

Ecologists note several problems with damming rivers. Dams disrupt the migration of fishes and other wildlife. They destroy forests and agricultural and recreational areas. They alter streams, causing disruption in plant and animal ecology as well as in other elements of the river ecosystem. Also, sediment is retained behind the dam, so water scours the streambed below the dam. Some scientists have questioned the net saving in GHG reduction due to the buildup of rotting vegetation that accumulates behind them.[79] Only 3 percent of US rivers are dammed, so it is estimated that hydropower could at least double its output of electricity.

Hydropower is clearly a renewable resource, and it would comply with the norms of sustainability and solidarity and with the adequacy

---

-Energy-Department-backs-plan-to-produce-algae-crude-oil/UPI-61091326752182/#, accessed January 31, 2012.

[78] Martin-Schramm, *Climate Justice*, 98–99.

[79] Fred Pierce, "Hydroelectric Dams Stoke Global Warming," *Albion Monitor*, August 28, 2000, http://www.monitor.net/monitor/0009a/dampollute.html, accessed February 1, 2012. Also see American Rivers, "The Ecology of Dam Removal: A Summary of Benefits and Impacts," February 2002, http://www.michigandnr.com/PUBLICATIONS /PDFS/fishing/dams/EcologyofDamRemoval.pdf, accessed February 1, 2012.

guideline. However, in compliance with the norm of sufficiency, care must be taken for other ecological harms to river life and endangered species.[80]

Geothermal

The western United States is prime territory for the development of geothermal energy sources.[81] A Massachusetts Institute of Technology study estimated that geothermal plants could generate enough energy (one hundred gigawatts) over the next fifty years to replace all of the nuclear power plants in the United States.[82] High drilling costs and the use of large amounts of water in areas that are often water stressed are problematic. Additionally, CO_2, mercury, and hydrogen sulfate are released during drilling. Drilling also risks setting off earthquakes, since sites good for this power source are near active seismic areas.[83]

Geothermal pumps can be used relatively risk free anywhere in the United States and are, according to the US Environmental Protection Agency (EPA), "the most energy efficient, cost effective, and environmentally clean space conditioning technology available."[84] Since the earth is at a constant temperature of about 50–75°F at five to ten feet below the surface, this technology can be used for heating and cooling.[85]

No doubt geothermal heat pumps satisfy all of the ecojustice norms and the guideline criteria. More doubtful is the situation with drilling associated with geothermal power plants. Participation requires that people most affected by any drilling would be consulted in advance of any activity and that the safety of local populations be given the highest consideration. Great care for ecosystems and for a safe, adequate, and accessible water supply is an additional decisive factor that must be addressed prior to drilling.[86]

---

[80] Martin-Schramm, *Climate Justice*, 100–101.

[81] See Charles W. Thurston, "Accelerating Geothermal Growth through DOE Initiatives," *Renewable Energy World*, January 26, 2012, http://www.renewableenergyworld.com/rea/news/article/2012/01/accelerating-geothermal-growth-through-doe-initiatives, accessed January 30, 2012.

[82] Martin-Schramm, *Climate Justice*, 102.

[83] Ibid.

[84] Cited in ibid., 103.

[85] See "Ground-Coupled Heat Exchanger," http://en.wikipedia.org/wiki/Ground-coupled_heat_exchanger, accessed February 1, 2012.

[86] Martin-Schramm, *Climate Justice*, 103.

Marine Energy

Energy generated by waves, tides, and ocean currents could readily meet 1 percent of all US electricity demands.[87] Tidal traps capture water at high tide and then release the water back to its source, generating electricity when passing through turbines on its way.[88] This process is being tested in New York's East River and in Tacoma, Washington, in Puget Sound.[89]

Problems faced in this field include the complex set of government agencies at many levels that have jurisdiction over the oceans and waterways and require permits before any energy development can take place. Ecological concerns include the potential harm of high voltage passing over the ocean floor and to the migration of fishes and whales. Costs are currently quite high per kilowatt-hour, ranging from twenty cents for tidal power to ninety cents for wave power.[90] Generally, there is potential here, and this kind of power could easily comply with the four norms and the energy guidelines. The difficulty remains that this technology is just in its infancy, and further research is needed to confirm these potentials.

Hydrogen

At first blush, hydrogen as a power source seems quite attractive from the moral point of view. However, even though it is the most abundant element on Earth, it does not exist in pure form anywhere. It needs to be extracted from water (H_2O), ammonia (NH_3), or other fossil fuels. Such extraction processes normally require the emission of GHGs, so the question becomes one of economy and net savings, especially in light of climate change concerns.[91] Further, difficulties include the reality that hydrogen is highly flammable and easily escapes storage containers. Hydrogen can be used in fuel cells or internal combustion engines, but it is currently very costly to produce.

---

[87] Ibid.

[88] See US Department of Energy, "Tapping into Wave and Tidal Ocean Power: 15% Water Power by 2030," January 27, 2012, http://energy.gov/articles/tapping-wave -and-tidal-ocean-power-15-water-power-2030, accessed February 3, 2012.

[89] Martin-Schramm, *Climate Justice*, 104.

[90] Ibid.

[91] Ibid., 105.

Generally, this energy source holds promise for the future. However, it too is in the infancy stages of research and development, and thus the potential for meeting the moral standard of the ecojustice norms and the energy guidelines we have been using needs to be revisited at a future date.

From the Writing of St. Francis

Thomas of Celano, The Remembrance of the Desire of a Soul *(1245–47)*, *CXXIV*[92]

When the brothers are cutting wood he forbids them to cut down the whole tree, so that it might have hope of sprouting again.

focus: renewable energy

Reflection and Application

If you are reading this book, you are part of the generations that need to make the transition from a fossil-fuel-based energy economy to an economy run on renewable energy. What is most difficult in any transition is to build the motivation in the minds of citizens who find it hard to believe change is a necessity, when by appearance there is still "plenty of oil to be had." Perhaps most instructive is to observe the debate that has surrounded the development of the tar sands in Alberta, Canada, and TransCanada's proposal to build the Keystone XL Pipeline to carry that Canadian crude oil 1,700 miles across the US heartland to refineries on the US Gulf Coast. In August of 2011, over twelve thousand people demonstrated in front of the White House urging denial of the permit for the pipeline. On January 18, 2012, President Obama denied permission for the Keystone XL Pipeline to be built as proposed.[93]

---

[92] Thomas of Celano, *The Remembrance of the Desire of a Soul* (1245–47), CXXIV, 165, in *Francis of Assisi: Early Documents*, vol. II, *The Founder*, ed. Regis J. Armstrong, J. A. Wayne Hellmann, and William J. Short (New York: New City Press, 2000), 353–54.

[93] Notably, in July of 2010 the US Environmental Protection Agency calculated that because "extraction and refining of Canadian oil sands crude are GHG-intensive relative to other types of crude oil . . . we estimate that GHG emissions from Canadian oil sands crude would be approximately 82% greater than the average crude

Controversy also loomed large in Canada concerning the overwhelming ecosystem damage in extracting the crude oil and the huge emissions of GHGs involved both in its extraction and in its use in vehicles. In January of 2009, Bishop Luc Bouchard of the Diocese of St. Paul in Alberta, Canada, published a pastoral letter entitled The Integrity of Creation and the Athabasca Oil Sands. The Diocese of St. Paul encompasses the northeastern portion of Alberta, which is the site of the Athabasca Oil Sands, the second largest deposit of oil in the world.

A Pastoral Letter:
The Integrity of Creation and the Athabasca Oil Sands[94]

It is estimated that the Athabasca Oil Sands hold about one trillion barrels of oil, with—theoretically—315 billion barrels extractable.[95] The bishop's analysis focuses on tar sands mining operations near Fort McMurray.[96] The pastoral explains why safeguarding the natural environment is a religious obligation; examines effects of oil sands development on the air, land, and water in northeastern Alberta; draws religious and moral conclusions from the analysis; recommends actions that must be considered if the integrity of the environment is to be respected; and suggests political and personal responses to this moral challenge.

Bishop Bouchard applies the seven major environmental ethical themes from Catholic social teaching on the environment to the tar sands situation. He then summarizes the impacts of the extraction of the oil sands and states his analysis of their moral implications. The bishop's

---

refined in the U.S., on a well-to-tank basis. To provide some perspective on the potential scale of emissions, 27 million metric tons is roughly equivalent to annual CO_2 emissions of seven coal-fired power plants." See the text of the report at http://yosemite.epa.gov/oeca/webeis.nsf/%28PDFView%29/20100126/$file/20100126. PDF?OpenElement, accessed February 3, 2012.

[94] See the full text of this pastoral letter of January 25, 2009, at http://www.diocese ofstpaul.ca/index.php?option=com_docman&task=cat_ view&gid=15&lang=en, accessed January 27, 2012. Permission to quote in the full second and third sections of the pastoral has been granted by Bishop Bouchard.

[95] To put this in perspective, the United States consumes 20.7 million barrels per day.

[96] See also the pastoral letter by Bishop Murray Chatlain, Roman Catholic Diocese of Mackenzie-Ft. Smith, April 15, 2009, at http://www.dioceseofmackenzie.com /nwt/files/Tar_sands_statement_on_letterhead.pdf, accessed February 3, 2012.

excellent and prophetic pastoral letter deserves lengthy citation of his own words.

The Environmental Impact of Oil Sands Development

Surface mining of oil sands is a multi-phased, complex operation:

- Large tracts of boreal forest are prepared for mining by draining off ground water, removing the trees and topsoil, and removing the "overburden" of muskeg, peat, sand, etc. in order to expose the underlying oil sands. To produce a barrel of oil requires excavating two tons of earth and muskeg.[97]

- The oil sands, which have firm sandstone like density, are then surface mined and crushed into a granular state, which is then mixed with water and solvents and piped to an on-site processing plant. Medium grade oil sands consist of 83% sand, 10% bitumen, 4% water and 3% clay.[98] On average, two tons of oil sands need to be mined and processed, for each barrel of oil produced.[99]

- At the plant site, the sand slurry is placed into tanks, where it is further mixed with hot water and sometimes caustic soda. Bitumen, a heavy viscous form of oil, floats to the surface, where it is skimmed off into holding tanks, then diluted to improve its flow, and finally piped to refineries; the sand settles out to the bottom of the tank and is removed and returned to the earth, leaving a murky middle layer (middlings) which constitute a mix of water, silt, clay, traces of chemicals as well as some bitumen. The middlings are processed to remove as much water as possible for recycling and then the remaining middlings are deposited into tailings ponds.

The environmental liabilities that result from the various steps in this process are significant and include:

---

[97] In a telephone interview with Bishop Bouchard, January 30, 2012, the bishop stressed that technical information cited in the footnotes of the pastoral are sources of the tar sands industry: "We cited the industry's own data to make our point." Pastoral endnote 22: Jennifer Grant, *Fact or Fiction: Oil Sands Reclamation*, Drayton Valley, AB: Pembina Institute, 2008, p. 6. Here and in subsequent citations of the pastoral endnotes, I have provided the full content of the bishop's endnote. Given the lapse of time, some internet web sites have changed. Thus, where possible, I have given the updated link that supplies similar information.

[98] Pastoral endnote 23: Alberta Department of Energy, "Alberta Oil Sands 2006 (updated December 2007) Edmonton, AB, 2007.

[99] Pastoral endnote 24: Jennifer Grant, *Fact or Fiction: Oil Sands Reclamation*, Drayton Valley, AB: Pembina Institute, 2008, 6.

Destruction of the boreal forest eco-system

All of the oil sands leases slated for development are in terrain classified as boreal forest. This type of ecological site is environmentally valuable because it has the unique ability to store large amounts of carbon in its bogs, peat, soil, and trees. The destruction of boreal forest reduces the earth's capacity to store carbon and releases greenhouse gases into the atmosphere as it is destroyed. The proposed oil sands projects, if all were to be activated, would remove an area of boreal forest eco-system equivalent in size to the state of Florida. . . .[100]

Potential damage to the Athabasca water shed

Two to four and a half barrels of water are required to produce a barrel of oil from oil sands.[101] This water is used to create the slurry of bitumen and oil that is heated and processed. . . . Despite impressive recycling efforts and improvements, for every barrel of oil produced approximately one barrel of water is contaminated in the process and deposited into a tailings pond. . . .[102] Cooperative ventures between industry, downstream First Nations and Metis communities, and the City of Fort McMurray are striving to arrive at manageable controls for water usage. But a recent report concluded that "Over the long term, the Athabasca River may not have sufficient flows to meet the needs of all the planned mining operations, and maintain adequate instream flows."[103] This possible shortage threatens fish, wildlife, downstream communities, and transportation in the Mackenzie delta.[104] Apart from the environmental issue

[100] Pastoral endnote 25: Sierra Club web site, "Tar Sands and the Boreal Forest," 2006. For similar and updated information, see Sierra Club, "Dirty Fuels: Tarsands; The Rainforest of North America," http://www.sierraclub.org/dirtyfuels/tar-sands/boreal.aspx, accessed June 27, 2012.

[101] Pastoral endnote 27: Sierra Club web site, "Tar Sands and Water," 2006. For similar and updated information, see Sierra Club, "Tar Sands Oil Poisons Our Air and Contaminates Our Clean Water," http://www.sierraclub.org/dirtyfuels/tar-sands/faces/intro.aspx, accessed June 27, 2012.

[102] Pastoral endnote 30: ibid.

[103] Pastoral endnote 31: Government of Alberta, Oil Sands Ministerial Strategy Committee, "Investing in Our Future: Responding to the Rapid Growth of the Oil Sands Development," 2006, 112.

[104] Pastoral endnote 32: Sierra Club web site, "Living Downstream—Growing Water Concerns in the NWT," 2006. For similar and updated information, see Michael Brune, "Tar Sands Pipelines Are Even Worse Than You Think," *Coming Clean* (blog), June 26, 2012, http://sierraclub.typepad.com/michaelbrune/2012/06/tar-sands-pipelines.html, accessed June 27, 2012.

of polluting one barrel of water, in order to produce a barrel of oil, the toxicity of the tailings ponds also represent[s] a very long term threat to the region's aquifers and to the quality of water in the Athabasca River due to the danger of seepage or a sudden and large catastrophic failure of a pond's enclosure.[105]

The release of greenhouse gases

Very large amounts of natural gas are required to heat water in order to process bitumen. By 2011, it is estimated that the then existing oil sands plants will burn enough natural gas to annually release 80 million tons of CO_2 into the atmosphere. This is far more than all of the CO_2 released annually by all of Canada's passenger cars.[106] The oil sands plants will then account for 15% of all of Canada's greenhouse gas emissions. At present, Alberta produces three times more per capita greenhouse gas emissions than the Canadian average and six times the West European average. . . . The bad news is that this reduction will not affect the total amount of emissions because new oil sands projects and expansions keep raising the total amount of emissions despite average per barrel reductions.

Heavy consumption of natural gas

To produce a barrel of oil processed from oil sands requires approximately one thousand cubic feet of natural gas per barrel. It is estimated that as proposed future oil sands projects come on stream, 20% of Canada's total natural gas production will be burned in order to extract bitumen. . . .[107] Also this high consumption of natural gas will likely raise its cost thereby promoting the use of coal and/or coal bed methane as cheaper alternatives. Coal derived energy is more environmentally harmful than natural gas. In summary, enormous quantities of clean natural gas are being burned to produce more environmentally damaging bitumen and the process is likely to bring about other adverse environmental effects.

---

[105] Pastoral endnote 33: Jennifer Grant, *Fact or Fiction: Oil Sands Reclamation*, Drayton Valley, AB: Pembina Institute, 2008, 42.

[106] Pastoral endnote 34: Sierra Club web site, "Tar Sands and Global Warming," 2006. For similar and updated information, see Sierra Club, "Background: Environmental Impacts of Tar Sands Development," http://www.sierraclub.org/energy/factsheets/tarsands.asp, accessed June 27, 2012.

[107] Pastoral endnote 35: Polaris Institute web site, "Dirty Little Secret: Canada's Global Warming Engine," Alberta Tar Sands Profile Series, 2007, http://dirtyoilsands.org/files/adirtylittlesecret-2.pdf, accessed June 27, 2012.

The creation of toxic tailings ponds

The "middlings" (water, suspended clay and bitumen) that are deposited into tailings ponds settle over time into a layer termed "mature fine tailings," which compact into a stable suspension that cannot at present be further recycled. This suspension is very toxic, containing naphthenic acids, phenolic compounds, ammonia-ammonium with traces of copper, zinc and iron as well as residual bitumen and naphtha.[108] Despite a great deal of research and effort, no fully effective means of neutralizing the toxicity of these tailings ponds has to date been devised, although some slow progress is being recorded.[109] There are two proposed treatments for these ponds. . . . The problem with these solutions is that the long term integrity of the containment structures is unknown. Toxic materials may in time seep into the Athabasca River polluting it and in succession the Slave River, the McKenzie River and the Beaufort Sea.[110] If a substantial leak of an end pit lake occurred, the result would be catastrophic. . . . There are now 5.5 billion cubic meters (175,000,000,000 cubic feet) of impounded tailings. This is slated to grow to 11 billion cubic meters. . . .[111] These toxic ponds will exist long after the plants have closed and will require one hundred years or more of supervision and maintenance.

Any one of the above destructive effects provokes moral concern, but it is when the damaging effects are all added together that the moral legitimacy of oil sands production is challenged. An even more alarming level of concern is reached when the scale of proposed future expansions (a quadrupling of the number of barrels per day from 1.25 to 5 million) is taken into account. It is then that the full environmental threat of the oil sands and the resulting gravity of the moral issue involved is most deeply felt.

The ecological objections and fears surrounding oil sands development outlined above are not contentious. Both industry and environmentalists . . . would agree that the above is a fair summary of the situation. The concerns environmentalists express are highly credible. The proposed additional oil sands projects are moving forward based

[108] Pastoral endnote 36: Jennifer Grant, *Fact or Fiction: Oil Sands Reclamation*, Drayton Valley, AB: Pembina Institute, 2008, 36.

[109] Pastoral endnote 37: Syncrude Canada Ltd. web site, "Tailings Management," 2006, http://www.syncrude.ca/users/folder.asp?FolderID=5913.

[110] Pastoral endnote 38: Jennifer Grant, *Fact or Fiction: Oil Sands Reclamation*, Drayton Valley, AB: Pembina Institute, 2008, 43.

[111] Pastoral endnote 39: Jennifer Grant, *Fact or Fiction: Oil Sands Reclamation*, Drayton Valley, AB: Pembina Institute, 2008, 39.

on the confidence that technological solutions will be found to these concerns. This drive to development ignores the fact that forty years of research into the oil sands, while it has led to a substantial reduction in some forms of pollution, especially air pollution and water usage, does not at present hold out the hope of reducing environmental harm to an acceptable level primarily because of the enormous scale and rapid development of the projects.

The moral problem does not lie in government and industry's lack of a sincere desire to find a solution; the moral problem lies in their racing ahead and aggressively expanding the oil sands industry despite the fact that serious environmental problems remain unsolved after more than forty years of on-going research. The moral question has been left to market forces and self-regulation to resolve when what is urgently required is moral vision and leadership.

I am forced to conclude that the integrity of creation in the Athabasca Oil Sands is clearly being sacrificed for economic gain. The proposed future development of the oil sands constitutes a serious moral problem. Environmentalists and members of First Nations and Metis communities who are challenging government and industry to adequately safeguard the air, water, and boreal forest eco-systems of the Athabasca oil sands region present a very strong moral argument, which I support. The present pace and scale of development in the Athabasca oil sands cannot be morally justified. Active steps to alleviate this environmental damage must be undertaken.[112]

In the next section of the pastoral, "An Action Plan to Safeguard Creation," Bishop Bouchard proposes ten ways the moral concerns need to be addressed:

1. A very prudent pre-cautionary approach should surround water issues.[113]

2. A rational limit must be placed on the size and quantity of tailings ponds.

3. A national program of energy conservation that includes ambitious auto fuel efficiency standards should be initiated to reduce Canada's use of oil and to promote the development of alternative energy sources.

---

[112] The emphasis is in the original text.

[113] Pastoral endnote 40: Kevin P. Timoney, "A Study of Water and Sediment Quality as Related to Public Health Issues, Fort Chipewyan, Alberta," Sherwood Park, AB: Treeline Ecological Research, 2007, 68–70.

4. The treaty rights of First Nations people to hunt wildlife and to fish have to be respected.[114]

5. Future oil sands developments must be paced so as to allow Canada to meet its international commitments.[115]

6. The enormous amounts of greenhouse gases created by the oil sands processing plants must be offset by national reductions.[116]

7. A land use plan should be created to protect the boreal forest eco-system.[117]

8. The Municipality of Wood Buffalo should be provided with adequate social resources and infrastructure in order to meet the educational, health, and social services requirements to service a large and a transient population.[118]

9. Foreign workers must be protected from exploitation and Alberta labor standards must not be lowered or compromised.

10. Future liabilities for the reclamation of the boreal forest eco-system, the tailings ponds, ground water and the Athabasca water-shed area must be covered by full cost bonding.[119]

[114] Pastoral endnote 43: Pope John Paul II, video address to First Nations and Metis people in Fort Simpson, NWT, 1984. Also see Carol Berry, "Alberta Oil Sands up Close: Gunshot Sounds, Dead Birds, a Moonscape," *Indian Country Today Media Network*, February 2, 2012, http://indiancountrytodaymedianetwork.com/2012/02/02/alberta-oil-sands-up-close-gunshot-sounds-dead-birds-a-moonscape-95444, accessed February 4, 2012.

[115] Pastoral endnote 44: Sierra Club web site: "Managing Oil Sands Development for the Long Term: A Declaration by Canada's Environmental Community," 2005; the updated link is http://www.pembinafoundation.org/pub/585, accessed June 25, 2012.

[116] Pastoral endnote 45: Cumulative Environmental Management Association, "Ecosystem Management Framework for the Regional Municipality of Wood Buffalo," Edmonton, AB, 2008, CEMA press release.

[117] Pastoral endnote 46: Government of Alberta, Sustainable Resources Development web site: "Draft Land Use Framework," 2008; the updated link is http://www.srd.alberta.ca/newsroom/ministersoffice/documents/srd-annualreport-2008-09.pdf, accessed June 27, 2012.

[118] Pastoral endnote 47: Tony Clarke, *Tar Sands Showdown: Canada and the Politics of Oil in an Age of Climate Change*, Toronto: James Lorimer and Co., 2008, 184–85.

[119] Pastoral endnote 49: Sierra Club web site: "Managing Oil Sands Development for the Long Term: A Declaration by Canada's Environmental Community," 2005, http://www.pembinafoundation.org/pub/585.

> *I believe that a serious commitment on the part of government and in-*
> *dustry must be made to satisfying the above requirements before any further*
> *oil sands plants or leases are considered for approval.*[120]

Though the US bishops have published no pastoral letter on the tar sands or on the Keystone XL Pipeline, the Catholic Coalition on Climate Change (to which the USCCB subscribes), Catholic college and university students,[121] and many religious orders, including the national Franciscan Action Network, strongly oppose the building of the pipeline based on Catholic social teachings.[122] For Catholics, people of other faith traditions, and people of good will, the pipeline has become a national symbol of the crossroads at which the United States stands concerning its energy future, and the debate is far from over.[123]

A Personal Reflection on the Keystone XL Pipeline

"God Saw Everything That He Had Made, and Indeed, It Was Very Good"
(Genesis 1:31)

A couple of years ago, I had the privilege of experiencing the spectacular beauty and grandeur of the Canadian Rockies in Alberta, Canada, for the first time. From the flowing bright green tall grasses of the plains at their base, the jagged light grey peaks thrust skyward, leading the eye upward to their melting snowcaps and on to the azure blue sky, dotted with cotton-ball-puffed clouds. In the most unexpected moments and to my delight I was treated to the magnificence of a waterfall cascading ice-cold ribbons of water hundreds of meters downward, forming whirlpools in the streams or rivers below. Later I hiked in Banff National Park,

---

[120] The emphasis is in the original text.

[121] See the web site of Jesuit-run Creighton University's Creighton Center for Service and Justice, "Sustainability—Keystone Pipeline Petition," October 5, 2011, http://blogs.creighton.edu/ccsj/category/justice-advocacy-priorities/sustainability-environmental-justice/page/2, accessed February 3, 2012.

[122] See the Franciscan Action Network, "No Flow for Keystone XL Pipeline," at http://www.franciscanaction.org/news/exec/No%20Flow%20for%20Keystone%20XL%20Pipeline, accessed February 3, 2012.

[123] See Dennis Sadowski, "Country's Debate over Keystone XL Pipeline Is Far from Over," *National Catholic Reporter*, January 27, 2012, http://ncronline.org/news/ecology/countrys-debate-over-keystone-xl-pipeline-far-over, accessed February 3, 2012. For current developments, see National Resources Defense Council web site, nrdc.org, accessed August 12, 2012.

to the Hoodoos Viewpoint,[124] along Tunnel Mountain Road, and then on to Moraine Lake and Lake Louise. There the bright aqua waters mirrored the snowcapped mountains, and gentle breezes wafted across the surface to the shores.

"The Whole Creation Has Been Groaning" (Romans 8:22)

But the next day, when circling northeastward toward St. Paul, taking the long route back to Calgary, the scenery shifted and revealed vistas of ecological destruction that were simply shattering! Huge tracts of land were being reduced to moonscapes because the "overburden" of water, soil, and ancient boreal forests (muskeg, peat, and sand) was ripped away—roots and all—and cast aside in heaps to expose the tar sands, the new "black gold." My heart cried out at this Baconian disaster in progress! This damage will certainly impact the ecological health of this region for generations to come—to say nothing of the overall damage the release of the CO_2 will inflict on the planet by contributing to global warming.[125]

Imperial Ecology versus Kinship of Creation

The irony is both tragic and profound. In contrast to the wisdom of St. Francis of Assisi, the philosophy of Francis Bacon (1561–26) opened the door to "imperial ecology."[126] Bacon held that humans are the lords and masters over nature. Technology was the means to that end. His writings

---

[124] Hoodoos are sandstone spires created over thousands of years by erosion and were believed to be spiritually significant by the forefathers of the First Nations.

[125] An overwhelming objection is that exploitation of tar sands would make it implausible to stabilize Earth's climate and avoid disastrous global climate impacts. According to the IPCC *Fourth Assessment Report*, the tar sands are estimated to contain at least 400 GtC (equivalent to about 200 parts per million [ppm] CO_2). GtC means gigatons of carbon.

See data at http://www.ipcc.ch/publications_and_data/ar4/wg3/en/contents.html, accessed June 27, 2012. Easily available reserves of conventional oil and gas are enough to take atmospheric CO_2 well above 400 ppm, which is unsafe for life on Earth. However, if emissions from coal are phased out over the next few decades and if unconventional fossil fuels including tar sands are left in the ground, it is conceivable to stabilize Earth's climate. See James Hansen et al., "Target Atmospheric CO_2: Where Should Humanity Aim?" http://pubs.giss.nasa.gov/cgi-bin/abstract.cgi?id=ha00410c.

[126] David Toolan, *At Home in the Cosmos* (Maryknoll, NY: Orbis Books, 2001), 48–49.

are full of metaphors of torturous violence: nature was to be "bound into service," "made a slave," "put under constraint," "squeezed and dissected," and "forced out of her natural state and molded" so that "human knowledge and human power meet as one." Bacon believed that using science in this way would produce a "blessed race of heroes and supermen."[127] Indeed, we humans have become *like* gods! We *have* gained "control" over the earth! We *do* know the fundamental workings of the major systems of land, water, and sky; indeed, *we are to blame* for many catastrophic events! Yet we are like adolescents who lack moral wisdom, and we choose to ignore the harms our pillage inflicts, for the sake of the comforts of the "good life." In the depths of our beings, we know that *we are responsible*, and this drives us to ever more vicious cycles of denial and false hope.

Genuine versus False Hope

In St. Francis's day, wood was central to medieval life, similar to the way that fossil fuels are central to us. Without wood, medieval societies would have collapsed; if we removed all oil-based products from our homes, we'd have precious little left. However, Francis set forth a relationship (sisterhood and brotherhood) that would sustain both people and trees in hope. This was a first and necessary step toward sustainable living. Indeed, the medieval ax devastated forests and harmed ecosystems. But today the conditions of the size, scale, and context of global warming create a distinct urgency Francis could never have known. Yet his call for hope is worth our consideration.

Francis was wise to point to hope, for hope makes all of life possible. The Bible is awash in symbols of hope. The First Testament points us away from political, economic, and military alliances that bring us false hope (Isa 31:1-3; 36:4-9; Hos 10:13). Also, in the First Testament, God and hope are virtually identified: God is the "hope of Israel" (Jer 14:8; cf. Ps 71:5). In the New Testament, God is a "God of hope" in whose presence we should "abound with hope" (Rom 15:13).

Jesus refers to all of this in his "inaugural address" in Luke 4:18-19. He specifically refers to Lev 25:23: "The land shall not be sold in perpetuity, for the land is *mine*; with me you are but aliens and tenants" (emphasis added). Key to genuine hope is a just and sustainable relationship with the land. Hope requires that we are not free to ravish the land with

---

[127] Ibid., 49.

unchecked license! Rather, only when we care for the land as God cares for us will we achieve joy and peace. When we try to buy hope and safety on the cheap, placing our own greed that satiates rather than provides sufficiency, we deceive ourselves into the false hope of finding happiness. We spiral downward into insensitivity to the needs of others and the inability to respond to anything but our fears and insecurities. It is fear and insecurity (not hope) that has long been considered a classic impediment to sound moral judgment. When we listen to the reasons proponents of the Keystone XL Pipeline give for mining the tar sands and for bringing that crude through to the United States, fears loom large, along with attitudes of control and domination.[128]

St. Bonaventure of Bagnoregio

As a university theologian, St. Bonaventure of Bagnoregio developed what St. Francis of Assisi taught about Christ, creation, creatures, and humans.[129] His love-oriented virtue ethics framework is known as the *imitatio Christi*—the following or imitation of Christ.[130]

IMITATIO CHRISTI AND VIRTUE ETHICS

The *imitatio Christi* has both an internal and an external dimension. Humans are embodied and spiritual earth creatures who seek union

---

[128] See, for example, Mark Green, "Energy Key: Keystone XL Pipeline," *Energy Tomorrow Blog*, June 10, 2011, http://energytomorrow.org/blog/energy-key-keystone -xl-pipeline/#/type/all, accessed August 14, 2012. Also see Procon.org, "Should the US Authorize the Keystone XL Pipeline to Import Tar Sand Oil from Canada?" http:// alternativeenergy.procon.org/view.answers.php?Question ID=001628, accessed February 3, 2012.

[129] See Kenan B. Osborne, ed., *The History of Franciscan Theology* (St. Bonaventure, NY: The Franciscan Institute, 1994), vii–ix. See Zachary Hayes, "The Life and the Christological Thought of St. Bonaventure," in Damian McElrath, ed., *Franciscan Christology: Selected Texts, Translations and Introductory Essays*, Franciscan Sources, no. 1 (St. Bonaventure, NY: The Franciscan Institute, 1980), 62–64. See also Timothy Johnson, "Lost in Sacred Space: Textual Hermeneutics, Liturgical Worship, and Celano's *Legenda ad usum chori*" (unpublished paper presented at the Thirty-Sixth International Congress of Medieval Studies, May 3, 2001, Kalamazoo, MI), 12; and E. R. Daniel, *The Franciscan Concept of Mission in the High Middle Ages* (New York: The Franciscan Institute, 1975), 48.

[130] Zachary Hayes, "Christ, Word of God and Exemplar of Humanity," *The Cord* 46 (1996): 6.

with God while in *this* world, which utterly bursts with the signs and wonders of God. Bonaventure says that we can learn how to live morally by studying the whole life of Jesus, the Word Incarnate, explained in the gospels and interpreted by St. Francis. Following in the footprints of Jesus takes us beyond a mere mimicry of his actions to *spiritual* transformation. There is a constant interplay between being good and doing what is good (ethical, external) and the process of our becoming good (spiritual, internal). In these two ways God's grace assists in the moral life.[131] Central to this transformation are the virtues of humility, poverty, obedience, and love.

HUMILITY

Humility is the virtue central to the God-human relationship. The English word for "humility" comes from the Latin word for "earth," *humus*. God, in the incarnation, entered our reality, choosing an intimate relationship with us *earth creatures*.[132] But, clearly, we are *not* God! Today we must reclaim our *creaturely* identity and use our considerable, though limited, scientific and technological prowess to care for one another and the planet.[133]

Humility is particularly important when contemplating massive and destructive projects such as tar sands extractions and the Keystone XL Pipeline.[134] As scientist R. Eugene Turner explains,

---

[131] Zachary Hayes, *The Hidden Center: Spirituality and Speculative Christology in St. Bonaventure*, Franciscan Pathways (St. Bonaventure, NY: The Franciscan Institute, 1992), 42.

[132] Bonaventure, *Sermon on the Nativity*, IX, 106, citied by Hayes, *The Hidden Center*, 42.

[133] Leonard J. Bowman, "The Cosmic Exemplarism of Bonaventure," *The Journal of Religion* 55 (1985): 187.

[134] Known hazards are clear and well documented, including, for example, Dr. James Hansen, "Silence is Deadly," June 3, 2011, http://www.columbia.edu/~jeh1/mailings/2011/20110603_SilenceIsDeadly.pdf, accessed August 7, 2011; Mark Guarino, "US: Canadian Oil Pipeline Hazardous to the Environment," *Christian Science Monitor*, June 4, 2011, http://www.csmonitor.com/Environment/2011/0604/US-Canadian-oil-pipeline-hazardous-to-the-environment, accessed August 7, 2011; Elizabeth McGowan, "Groups Demand More Time and Public Say in Keystone XL Pipeline Review," InsideClimate News, April 7, 2011, http://insideclimatenews.com/news/20110407/public-keystone-xl-pipeline-environmental-review-clinton, accessed August 7, 2011; and Elizabeth McGowan, "Nebraska Lawmakers Plead with Secy. Clinton to Delay Keystone XL Decision," *InsideClimate News*, June 3, 2011 http://

> Embracing doubt, a signature of strength of science, is an essential
> core component of an ignorance-based world view (IBWV) that as-
> sumes the areas of certainty are small and relative. The contrasting
> knowledge-based world view (KBWV) assumes small and mostly
> insignificant knowledge gaps exist. When the KBWV is combined
> with a sense of urgency to "do something," then the intellectual
> landscape is flattened, the introduction of new ideas is impeded,
> monitoring and adaptive management is marginalized, risky behav-
> iors continue, and social learning is restricted.[135]

Christian environmental ethics is normatively rooted in values that
strongly embrace prudence and the precautionary principle when dealing with questions of great complexity, the unknown, or the unknowable.
Thus, an IBWV approach is clearly the preferred methodology for the
issue of the tar sands and the Keystone XL Pipeline project. The central
value of the world as a sacramental universe requires upholding claims
of the intrinsic *and* instrumental value of the Canadian boreal forests and
watersheds, as well as US farmlands, aquifers, and waterways. Moreover,
the values of authentic development and sustainability require that the
environmental impact of human constructions not endanger human life
or unnecessarily wreak damage on the natural environment. Further,
development of public policies and their enforcement that prevent destruction and limit vulnerability, thus securing public safety for all citizens without prejudice, is demanded by the norms of justice, participation,
and the preferential option for the poor.

It is precisely due to situations as those discussed above that member
states of the United Nations mandated the elaboration of the 2005 report
The Precautionary Principle.[136] The precautionary principle deals with the
complexities of economic activities that would exploit natural resources
using technologies that could result in serious and/or irreversible

---

solveclimatenews.com/news/20110602/nebraska-senators-hillary-clinton-keystone
-xl-pipeline, accessed August 7, 2011.

[135] R. Eugene Turner, "Doubt and the Values of an Ignorance-Based World View
for Restoration: Coastal Louisiana Wetlands," *Estuaries and Coasts* 32 (2009): 1054.

[136] See World Commission on the Ethics of Scientific Knowledge and Technology
(COMEST) and United Nation Education, Scientific and Cultural Organization
(UNESCO), *The Precautionary Principle*, available at http://unesdoc.unesco.org
/images/0013/001395/139578e.pdf, accessed December 24, 2010. See also the Commission of the Bishops' Conferences of the European Community (COMECE), A
Christian View on Climate Change: The Implications of Climate Change for Lifestyles
and EU Policies (Brussels, Belgium: COMECE, 2008), 17.

harm.[137] The objective of the precautionary principle is to provide guidance in cases of risk where outcomes and probabilities are not well known. "The unquantified *possibility* of risk is sufficient to trigger the consideration of the [precautionary principle]. . . . Interventions are required before possible harm occurs, or before certainty about such harm can be achieved (that is, a wait-and-see is excluded)."[138]

POVERTY

Bonaventure holds that material poverty (Christian simplicity) must go hand in hand with humility. Many of us materially wealthy people know only a false (material) poverty; we have the illusion of never having enough "stuff," and we are always ultimately craving something more. This is spiritual poverty. Today we must choose to live with what is sufficient for a life of dignity and what is ecologically sustainable! Key to the virtue of poverty is being confident in God's generosity, ready with open hands and heart, and ready to give away whatever we can to another in need (Matt 10:8). Today this means limiting our consumption of energy from unsustainable sources and working to develop renewable energy sources and ways of sustainable living.

OBEDIENCE

"Obedience" comes from the Latin *oboedire*, "to pay attention" or "to hear." Jesus Christ modeled this virtue by listening to his Father's will (see Heb 10:7, 9; John 14:31; 5:30) and by caring for the needs of people and nonhuman others.[139] Today we must heed the groaning of the suffering earth, become ecologically literate, engage in prayerful discernment, and then act to halt environmental destruction. There is an intimate relationship between the virtues of obedience and prudence. You cannot have one without the other!

---

[137] COMEST and UNESCO, *The Precautionary Principle*, p. 8. See the 1972 Polluter Pays Principle, which requires that the costs of pollution be borne by those who cause the pollution. See also the 1992 Earth Summit, Agenda 21, as a principle of sustainable development. Today it is a generally recognized principle of international environmental law. Also see the United Nations Conference on Environment and Development's 1992 *Rio Declaration on Environment and Development*.

[138] COMEST and UNESCO, *The Precautionary Principle*, 13.

[139] Hayes, *The Hidden Center*, 37. Bonaventure's commentary on Luke stresses Jesus' obedience to people.

Prudence is a classical virtue in Christian environmental ethics based on Aristotle's *phronêsis*, or practical wisdom, and found in the works of Thomas Aquinas.[140] According to the *Catechism of the Catholic Church*, article 7, no. 1806:

> *Prudence* is the virtue that disposes practical reason to discern our true good in every circumstance and to choose the right means of achieving it. . . . Prudence is "right reason in action" (Aquinas, *STh* II-II,47,2). It is not to be confused with timidity or fear, nor with duplicity or dissimulation. . . . It guides the other virtues by setting rule and measure. It . . . immediately guides the judgment of conscience. The prudent man determines and directs his conduct in accordance with this judgment. With the help of this virtue we apply moral principles to particular cases without error and overcome doubts about the good to achieve and the evil to avoid.[141]

When prudence is used in environmental ethical analysis, it functions to conserve known values while remaining open to new knowledge.[142] In the case of the Keystone XL Pipeline, known values include the intrinsic value of the 1,300 miles of privately owned land and the five hundred miles of prime farmland of the "breadbasket" of the United States that the pipeline will traverse, as well as the Yellowstone River and the Ogallala Aquifer, which provides roughly 30 percent of all the water used for irrigation on American farms. It is this very section of US

---

[140] See T. Gilby, s.v. "Prudence," *New Catholic Encyclopedia*, vol. 11, 2nd ed. (Detroit: Gale, 2003), 787–92. Also see Scott Carson, s.v. "Phronêsis," *Encyclopedia of Philosophy*, ed. Donald M. Borchert, vol. 10. 2nd ed. (Detroit: Macmillan Reference USA, 2006), 27–28. See also examples of secular environmentalists' value for prudence: Nigel Dower, "Ethics and Environmental Futures," *International* 21 (May 1983): 29–44; John R. E. Bliese, "Traditionalist Conservatism and Environmental Ethics," *Environmental Ethics* 19 (Summer 1997): 135–51; Charles J. List, "The Virtues of Wild Leisure," *Environmental Ethics* 27 (Winter 2005): 355–73; and Vasileios E. Pantazis, "Reverence ('Ehrfurcht') for the Living World as the Basic Bioethical Principle: Anthropological-Pedagogical Approach," *Ethics, Place and Environment* 12 (June 2009): 255–66, especially 262.

[141] See http://www.usccb.org/catechism/text/pt3sect1chpt1art7.shtml, accessed December 24, 2010.

[142] See "Scientific Knowledge and the Virtue of Prudence," 10–11, in NCCB/USCC, *Global Climate Change: A Plea for Dialogue, Prudence, and the Common Good*, June 15, 2001, http://www.usccb.org/sdwp/international/globalclimate.shtml, accessed December 24, 2010. See also Steven Bouma-Prediger, "Why Care for Creation? From Prudence to Piety," *Christian Scholar's Review* 27 (Spring 1998): 277–97.

farm country that John Paul II spoke of in his homily at Living History Farm on October 4, 1979, when he said,

> The land must be conserved with care since it is intended to be fruitful for generation upon generation. You who live in the heartland of America have been entrusted with some of the earth's best land: the soil so rich in minerals, the climate so favorable for producing bountiful crops, with fresh water and unpolluted air available all around you. You are stewards of some of the most important resources God has given to the world. Therefore conserve the land well, so that your children's children and generations after them will inherit an even richer land than was entrusted to you. But also remember what the heart of your vocation is. While it is true here that farming today provides an economic livelihood for the farmer, still it will always be more than an enterprise of profit-making. In farming, you cooperate with the Creator in the very sustenance of life on earth.[143]

In a time of global food insecurity, record climatic warming resulting from fossil fuel use, and the disastrous safety record of catastrophic oil spills from pipelines, prudence and obedience call for a halt to this entire project.[144] Time, talent, finances, and research measures should be directed to renewable fuels sources that are not heavy carbon producers.

LOVE

Having first received God's love, humans then share it among themselves and with all of creation (John 13:34-35).[145] But humans love imperfectly; so justice and the discipline of law is necessary. Christ is the ultimate norm and negotiator of justice (love).[146] Today we must relate to the non-

---

[143] See full text of the homily at http://www.vatican.va/holy_father/john_paul_ii/homilies/1979/documents/hf_jp-ii_hom_19791004_usa-des-moines_en.html, accessed February 4, 2012.

[144] See Pope Paul VI, address to World Food Conference in Rome, November 9, 1974. See also the regional pastoral letter issued by the bishops of Colorado, Illinois, Indiana, Iowa, Kansas, Minnesota, Missouri, Nebraska, North Dakota, Wisconsin, and Wyoming, Strangers and Guests: Toward Community in the Heartland, May 1, 1980.

[145] Hayes, *The Hidden Center*, 38–39. In Bonaventure's speculative theology and spirituality, love drives the Christ mystery.

[146] Ibid., 202–3. Hayes cites *Hex.* 1, 31–33 (V, 334); Aristotle, *II Ethics*, c. 6; and *Hex*.1, 34–36 (V, 335).

human world with justice and love, as God relates to us. Today we need to create and enforce policies and laws that keep air, water, and soils pure; that sharply restrict the plundering and warming of the planet; and that support the restoration of environmental damage.[147] Or, as a World Council of Churches poster puts it, "Love your neighbor. Halt global warming!"

IMITATIO CHRISTI: VIRTUE ETHICS, TAR SANDS, THE KEYSTONE XL PIPELINE, AND GLOBAL WARMING

Like St. Francis of Assisi, Bonaventure holds a hope-filled, positive, and radically relational view of God, creation, redemption, and ethical praxis.[148] Each creature responds to God's love in its unique way. The incarnation unites humans with the whole cosmos, and Jesus Christ incarnate embodies and exemplifies the norm and standard for all ethical relations. Humans can read the signs of the divine in creation and then *act* morally.[149] By following Jesus, humans can participate with Christ and become cocreators and coredeemers of the cosmos.

Bonaventure shows how at the root of the Gospel mandate of poverty there lies a recognition that God's love is expressed in all of creation,

---

[147] Hayes, *The Hidden Center*, 39. The spiritual life in Christ is a journey deeper into the foundational realities of the world. Understanding those realities also shapes Christian ethics. "To perceive the life of Christ as a paradigm is to accept its fundamental values as normative for human life. The fundamental attitude and values of Christ must be so personalized in one's life that they truly define one's relationship to reality."

[148] See Leonardo Boff, *Cry of the Earth, Cry of the Poor*, trans. Phillip Berryman (Maryknoll, NY: Orbis Books, 1997), 174–86. John Duns Scotus and Chardin make this link even more explicit. See John 1:3, 14; Heb 1:2; Col 1:15-20; Eph 1:3-14; Rev 1:8; 21:6. Also see Ilia Delio, *A Franciscan View of Creation: Learning to Live in a Sacramental World*, The Franciscan Heritage Series, vol. 2 (St. Bonaventure, NY: The Franciscan Institute, 2003), 31: "Bonaventure consistently claims that Christ belongs to the very structure of reality—as the Word, to the reality of God; as the Incarnate Word, to the reality of the universe created by God. It is Christ who reveals to the world its own meaning." See also Zachary Hayes, "Christology-Cosmology," in "Franciscan Leadership in Ministry: Foundations in History, Theology, and Spirituality," *Spirit and Life: A Journal of Contemporary Franciscanism* 7 (1997): 41–58.

[149] See discussion of "deep incarnation" in Denis Edwards, *Ecology at the Heart of Faith* (Maryknoll, NY: Orbis Books, 2006), 58–60. Also see Duncan Reid, "Enfleshing the Human," in *Earth Revealing—Earth Healing: Ecology and Christian Theology*, ed. Denis Edwards (Collegeville, MN: Liturgical Press, 2000), 69–83. See Neils Henrick Gregersen, "The Cross of Christ in an Evolutionary World," *Dialog* 40 (2001): 205.

including human life, and is *pure gift*.[150] Indeed, in Christ incarnate the
entire cosmos is united and transformed.[151] Bonaventure states: "All
things are said to be transformed in the transfiguration of Christ. For as
a human being, Christ has something in common with all creatures. With
the stone he shares existence; with plants he shares life; with animals he
shares sensation; and with the angels he shares intelligence. Therefore,
all things are said to be transformed in Christ since—in his human nature—he embraces something of every creature."[152] Through Christ Jesus,
our relationship with God brings us into relationship with the world.
That relationship requires humility, poverty of spirit, austerity of life,
and genuine charity (John 13:34-35).[153] Considering Bonaventure's grasp
of the cosmos and his open attitude toward science,[154] I think that if he
were present here today, he would hold that his love-centered virtue
ethics require that we act to halt global warming.[155]

Today I believe the ecological footprint of tar sands mining and the
Keystone XL Pipeline is far too large. This energy source has a size, scale,
and potential GHG impact on climate change that is ultimately detri-
mental to both the United States and Canada, taking us in the opposite
direction from conservation, efficiency, and living within the limits of
our common planetary home. We must follow the wisdom of St. Francis:
"When the brothers are cutting wood he forbids them to cut down the
whole tree, so that it might have hope of sprouting again."[156] We must

---

[150] Hayes, "Christ, Word of God and Exemplar of Humanity," 11.

[151] See Bonaventure's *Disputed Questions on Evangelical Perfection*. Here we can see
the influence of Pseudo-Dionysius on Bonaventure. See Jose de Vinck, *Introduction
to the Works of Bonaventure*, trans. J. Guy Bougerol (Paterson, NJ: St. Anthony Guild
Press, 1972), 40.

[152] Bonaventure, *Sermo I, Dom II*, in Quad. IX, 215–19, quoted in Hayes, "Christ,
Word of God and Exemplar of Humanity," 13.

[153] Hayes, *The Hidden Center*, 39. Hayes cites *Dom. IV in Quad. I* (IX, 232).

[154] Zachary Hayes, "The Cosmos, A Symbol of the Divine," in *Franciscan Theology
of the Environment: An Introductory Reader*, ed. Dawn M. Nothwehr (Quincy, IL: Franciscan Press, 2002), 249–67.

[155] See Intergovernmental Panel on Climate Change, *Climate Change 2007: Synthesis
Report; Summary for Policymakers*. See also Gerald Baum, Monika Hellwig, and W.
Malcolm Byrnes, "Global Climate and Catholic Responsibility: Facts and Responses,"
Journal of Catholic Social Thought 4 (Summer 2007): 313–401; and Elizabeth A. Johnson,
"An Earthy Christology: 'For God So Loved the Cosmos,'" *America* 200/12, whole
no. 4852 (April 13, 2009): 27–30.

[156] Thomas of Celano, *The Remembrance of the Desire of a Soul* (1245–47), CXXIV, 165,
in FAED, vol. II, *The Founder*, ed. Regis J. Armstrong, J. A. Wayne Hellmann, and
William J. Short (New York: New City Press, 2000), 353–54.

not continue to wreak irreparable damage on the ecosystems of the tar sands and knowingly continue to emit enormous amounts of GHGs while extracting oil that will, in turn, emit even more GHGs when used to fuel cars and trucks, risking permanent destruction of America's breadbasket in the process.

Questions for Reflection and Discussion

1. Do you know what renewable energy sources your utility company utilizes?

2. In what way are massive projects that damage or destroy Earth's ecosystems idolatrous?

3. What concrete steps will you take to conserve energy and avoid fossil fuel use?

4. What is most difficult for you when contemplating living with less oil dependency?

5. Do you agree that it is immoral to proceed with oil sands production? Explain.

Suggestions for Action

1. Download the US Department of Energy's "EnergySavers" guide at http://www.energysavers.gov/pdfs/energy_savers.pdf.

2. Join a car cooperative; group errands together so that you make fewer trips in your vehicle.

3. Explore the web site of Interfaith Power and Light at http://inter faithpowerandlight.org.

4. Explore the US Department of Energy science education page at http://energy.gov/science-innovation/science-education.

5. Avoid using plastics; purchase products made from recycled and natural materials.

6. Trade in your vehicle for a more fuel-efficient one.

7. Purchase non-petroleum-based personal care and cleaning products.

Prayer

Most High and Glorious Creator, we give you thanks and praise
For the sun above us;
For the warm ground beneath us;
For the freedom of the wind around us;
For the power of the rivers that rush by us;
For the strength of the waves and the rhythm of the tides beyond us.
Grant us the wisdom to use energy sources safely and wisely.
Bless researchers with integrity,
and inspire them to develop efficient sustainable ways
to use your power-full gifts.
We ask all of this in unity with the Spirit who sustains us and
in the name of Jesus who empowers us. Amen.

Sources for Further Study

Amnesty International. *Nigeria: Petroleum, Pollution and Poverty in the Niger Delta.* London: Amnesty International Publications, 2009. Download at http://www.amnesty.org/en/library/asset/AFR44/017/2009/en/e2415061-da5c-44f8-a73c-a7a4766ee21d/afr440172009en.pdf.

Gasaway, Richard. *An Inconvenient Purpose: Linking Stewardship and Alternative Energy.* Enumclaw, WA: WinePress Publishing, 2009.

Goodell, Jeff. *Big Coal: The Dirty Secret behind America's Future.* New York: Houghton Mifflin, 2006.

Lester, Richard K., and David M. Hart. *Unlocking Energy Innovation: How America Can Build a Low-Cost, Low-Carbon Energy System.* Cambridge, MA: MIT Press, 2012.

Martin-Schramm, James B. *Climate Justice: Ethics, Energy, and Public Policy.* Minneapolis: Fortress Press, 2010.

Tamminen, Terry. *Lives per Gallon: The True Cost of Our Oil Addiction.* Washington, DC: Island Press, 2006.

Norms, Themes, and Guidelines for Energy and Climate Policy

Energy Policy

Ecojustice Norms	Sustainability	Sufficiency	Participation	Solidarity

Themes—USCCB, Renewing the Earth (1991)	Energy Policy Guidelines*		
Catholic Social Teaching	Option for the Poor	Equity	Peace
Sacramental Universe	Authentic Development	Efficiency	Cost
Respect for Life		Adequacy	Employment
Planetary Common Good	**Public Policy Criteria**	Renewability	Flexibility
A New Solidarity	Consumption and Population Growth	Appropriateness	Timely Decision Making
Universal Purpose of Created Things	A Web of Life	Risk	Aesthetics

Climate Policy

Themes—USCCB, Global Climate Change (2001)	Climate Policy Guidelines*
Scientific Knowledge	**Temporal Dimensions**
Virtue of Prudence	Current Urgency
Universal Common Good	Future Adequacy
Stewardship of Creation	Historical Responsibility
Restraint and Moderation	Existing Capacity
Authentic Human Ecology	Political Viability
Protection of Environment for Future Generations	**Structural Dimensions**
Population and Authentic Development	Scientific Integrity
Reduction of Poverty	Sectoral Comprehensiveness
Importance of Education and Social Conditions	International Integration
Caring for the Poor and Issues of Equity	Resource Sharing
Solidarity	Economic Efficiency
Shared Responsibility for Burdens and Benefits	**Procedural Dimensions**
Shared Technologies	Policy Transparency
United States Must Lead	Emissions Verifiability
Climate Refugees and Poor Are a Priority	Political Incorruptibility
Sustainability	Implementational Subsidiarity

*James B. Martin-Schramm, *Climate Justice: Ethics, Energy, and Public Policy* (Minneapolis: Fortress Press, 2010), 38–39, 42–44, 46, and 119. Used with permission.

Afterword

A Call to Penance for Justice, Peace, and the Integrity of Creation

An Internet search on the topic "ecology" yields well over twenty-four million hits. It seems that a lot of people—both lay people and experts—are concerned about the environment and are seeking ways to preserve it and to use the resources of nature sustainably. As I have expressed in various ways throughout this book, I agree there is an environmental crisis. Yet I firmly believe Christianity, particularly the values, vision, and spiritual resources of the Franciscan charism, holds promise toward bringing it to an end. But what *do* Christianity and the Franciscan way of life have to say to people and a planet threatened (often as a result of humanity's "successes") with their demise?

First and foremost, we bring the Gospel of Jesus Christ, which announces the radical relationship of everything and everyone in God, as it is proclaimed in the doctrines and stories of creation, incarnation, and redemption. This ancient wisdom defines us and our call to be the guardians of creation. But for us today, the greatest significance of the Gospel is its power to instill in us a profound refusal to abandon faith and hope in the resurrection of Jesus Christ as the revelation of God's gracious intention toward the flourishing of all of creation. This is the ancient, but ever-new, wisdom we offer the world!

I find it impossible to imagine that we can live long in pervasive doubt and fear about this hope if we, like St. Francis and St. Clare and the throngs who have gone before us, hold fast and "follow in the footprints of Jesus." This is our lifeblood and our identity. But there is no Christianity if there is no discipleship. Thus, we are also called to nurture this hope through intentional theological study (adult faith formation, Bible study, social ministry education) and spiritual formation (prayer, spiritual direction, participation in the sacraments). In these ways we open ourselves to the Spirit who provides us with insight and wisdom to bring the ever-ancient but ever-new Gospel to our world.

In the early days of the Catholic environmental movement, Michael J. and Kenneth R. Himes responded to our question by citing the late Richard McCormick, who held that Christianity is "more a value raiser than a problem solver."[1] They highlighted Christianity's contribution of the notion of kinship that comes down to us through the creation stories of the Hebrew Scriptures, the early Christian writers, and saints such as Augustine and Francis of Assisi. As we have seen, a profound and definitive shift away from traditional US notions of self-interest and giving nature only instrumental value is central to other changes that are needed for the life of the earth. It is imperative that humans realize their origins as beings created in the image of God, who has been revealed as a radically relational being. Additional clues for the kinship between humankind and otherkind come in Genesis 2:18, where God invites the human to name the animals—not to gain power over them, but rather to form a lasting bond of intimate companionship with them.

It is this very human need for something beyond themselves that indicates yet another important truth about human existence, namely, that humans are finite and contingent. In other words, poverty is in a sense our true condition, yet we are enriched and nourished through the love of God, who is forever. One of the primary modalities God uses to sustain humans is their relationship with the created world. God's goodness and grace is known and revealed through creation, making it, in essence, sacramental. The Himes brothers remark, "Francis of Assisi's interweaving of poverty with the brotherhood and sisterhood of all creatures is profoundly Catholic because it is profoundly sacramental."[2] All of creation has value in itself and as a revelation of the Creator.

This insight about the sacramental character of creation gains force when considered along with Catholic social teaching. Pope Pius XII, for example, held that the right to private property is only secondary when

---

[1] Michael J. Himes and Kenneth R. Himes, "The Sacrament of Creation: Toward an Environmental Theology," in *Franciscan Theology of the Environment: An Introductory Reader*, ed. Dawn M. Nothwehr (Quincy, IL: Franciscan Press, 2003), 346. This article originally appeared as "The Sacrament of Creation," *Commonweal* 117 (January 26, 1990): 42–49.

[2] Ibid., 351.

measured against the common good.[3] No element of creation can live fully by itself. Kinship with other-than-human elements of creation implies that humans expand their moral imagination, engage in mutual relationship with them, and give moral standing to them (for their own sake). Once rights to moral standing are recognized, those rights must be promoted and protected. Often, such promotion and protection requires political action, not from an ideological position, but from an inclusive position on social justice.

Indeed, Keith Warner has suggested that it is this kind of unified stance toward addressing the environmental issues of today that flows naturally from the values inherent in the Franciscan charism.[4] He raises up three predominant themes that are part and parcel of the Franciscan tradition: concern about relationships; the life of penance; and an attitude of respectful deference toward the other. All human relating needs to be inclusive; it must consider how actions and decisions made within one relationship will impact all other possible relationships between humans and God, among humans, and between humans and the other-than-human creatures. Francis's practice of penance was grounded in a value base deeply rooted in God's love, demonstrated in the incarnation. Francis responded to God's love in acts of humility, simplicity, service to the poor, hospitality, and peacemaking.

So too today, where ecological, economic, social, and political issues are intertwined and complex, a holistic method, modeled by Francis's integrated approach to God and the created world, is needed. Many people of good will are already engaged in actions toward making the world more whole and holy—safeguarding human rights of migrants and climate refugees, protesting war, advocating for the poor and oppressed, or testifying against environmental destruction and promoting ecojustice in energy policies. Yet there is evidence to show that stopping a war does not necessarily shift a nation's economic priorities toward ecojustice or eliminating poverty. Nor does the priority of eliminating poverty require development and industrial growth that respects the integrity of the environment. And, especially because of global warming and climate change, destruction of ecosystems frequently necessitates a shift in human population and poses a risk for an occasion for war. The

---

[3] See, for example, Pope Leo XIII, *Rerum Novarum*, 19; Pope Pius XII, radio message, *La sollenità della Pentecoste*, 198–99; and Pope John XXIII, *Pacem in Terris*, 62–65.

[4] Keith Warner, "Get Him out of the Birdbath! What Does It Mean to Have a Patron Saint of Ecology?" in *Franciscan Theology of the Environment*, ed. Nothwehr, 373.

work taken up on behalf of social justice, peacemaking, or advocacy for the environment must each consider the interrelationship of justice, peace, and the integrity of creation.

Yet, as the late nationally known entomologist and university educator James F. Edmiston showed, in order to champion someone or something, one must know the subject quite intimately. He claimed that of the approximately one hundred million animal species, most ordinary people know only a few. Indeed, the animals most people will name when asked (cats, dogs, bears) show our own vertebrate bias. Colorful butterflies and moths receive some attention, but only because they stimulate our emotions through the visual spectrum.[5] Edmiston continued, "To personally know other creatures that are not like us can enable us to appreciate how our life interacts with millions of other life forms."[6]

Francis of Assisi provides a clear example of one who knew numerous creatures for their own sake, but also as revealers of God. From Francis's experiences, a spiritual and intellectual tradition emerged, and his legacy is found in the work of Bonaventure, John Duns Scotus, and their successors. This spiritual and intellectual tradition enriched Edmiston's own life and work as an entomologist, and he developed a "theology of biodiversity." Yard sweeps, soil extractions, and stream walks are three respectful and lightly intrusive ways for people of all ages to begin to know the vast diversity of the nonhuman world and then to begin to understand the world from the perspective of the other creatures of creation. Edmiston concluded: "Building relationships with other species can help rejoin information with the soul, . . . can promote connecting our spirituality with science, . . . [and] will promote receptivity to national and international policies that can reduce the reduction of biodiversity."[7]

One way that formal Franciscan religious order communities and others inspired by the charism of Francis and Clare of Assisi from around the globe have begun to bring their familiarity with the nonhuman perspective to bear especially on international policies is through the work of Franciscans at the United Nations.[8] Earth sciences professor Margaret

---

[5] James F. Edmiston, "How to Love a Worm? Biodiversity: Franciscan Spirituality and Praxis," in *Franciscan Theology of the Environment*, ed. Nothwehr, 379.

[6] Ibid.

[7] Ibid., 388.

[8] See the web site for Franciscans International at http://www.franciscansinter national.org, accessed February 11, 2012.

Pirkl, OSF, one of the founders of this effort, engaged in the pioneering work at the UN, particularly in the 1982 breakthrough document "The World Charter of Nature."[9] The seven major points that frame the document clearly reflect the Franciscan vision and values. Ever since then, the Franciscans at the UN have not only been involved in developing a theoretical base for safeguarding the integrity of creation; they have promoted and participated in hundreds of direct actions on the "Earth Charter."[10]

While much good can be done within existing institutions such as the UN, the influence of social and political structures that operate from an exclusive and nonparticipative power base still firmly dominates economic and government systems. Not infrequently, environmental concerns are simply ignored by those in power, or compromises are made that lead to less than satisfactory solutions. The human conversion to an attitude that values the power of mutual relations has barely begun. And certainly, as we confront climate change and the transition to sustainable energy and firmly assert and achieve the human rights to water and food, ethical reflection for the future must join the option for the poor with the integrity of creation.

Many people of faith, including lay Catholics and various religious orders within the church, have begun to tap their particular potential to contribute to the resolution of the complex environmental issues of our day. The Benedictines and the Franciscans were among the first to recover their spiritual, intellectual, and practical heritage. These two major traditions are firmly rooted in the Christian and Hebrew Scriptures and in the doctrinal traditions of the church. The Benedictines stress the relationship in which humans are stewards and owners of the land, while the Franciscans focus on the mutual relationship of humans with nonhumans and the role of humans as sojourners on the land. Certainly, gifts of all charisms are needed in our ecologically threatened world. Perhaps it is the case that the language of Benedict can more easily bridge the gap that exists between the utilitarian and the steward, but it is the Poor Man of Assisi who holds forth the kinship paradigm and the kind of power needed for the future.[11]

---

[9] See Margaret Pirkl, "Care of Creation: Working with the United Nations," in Franciscan *Theology of the Environment*, ed. Nothwehr, 391–402.

[10] See the Earth Charter Initiative, http://www.earthcharterinaction.org/content, accessed June 27, 2012.

[11] Dawn M. Nothwehr, "Benedictine Responsibility and Franciscan Mutuality: Perspectives on the Relationship between Humans and the Environment," in *Franciscan Theology of the Environment*, ed. Nothwehr, 403–31.

Giovanni Francesco di Bernardone's search for "something more" than wealth maintained through bloodshed and clever manipulations of the mercantile market was intentional, self-disciplined, and the subject of his entire life. As he grew, he became an ontological poet and a nature mystic who began to comprehend God's loving transformation of the universe and the interrelatedness of all beings. His was a spiritual journey of conversion, penance, and praise. What is important for us is to realize that though this journey was arduous, it was also profoundly joyful and satisfying!

Christians have a long tradition of penance and reconciliation that dates back to our Jewish roots, to the life and ministry of Jesus and his saving death and resurrection. The God we claim to worship is the God who time and time again forgives and gives us yet another chance! Conversion of heart requires disciplined training, similar to that of any Olympic athlete who wants to win the gold. Physical discipline and a focused imagination are needed. In our ecologically threatened age, it is also important for us to realize that our encounters with God will make us internally strong, expand our insights, and activate our moral imaginations so that we can know what is good and right. Yet we will *always* have the choice of whether or not to take up the courage and fortitude God offers that enables us to act and do what is morally good. But when we choose to follow in the footprints of Jesus, we soon discover a deep empowering confidence because we do not journey alone. The footprints we follow are created by the nail-pierced feet of the one who came to dwell with us and who knows "the joys and the hopes, the griefs and the anxieties of the [people] of this age, especially of those who are poor or in any way afflicted."[12] It is he who will continue to guide us.

"The Testament" of Francis tells us that he responded to God's call to do penance.[13] To do penance means to embrace a life of loving relationship with God, to see the world as an expression of the Creator's goodness, and to live in hope of the fulfillment of the reign of God. Francis shows us that a life of penance is a journey of faith that climaxes in conversion, a new way of knowing, and a greater sensitivity to the voice of God within ourselves and all of creation. Most importantly, this conversion leads to action.

[12] See the Second Vatican Council, *Gaudium et Spes*, no. 1, at http://www.vatican.va/archive/hist_councils/ii_vatican_council/documents/vat-ii_cons_19651207_gaudium-et-spes_en.html, accessed February 11, 2012.

[13] See Francis's "The Testament" (1226), 1–3, in Regis J. Armstrong, J. A. Wayne Hellmann, and William J. Short, eds., *Francis of Assisi: Early Documents*, vol. I, *The Saint* (New York: New City Press, 1999), 124.

So let us begin, as St. Francis did, with an act of penance. I invite you to join with me and my religious community, the Sisters of St. Francis of Rochester, Minnesota, in praying "The Way of the Cross and the Suffering Earth." Let us support one another in engaging the ecological issues of our day in confidence that nothing—neither life nor death, neither the present nor the future, no power or energy or cosmic force—will separate reality from the love of God that comes to us in Christ Jesus (Rom 8:38-39). We do this together as deeply committed Christians, motivated by hope in the resurrection!

Clairvaux McFarland, OSF, "Crown of Thorns around the Earth." Used with permission.

"The Way of the Cross and the Suffering Earth"
by
the Sisters of St. Francis, Rochester, Minnesota[14]

Prelude: The Way of the Cross and the Suffering Earth

Reflection

"If we could but see the earth as a totality—the complex interconnected-ness of all creatures throughout time, we would tremble in awe and ado-ration, and we would weep for our ignorance in the misuse of her gifts and resources."

Mary Southard, CSJ[15]

Prayer

Jesus, violated, made more precious in your violation, you beg us today to see your strangled earth, its blue beauty raped by the thorns of our environmental sin. As we follow on this way of penance for a nuclear age, this cosmic examination of conscience, point us to the hope that we can repent, rebuild, and return the earth to you whole and beautiful.

1. Jesus Is Condemned to Death

Reflection

We tolerate, don't think about, disregard these things we see as common, ordinary, and plentiful. We throw away because there is always more. We see resources not as gift but as our belongings to do with as we wish. Consequently, we burn, plunder, toss, discard, waste until the scarcity is before our eyes. It is then we begin to realize resources as gift.

---

[14] These reflections were created by Members of the Water Forum, Sisters of St. Francis, Rochester, MN, Spring 1989. Artwork is by S. Clairvaux McFarland, OSF. You are encouraged to pray with these often, but in justice, please give credit where credit is due.

[15] This quote appears on a calendar that is self-published by Mary Southard, CSJ. It is used with permission of the author.

Prayer

Abba, in your generosity you gave us abundance to meet our needs. You gave us Jesus as gift, the earth as gift. Forgive us our sin of abuse. Increase our awareness of the value of your gifts of Jesus and the earth, lest we destroy all that gives us life. + Amen.

S. Ruth Peterson

2. Jesus Is Made to Bear the Cross

Reflection

Jesus, as your body was jerked around in the beginning of this painful journey, so do we abuse your earth. Rough hands dug into your arms, arms that long to hold our earth, as we bury contaminated trash that is causing deep wounds. . . . The cross pressed on your shoulder was once a beautiful tree which you created to enhance life. It was fashioned into an instrument of destruction just as we destroy by our careless use of paper products. . . . You were whipped to move forward under the weight of the cross, barely able to breathe because of the blows. Thoughtlessly, we pollute the air, setting in motion our own process of death. . . .

Prayer

Jesus, the good earth, like you, is suffering for our sins of thoughtlessness and wastefulness and our wanton way of taking the easy way out. We pray for the grace to take our sins upon ourselves and become informed, concerned, and responsible codwellers on this beautiful gift of your planet Earth. + Amen.

S. Victorine Honermann

3. Jesus Falls the First Time

Reflection

God, Creator, you have given us the sun, air, water, light. Through creation, the earth provides the gifts of life. All these are given to us that we may preserve and recreate these into gifts for the good of others.

Prayer

Jesus, in your humanity I see you completely exhausted. You fall, you touch, you bless the earth that brings forth life. You are the gift of life to us, human and divine. In my humanity I come to know my weakness, my strengths. In my falls and as I see another fall, may our presence to one another be the gift that helps us rise from our fall to new life in Christ and for Christ. + Amen.

S. Verona Klein

4. Jesus Meets His Mother

Reflection

Earth, you are Mother; how can this be? I look at your scarred, disfigured body. How can this be done to my Mother—you who hold within your tender bosom the bodily remains of those I love, you who hold the wealth that divides nations and the missile silos that house the destructive forces that destroy your Son-like inhabitants as well as all the beauty and superabundance with which your Creator has adorned you?

You long to hold all, sacred in your embrace, but we continue our violence in the name of indifference, progress, and power. Your pain, her pain, meets the awesome gaze of the suffering Jesus. In his consuming love, he embraces the added pain and continues his salvation journey. I stand indifferent as a bystander watching this encounter. What keeps me from being a participant in my *Sister, Mother Earth's* pain—indifferentism, unconcern, busyness, laziness?

Prayer

Lord Jesus, you meet the painful gaze of your dear mother. You, the compassionate one, the Savior, do not save your Mother from this humiliation, this brokenness. She likewise has been invited to share the plan of redemption. She helplessly unites her being with yours in this violence that destroys so sacred a body. Her body as well is torn, bruised as she experiences the abuse laid on her Son. Mother Mary, Mother Earth, give me a heart of flesh, of compassion that brings me to reverence, to meet *all things* with grace, as you met your Son. + Amen.

S. Clairvaux McFarland

5. Simon Helps Jesus Carry the Cross

Reflection

What I said was that somebody else should do it. I didn't want a landfill, a waste incinerator, a recycling plant in my backyard. And I told them not to preach to me about sorting and bagging newspapers or washing aluminum cans; I was impatient with flattening tin and cleaning jars and bottles. It's all nonsense, EPA scare stuff, somebody's pet "greenhouse warming" project. Even the scientists don't agree about it. That was what I thought; that was how I lived, uncaring about the burden I laid on others, on the next generation. . . .

Prayer

Lord Jesus, as Simon took up your cross, he must have done so in reluctance, in fear, maybe in resentment—it couldn't have been convenient. He didn't recognize you as God . . . as I don't always see you, suffering, in the incredible devastation of your creation. Forgive me for that; help me to pick up my share of the burden, to renew the face of the earth. + Amen.

S. Eileen Haugh

6. Veronica Hands Her Veil to Jesus

Reflection

Out of legend, though metaphorically true in name, Veronica enters the passion story. In the Middle Ages, a veronica *was* an image of the face of Christ. She comes pushing her way through the crowd, ripping the veil from her head—or so one is free to surmise—and offering it to the sweating, bloody Jesus. In Romano Guardini's little book of meditations, this compassionate woman's hair floats free, in defiance of the Jewish taboo. A second meaning of Veronica derives from the plant whose name comes from the L. *verus*, veronica: a member of the speedwell family with small pastel flowers. In this beginning of summer, it is beautiful to think of the Lady Veronica's gesture of "speedwell" to Jesus as he mounts Calvary. The earth itself, through her, extends to its Lord sympathy and grateful love.

Prayer

We, too, can respond in an extension of the words of Guardini: "O make me also free!" When I am in the midst of suffering and apt to become blind and indifferent toward those about me, then keep my eyes clear. Teach me to notice each aspect of our earth's beauty as it reflects Christ's unconditional love; teach me to be grateful for this praise! Above all, help me to be through grace as Veronica was, a risk taker for the sake of the Lord Jesus. + Amen.

S. Bernetta Quinn

Song (Tune of Adoro Te*)*

For the beauty of the earth, sing oh sing today.
Of the sky and at our birth, sing oh sing always!
Nature human and divine all around us lies;
God of all, to thee we raise grateful hymns of praise.

7. Jesus Falls a Second Time

Reflection

Jesus, we see reluctant Simons in our day and the acts of service done for you by many Veronicas. Yet the cross becomes heavier and your body weaker through our increased exploitation and greed, our misuse of your gifts of nature, our carelessness and wastefulness, and our indifference to the evils around us.

We see you fall again in the victims of our exploitation, those suffering from our misuse of the gifts of nature, those who are deprived of basic needs because of our carelessness and wastefulness, and those who suffer oppression because of our indifference to the evils around us.

Prayer

Jesus, forgive us! Help us to understand! + Amen.

S. Joseen Voght

8. Jesus Meets the Women of Jerusalem

Reflection

Women! Women! Women! The women were always around, helping Jesus. The children that Jesus told the Jerusalem women to weep for include the children of today who have asthma because of unholy emissions from a nearby Coca-Cola plant. The children have to move from their paid-for home, their school friends, and a caring community. Other children and women are weeping because of the polluted water that they are forced to drink. Nothing is done to help them. Inwardly, today's women are weeping because of the asbestos or radon in their homes. These two hidden elements cause sickness.

Prayer

Bloody body of our crucified Savior, please inspire those who pretend to help us to really do something about all these things. Help our leaders to cast politics aside and *risk* for the future of our children. + Amen.

S. DeLellis Hinrichs

9. Jesus Falls a Third Time

Reflection

Falling again? Falling and falling and falling—what is it about this station of Jesus' third fall that is so "attractive" to the peoples of Latin America and of other third-world countries? Why all the bloody life-sized statues of Jesus with knees scraped to the bone, a back deeply gouged by the weight of his burden, a look of unutterable anguish on his face? Could it be that this is the station the people know best through their own experience? How many times have they fallen under the weight of the far-reaching implications of those greedy multinational companies who have tricked them out of their land and livelihood in order to lay a pipeline or grow a fast, one-crop cash product that soon ravages the land of all its nutrients, leaving the earth barren and useless? And it happens again . . . and again . . . and again!

Prayer

Jesus, in those years of growing up and young adulthood, you knew the satisfaction of working with your hands and providing for family needs, even in the midst of poverty. Later, you ached as you saw human greed despoiling the pride and property of the simple workers of the day. I beg you to sensitize me to the ways that I unwittingly participate in this same activity today, through my unthinking purchases of produce and products that send the poor and simple of our globe crashing to their knees once more. Forgive my comfortable apathy toward the socio-economic realities of our global family, and grace me to make choices out of justice and love. + Amen.

S. Valerie Usher

10. Jesus Is Stripped of His Garments

Reflection

[Read as alternating sides.]

1. I am a hill in Kentucky with rich, black soil, trees, and forest life.
2. You are stripped by miners, robbed of your coal, and left as an ugly, spoiled scar.

1. I am the ozone layer. Though invisible, I am vital for the protection and balance I provide.
2. You are stripped through misuse of contaminants. You are deteriorating into uselessness.

1. I am a tropical rain forest, lush, green, producing oxygen and moisture.
2. You are stripped. For lumber and paper, your trees are taken, leaving you bare.

1. I am, for example, a Texas red wolf, a pocket gopher, a silver trout, a California grizzly, a passenger pigeon, and a gray whale of the Atlantic.
2. You are stripped by hunters and marauders of your habitat. You are forever dead—extinct.

1. I am the earth—strong, living in the gentle cycle of seasons with a wise, ingenious interdependence. . . .
2. You are stripped, naked, and vulnerable—a victim of violence and deprivation. Beautiful and strong, you are yet so fragile and wounded.

Prayer

Creator God, Earth stands naked and vulnerable before us. Grant us the humility to be stripped and to stand with her in mutual respect. Let us be in awe of, and moved by, her beauty. Allow us to surrender our human strength and power to her wiser and gentler ways. Let us sacrifice those habits that lead to her destruction. We remember our own vulnerability and need as we stand in relationship to your creation. Purify us that we may be worthy to share our life with the earth, and give us all, earth and human alike, strength through our weakness. + Amen.

Janet Cramer

11. Jesus Is Nailed to the Cross

Reflection

A tree or two trees were cut to form the instrument of execution upon which Jesus was hung until he died. From that time on, the wooden cross has been a symbol of Christ's death, but the tree has always been a symbol of life, and the cross, too, is a symbol of the life that Christ won for us. The cross and the empty tomb are images of death/resurrection and give meaning to our own sufferings and death. In this century, the life of trees in all parts of the world is being cut short, is being twisted into forms of exploitation, and the death of trees is seriously affecting the ecosystems of the planet. The rain forests of the Amazon, Africa, and Southeast Asia are the habitats of myriad forms of life: birds, medicinal plants, insects, flowers, animals—all living together in a joyful network of shared life. We are cutting them down at an alarming rate. . . .

LORD, HAVE MERCY. CHRIST, HAVE MERCY. LORD, HAVE MERCY.

Too many trees have been cut down in China, in the Philippines, in parts of the United States; the roots that held the soil are gone; there is wholesale erosion; the soil washes away; there is nothing to stop the floods. . . .

Lord, have mercy. Christ, have mercy. Lord, have mercy.

We use so much paper and then throw it away; each day we create mountains of paper waste—and paper comes from trees. Trees are sacrificed to some of our greed, to our carelessness. . . .

Lord, have mercy. Christ, have mercy. Lord, have mercy.

Song

Were you there when they nailed him to a tree?
Were you there when they nailed him to a tree?
Oh! Oh! Oh! Sometimes it causes me to tremble, tremble, tremble.
Were you there when they nailed him to a tree?

Prayer

The cross of Jesus is a symbol of the pain and suffering of Jesus. It is also a symbol of the suffering of trees, those givers of life. God of compassion and love, soften our hard hearts so that we will be able to love and care for every living creature. Forgive us our sins against life. Heal the violence in our minds and hands. We ask this through Jesus and the Holy Spirit. + Amen.

S. Carlan Kraman

12. Jesus Dies on the Cross

Reflection

Refrain [repeat after every four stanzas]: Jesus dies on the cross, and the dying of Jesus continues today.

> In the gradual extinction of many species of animals, fish, birds, plants, and other forms of life;
> in the contamination of life-giving waters, making them no longer compatible with sustaining life;
> in every tree carelessly and wastefully chopped down;
> in the erosion of fertile lands and the depletion of vital elements in the soil. . . .

Refrain

In the polluted air of our industrialized civilization;

in the creation of wastelands that mar the earth;

in the deadliness of acid rain and other poisonous chemicals showered upon Earth and all her inhabitants;

in the overabundance of noise and haste that deafens the ear and blinds the eye to beauty. . . .

Refrain

In the poisoning of fruits and vegetables with pesticides and insecticides, making them unfit for human and animal consumption;

in the premature termination of life as children and young people fall prey to contamination and pollution;

in the destruction of the ozone layer, causing the deadly phenomenon known as the greenhouse effect;

in every lake, river, stream, or ocean glutted with the garbage of our technological society. . . .

Refrain

In the exploitation of developing nations by using them as dumping grounds for unwanted wastes and by limitlessly devouring their valuable natural resources;

in every flower nipped in the bud by uncaring minds, hearts, hands, and feet;

in the stockpiling of garbage and hazardous wastes that smear the land and shed deadly poisons in all directions;

in the silencing of minds and voices that care enough and are courageous enough to dare to take the risk of speaking out for change. . . .

Pause for Silence

Prayer

In our very midst, Jesus dies yet today. Will we stand by and let the dying continue? Or are we willing to change our attitudes and ways? Will we let the profound experience of innocent dying awaken us to a new way of being that promotes life rather than death? May we let God's words echo in our hearts: "I set before you life or death, blessing or curse. Choose life, then, so that you and your descendants may live" (Deut 30:19). + Amen.

S. Mary Ann Dols

13. Jesus Is Taken Down from the Cross

Reflection

The tree held Life and now releases the source of its energy, Jesus, to form a link with all humankind through the loving ministrations of Mary, his mother; Nicodemus; and Joseph of Arimathea, who held the seed of belief for so long in a silent place. How light the burden for the rock that must have "reached" to hold the resting body and was thus graced.

Prayer

As a part of the cosmos, we too hold our hands and hearts and being to receive the body of Jesus and recall that a wooden cross and a rock before us held the sublime treasure. On this day of darkness, may the seeds of light and strength be nourished for blossoming in the universe. + Amen.

S. Valerie Olson

14. Jesus Is Laid in the Tomb

Reflection

Just as the Crucified One was lovingly entrusted to the darkness and aloneness of an earth tomb and was raised from the dead, so does nature find new life through dormancy and the active rest of Earth's self-healing power. The darkness time in a chrysalis necessary for the emergence of a magnificent monarch cannot be hurried. Whenever anything returns to Earth, there is a chance for new life. Rainwater that has collected toxic chemicals is purified by its long, dark, quiet trickling through layers of soil and rock to its place in the water table or aquifer. This purified water quenches human thirst and the thirst of other creatures. Sad to say, we humans are now causing large-scale changes that poison the earth at a rate to which she cannot adjust.

Prayer

Forgive us, God, for upsetting the natural cycles that lead to healing; help us to open our eyes, and give us the courage to change our lifestyle.

[Read as alternating sides.]

1. If we change, Earth's power of self-healing will naturally continue
2. according to your loving plan.

1. If we do not change, Earth in frustration will become a tomb without the promise of life.
2. We understand that this will be inevitable.

All: Be with us, O God, as we ponder these realities. *The choice is ours.*

Song

Were you there when they laid him in the tomb?
Were you there when they laid him in the tomb?
Oh! Oh! Oh! Sometimes it causes me to tremble, tremble, tremble.
Were you there when they laid him in the tomb?

S. Franchon Pirkl

15. The Resurrection of Jesus

Jesus is risen! Jesus is risen! Alleluia, alleluia, alleluia!
Jesus' death:
scourged,
broken,
shattered,
thirsty,
wounded.
DEATH.

Earth's death:
scourged ozone,
shattered rain forest,
dead species,
thirsty, sparse water,
broken soil,
wounded air.
DEATH.

Jesus, Triumphant One, Risen One, come
    to mend, to give new life, to liberate us. . . .
Resurrect our complacency so that we may heal the wounded earth.
Awaken us to endure wholeness for the earth that is dangling,
    fragile, bleeding, and dead.
Transform us and thrust us into responsibility of
    mending what is torn, wasted, and wasting away—give back life.

Prayer

Jesus, Triumphant One, Risen One—alleluia!
Your death brings life: liberate us, transform us, give us courage to heal
    the suffering earth.
Jesus, Risen One, bring about through us a new creation!
Come give life, give love, to Earth. . . .
Alleluia! Alleluia!
Jesus is risen! + Amen, Alleluia!

S. Adelia Marie Ryan

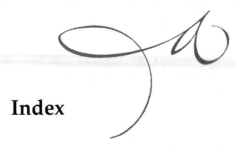

Index